Honor and Shame in Western History

This book covers a wide range of topics related to honor and shame in European historical societies: history of law and literature, social and ancient history, as well as theoretical contributions on the state of research and the importance of honor and shame in traditional societies.

Honor and Shame in Western History brings together 14 texts of interdisciplinary scholars from Europe and North America. It covers a wide range of topics related to honor and shame in historical societies. The contributions cover periods of Western history from Greek and Roman times to the nineteenth century and many of them integrate the concept of a "deep history" of honor and shame in social interaction.

The book is essential for a broad audience interested in social history and the history of emotions.

Jörg Wettlaufer is head of the Digital Academy at the Academy of Sciences and Humanities in Lower Saxony at Göttingen, Germany. He is doing research in the history of law, evolutionary anthropology, and digital history with a focus on the social usage of shame in medieval society.

David Nash is Professor of History at Oxford Brookes University. He has written and published extensively on the history of atheism, blasphemy, and shame. He has advised governments in the UK, the European Union, and Australia on the issue of blasphemy laws and their repeal.

Jan Frode Hatlen is head of the Department of Historical and Classical Studies, at the Norwegian University of Science and Technology (NTNU). He earned his PhD in history from NTNU in 2015. His research ranges from gender and honor in Late Roman society, to learning and teaching history in higher education.

Routledge Studies in Cultural History

Cultural Representations of Piracy in England, Spain, and the Caribbean
Travelers, Traders, and Traitors, 1570 to 1604
Mariana Cecilia Velázquez

Sport and the Pursuit of War and Peace from the Nineteenth Century to the Present
War Minus the Shooting?
Edited by Martin Hurcombe and Philip Dine

Staging Slavery
Performances of Colonial Slavery and Race from International Perspectives, 1770–1850
Edited by Sarah J. Adams, Jenna M. Gibbs, and Wendy Sutherland

Honor and Shame in Western History
Edited by Jörg Wettlaufer, David Nash, and Jan Frode Hatlen

Modern Murders
The Turn-of-the-Century's Backlash Against Melodramatic and Sensational Representations of Murder, 1880–1914
Lee Michael-Berger

Histories, Adaptations, and Legacies of *Tinker Tailor Soldier Spy*
Randal Rogers

A History of the Cultural Travels of Energy
From Aristotle to the OED
Peter Hjertholm

For more information about this series, please visit: https://www.routledge.com/Routledge-Studies-in-Cultural-History/book-series/SE0367

Honor and Shame in Western History

Edited by
Jörg Wettlaufer, David Nash, and Jan Frode Hatlen

NEW YORK AND LONDON

First published 2023
by Routledge
605 Third Avenue, New York, NY 10158

and by Routledge
4 Park Square, Milton Park, Abingdon, Oxon OX14 4RN

Routledge is an imprint of the Taylor & Francis Group, an informa business

© 2023 Taylor & Francis

The right of Jörg Wettlaufer, David Nash, and Jan Frode Hatlen to be identified as the authors of the editorial material, and of the authors for their individual chapters, has been asserted in accordance with sections 77 and 78 of the Copyright, Designs and Patents Act 1988.

All rights reserved. No part of this book may be reprinted or reproduced or utilized in any form or by any electronic, mechanical, or other means, now known or hereafter invented, including photocopying and recording, or in any information storage or retrieval system, without permission in writing from the publishers.

Trademark notice: Product or corporate names may be trademarks or registered trademarks, and are used only for identification and explanation without intent to infringe.

ISBN: 978-0-367-90148-6 (hbk)
ISBN: 978-1-032-43469-8 (pbk)
ISBN: 978-1-003-02291-6 (ebk)

DOI: 10.4324/9781003022916

Typeset in Sabon
by Taylor & Francis Books

Contents

List of Figures vii
List of Contributors viii
Acknowledgments x

Introduction 1
JÖRG WETTLAUFER, DAVID NASH, AND JAN FRODE HATLEN

PART I
Honor and Shame: Concepts and Challenges 7

1 The Unwieldy Phenomenon of Honor 9
   DAGMAR BURKHART

2 Shame: A Social Emotion and Its Cultural Concepts in a Historical (European) Perspective 27
   JÖRG WETTLAUFER

3 Zero-Sum Emotions and Shame–Honor Dynamics 45
   RICHARD LANDES

PART II
Honor and Shame in Traditional European Societies 79

4 Honor–Shame Dynamics in Late Antiquity: Balance and Control 81
   JAN FRODE HATLEN

5 Gregory of Tours on Sichar and Chramnesind 97
   RICHARD LANDES

6 Better to die in honor than to live in shame?: A Comparative Approach to the Literary Dynamics of Honor and Shame in French Chanson de Geste, Romance, and Fabliau (Twelfth to Thirteenth Centuries) 107
LISA SANCHO

7 The Dynamics of Gender-Specific Honor and Shame in the Middle Ages: The *Nibelungenlied* as Example 124
JUTTA EMING

8 The Emergence and Social Usage of Shaming Punishments in the Twelfth and Thirteenth Centuries in Northwest European Cities 140
JÖRG WETTLAUFER

9 Christian Humility, Papal Humiliations: An Honor-and-Shame Criterion in the Church's History Grand Narratives 159
BÉNÉDICTE SÈRE

PART III
Honor and Shame in Modernity 169

10 Collective Shame in the Modern World: The Case of Blasphemy Laws and Tolerant Sensibilities 171
DAVID NASH

11 The Culture of American Dueling under Attack: The 1856 Public Beating of an Abolitionist Massachusetts Senator by a South Carolina Congressman 187
KENNETH S. GREENBERG

12 Brought Up with Shame: Trans-Generational Perspectives on Disciplinary Correction in Finland during the Twentieth and Twenty-First Centuries 203
SATU LIDMAN

13 Plato, MeToo, the Honorable, and the Others 223
HEGE DYPEDOKK JOHNSEN

14 Shame, Modernity, and Postmodernity in Britain 241
DAVID NASH

Index 257

Figures

8.1 Soester "Nequam"-book, early fourteenth century. Das Soester Nequambuch, hrsg. v. d. Historischen Kommission für die Provinz Westfalen, Leipzig 1924, Fig. XIII, fol. 46r. in the original Ms. 144
8.2 Herzog August Bibliothek Wolfenbüttel, Cod. Guelf. Aug. 3.1 2, fol. 42v. Last quarter of the fourteenth century. The content refers back to the thirteenth century (Scheele, 1998). © Herzog August Bibliothek Wolfenbüttel: http://diglib.hab.de/?db=mssid=3-1-aug-2f. 146

Contributors

Dagmar Burkhart is Professor Emeritus of Slavic Literatures and Cultural Anthropology. She was Chair of the Department of Slavic Studies at the University Mannheim. She published books and articles on the gender specific and intercultural history of honor and shame codes (focus: Germany, Russia, and the Balkans). For a list of publications: dagmar-burkhart.de or dagmar-burkhart.jimdofree.com.

Jutta Eming holds a Chair for Medieval German Literature and Language at Freie Universität Berlin. Her main areas of research are novels of the High and Late Middle Ages, sacred plays, short stories, genre theory, gender studies, theories of the miraculous, emotionality in medieval literature, literature and knowledge; literature and adventure; concepts of the magical in medieval and early modern culture and literature, temporality and medievalism, and sustainability and cultural heritage in the humanities.

Kenneth S. Greenberg is Distinguished Professor of History, Emeritus at Suffolk University. He has written and edited many books and articles on enslavement in the antebellum South. His special focus includes honor and slavery, the political culture of American slavery, and the Nat Turner rebellion of enslaved people in 1831 Virginia.

Hege Dypedokk Johnsen is Associate Professor in philosophy at the Norwegian University of Science and Technology (NTNU). She holds a PhD from Stockholm University. Her philosophical interests include ancient philosophy (especially Plato), philosophy of love, moral psychology, early modern philosophy, and feminist philosophy.

Richard Landes is a medieval historian living in Jerusalem. He writes on the 11th century, millennialism, shame-honor culture, demotic religiosity, media coverage of the Middle East, and 21st century Global Jihad. He recently published *Can "The Whole World" Be Wrong? Lethal Journalism, Antisemitism and Global Jihad* (2022).

Satu Lidman is Adjunct Professor and independent scholar based in Finland. Her research interests include gender, bodiliness and aspects of violence in historical and present-day contexts of criminal law, human rights, and attitudinal change. For the full list of publications in English, German, and Finnish see: www.lidman.fi.

Lisa Sancho earned her Ph.D. in medieval French literature (2022). Her research focuses on representations and conceptions of shame in 12th and 13th century oïl language fictional literature.

Bénédicte Sère is Professor at the University of Paris Nanterre and senior member of the Institut Universitaire de France. She is currently Visiting Professor at JTS/ University of Columbia (NYC). She wrote several books on the history of friendship, honor and shame, and polemics, regarding church history and medieval papacy.

Acknowledgments

The editors would like to thank the Centre for Interdisciplinary Studies (ZiF) and its team for the generous support of the workshop "Honor–Shame Dynamics in Western History" held between June 14 and 16, 2018 at Bielefeld, Germany. This workshop was organized by Richard Landes (Israel) and Jörg Wettlaufer (Germany) and the majority of the collected papers published in this volume have been prepared for and presented in this context. We would also like to thank the publisher Routledge and especially Max Novick for accepting this book in the "Studies in Cultural History" series. Finally, we would like to express our gratitude to all those who supported this publication in one or another way, gave feedback, and reviewed earlier versions of the collected papers.

We think we can speak for all contributors when we share our hope that this book will further stimulate research in this extremely interesting and challenging field of cultural history. We would love to see more comparative work, both empirical studies and reviews of existing work, not limited to the Western hemisphere but extending to all cultural backgrounds and all periods of history.

We would like to dedicate this book to Werner Paravicini in honor of his 80th birthday in October 2022. His continuing work on the history of the nobility in late medieval Western Europe and the importance of honor for this group inspired some of us to look deeper into the history of emotions and their role in human social interaction, past and present.

Introduction

Jörg Wettlaufer, David Nash, and Jan Frode Hatlen

This book seeks to bring comparative perspective to the idea that honor and shame are two fundamentally important and closely related concepts of human social experience with a diverse and important history. Both vital responses are rooted in the social existence of mankind–human life is embedded in social interaction, attribution of respect and contempt. What is of particular importance is that the historical significance of this interrelationship has been fundamentally under-researched.

The drive to acquire and uphold honor and to scrupulously avoid shame has been of tremendous influence for the social makeup of past societies from the dawn of humankind on into the postmodern world of social interaction. Since the Neolithic era, these dynamics have developed, and left behind a wide range of evidence of both the basic patterns, and the efforts (of varying success) to change those dynamics. In more recent historical times (the last four millennia) these dynamics have evolved, refined, found new equilibria, defined, contradicted, and shaped historical decisions and behavior.

This volume brings together acknowledged experts from various disciplines on the topic of honor and shame in Western history. The majority of the contributions are based on papers presented at the workshop "Honor–Shame Dynamics in Western History" between June 14 and 16, 2018 at the Centre for Interdisciplinary Studies (ZiF) at the University of Bielefeld, Germany. The workshop was organized by Richard Landes and Jörg Wettlaufer and was generously supported by the ZiF. Without the support of Marina Hoffmann (ZiF) it would not have been possible to bring together specialists from all over the world on this topic.[1] Two contributions, by Hege Dypedokk Johnson and Jutta Eming, were integrated during the planning of this volume. The concept of the workshop and this book owes many inspiring and sometimes also controversial ideas to Richard Landes, Co-Convener of the Bielefeld Conference and provider of many important insights and thoughts on the topic. Although the editors profoundly disagree with the application of his research on the honor–shame dichotomy to political problems of the Near East, we would like to thank him nevertheless for sharing his sometimes provocative ideas and concepts with us.

DOI: 10.4324/9781003022916-1

In current research, honor and shame have been tackled mostly independently and within the narrow borders of historical disciplines. Only anthropological research and *deep history* have addressed the intersection of the two antagonistic concepts and discussed honor and shame on the level of cultural concepts that shape societies. On one whole, however, while honor and shame and associated issues (such as guilt) get a great deal of attention from anyone discussing social dynamics, they are less frequently the specific object of study, even in current anthropology. By and large scholars focus on one dimension of the dyad—honor *or* shame—without necessarily paying much attention either to the opposite element or their dynamic relationship.

Both honor and shame are "other-directed" and therefore, ultimately, dimensions of social interactions. They are primary in the sense that pride and self-confidence—emotions related to the enduring state of honor—and shame go back to our earliest feelings about ourselves. Shame in particular has a visceral, almost ontological status: experience of shame involves the whole person. Shame concerns specifically shared norms and moral values of members in a social group. What (we think) others think about us is the driving force behind the shame experience: *they*—the members of the group—deliver both honor and shame through this internalized mechanism, and dominate the concerns of those for whom the most important matters are gaining/maintaining honor and avoiding/purging shame. People thought shameful by their honor-group feel bad about themselves even when innocent of wrongdoing or stigma.

Furthermore, both terms represent social concepts and emotional states in individuals at the same time, including overlapping semantic fields, and therefore have divergent translations in different languages and different historical periods. Some examples here briefly illustrate the complexity that the book seeks to make evident for its audience. While the direct antonym of honor (*Ehre*) is dishonor (*Unehre*), the English "shame" can represent both the feeling of *Scham* and the social stigma of *Schande* (disgrace) in German. The latter sense is also antonymic to honor in German. Honor and pride are closely related but distinct concepts in many European languages. Both come with emotional states, but less so for honor, which is, in Pierre Bourdieu's words, a symbolic capital that can be employed in social interactions for the benefit of those in possession of it (Bourdieu, 1984). With honor comes the feeling of dominance and righteousness, while with shame there is a close association with humiliation and debasement. Again the different languages grasp these semantic fields with distinctive vocabulary. Honor and shame are typical homonyms in English, incorporating different concepts in one word. In French, for example, shame can be described by several expressions with different origins in Latin. While *pudeur* signifies the shame of the body, *honte* and *vergogne* are more morally loaded and related to the Latin concept of *verecundia*. Arabic also has multiple terms for both sides of the dyad. Furthermore, the semantic fields of these words in classical times have changed during the long Roman Empire. Given these semantically overlapping expressions and shifting meanings, both the concept and the experience of honor and shame have been extremely difficult to tackle in the broader context of cultural history. To complicate matters further, scholars have found the dynamics in honor cultures useful in explaining dynamics where the semantics are not visible in the source material. By generalizing ideas of honor in honor groups and societies, conceptual approaches have been used as a heuristic model in order to understand human behavior (on the distinction between semantic and conceptual approaches to honor, see Stewart 1994: 5). This book takes up the challenge to untangle the concepts because of the predominant importance of these concepts in traditional Western societies and beyond.

Shame and honor can be attributed not only to individual people but also to actions and whole groups. This bidirectional feature of the concepts of honor and shame allows multiple perspectives and dimensions. The underlying social and neural mechanisms governing feelings and perceptions of shame and honor are inherited from the shared human bias toward social interaction and group-oriented life forms. It is important to understand the origin of these concepts and to understand them as productive and adaptive in a way that establishes them as integral parts of human cultures. In human history these mechanisms have been refined and ritualized, playing an important role in both individual and group dynamics.

On these conceptual bases the contributions to this volume aim to understand better how the dynamic relationship between honor and shame has been implemented in the cultural makeup of groups and whole societies. By using (mostly) examples from well-researched European history the essays contribute to understanding diachronic adaptations of the concepts to changing cultural and natural landscapes. They look out for recurring patterns in the way honor and shame are embedded into the dynamic cultural context. From this we learn more about the identity of those groups using honor and shame establishing and operating a society in the historical past.

The book is divided into three parts. Part I tackles concepts and challenges of both honor and shame in three contributions. Dagmar Burkhart's essay opens up the discussion on the semantic field of honor in European languages incorporating both internal (moral values) and external (reputation) honor. She illustrates the "unwieldy phenomenon of honor" through an analysis of two literary texts published at a distance of roughly one hundred years, demonstrating the range of concepts of honor in different periods of Western society: Theodor Fontane's *Effi Briest* (Germany), published in 1895, and J.M. Coetzee's *Disgrace* (South Africa), from 1999.

Jörg Wettlaufer's contribution introduces shame as a human emotion in the intersection between biology and culture by giving an overview of recent theories of self-conscious emotions and putting shame in the context of the social functions of shame in historical societies from an evolutionary and deep history point of view. According to his research the European cultural concept of shame has been shaped strongly through the Christian religion and its morality, exploiting its potential to strengthen group coherence (through the internalization of norms) and to promote cooperation.

In the third contribution of this first part, Richard Landes presents an original theory about the development of the honor–shame dyad in European and Western societies from the tribal warrior age to modern times. This *longue durée* perspective on zero-sum emotions and shame–honor dynamics introduces new terms and definitions to describe what Landes interprets as a constant evolution in law, religion and social relationships during the last millennia. It is a thought-provoking and controversial narration of Western history through the lens of honor–shame dynamics of the heroic age to modernity.

Part II of the book contains exemplary contributions on honor and shame in traditional European societies, from Late Antiquity through to the Middle Ages. Jan Frode Hatlen's chapter discusses honor and shame in relation to gender roles in Late Antiquity. He argues that honor can dictate behavior and emotional experiences. However, attempts to injure honor may have little effect if the honor codes are not understood or respected by all parties.

In his chapter "Gregory of Tours on Sichar and Chramnesind," Richard Landes applies his model of "primary honor codes" to Late Ancient Gaul. He argues that primary honor codes can "mutate" when societies become more stratified, and that honor becomes a marker for superiority.

Lisa Sancho explores the ideological phrase often found in French medieval literature: "Better to die in honor than to live in shame." Her discussion shows that honor and shame were part of a number of competing discourses, and the relation between honor and shame highly dynamic. Though honor is generally conceived of as a value and shame as a counter-value, the axiology can sometimes be completely reversed, with shame becoming honorable and vice versa.

Following up the topic of medieval literature, Jutta Eming also demonstrates that honor and shame in the Middle Ages were complex, and that gender roles were not as obvious as one might think. Her argument is developed through a close reading of the tragic plot of the Nibelunglied, a story from around the year 1200 partially based on oral traditions.

Honor and shame were not mere literary ideas in the Middle Ages. Jörg Wettlaufer illustrates this in his chapter on the emergence and usage of shaming punishments. His study of penal law with a focus on the Holy Roman Empire shows how social shaming punishments were part of the development of the jurisdictional culture in European cities.

In the concluding chapter of this second part headlined "The Pope in the period of the Great Schism," Bénédicte Sère discusses honor and shame dynamics and the role of both concepts in the institution of papacy. As a scholar of medieval religious studies, she argues that power in this sphere was constructed in a tension between honor and humility.

Part III looks at the concepts of honor and shame operating within the transition to modernity. David Nash's chapter explores how shame operates within the logic of blasphemy laws. These have regularly made use of shame as method of manipulating behavior to achieve specific aspirations and outcomes. Medieval minds were persuaded to take action against the blasphemer because they suspected the Almighty would enact providential judgment and shame down upon them. Within modernity, shame indicted those in positions of power who failed to protect religious beliefs from the questioning and assaults of blasphemers. Later on shame has been a thoroughly modern tool fundamental to the pursuit of "modern" liberal values ranged against what are seen as "anachronistic" forms of intolerance.

Kenneth Greenberg's chapter examines the unraveling and ambivalent nature of shame and honor codes in mid-nineteenth century America, using an instance of "dueling" in which a Northern abolitionist congressman was caned by a Southern pro-slavery congressman. The incident highlights the clash of two societies and in particular showcases the South—a place where dueling and honor cultures ran deep and still made perfect sense in a world on the cusp of modernity. This was further emphasized by reactions from the North, which saw this culture as incongruous and backward.

Satu Lidman investigates the consequences of shame's appearance within forms of corporal punishment in late twentieth-century and twenty-first-century Finnish society. She focusses upon the difficulties of legislating seeking to intrude into the private world of familial relations and power structures. In particular, it notes that legislation does not always succeed or produce the desired outcome politicians and societies actively crave—leaving children too often shamed and isolated. The chapter examines how generational continuity has been a transmissive factor in the continuity of physical violence within the family, but concludes by asking how this chain can and should be broken through recognition of the rights of the child.

Hege Dypedokk Johnsen spotlights upon the often highly gendered dimensions within sexual assault where shame appears to function "incorrectly." Her analysis ranges between ancient and modern to investigate how shame exists within the context of sexual crimes. Drawing on insights present in Plato's Laws, Johnsen investigates the "shame paradox" whereby the victim in sexual assault feels shame, arguably more acutely than the transgressor. The chapter concludes by looking at naming, vocalizing, and identifying strategies, which it is argued is the most effective method of breaking down the "paradox." Thus, both historical and contemporary investigation should set itself the goal of either uncovering these strategies or encouraging them.

David Nash's final chapter in this book is a dialogue with both liberalism in nineteenth-century England and the ideas on humiliation recently published by Ute Frevert. The chapter notes that civilization's crusade to remove shame from human interactions was something of a veil concealing the fact that liberalism required its own forms of coercion to enforce the benefits of modernity. Class, a product of modernity, became a tool whereby individuals policed their own interactions and aspirations within a bourgeois world. The chapter ends by speculating on the enduring usefulness of shame as a manipulative social tool that perhaps points to imperatives that so regularly refashion and reinvent it.

With the publication of this conference volume we would like to encourage more interdisciplinary and comparative research on the topic of honor–shame dynamics in Western Europe and beyond. We think and hope that the contributions will prove that the conceptual approach of looking at this topic from an evolutionary and deep history point of view is most promising for future interdisciplinary historical research.

Note

1 Parts of the Introduction are based on the application written by Richard Landes and Jörg Wettlaufer in 2017 for the workshop "Honor–Shame Dynamics in Western History" at the ZIF Bielefeld in June 2018. Further information about the conference can be found at https://shamestudies.de/conferences/bielefeld-2018/.

References

Bourdieu, P. (1984). *Distinction: A social critique of the judgement of taste*. Harvard University Press.

Stewart, F.H. (1994). *Honor*. University of Chicago Press.

Part I

Honor and Shame: Concepts and Challenges

1 The Unwieldy Phenomenon of Honor

Dagmar Burkhart

> One may assume that there is an overarching model of social communication in which honor, as a lexeme and as a concept, forms part of the common vocabulary of a cultural community and is considered part of its "symbolic capital."
>
> (Bourdieu, 1984)

The Semantics and Pragmatics of Honor: Inspection of the Western— in Particular the German—Concept

Because honor is something that has been discursively constructed, it will appear in a wide variety of discourses. If we take discourse to mean the regular communications which are linked to a specific tradition of common knowledge and social values (axiologies) then honor may occupy different levels of discourse:

- the level of objective speech, in which the specific lexeme honor that is in general use and thus valid for the discourse community has its place as part of the vocabulary and is found in word fields or word families, and used orally or in written form;
- a first meta level of rule books for honorable behavior, in which standards of etiquette and regulations regarding ceremonies are written down and deal with separate layers of society or address any conceivable situation of social communication;
- a second meta level of philosophical, religious, ethical, and sociological writings or works of political science and jurisprudence, in which the writers reflect on the concept of honor, its semantic range and its value in the proximity of ethics, morality, justice, and dignity; and
- a third meta level of fictional works, in which honor is a topic and motif in drama and films, in verse poems, in novels, stories, and novellas.

The Duality of Internal and External Honor

The semantics of the term honor (in German *Ehre*) shimmer in many hues and therefore there is a certain sense of confusion in defining this unwieldy

DOI: 10.4324/9781003022916-3

phenomenon that is so hard to pin down, a problem that has existed since before the dawn of the modern age. What was *Ehre* (honor), and what did it really mean in pre-modern or modern society, or in a functionally differentiated society? Self-esteem coupled with a claim to social recognition? A collection of ritual patterns for one's actions? A system of values that guaranteed the individual and the group their due share of esteem? An extremely vulnerable possession to be defended at all costs?

The semantics and pragmatics of the notion and lexeme *Ehre* (honor) appear in multivalent and polysemic fashion. This is partly explained by the fact that the German word *Ehre* (likewise honor in English and *honneur* in French) is a homonym; i.e., it stands for two different concepts although spelling and pronunciation are identical:

- *Ehre* can mean something one might call internal honor, or the characteristics that underlie a person's good reputation and entitle them to the respect and esteem of society; his or her moral values and conduct, conscience, virtue, decency, self-esteem and integrity, honesty, sense of shame, and the maxims of ethical, temperate behavior.
- At the same time *Ehre* can mean external honor, the recognition and esteem of others, reputation, renown, a person's prominent social standing as shown by public recognition in the form of honors and awards or broad public approval of someone's special achievements, the respect shown by society, a person's fame or celebrity status.

Starting around the thirteenth century, when, under the influence of scholasticism (e.g., Thomas Aquinas), the term *Ehre* (honor) in the sense of "public regard" was widened to include a moral element, the division between internal and external honor became a concept in German-speaking cultural areas too. Apart from internal/outward honor, German-speakers today will also refer to "intrinsic," "subjective" honor (i.e., based on a person's inner values and moral standards) and "extrinsic," "objective" honor (granted on the basis of possessions, parentage, age, achievements, etc.).

An individual possesses his/her internal honor and as a rule takes pains to preserve it, whereas outward honor is something that must be granted by other members of the society, in public recognition of achievement or services. This extra amount of honor as an expression of social esteem may take the form of material goods or an increase of symbolic power when the subject is offered public office, a title, an order of merit, or a higher rank in the social hierarchy. However, society could and can strip people of their honor (ostracize or denounce them) which means shame or disgrace (*Schande*) and dishonor (*Ehrlosigkeit*; infamy, outlawry) or "social death" (through slander, withdrawal of civic rights, etc.).

In certain cases it may be possible to defend or regain one's honor, to be rehabilitated—in bygone days by dueling, in modern times by retracting or correcting an utterance in the sense of a public apology to the injured party.

Thus the concept of honor is both a timeless ideal system of standards, as well as one that may be interpreted in various ways in specific social functions and behavior contexts, which is communicated through discourse as a code or semiotic system.

However, in the case of honor, there is not necessarily a cause-and-effect relationship: it is possible to have outward honor without internal honor, in other words fame without honor, as when people speak of a false "man of honor" or use irony to convey a deliberate untruth. One example of this is Mark Antony's funeral oration on Caesar in Shakespeare's *Julius Caesar*, with the repetitions of "And Brutus is an honorable man!"—statements which only seem to flatter. Conversely, someone's internal honor may bloom hidden from view, unrecognized and unappreciated by the public. In 1936, during the Nazi dictatorship, Walter Benjamin gave his collection of letters called *Deutsche Menschen* the subheading "Honor without fame, greatness without splendor, dignity without recompense" when seeking to preserve in the present some past examples of Germany's humane attitudes.

Proverbs from many sources, often a yardstick for conservative values, have defined the axiological priority of internal before outward honor as follows: "*Ehre dem Ehre gebührt*" (Honor to whom honor is due, *Romans* 13, 7), "*Ehre geht den Ehren vor*" (Honor before honors), "*Ehr' und Eid gilt mehr als Land und Leut'*" (Oath and honor above country and kin), "*Ehre folgt dem, der sie flieht, und flieht den, der sie jagt*" (Honor follows him who shuns it and shuns him who chases after it).

Honor clearly has much to do with oral speech and discourse. It is verbalized in what people say about someone else, what "one" (the social group) says about a person. This becomes apparent by examining the etymology of German honor lexemes like *Ruf* (reputation) and *Ruhm* (fame).

An inadmissible redefinition of the concept of *Ehre*/honor is seen in some publications or reference works such as the sociology lexicon *Lexikon Gesellschaft* (1992) where *Ehre*/honor is replaced by *Würde* (dignity) on the grounds that the concept of honor is obsolete and its perversion during the Nazi era has rendered it unacceptable. But *Ehre* is not the same as *Würde* because there are a number of specific characteristics to distinguish the two concepts. *Würde*, etymologically related to the adjective "*wert*," English "worth(y)," is rooted in the Christian tradition that man is made in the image of God, which therefore sets him apart from all other living creatures. Whereas in ancient Rome and medieval Europe *Würde* (*dignitas*) was very akin to the concept of external honor in the form of rank and reputation, people began in the eighteenth century to see *Würde* (dignity) as a value to be accorded to every person, even the criminal whose honor is lost, but not his *Würde*, purely because he is a human being. The Enlightenment concept of *Würde* is encapsulated in Immanuel Kant's concept of the dignity due to every person as a moral, rational being.

As *Würde* in the sense of human dignity has been considered a basic human right since the Enlightenment, it is with good reason that Article 1 of the *Grundgesetz* (Basic Law) of the Federal Republic of Germany is: "The dignity of human beings is inviolable" (see also "All human beings are born free and equal in dignity and rights," Art. 1, United Nations' *Universal Declaration of Human Rights*). By contrast with the egalitarian concept of *Würde* (dignity), *Ehre* (honor) is a social and psychological concept and subject to change over the course of history; it is practiced by each society or class within that society according to written or unwritten codes of honor.

The treatment of various concepts of honor has become a very fruitful field for analysis, and is now part of the canon of research paradigms when describing historic and recent societies and cultures. In connection with their research, historians, sociologists, and cultural anthropologists considered *Ehre*/honor primarily as a characteristic that differentiated social classes or estates. They saw *Ehre*/honor as a central concept, above all a value that was intrinsic to feudalism and—according to Max Weber—survived the transition from "the three estates" (Weber, 1980: 538) to a society stratified by class, from a feudal to a capitalistic model, more or less intact. The sociologist Georg Simmel, for whom *Ehre*/honor is situated somewhere between justice and morality as part of common decency, speaks of a "normative system of control" (Simmel, 1992: 78). In modern society, however, he believes that this no longer applies to the whole of society, but only to specific groups. By contrast Ludgera Vogt and Arnold Zingerle, representatives of the more recent practice of sociology, see honor as an "archaic moment" that exists in the present in many, contradictory forms (Vogt & Zingerle, 1994). Julian Pitt-Rivers—accompanied by John Peristiany in asserting that there is a Mediterranean honor and shame—offers a definition of honor in terms of three facets: "a sentiment, a manifestation of this sentiment in conduct, and the evaluation of this conduct by others" (Pitt-Rivers, 1968: 503). Pierre Bourdieu refers to "symbolic capital," which has roots in economic, social, and cultural capital, as "the acquisition of a reputation for competence and an image of respectability and honorability" (Bourdieu, 1984: 291). And Frank Henderson Stewart, who is mainly concerned with "personal honor," roughly characterizes this kind of honor as "a right to respect" (Stewart, 1994: 54, 145).

Ways in which the Concept of Honor Depends on the Temporal, Social, and Political Context

Max Scheler declared that, "It is not honor, but that onto which men pin their honor which is changeable" ("*Nicht die Ehre ist veränderlich, sondern worin die Menschen ihre Ehre setzen*") (Scheler, 1957: 153), and this lucid sentence conveys two meanings:

The phenomenon *Ehre*/honor consists both of constant elements and of variables. The constants, or categorial structure, of the phenomenon are that when a person subscribes to shared values on which to base his/her *Ehr-Würdigkeit* (i.e., the state of being worthy of honor) his fellow beings are bound to recognize this worth or value, thereby constituting the means to obtain an adequate social standing. Variability, by contrast, determines which types of expression are semantically allocated to historical concepts of honor; i.e., they are dictated by axiological rules, which can vary greatly in different cultures, epochs, and social groupings (family, class, nation).

Much that once was considered as honorable practice—for example participation in prostitution for ritual reasons (key word: piety), the practice of extracting blood revenge to restore injured family honor (pride), the public humiliation and mutilation of offenders (law), denying social and other rights to "dishonorable trades" (status), etc.—is now considered axiologically unacceptable in accordance with modern, i.e., humanist and enlightened, ethical standards. That is, variables are dependent on two different factors: time, which reveals varying forms of honor and values on the *diachronic, temporal* plane, and, on the other hand, the social or political factor, which acts on the *synchronous* level of the simultaneous to bring about gender-specific (men's honor or woman's honor) and group-specific valuations or, to be more precise, inter- and intra-social valuations of honorability.

An example of the *temporal* dimension may be found in the way that service activities have been valued in different ages: in antiquity services were performed by slaves (who were "ehrlos," i.e., *honorless*) and such tasks were beneath the attention of a free citizen; during the medieval period, Christian and knightly traditions based on a belief in the hierarchy of power and the value of loyalty elevated the axiological concept of service to a central position, meaning that service to others was seen as a worthy task for every layer in the hierarchy. Offering someone of superior status a cup at table, carving meat, helping him into his armor, holding his stirrup (in German the latter—*Steigbügelhalter*—is now used metaphorically and is negative in meaning) was common practice and considered an honorary post (*Ehrenamt*). Titles such as *Mundschenk* (cup-bearer), *Truchsess* (seneschal), *Kämmerer* (chamberlain), and *Marschall* (marshal) are reminders of these services.

In a feudal society members of the nobility were accorded special honor purely due to their noble birth, but in today's egalitarian, functionally divided society pedigree alone does not automatically entitle someone to especial respect or a position of honor. In a society divided into estates or classes, however, yardsticks such as "high birth," possessions, profession, or post determined the value of a person.

On the other hand, one can find many examples of synchronous, i.e., *simultaneously* co-existing, social or political dimensions of honor. Social fringe groups and (in German-speaking areas) "*unehrliche Leute*" (dishonest people) who have been judged "*nicht-ehrbar*" (dishonorable) by the representatives of groups privileged by law and society, may well, however, have their own code of honor (e.g., executioners, thieves, whores, and rogues) and behave "*ehrlich*" (honestly) when in the company of their fellows (in the original meaning of *ehrlich*, namely "*ehrbar*," honorable).

The most striking *political* example may be observed in the opposed, synchronous concepts of honor held by both regime and Resistance during the Nazi dictatorship. Whereas for the Nazis honor was to be seen in loyalty to a totalitarian regime based on racial ideology and to the "Führer" as the embodiment of national honor, the civilian and military adherents of the Resistance saw their honor in removing the criminal dictatorship from power and restoring the rule of law. Thus two different "honor groups"[1] confronted each other.

On the one side stands the nationalistic, racist Nazi concept of "Blood and honor." In his 1930 book *Der Mythus des 20. Jahrhunderts*, Alfred Rosenberg supplied the Nazis with an underpinning for their ideology of the superiority of the Germanic race and honor. In 1935 the Law for the Protection of German Blood and German Honor was passed at the party rally in Nuremberg, prohibiting marriage between Jews and people of "German blood"; any violation of this law was criminalized as a "shameful act" punishable by imprisonment with hard labor. In the aftermath of the "shameful diktat" (Schanddiktat) of the Versailles treaty, popular support for the Nazis grew steadily because they regarded national honor as the supreme goal of their actions and promised that Germans would cease to be a people without honor. "Enemies of the Reich," such as Jews, Sinti, and Roma, people stripped of their citizenship, and emigrants were declared to be without honor (*ehrlos*). The motto of the SS was "Our honor is loyalty" (*Unsere Ehre heißt Treue*) and the Hitler Youth daggers were marked with the words "Blood and Honor" (*Blut und Ehre*). In 1936 the Nazi Party held its "Rally of Honor," so called because the Party elite felt that the occupation of the Rhineland had restored German honor. When, on September 1, 1939, Hitler announced in the Reichstag that German troops had marched into Poland, his reason for the invasion was an alleged sequence of Polish measures to suppress all things German which Germany, as a "major and honorable power," could not allow to go unpunished. When German soldiers were killed in battle, the standard euphemism was "fallen on the field of honor."

This perverted travesty of a system of honor and morality, which claimed the lives of millions of people in Europe between 1933 and 1945, finds especially chilling expression in the secret *Posener Reden* ("Posen Speeches") held by Heinrich Himmler, the leader of the SS, between October 4 and 6, 1943 in the town hall of Posen, a Polish city (Poznan) that had been incorporated into the German Reich. The first speech was held before SS officers, the second before high-ranking officials, "Reichsleiter," "Gauleiter," and government representatives. They are among the most important of his speeches during the war years, revealing his role as the architect of the "final solution to the Jewish question" and as a man fired by his vision of a future "SS state" founded on a racial elite. Above all, the first speech shows Himmler's efforts to appeal to his audience's sense of honor and to enjoin the SS members to continue the task of exterminating the Jews:

> One basic principle must be the absolute rule for the SS men: We must be honest, decent, loyal and comradely to members of our own blood and to nobody else. [...]
> I am now referring to the evacuation of the Jews, the extermination of the Jewish people. It's one of those things that is easily said: "The Jewish people are being exterminated", says every party member, "this is very obvious, it's in our program, elimination of the Jews, extermination, we're doing it, hah, a small matter." [...] But none has observed it, endured it. Most of you here know what it means when 100 corpses lie next to each other, when there are 500 or when there are 1,000. To have endured this and at the same time to have remained a decent person – with exceptions due to human weaknesses – has made us tough, and is a glorious chapter that has not and will not be spoken of.
> (IMT, 1989, 29, pp. 123, 145–146)

This speech contains the absolute perversion of positive values such as "decency," "honor," "fulfilment of duty," and "loyalty"—by applauding perseverance in the business of mass murder. This horrific, new linking of murder and honor, of crime and decency, is exactly what constitutes the core of the Nazi perpetrator mentality.

The other "honor group" during the Nazi era was recruited from the opposition to the criminal regime. Resistance by the few was, however, contrasted with the majority of the population who adjusted to life under the regime, either from ignorance or as an act of self-preservation. In 1939 the laborer Georg Elser attempted to assassinate Hitler, Göring, and Himmler in Munich's Bürgerbräu beer cellars, in order to prevent war and bloodshed, and in the latter years of the war resistance stirred again. Above all, after reports of crimes committed by the Wehrmacht against the civilian population of the occupied Eastern regions started to circulate, opponents of the Nazi regime began to coalesce into a political opposition which replaced Nazi concepts of racial honor with their own, ethics-based concept of individual and national honor or shame. The small, radical part of the resistance movement was drawn from the military, civil service, and both major churches; they included liberals, conservatives, socialists, trade unionists, and laborers, all following the dictates of conscience to join in removing the totalitarian government from power. Their actions were based on the underlying concept that natural law permits tyrannicide, which Catholic doctrine also allows, if the assassination will create a new order and restore just rule. Correspondingly, the motives of those who advocated active resistance were based on internal and external honor; of these people, special importance was attached to the members of the "Kreisau Circle" and above all the "Men of the 20th July 1944" whose bomb attack only narrowly failed. Shortly before the assassination attempt, conservative colonel Claus Schenk Graf von Stauffenberg expressed an ethical justification for his heroic deed, for which he paid with his life:

It is time to take action. However, whoever dares to act needs to be aware that he is likely to go down in German history as a traitor.[2] But if he failed to act, he would be betraying his own conscience. [...]

I would not be able to look the widows and orphans of the fallen in the eye if I did not do everything I could to stop this senseless sacrifice of human life.

(Kramatz, 1965: 201, 132)

Henning von Tresckow wrote in a letter that he considered the assassination attempt to be necessary in order to prove "to the world and history that the German Resistance dared to take decisive action at the risk of their own lives" (Fest, 2004: 176) And Carl Friedrich Goerdeler wrote in his position paper for the government of the UK: "The German people must and will liberate itself from a system that, shielded by terror, commits heinous crimes and has destroyed the legal structure, honor and liberty of the German people" (Gillmann & Mommsen, 2003: 945). Despite the failure of the coup of July 20, 1944, in whose aftermath a large number of people were arrested and executed, "it should be the historian's first duty to pay tribute to those men who worked for the day of deliverance from tyranny and shame, for an end to the shedding of blood and for the cleansing of the German name" (Rothfels, 1962: 11).

The Phenomenon of Ehre/Honor or Schande/Shame and Its Treatment in Theodor Fontane's Effi Briest and J.M. Coetzee's Disgrace

The following text analysis specifically looks at two works from different epochs and different cultural environments – Germany at the end of the nineteenth century and post-Apartheid South Africa a century later – in order to illustrate the range of concepts covered by the notion of honor and its antipode, dishonor.

Both novels are exemplary, each in its own way: Fontane's *Effi Briest* is exemplary of the imperial, realistic literature of the Wilhelminian Empire with its omnipresent, imperative code of honor; Coetzee's *Disgrace* is exemplary of post-empire literature in the Republic of South Africa, with its broken protagonists and ambivalent code of honor. These two narrative texts were chosen because they illustrate, each in its own specific manner, aspects of the contrasting pairs honor/shame, internal/external honor, male/female honor, upper/lower class, humankind/animals, naturalness/social constructs, and power/impotence.

Theodor Fontane's Effi Briest (1895)

Theodor Fontane's (1819–1898) works of literature describe individuals in social entanglements and conflicts of honor which reveal patterns that remain basically unchanged to this day. In his socially critical writings

Fontane often took honor as his subject matter; for example, in his 1882 novel *L'Adultera*, which was based on an authentic case of adultery and subsequent duel that happened in Berlin society circles (the "Ardenne Case"). Another example is the story *Schach von Wuthenow* (1883) in which Fontane diagnoses the aristocratic officer Schach as displaying symptoms of false honor, which is nothing but vanity, and examines the questionable rules of *honnêteté* as it is demanded by the king. In 1895 the most important of Fontane's works on the topic of honor was published: *Effi Briest* [3]— written in the tradition of novels about adultery, such as Gustave Flaubert's *Madame Bovary* (1856/57) and Lev Tolstoy's *Anna Karenina* (1875/77).

The plot of the novel sees 17-year-old Effi von Briest entering into a marriage her parents have arranged with the ambitious Baron von Innstetten, who is 20 years older than she. Innstetten is primarily interested in his career (he is a Landrat or district administrator) and takes Effi away from Brandenburg to his house in Eastern Pomerania, where she is almost completely isolated, bored, and prey to superstitious fears. Even motherhood does little to alter the young woman's emotional state. Neglected by her husband she drifts somewhat half-heartedly into an affair with Captain Crampas, a manipulative womanizer. Their adulterous meetings come to an end when Innstetten is promoted to a ministry position in Berlin. Six years later Innstetten happens to find love letters written by Crampas to Effi and challenges him to a duel. Crampas is fatally wounded and dies, Innstetten divorces Effi and is granted custody of the child. Ostracized by Berlin society, Effi becomes increasingly ill. Her doctor insists she should return to her parents' house, where she dies at the age of 26.

All the characters in the novel and the ways in which they are depicted are defined by the core conflict between the "natural" and the conventional, by natural feelings in contrast with social standards of honor with which people are obliged to comply. Each character represents one of these two categories. Thus Innstetten is categorized as the "man of character," the "man with principles" (p. 25), "high principles" (p. 26), the "*Ehrenmann*" ("He has his honor," p. 95), whereas Effi is the "*Tochter der Luft*" ("always flying through the air," p. 4), the "*Naturkind*" ("child of nature," p. 28). The stage on which the lives of the novel's characters are played out, ending in success or failure, is thus set between the two opposites, "Nature" and the "Natural," in the powerful Rousseauian tradition on the one side and "Society" with its prevailing morality and concepts of honor on the other. The fact that Fontane always uses dogs to reveal what is "natural" betrays his skeptical view of human society whose emotional world is, as the author writes in a letter, "untrustworthy" ("*windig*") (Zuberbühler, 1991: 81). In *Effi Briest* Rollo, Baron von Innstetten's Newfoundland dog becomes the loyal companion of the childlike protagonist, whom her mother describes as "wild". The dog immediately senses that Effi is a kindred spirit and when "she held out her hand to him, he gave it a friendly lick" (p. 38). Rollo, together with Effi, the "child of nature," her father, her cousin Dagobert, the apothecary Gieshübler, the nanny Roswitha, and, to a certain degree, the irresponsible Crampas are all characters with an affinity for the natural; they are contrasted in the novel with those who represent social standards—Innstetten, Effi's mother, the country nobility, the housemaid Johanna, daughter Annie, and the upper echelons of Berlin society.

In this framework of regulation by the constraints of society's concept of honor a key topic for discussion is the rigid set of sexual morals, especially as applied to women whatever their social class. Roswitha, for example, tells her mistress Effi that she is ostracized in her home village and that her father almost killed her with a red-hot iron bar when he heard she was expecting an illegitimate child. "And I had a younger sister, and she kept pointing at me and saying 'shame on you!' And then, when the child was about to come, I went into a barn nearby because I didn't dare have it at home." And "on the third day they took the child away, and when later on I asked where it was, they told me it was in good hands" (p. 142). It is true that Effi's standing, as a married, well-off and respected member of high society is considerably more comfortable than that of Roswitha. But by embarking on a secret affair with Crampas she has violated convention and external honor. Therefore, she is increasingly plagued by the fear that one day her adultery will be revealed and all will be lost. In a moment of self-recognition in front of the mirror she feels "as if someone were looking over her shoulder" (p. 135). She understands that it is her bad conscience, because she knows she is guilty and her family's reputation is at stake. And in her farewell letter to Crampas just before leaving for Berlin, she blames herself for the affair. "The guilt is all mine" (p. 152). On the evening of their departure Effi reflects once more on her internal honor and the question of shame and guilt ("bearing this guilt inside me," p. 175). "Just as I don't feel true remorse, I don't feel true shame. I just feel ashamed because of the eternal lies and deception; I always took pride in the fact that I couldn't lie and didn't need to lie." She is shocked by her own lack of moral shame: "Yes, I'm tormented by fear and shame at my deception, but shame at my guilt, that's something I *don't* feel, or not real shame, or not enough, and the fact that I don't feel it is killing me" (p. 176). Having been socialized in a Christian culture of sin and guilt and in view of the prevailing concepts of honor, she should be feeling deep shame and remorse. Since this is not the case, the reader understands that Effi, married by her parents to Innstetten who was "cold as a snowman" (p. 52), feels cheated of true love and happiness in her life and that her love affair with Crampas is justified as compensation for her loss. Talking to her mother shortly before her death, Effi portrays Innstetten as a man of honor but incapable of love. "There was much that was good in his nature, and he was as noble as anyone can be who lacks true love" (p. 237).

Although Innstetten could have regarded Effi's adultery as a thing of the past and forgiven her, and although he claims to harbor no thoughts of revenge and still loves Effi (pp. 188–189), he decides to satisfy the injury to his internal and external honor by dueling with Crampas. Agitated and upset he calls for his friend Wüllersdorf, saying, "I've been hurt, I've been shamefully deceived" and there is a "stain on my honor." He is aware that as a social being he must comply with the conventions of Wilhelmenian society in terms of respect and external honor: "We're not just separate individuals, we're part of a whole, and we must always consider the whole, we're entirely dependent on it." Because "there's a something that has developed in our society," and "that—tyrannical, if you like—social something [*"Gesellschafts-Etwas"*] is not concerned with charm, nor with love, nor with the lapse of time. I have no choice. I have to" (pp. 189–190), he explains to his friend Wüllersdorf and asks him to take his demand for a duel to Crampas and also to act as his second. Wüllersdorf agrees, but expresses his doubts about the principles behind the obsolete institution of the duel of honor: "Our cult of honor is worship of a false idol, but we have to submit as long as the idol rules" (p. 191).

In the context of this aristocratic, military cult of honor, Kaiser Wilhelm I (1871–1888) in fact obliged "all officers to duel, when he declared that he would tolerate in his army neither an officer who injures the honor of a comrade, nor an officer who is not able to uphold his honor" (Frevert, 1991, p. 113). Innstetten's guilt consists of the fact that in consideration of his career, and fearful of losing his reputation, he sacrifices to this idol, although from the ethical and rational point of view he despises it.

Effi's mother Luise von Briest is also obedient to the rules of external honor, by refusing to allow her daughter back home for fear of being excluded from polite society: "We cannot offer you a quiet corner in Hohen-Cremmen, a refuge in our house, for that would mean shutting the house off from all the world, and we are definitely not inclined to do that" (p. 205).

After Effi has been stigmatized as an adulteress and divorced woman, avoided by Berlin society and, as a dishonored woman not even permitted to do charitable works (p. 214), she wishes to contact her daughter Annie. After the meeting, bitterly disappointed by Annie's cold, unnatural and affected manners, which speak of Innstetten's upbringing and influence, Effi rails against him and the values he represents in an inner monologue: "I thought he had a noble heart and always felt small beside him; but now I know that it's him, he's the one who is small-minded. And because he's small-minded, he's cruel." Effi believes that Innstetten's lack of internal honor leads to his craving for honor, his desire for a career and external honors: "He just wanted to get on in the world, that's all.—Honor, honor, honor ... and then he shot the poor man dead, a man whom I didn't even love." Finally, addressing Instetten she says: "I loathe what I did, but what I loathe even more is your virtue. Away with you" (pp. 221–222).

In the last part of the novel—following their doctor's advice the ailing Effi is allowed to live once again at her parents' home—the author again contrasts internal and external honor in a most effective manner. On one and the same day Innstetten, living an arid, lonely life, receives two letters: one informs him that the Kaiser has awarded him the order of the Roter Adler (red eagle) for his services. The second is from the straightforward, good-hearted Roswitha, who has remained loyal to Effi both in Berlin and at her parents' house. She asks him to send Rollo to Effi, because she urgently needs a companion on her lonely walks and, after all, the loss of social honor and standing mean nothing to animals. "That's the good thing about animals that they're not concerned about that kind of thing" (p. 231).

When Innstetten has read Roswitha's letter which is a testimony to her superior humanity and internal honor, he finds external honors and "all that glittering show" to be so lacking in meaning that he throws the "Order of the Red Eagle" to the ground in a fury, crying out, "Stay there until you turn *black*." Talking to Privy Councillor Wüllersdorf afterwards, both agree on the topic of Roswitha: "We're no match for her" (p. 231). Like Rollo, Roswitha stands for those who place natural affection and unconditional loyalty above social concepts of honor or morality, to which Effi Briest has fallen victim. "The 'ladies man' Crampas and the career man Innstetten— Effi's self-fulfilment as a woman is crushed between these two models of manliness" (Mecklenburg, 2018: 141).

All three main characters are caught, each in a different way, in the maelstrom of the two dominant discourses (in their political, ethical, and cultural dimensions), namely the discourse on honor and the Rousseauian discourse. Natural feelings or naturalness are contrasted with striving to gain and preserve external honor, thus creating a conflict which all three characters fail to resolve. Last but not least, the novel is a passionate plea to end the irrational institution of dueling, criticism of which had been growing steadily since the Enlightenment debate (Burkhart, 2006: 84–88, 100–106; Appiah, 2010: 31–51), leading to the foundation of anti-dueling associations (in England 1844, in Germany not until 1902).

J.M. Coetzee's Disgrace (1999)

J.M. Coetzee's (1940—) novel *Disgrace*,[4] set in post-apartheid South Africa, is a complex text that unites a large number of aspects and dimensions in its plot:

The protagonist David Lurie is a professor of literature in Cape Town; after two failed marriages he lives alone. A brief affair with a colored girl, Melanie Isaacs, one of his students, results in his dishonorable dismissal from the university. The 52-year-old is particularly reproached for refusing to show any remorse, but he sees himself as a servant of Eros, just like Lord Byron. Lurie takes refuge with his daughter Lucy, who runs a small, provincial organic farm. She makes her living by selling flowers and vegetables on the market and by running boarding kennels for watchdogs. She has a black neighbor and farmhand, Petrus. Her closest friends are Bev and Bill Shaw, who operate a veterinary clinic and animal shelter; like Lucy, they are animal rights advocates. During Lurie's stay, three black men force their way onto the farm and rape Lucy. The men also injure David, kill the dogs and escape from the farm in David's car. Petrus is away from the farm when the attack takes place. Lucy recovers only slowly from the attack but refuses to report the rapists and give up the farm. When it becomes apparent that she is pregnant, David tries once again to persuade her to leave the land. But Lucy meekly accepts her fate. In her eyes, relinquishing her independence is the price for being able to stay on the piece of land she loves. She places herself under the protection of Petrus and transfers ownership of the farm to him, although one of the perpetrators is distantly related to Petrus. David returns to Cape Town to discover that his apartment has been ransacked. He visits Melanie and her family and asks forgiveness for what he has done to them. On the farm he takes on menial tasks and is a voluntary assistant to Bev Shaw. In his free time he tries to compose a chamber opera, but finally gives this project up.

Honor and shame are the main issues in this novel, as its title *Disgrace* indicates. Usually the terms "disgrace" and "shame" appear together, because, as a rule, a sense of shame follows disgrace. David Lurie, however, a self-righteous egomaniac, feels no sense of shame for having seduced and used Melanie, which his position of power enabled him to do. "Not rape," Lurie states, "not quite that, but undesired nevertheless, undesired to the core. As though she had decided to go slack, die within for the duration, like a rabbit when the jaws of the fox close on its neck" (p. 25). However, when Lucy is raped he changes his attitude, having become a victim instead of a perpetrator. He takes the attack on his daughter personally, "Lucy's secret; his disgrace" (p. 109). David Lurie, locked in the bathroom and injured, is unable to rush to his daughter's aid and experiences his helplessness as shameful and disgraceful. Now, after the traumatic attack on Lucy, he becomes aware that it was disgraceful of him to have an affair with one of the students because they are almost completely at his mercy. Only now does he begin to understand the true dimension of his past acts, and feels shame at the offense he has caused Melanie and her family. "If I was you, I'd be very ashamed of myself" (p. 38), Melanie's father had told him before reporting him for sexual harassment to the Dean of the university, although at that point in time David's arrogance prevented him from realizing his moral failing.

In *Disgrace* the honor–shame code is embedded in political, post-colonial, philosophical, and psychological discourses which serve as parables for constant themes of human existence—power and impotence, power and subjugation. As in Coetzee's prose work likewise published in 1999, *The Lives of Animals*, the question of the relationship between humans and animals and its ethical implications is likewise a key issue in *Disgrace*. From the political perspective, the novel paints a gloomy picture of South Africa's progress since the end of apartheid (1994), highlighting the failure to achieve integration. Violence has now found new perpetrators and chosen new victims, whose physical existence and honor are at stake. In Melanie's case

David Lurie found himself confronted by an organization called Women Against Rape. The group's acronym is WAR, and its members wage war until the enemy has been successfully stripped of his social standing. David Lurie, in disgrace, sees no alternative but to retire to the countryside. And there, out of the blue, war is waged against Lucy. The three black men, who have forced their way into the house on a pretext, mishandle not only David and lock him in a room, but they violate Lucy in order to teach her, the white lady farmer, a lesson and to demean her. To Lucy however, the rape is not as bad as the hatred expressed in the act, "'the shock of being hated, I mean. In the act'" (p. 156), she says. Nevertheless, as if taking upon herself the guilt of the white people during apartheid, she rejects her father's advice to sell the farm and move to Holland or somewhere else. She does not report the rape to the police, merely the theft of objects, in order to obtain money from the insurance company. It remains unclear whether Petrus, her black neighbor and farmhand, had any indirect involvement in the crime. Lucy draws up a new survival plan which results in her transferring the title deeds of the farm to Petrus in return for his protection. She explains what she considers to be the rapists' understandable and justified motives in this way, "'They see me as owing something. They see themselves as debt collectors, tax collectors. Why should I be allowed to live here without paying?'" (p. 158) Later she reiterates that living in South Africa requires one to tolerate brutalization and humiliation, and that this is the price for the right to stay on this piece of land as an unmarried, white woman. "'Yes, I agree, it is humiliating. But perhaps that is a good point to start from again. Perhaps that is what I must learn to accept. To start at a ground level. With nothing. No cards, no weapons, no property, no rights, no dignity'. 'Like a dog?' 'Yes, like a dog'" (p. 205). Responding to her father's insistence that justice should be done and the perpetrators punished, she says she is "prepared to anything, make any sacrifice for the sake of peace" (p. 208).

Not only has Lucy been raped, she has also, it transpires, been made pregnant. But she refuses an abortion; she will have the child and it will be colored: a life-long embodiment of her shame. She counters her father's objections by saying she trusts in Nature that will allow motherly love to grow (p. 216).

Lucy, the emancipated white woman who, in the immediate aftermath of the rape no longer wishes to go to the market and show herself in public "because of the disgrace, because of the shame" (p. 115), accepts the new balance of power. She insists that this is her own private affair (p. 112). The narrator adds no comment, letting the statement stand. But nor does he deny the supposition that paying this price to stay in the country could well be valid not only for Lucy but for other white people too, such as David. When Petrus wants to lay a new water pipe, David will be his "*handlanger*" (p. 136).

The novel *Disgrace* is the complex treatment of issues regarding political, historical, and ethical responsibility, but above all of the paired questions of honor and shame. Commenting on the title and main motif of *Disgrace*, David Attridge remarks that the antonym of *disgrace* is not *grace*.

> The opposite of disgrace is something like "honor"; the OED definition of "disgrace" links it frequently with "dishonor". Public shame, in other words, is contrasted with, and can only be cancelled by, public esteem, disgrace is redeemed by honor. Lurie spurns the opportunity to escape disgrace by means of public confession, and he makes little attempt to regain a position of public honor after his shaming.
>
> (Attridge, 2005: 178)

Instead of attempting the impossible task of regaining external honor, "public honor," and being rehabilitated at the university, David Lurie sets out to reclaim and rebuild self-esteem and internal honor through self-abasement and by relinquishing power. "I am sunk into a state of disgrace from which it will not be easy to lift myself. It is not a punishment I have refused. I do not murmur against it. On the contrary, I am living it out from day to day, trying to accept disgrace as my state of being. Is it enough for God, do you think, that I live in disgrace without term?" (p. 172) Lurie asks Melanie's father. The *metanoia*, or inner reform and change of heart that David Lurie wishes to demonstrate also finds its expression in gestures: in order to obtain the forgiveness of Melanie's family for his dishonorable conduct, "he gets to his knees and touches his forehead to the floor" (p. 173).

Lurie is striving for secular redemption, not salvation in any religious sense: "The question of (secular) salvation is one of the most difficult ones in Coetzee's writings," stresses Richard Alan Northover. "It is not clear why a secular writer like Coetzee should feel the need to use the biblical narrative of the fall, grace and redemption at all." It is fair to ask, then, "what exactly his protagonists need to be saved from. Is it from their guilt at being (unwillingly) complicit in exploitative and brutal social, political and economic structures" such as colonialism, apartheid and the industrialized farming of animals? Or is Coetzee concerned "with the salvation not only of his protagonists but also of the entire world they inhabit?" Northover comes to the conclusion that "the state of disgrace in *Disgrace* is realised at all levels, that the novel depicts an entire world in a fallen state requiring salvation, but without the possibility of divine intervention or grace" (Northover, 2009: 202).

Dogs play a relevant role in the plot of *Disgrace*. In this novel dogs serve as a metaphor for impotence. They are completely dependent on the humans who give them a home. The paradox is that Lucy and Bev, later David too, reveal their humanity in their treatment of the dogs. When David has become a volunteer at the animal shelter he calls himself, as Petrus used to earlier (p. 64), a "dog-man" (pp. 129, 146). His task is to transport to the crematorium the bodies of animals who have been put down. Dogs, according to Bev, who runs the clinic for unwanted, sick, or stray animals, can smell thoughts. That is why she administers lethal injections to the dogs herself, so that she can talk to them, stroke and comfort them and maintain the dogs' last remnants of dignity. When David Lurie sees how the crematorium workers wield shovels to smash the stiff cadavers in the sacks, to make it easier to push them into the furnace, he undertakes this job too. In self-critical manner he asks himself,

> Why has he taken on this job? To lighten the burden on Bev Shaw? For that it would be enough to drop off the bags at the dump and drive away. For the sake of the dogs? But the dogs are dead; and what do dogs know of honor and dishonor anyway? For himself, then. For his idea of the world, a world in which men do not use shovels to beat corpses into a more convenient shape for processing.

In his self-ironic view he is not only "a dog-man: a dog undertaker, a dog psychopompos," but has become an absurd saint, "He saves the honor of corpses because there is no one else stupid enough to do it" (pp. 145–146).

The young black men who raped Lucy kill her dogs too—taking pleasure in their cruelty—"contemptible, yet exhilarating, probably, in a country where dogs are bred to snarl at the mere smell of a black man" (p. 110). Dogs are used by white people as a tool to wield power, they perform what their master commands and in this function they fall victim to the revenge extracted by the black men.

To Lurie, the aesthete, having sex with the unattractive Bev Shaw, whom he respects for her animal rights advocacy and internal honor, is a retrograde step, a kind of "going to the dogs," but he is still prepared to accept the situation. "Let me not forget this day, he tells himself, lying beside her when they are spent. After the sweet flesh of Melanie Isaacs, this is what I have to get used to, this and even less than this" (p. 150).

But someone like David Lurie, who has lost his honor in the eyes of society, can only try to regain his internal honor through radical self-abasement that then leads to redemption. Authors such as Dostoevsky and, in the same tradition, Coetzee have offered non-theological interpretations of a term found in the *Letter to the Philippians* (2:5–11), i.e., *kenosis* (self-renunciation), which illustrates what lies behind the spiritual passage of the characters in their novels. Michael S. Kochin quite rightly refers to Coetzee's *Disgrace* as "postmetaphysical literature" (Kochin, 2004: 4).

David Lurie (David) battles with his former self (Goliath) as it were, not with a dueling opponent as does Innstetten in *Effi Briest*. He accepts that he cannot regain his social reputation, because "the scandal will follow him" and he is "no longer marketable" (p. 89). He also accepts that his project to compose an opera called *Byron in Italy*, which he once imagined would bring fame and honors, is a failure. "It would have been nice to be returned triumphant to society as the author of an eccentric little chamber opera. But that will not be" (p. 214). At the end of the novel he gives up the last power he still possesses; that of sparing the life of his favorite dog. "'Are you giving him up?'" Bev Shaw asks. "'Yes, I am giving him up'" (p. 220) are the last words he speaks in the novel.

Impotence or a refusal to exercise power is the ideal of a state of internal honor—as practiced by the Cynics or dog-philosophers of antiquity. The name is derived from *kyon*/κύων (dog), and the name thus expresses the Cynic reduction of life to its animal elements as a break with every form of human convention. Rejection of society entails forgoing the material goods it offers, abstinence of the type practiced by Diogenes who decided to live without desires and thereby achieve spiritual autarchy.

This reference to the Cynics can help to understand the concept of salvation that Coetzee has developed in *Disgrace*; it shows not only in David Lurie's care of the dogs in the animal shelter but also in the fact that he must learn to free himself of his devotion to Eros, which was the cause of his "fall from Grace." Therefore, he is admiring of Petrus as a man:

> If there is such a thing as honest toil, Petrus bears its marks. A man of patience, energy, resilience. A peasant, a *paysan,* a man of the country. A plotter and a schemer and no doubt a liar too, like peasants everywhere. Honest toil and honest cunning.
>
> (p. 117)

In the final analysis he respects his daughter too, who has practiced autarchy (in the Cynic meaning) on her patch of land through hard work on the farm and an ethical lifestyle including vegetarianism and respect for animal rights. Her ideal of organic farming and respect for life in "a new world" (p. 117) are closely bound up with her land. If she had left the farm following the rape "she would have given up her dream to create a better world and capitulated to violence. Her stubborn, Cynical refusal to budge and her persistence despite personal violation make her the real hero of the novel," as Northover so rightly remarks (p. 247). By recognizing the new black rulers of the country, represented by Petrus (whose biblical name means "rock"), Lucy, the white woman, who feels ashamed of the colonial past and finally cedes her right to the land to those who, in her view, have a prerogative to it, is attempting to pay honor to her name—Lucia, the illuminated one, the enlightened; Lurie's name however, has overtones of "lure" and of "lurid."

Notes

1 The term "honor group" refers to "a set of people who follow the same code of honor and who recognize each other as doing so" (Taylor, 1985: 55).
2 The reference is to what would be seen as a dishonorable breach of the soldier's oath of loyalty to his commander in chief, i.e., Hitler.

3 The quotations are taken from Mike Mitchell's translation of *Effi Briest* (Oxford University Press, 2015).
4 Quotations are taken from the 1999 edition of *Disgrace* published by Martin Secker & Warburg.

References

Appiah, K.A. (2010). *The Honor Code*. W.W. Norton & Company.
Attridge, D. (2005). *J.M. Coetzee and the Ethics of Reading*. University of Chicago Press.
Benjamin, W. (1936). *Deutsche Menschen: Von Ehre ohne Ruhm, von Größe ohne Glanz, von Würde ohne Sold*. Vita Nova.
Bourdieu, P. (1984). *Distinction: A social critique of the judgement of taste*. Harvard University Press.
Burkhart, D. (2006). *Eine Geschichte der Ehre*. Wissenschaftliche Buchgesellschaft.
Fest, J. (2004). *Staatsstreich: Der lange Weg zum 20. Juli*. Siedler.
Frevert, U. (1991). *Ehrenmänner*. C.H. Beck.
Gillmann, S., & Mommsen, H. (eds.) (2003). *Politische Schriften und Brief Carl Friedrich Goerdelers*. K.G. Saur.
IMT (1989). *International Military Tribunal Nuremberg: The Nuremberg Trials*. Vol. 29: *Documents and other proofs*. Delphin. https://phdn.org/archives/holocaust-history.org/himmler-poznan/speech-text.shtml [31.05.2020]
Kochin, M.S. (2004). *Postmetaphysical Literature: Reflections on J.M. Coetzee's Disgrace. Perspectives of Political Science*, 33, 4–9.
Kramatz, J. (1965). *Claus Graf von Stauffenberg: The Life of an Officer, 15 November 1907–20 July 1944*. Bernard & Graefe.
Mecklenburg, N. (2018). *Theodor Fontane: Realismus, Redevielfalt, Ressentiment*. Metzler.
Northover, R.A. (2009). *J.M. Coetzee and Animal Rights: Elizabeth Costello's Challenge to Philosophy*. University of Pretoria Press.
Peristiany, J.G., & Pitt-Rivers, J. (eds.) (1991). *Honor and Grace in Mediterranean Society*. Cambridge University Press.
Pitt-Rivers, J. (1968). Honor. *International Encyclopedia of the Social Sciences*, 6. David L. Sills (ed.). Macmillan, Free Press, 503–511.
Rothfels, H. (1962). *The German Opposition to Hitler*. Henry Regnery Company.
Scheler, M. (1957). *Über Scham und Schamgefühl* [1913]. Gesammelte Werke in 15 Bdn., 10. Francke, 65–154.
Simmel, G. (1992). *Soziologie* [1908]. Suhrkamp.
Stewart, F.H. (1994). *Honor*. University of Chicago Press.
Taylor, G. (1985). *Pride, Shame and Guilt: Emotions of Self-Assessment*. Clarendon Press.
Vogt, L. (1997). *Zur Logik der Ehre in der Gegenwartsgesellschaft*. Suhrkamp.
Vogt, L., & Zingerle, A. (eds.) (1994). *Ehre – archaische Momente in der Moderne*. Suhrkamp.
Weber, M. (1980). *Wirtschaft und Gesellschaft* [1922]. Niemeyer.
Zuberbühler, R. (1991). "Ja, Luise, die Kreatur." *Zur Bedeutung der Neufundländer in Fontanes Romanen*. De Gruyter.

2 Shame

A Social Emotion and Its Cultural Concepts in a Historical (European) Perspective

Jörg Wettlaufer

Introduction

This introductory chapter aims at giving us a solid understanding of what shame both biologically and socially means in the context of this volume and why it is difficult to approach the social concept of shame, like honor, throughout history. Nowadays, we have a reasonable understanding of the physiology of the shame reaction in humans, but our knowledge about the neurophysiology of the moral emotions in the brain is still relatively poor compared to other aspects of our cognitive and emotional abilities. With the biological bases of these emotions comes the insight that there must have been (and probably still is) some adaptive value in the ability to feel these emotions. The best candidate for such an added value seems to be the ability of shame to support cooperation in groups. We will see later why that is and how the socio-cultural functionalities of shame stretch far beyond that one capacity. The chapter concentrates on Western culture (like the whole book) and adopts a perspective of deep history, integrating through anthropological reasoning also prehistory and periods before the invention of writing (Shryock & Smail, 2011; Smail, 2007). To condense this long period of time into a book chapter, the text can obviously not always go into minute detail but will sketch very broadly the development of research on shame in historical perspective in the last decades. It will also deliver some references to important theories that I consider crucial for the understanding of the cultural history of shame in the European context.

The Biology of Shame

Let's consider first how the natural history of shame, the underlying moral and self-conscious emotion, is understood today. Of course, one will find many different definitions in the relevant disciplines, but there are also some aspects that most scientists agree upon nowadays. It is undisputed that shame is an unpleasant feeling; an emotion with a strong bodily component. It is very probably caused by an interaction of the limbic system with the orbitofrontal cortex that acts directly on the sympathetic nervous system and causes blushing, as neuroscience tells us (Beer et. al., 2003). But there are even more visible signs of shame.

In the condition and experience of shame, people lower their faces, drop their shoulders, and give the impression that they want to vanish into the ground, presumably because it is rooted in appeasement behavior already known in primates. This theory was put forward by Daniel T. Fessler in 2007. He claims that "human shame is a bipartite emotion consisting of an ancient, or ancestral, component that is shared with nonhuman primates, and a novel, or derived, component that is likely unique to our species" (Fessler, 2007: 176). On the bases of this theory, one can distinguish between a phylogenetic older appeasement-shame and a younger conformity-shame: two different sides of the very same emotion (Fessler 1999, 2007; Fessler & Haley, 2004). This is also supported by linguistic data. The polysemy of shame terms incorporating shame as an emotional state and the feeling of reverence at the same time around the world and also through time supports Fessler's theory (Fessler, 2004; see also Wettlaufer, 2008; Wettlaufer & Nishimura, 2013). Apart from the polysemy of shame words itself there is more linguistic support through the observation of shame-related terms like "blushing" cross-culturally. The blush is present in all cultures and ethnic groups (Casimir & Schnegg, 2002). Blushing for shame is regulated by the sympathetic nervous system (Mariauzouls, 1996). Given how deeply this emotion is rooted in the human nervous system and brain, there is no doubt that it has been selected in an evolutionary process and thus is a functional adaptation. Cooperation is a very likely candidate for the selection pressure that shaped the ability to feel shame, because it is an effective but not physically wounding punishment for non-conformity to the norms of a group that one is identifying with. This makes shame culturally flexible (with no fixed rules on what to be ashamed of), yet effective in all possible environments and groups of all sizes that share common norms and moral standards (Boehm, 2012; Bowles & Gintis, 2011: 186–198; Engelen et al., 2009).

Briefly, we can say that shame consists of a physical reaction to a transgression of cultural norms, and is elicited by behavior that is deemed inappropriate in terms of in-group norms. This makes shame, as other emotions, a mediator between the human body and the human capacity for culture in its broader sense. It is not by chance that shame is the emotion that is characterized in the Bible as the sign of human condition itself, the distinctive marker between man and animal (Scheler, 1913: 69). Nudity, in the sense of not wearing a distinctive cultural marker, is associated with shame in all traditional cultures because it presents the body in its natural state – which lacks the distinctive feature of human kind, the alteration caused by the apple from the tree of knowledge – as the Bible puts it.

> Nude bodies remind us of the natural layer upon which humanity is built, as they react to stimuli from a basic domain of life that even a strong tool like shame for self-control cannot easily cope with: sexuality

and procreation. This shame – related to the human body – can also be understood in terms of consciousness about the additive character and fragility of emotion-based normative control that guides humans in their social relationships and makes interactions so different from what the great apes, for example, show us. At least it gives us the possibility to act differently.

(Wettlaufer, 2016a: 36; c.f. Bauks, 2011, Bologne, 1999)

But how do we learn about these rules and know what to be ashamed of? Following such rules is a skill that has been learned during infancy and childhood through good examples or shaming by a caregiver (Griffin, 1995; Lewis, 1992; Schore, 1998; Stipek, 1995). This is universal and can be found in all cultures, although some East Asian and Pacific cultures really seem to play on the use of shame in education more than others.[1] At the end of adolescence, the most important threshold to becoming an accepted member of the group of adults is not sexual maturity but the ability to control body and mind according to the rules and norms internalized during infancy and adolescence, in order to perform as an effective member of the team. In many societies, this transition is marked by so called *rite de passage* (Van Gennep). The early medieval Welsh law governing women gives a stunning definition of female "shame" in such a setting. Shame is related to women's bodies and the laws of Hywel Daa[2] associate particular payments to the transition from a virgin to a married woman:

> The three shames of a girl are: One is that her father tells her, "I have given you to a husband", the second is, when she first goes to bed to her husband, the third is when she first rises from the bed to the midst of people. For the giving, her *amobr* is paid. For her virginity her *cowyll*; for her shame her *egweddi*.
>
> (Owen, 1980: 49)

It is of course not easy to grasp the original meaning of those words translated as "shame" in this context. The first shame, the announcement of the betrothal, might be understood as a first indication of the girl's transition in her life cycle and therefore only anticipating the prospective "shame" through the consummation of marriage. But why has sexuality, obviously one of the most natural things in life, been shameful at all in this cultural setting? This can only and has to be understood in the social and cultural context of the Welsh Christian kingdom of the early Middle Ages.

From Bio-Emotions to Socio-Symbolic Concepts and Cultural Adaptations—Shame and Honor as Socio-Symbolic Categories

At this point we have to emphasize an important distinction between shame in the sense of "dishonor" as a socio-symbolic category and the meaning of shame as signifying an emotional inner state (Casimir & Jung, 2009: 230). When talking about honor and shame in history we have to be clear about what we refer to. In most cases we will only be able to observe how people act and react within these cultural categories. The underlying emotional state stays hidden. Only autobiographical texts confessing the inner state of a person or attributions of this inner state by other people allow us, through the filter of text or images, to catch a glimpse of those volatile bodily emotional experiences. The fascinating thing about this distinction is that emotions and their socio-symbolic concepts act almost independently from each other, but one cannot exist without the other. The adaptation that molded shame as an emotion (presumably sustaining cooperation and group norms) can be similar in the cultural usage or indeed totally different. In Chapter 8 of this volume I give an example of how shame was used, through the Christian interpretation of confession and penance, to support cooperation and trust within medieval towns. But at the same time shame and humiliation was used constantly as a means in the struggle for power and resources. As sociologists and historians point out, shame and status are as close as honor and status (Frevert, 2017, 2020; Harré, 1986; Harré & Parrot, 1996; Miller, 1993; Neckel, 1991). Honor and shame tend to play an important role for gender roles in traditional societies. So far, the examples suggest that shame is mostly understood in a negative sense: something that has to be avoided. But shame also has a positive perspective in both the biological and the historical dimensions. The adherence to group norms appears as a selective advantage for this emotional trait and the obsession with "shamefastness" and the preservation of female honor in the later Middle Ages is just one more example for these many faces of shame in the cultural makeup of societies (Flannery, 2020). We can easily add more examples. In Ancient Greek there was a larger variety of rather positive meanings of shame, which also includes semantic fields such as awe, pity, consideration, sense of honor, or respect. David Yeandle points to this ambivalence of shame in his work on the semantics of "schame" in Old and Middle German (Yeandle, 2001). On the one hand, shame expresses itself as an unpleasant sensation, on the other hand, it is also understood as a virtue.

The integration of cultural history and evolutionary biology called "evolutionary (cultural) history" allows us to see the broader picture of shame in a truly anthropological perspective (Wettlaufer, 2015).[3] There is no direct or simple analogy between the biological and the cultural functions of shame, but as cultural traits tend to be adaptive in traditional societies, it is worth checking if such analogies of the biological adaptation with the cultural "exploitations" can be found in (deep) history.

The Semantics of Shame across Languages and Time

To grasp the meaning and the social use of emotions in a historical dimension, one should first and foremost turn to the semantics and the change of meaning of emotion terms in historical texts. It is obvious that English "shame" differs semantically from the corresponding words in other languages (cf. Hurtado-de-Mendoza et al., 2013; Krawczak, 2014; Rusch, 2004). While in German the direct antonym of honor (*Ehre*) is dishonor (*Unehre*), the English "shame" can represent both *Scham* and *Schande* in German. Honor and pride are closely related but refer of course to different, partially overlapping concepts. In French shame can be translated with several expressions originating in different Latin words. While *pudeur* means the shame of the body (Bologne, 1999), *honte* and *vergogne* are morally charged and refer to the Latin concept of *verecundia*. Also Arabic language has several terms for both sides of the dyad (Al-Jallad, 2002). To make communication about emotions even harder, the semantic fields of these words have changed over time. Given these semantically overlapping expressions and changing meanings, both the concept and the experience of honor and shame are extremely difficult to describe for past times.[4] To illustrate the challenge, I refer to the work of Hurtado de Mendoza and colleagues on the lexicographical analysis of the concepts of English "shame" and Spanish *vergüenza*. They describe the semantic variation across two languages and over time. Their aim is to warn against using a simple translation of emotion terms in psychological studies, but for historians the problem is even more crucial. The very understanding of source material is at stake and a rigorous application of historical semantics is needed.

Another example from corpus linguistics would be the distribution of words for shame and guilt in Old English texts in the Early and High Middle Ages (before 850 to 1150) in a corpus of legal, religious, and other secular texts (Fabiszak, 1999; Fabiszak & Hebda, 2006; 2010). One result of these studies is that shame appears in particular in the religious context before it enters the legal sphere in the later period of the observed timespan. This "evolution" cannot be observed for guilt (Fabiszak & Hebda, 2006: 8).

Given these restrictions we may wonder how to communicate about culturally loaded polysemic emotion terms in different languages at all. How should it be possible to find a commonly accepted definition of an emotional concept like shame?[5] Nevertheless, we need to take up this challenge because of the predominant importance of these concepts in traditional Western societies and beyond. There is no other way to understand shame or honor in the past than to understand their meaning within their specific cultural context. Etymology and historical semantics are today and will be in the future the key methods for the history of emotions.

Shame (and Honor) in History—Fluctuating Semantic Fields in Changing Social Contexts

From what is said above it appears that the first step to reveal the history of honor and shame is to identify the relevant terminology and understand the respective etymology. In English, for example, we have the relatively simple case of a few words in the semantic field of shame, some originating in Germanic languages, others in Latin. The Old English *scamu, sceomu*, "feeling of guilt or disgrace; confusion caused by shame; disgrace, dishonor, insult, loss of esteem or reputation; shameful circumstance, what brings disgrace; modesty; private parts," from Proto-Germanic **skamo* (source also of Old Saxon *skama*, Old Norse skömm, Swedish *skam*, Old Frisian *scome*, Dutch *schaamte*, Old High German *scama*, German *Scham*), is the most prominent in this cluster.[6] Closely related are embarrassment, blush, humiliation, dishonor, and so on, with subtle differences in orthography and historical relevance. Embarrassment, for example, is virtually nonexistent before 1750 and has a peak around 1840 in English written language.[7] For the blush it is similar, but with a first and higher peak around 1600. Shakespeare is not without responsibility for this. This inquiry can be done for every word and concept related to honor and shame and demonstrates how far we get with a purely quantitative approach in search for a better understanding of emotion terms in history. Context matters more than everything in this task and we desperately need more and deeper investigation of the historical semantics of those concepts in order to interpret the appearance of emotion terms in the source material.[8]

A semantic analysis of the terms for shame in Classical Roman times (*pudor, verecundia*, and *reverentia*) shows that especially *verecundia* incorporates aspects of *reverentia* in the works of Livy (59 BCE–17 CE) and Valerius Maximus (Kaster, 2005; Vaubel, 1969). Thus we can observe a strong polysemy of *verecundia* in classical Latin, encompassing various meanings such as reverence, shame, awe, and so on (Thomas, 2007). In the Middle Ages, one more word for shame appears in the religious context: *erubescentia*. Again the meaning is changing over time and distinct from the other Latin words used in the semantic field of shame. One popular definition of the difference between *verecundia* and *erubescentia* goes at follows:

> Shame was considered to be a form of fear and was signified by two Latin terms, *erubescentia* and *verecundia*. *Erubescentia* was the fear of censure for performing a foul deed in future. *Verecundia* was the fear experienced in regard to a foul deed already performed.
> (Payer, 2009: 55)

In the early Middle Ages, several aspects of honor and shame became more and more important through the rise of Christianity. The Bible speaks abundantly about shame and therefore the topic, like the book, is important up to now. Almost every aspect of shame in the Old and New Testament has been studied from the Middle Ages onwards. I limit the incomplete list to the newest and most relevant references (Bechtel, 1991, 1994; Burrus, 2007, 2013; Finney, 2013; Fletcher, 2004; Harper, 2013; Hobbs, 1997; Kazen, 2019; Lawrence, 2003; Lemos, 2006; Matthews & Benjamin, 1996; Moxnes, 1996; Nojima, 2011; Stiebert, 2000, 2002).

In Christian medieval theology, shame was also often referred to as a kind of confusion (*confusio*) of the mind, which allows for reorientation. The perspective of Aristotle, who qualified it as a virtue, was also popular.[9] However, shame also became an important obstacle in the context of confession (people do not confess their sins because of shame). Equally important was a theological discussion about the function of shame in relation to penance in the high middle ages. Shame itself became a part of penance and paved the way for the forgiveness of sins (Johnston, 2005: 55–57; Wagner, 1995). This view was later challenged in the fourth Lateran Concile (1215) which commanded yearly confession to a priest. The theological discussion had a direct influence on the design and development of public criminal law in large parts of Western Europe, because the concept of the remission of sins through confession to laypeople (in the absence of priests) and the similar effect of shame opened up new possibilities for a Christian way of enforcing law in a secular context (cf. Wettlaufer & Nishimura, 2013; Chapter 8 in this volume). Public criminal law borrowed from these ideas and developed in the burgeoning cities of Western Europe with a new concept of punishments based on public penance and confession for manifest sins against the Christian community (Wettlaufer, 2011; 2016b with further evidence). The resulting practice of shaming punishments (public shaming at pillories, public parades, and the like) was only given up during the eighteenth and early nineteenth centuries in most parts of the Western world.

With punishment comes humiliation. Shame as a means of the humiliation of others is probably as old as the emotion itself and comes in different flavors, not only through punishment. A first analysis of humiliation itself was done for Icelandic society of the Middle Ages by William Ian Miller in 1993. Other recent studies have broadened the view on shame and/or humiliation to French and German Literature of the Middle Ages (Eming, 2006; Flannery, 2012, 2020; Gvozdeva & Velten, 2011; Kollmann, 2009; Krause, 2006; Mecklenburg, 2007; Zink, 2017) or take an approach from psychology and the social sciences (Svindseth & Crawford, 2019). Although the concept is very old; the word embarrassment appears relatively late in English works.[10] Particular studies have been dedicated to shame in Shakespeare, covering also other aspects of shame than its humiliating manifestation (Boose, 1991; Fernie, 2003).

In fact, the whole Renaissance and Early Modern period is extensively concerned about honor and shame. Without being able to exactly quantify the effect, I suggest that one peak of this is around 1500. It might be that this impression is an artefact of my personal preferences, but at least in sources in the history of law from the rising European cities it is obvious that questions of honor and the willingness to use shame and shaming in social relations have a clear peak in the fifteenth and sixteenth centuries.[11] Before looking closer at the big picture of Modern history, I should mention two other recent studies that have been dedicated to the history of shame and humiliation (*Demütigung*) and tackle also more recent times, namely the twentieth and twenty-first centuries. Ute Frevert seeks for an explanation of the relative absence of practices of public humiliation by authorities and governments in the contemporary world Western world, stressing the rise of the idea of the "*Menschenrechte*/human rights" for an explanation (Frevert, 2017; 2020; see also David Nash's Chapter 14 on shame and modernity in this volume). Looking back at what has been said so far in this chapter, one might add another, more obvious line of reasoning: the process of secularization from the Enlightenment onwards. The secular trend eroded the very basis of public shaming and humiliation—the connection to sin and penance that had been relevant during the mediaeval and Early Modern period. Modernity has found other, less public means to discipline their subjects. Another reason is the dissolution of group structures with shared normative values and the transformation of societies to national, global, and liberal entities (Wettlaufer, 2021).

While the disappearance of shaming practices in law during the nineteenth century is undisputed, the relevance of shame itself in social relations is seen more controversially. Peter Stearns wrote a brief history of shame in 2017, concentrating on the history of shaming practices but also introduces psychological and ontogenetic perspectives. He argues that shame has been "ubiquitous" throughout history and therefore is in line with anthropological perspectives on honor and shame. He emphasizes the importance of these emotions in traditional societies, but also tackles the questions already asked by Frevert about obvious changes in the last two centuries in Western societies. In painting the very big picture, Stearns leaves many blank spaces and Ulte Frevert is right in criticizing this (Frevert, 2018: 317–318).

Still on the same line are a series of investigations into the importance of shame in criminal history, including blasphemy (Nash, 2007; Schwerhoff, 2005). David Nash, one of the co-editors of this book, has devoted several studies to this topic and investigates the importance of shame in modern criminal justice (Nash & Kilday 2010a/b; Rowbotham, Muravyeva, & Nash 2013; Zhao, 2016). This focus can be explained by the popularity of one of the major theories of modern criminology, namely the concept of reintegrative shaming by John Braithwaite (Braithwaite, 1989), who also wrote an interesting historical essay on shaming (Braithwaite, 1993). Given the modern debate about (reintegrative) shaming, the discussion soon became a political touchstone. Martha Nussbaum's "Hiding from Humanity: Disgust, Shame and the Law" from 2004 is the most prominent cornerstone of this discussion, which divides (mostly American) liberal Democrats and conservative Republicans about the question of the adequacy of shaming punishments in the modern law-enforcement regimes of (liberal) societies (Kahan, 2006; Markel 2001; Massaro, 1991; Nussbaum, 2004).

Closely related to shifts in levels of embarrassment and shame have been the influential ideas of Norbert Elias about the civilizing process (Elias, 1939). The reception of this theory started only in the seventies, after the second edition had been published in 1969. Standards of behavior have obviously changed over the last centuries. Milestones of European civilization have been said to be the widespread use of fork and knife at table and the control of the digestive signs of the body – to name just a few markers. Bodily functions, table manners and forms of speech were gradually transformed by increasing thresholds of shame and repugnance, working outward from a nucleus in court etiquette. The internalized "self-restraint" was imposed by increasingly complex networks of social connections leading to the construction of the modern state and transition of man from the warrior of the Middle Ages to the civil man of the end of the nineteenth century. Shame and embarrassment play a central role in this supposed transition process and are at the core of the internalization process that leads, in theory, to an increasing importance of what is called conscience (*Gewissen*).[12]

As nicely as this teleological construct fits in our Western self-identity in the mid-twentieth century, a few questions can be posed from an anthropological point of view (Duerr, 1988–2005, Paul, 2007). In fact, we already described shame and internalized self-control as universal features with benefits for groups and societies around the world and in all ages (even prehistorical). It is hard to believe that this basic feature of the human condition developed continuously in one direction in one ethnic group. What remains from Elias's theory today is the valuable observation that cultural standards for body shame and embarrassment seem to fluctuate strongly over time. For what we feel shame or honor or another connected moral emotion is indeed directly related to the cultural development within a given social group.

There has been a lot of discussion about honor and shame in the Mediterranean from the 1950s onwards (Peristiany, 1964). Similar discussions are still ongoing about different concepts of honor and shame in the South and North of the United States, mostly related to honor killings. (Nisbett & Cohen, 1996). There are of course cultural differences in the importance of honor/shame that can be pinned down both geographically and chronologically. Anthropological explanations based on economic and kinship systems can only partially explain those patterns. The unity of the Mediterranean has been doubted more than once and the explanations of particularly strong patterns of honor and shame in this region have been puzzling researchers for decades now. Looking closer, the effect seems to be not regional but rather historical. Anthropologists did their research on "traditional" societies catching a glimpse of the former importance of these concepts in many cultures, persisting more strongly in modernity in some regions compared to others.

We have browsed through a group of theories related to the social and cultural functions of shame and honor. There are, of course, many more aspects and theoretical approaches around. It is not possible to mention or to discuss all in this introduction to shame; instead I will confine myself to naming just a few prominent thinkers like Spinoza, Descartes, Hobbes, and Simmel, who contributed to this debate. The philosophical debate is still ongoing (see Zahavi, 2020 for a recent overview) and started with Aristotle and the Greek philosophers. Some of the most valuable contributions to the discussions have tackled the meaning of shame in Ancient Greek society (Alric, 2001; Cairns, 1993; Erffa, 1937; Maresca, 2006). The reception and interpretation of those concepts in later periods cannot be underestimated for the development of the European concept of honor and shame in modern history.

Recently one central aspect of shame, the ability to support conforming behavior at the group level has been emphasized in the context of the common good debate. The challenges of climate change and ecology can be described in terms of the common good dilemma and in this context honor and shame seem to be valuable assets to support behavior with long-term benefits for the group, making negative output in the short run more acceptable (Jacquet, 2015). Shame is associated with many activities that are seen as detrimental for the environment, such a flying (Flugscham), wasting energy, or resources. While this looks like an excellent idea at first sight, looking closer reveals major obstacles to the use of shame actively in the environmental debate. Shame and shaming bears the danger of exclusion from the group and stigmatization. Therefore, honor might be the better choice in this context.

Shame and Guilt

Before I conclude I would like to add a few words about shame and guilt. The scientific literature on the relation and distinction between shame and guilt is abundant. However, it is not clear that there is a clear distinction at all, at least on the neural level (see Bastin et. al., 2016; Michl et al., 2014; Takahashi et al., 2004). Although it is difficult to distinguish the emotions of shame and guilt on the neural level, there is considerable semantic difference in many languages (Jaffe et al., 2014).

Without diving into the long debate about the relation of shame and guilt it is worth investigating one author who has elaborated upon today's understanding of the relationship between these two concepts. Opposed to guilt, shame always affects a person's identity as a whole, as Helen B. Lewis pointed out from a psychoanalytical point of view:

> The experience of shame is directly about the self, which is the focus of evaluation. In guilt, the self is not the central object of negative evaluation, but rather the *thing* done or undone is the focus. In guilt, the self is negatively evaluated in connection with something but is not itself the focus of the experience.
>
> (Lewis, 1971: 30)

25 years later, another influential scholar, June Price Tangney, developed this distinction further in describing the shame reaction in more detail:

> In shame, the focus of the negative evaluation is on the entire self. Following some transgression or failure, the entire self is painfully scrutinized

and found lacking. With this painful self-scrutiny comes a sense of shrinking, a feeling of being small, and a sense of worthlessness and powerlessness. Shame also involves the imagery of being exposed before a real or imagined disapproving audience. Although empirical findings indicate that shame can be experienced when a person is alone ... shame typically involves an awareness of how the defective self may appear to others. Not surprisingly, the shame experience is often accompanied by a desire to hide-to sink into the floor and disappear. And ... shame can engender a hostile, defensive type of anger ... presumably aimed at a real or imagined disapproving other.

(Tangney & Fischer, 1995: 344; c.f. Katchadourian, 2009: 24–25)

Taking into account the evidence that we have so far from Psychology, Neuroscience, and Physiology, the distinction between shame and guilt seems to be a question of perspective. Depending on the context, sometimes the rational guilt is dominant, sometimes the more self-related shame. There is no reason to think that this relation between shame and guilt has changed over time.

Conclusion: The Many Faces of Shame

We have presented shame as a social emotion, grounded in a biological adaptation to promote cooperation in groups. Furthermore, we have distinguished between the emotional experience of shame itself (that cannot be reconstructed within the means of historical research) and the socio-cultural impact of the ability to feel shame and honor. In historical research, embedded in deep history and inspired by this bio-cultural approach, the major challenge is the semantic flexibility and polysemy of emotional concepts through time. Only a rigorous contextualization of emotional terms with the methods of historical semantics and corpus linguistics can help us to approach and understand the meaning of honor and shame and their neighboring concepts in distant cultural settings. This approach is very similar to the methods of cultural anthropology and only differs in the acquisition of the information, which in most cases can only be acquired indirectly through source material and other relics of the given period of time. Prominent fields of research have so far been shame and humiliation in the context of punishment and religion in the sense of a moral emotion. There is some work related to shame and the body, including sociological theories about the cultural development of Western civilization at large. Although shame is described today mostly as a negative experience one should avoid, shame had and still has positive connotations in the Christian religion. Following the Christian tradition, it was seen as an expression of the ability to make moral decisions. We have to take into account that in other cultural settings, especially in European history, shame had a much more positive connotation than it has today – understood as an unpleasant feeling that we seek to avoid. In Shakespearean times the blush was a positive sign of inner arousal and this holds also true for the female blush in the nineteenth century (Wierzbicka, 1999: 109). Shame had different functions for the sexes and has been in particular associated with female chastity in the past.

Finally, shame cannot be analyzed and understood without the contrasting concept of honor. An Ethiopian proverb puts it like this: "Where There Is No Shame, There Is No Honor" (Vila, 2004). This holds also true for Western history.

Notes

1 For a recent discussion with references to the older literature on shame and guilt cultures see Röttger-Rössler (2020). For a comparison of Western and Eastern cultures and an integrated theory see Mascolo et al. (2003).
2 King Hywel Daa died in 950; the law attributed to him was codified and written down in the twelfth and thirteenth centuries.
3 For more information on this methodological approach see https://evohist.org.
4 For an approach in corpus linguistics see Tissari (2006).
5 See also Kollareth et al. (2019).
6 https://www.etymonline.com/word/shame and *Oxford Concise Dictionary of Etymology* (1994: 433).
7 Google Ngram Viewer English Corpus 2019 (https://books.google.com/ngrams/). This result, as always with ngrams by Google, should be interpreted with some reservation because of the limited documentation of the corpus. The first known written occurrence of embarrass in English can be found in a diary in 1664. The word derives from the French word *embarrasser*, "to block" or "obstruct."
8 See for words of the shame/*Scham* family Birnbaum (2015); Jorgensen (2012); Palmer (1993); Tissari (2006).
9 Thomas Aquinas, *Summa Theologiae*, 2a2re, 144. Gilby (2006: 54–69). See also Teetaert (1926), Miner (2009), and Engelen (2009).
10 https://www.etymonline.com/word/embarrassment. It appears first in the late seventeenth century. Earlier words expressing the same meaning include banishment and *baishednesse* (late fourteenth and mid-fifteenth centuries).
11 Although a bias cannot be ruled out and the question merits a more profound investigation, the material I collected in the context of the project on "Enforced shame and redeeming repentance. On the social use of an adaptive emotion in the Middle-Ages and Early Modern times" points in this direction.
12 C.f. Voland and Voland (1993, 2014).

References

Al-Jallad, N.T. (2002). Shame in English, Arabic, and Javanese: a comparative lexical study, PhD thesis, University of Delaware.

Alric, J. (2001). Hector au pied du mur – Honte, honneur, aidôs dans la vie intime, familiale et publique en Grèce ancienne, *L'atelier du roman*, 26, 221–231.

Bastin, C., Harrison, B.J., Davey, C.G., Moll, J., & Whittle, S. (2016). Feelings of shame, embarrassment and guilt and their neural correlates: a systematic review. *Neuroscience & Biobehavioral Reviews*, 71, 455–471. https://doi.org/10.1016/j.neubiorev.2016.09.019.

Bauks, M. (2011). Nacktheit und Scham in Genesis 2–3. In Bauks, M. & Meyer, M. F. (eds.), *Zur Kulturgeschichte der Scham* (pp. 17–34), Archiv für Begriffsgeschichte, Sonderheft 9.

Bechtel, L.M. (1991). Shame as a sanction of social control in biblical Israel: judicial, political and social shaming, *Social Scientific Old Testament criticism*, 49, 47–76.

Bechtel, L.M. (1994). The perception of shame within the divine–human relationship in biblical Israel. In L.M. Hopfe (ed.), *Uncovering Ancient Stones: Essays in Memory of H. Neil Richardson* (pp. 79–92).

Beer, J.S., Heerey, E.H., Keltner, D., Scabini, D., & Knight, R.T. (2003). The regulatory function of self-conscious emotion: insights from patients with orbitofrontal damage. *Journal of Personality and Social Psychology*, 85(4), 594–604.

Birnbaum, T. (2015). Naming shame: translating emotion in the Old English Psalter Glosses. In Jorgensen, A., Wilcox, J. & McCormack, F. (eds.), *Anglo-Saxon Emotions: Reading the Heart in Old English Literature* (pp. 109–126), Ashgate.

Boehm, C. (2012). *Moral Origins: The Evolution of Virtue, Altruism, and Shame*, Basic.

Bologne, J.-C. (1999). *Histoire de la pudeur*, Librairie Académique Perrin.

Boose, L.E. (1991). Scolding brides and bridling scolds: taming the woman's unruly member. *Shakespeare Quarterly*, 42(2), 179–213.

Bowles, S. & Gintis, H. (2011). *A Cooperative Species: Human Reciprocity and Its Evolution*, Princeton University Press.

Braithwaite, J. (1989). *Crime, Shame and Reintegration*, Cambridge University Press.

Braithwaite, J. (1993). Shame and modernity, *The British Journal of Criminology*, 33 (1), 1–18.

Burrus, V. (2007). *Saving Shame. Martyrs, Saints, and Other Abject Subjects*, University of Pennsylvania Press.

Burrus, V. (2013). Bodies, desires, confession: shame in Plotinus, Antony and Augustine. In Sère, B., Wettlaufer, J. (eds.) *Shame between Punishment and Penance: The Social Usages of Shame in the Middle-Ages and Early Modern Times* (pp. 23–48), SISMEL – Edizioni del Galluzo.

Cairns, D.L. (1993). *Aidos: The Psychology and Ethics of Honour and Shame in Ancient Greek Literature*, Oxford University Press.

Casimir, M. & Jung, S. (2009). "Honor and Dishonor": Connotations of a socio-symbolic category in cross-cultural perspective. In Röttger-Rössler, B. & Markowitsch, H. (eds.) *Emotions as Bio-cultural Processes* (pp. 229–280), Springer.

Casimir, M. & Schnegg, M. (2002). Shame across cultures: the evolution, ontogeny and function of a moral emotion. In Keller, H., Poortinga, Y.H. & Schölmerich, A. (eds.), *Between Culture and Biology: Perspectives on Ontogenetic Development* (pp. 270–300), Cambridge University Press.

Duerr, H.-P. (1988–2005). *Der Mythos vom Zivilisationsprozess*, Vol. 1–5, Suhrkamp.

Elias, N. (1939/1969). *The Civilizing Process, Vol. I. The History of Manners* (1969); *Vol. II. State Formation and Civilization* (1982). Blackwell.

Eming, J. (2006). *Emotion und Expression: Untersuchungen zu deutschen und französischen Liebes- und Abenteuerromanen des 12. - 16. Jahrhunderts*, De Gruyter.

Engelen, E.-M., Markowitsch, H., Scheve, C., Röttger-Rössler, B., Stephan, A., Holodynski, M. and Vanderkerkhoeve, M. (2009). Towards conceptual foundations for bio-cultural research on emotions. In Röttger-Rössler, B. & Markowitsch, H.J. (eds.), *Emotions as Bio-Cultural Processes* (pp. 23–53), Springer.

Engelen, E.-M. (2009). Anger, shame and justice: the regulative function of emotions in the ancient and modern world. In Röttger-Rössler, B. & Markowitsch, H.J. (eds.), *Emotions as Bio-Cultural Processes* (pp. 395–413), Springer.

Erffa, C.E. von (1937). Aidos und verwandte Begriffe in ihrer Entwicklung von Homer bis Demokrit, *Philologus Supplementband*, 30. Dieterich.

Fabiszak, M. (1999). A semantic analysis of emotion terms in old English, *Studia Anglica Posnaniensia*, XXXIV, 133–146.

Fabiszak, M. & Hebda, A. (2006). Emotions of control in Old English: shame and guilt, *Poetica*, 66, 1–35.

Fabiszak, M. & Hebda, A. (2010). Cognitive historical approaches to emotions: pride. In Winters, M.E., Tissari, H. & Allan, K. (eds.), *Historical Cognitive Linguistics* (pp. 261–297), De Gruyter.

Fernie, E. (2003). *Shame in Shakespeare*, Routledge.

Fessler, D.M.T. (1999). Toward an understanding of the universality of second order emotions. In Hinton, A. (ed.), *Beyond Nature or Nurture: Biocultural Approaches to the Emotions* (pp. 75–116), Cambridge University Press.

Fessler, D.M.T. (2004). Shame in two cultures: implications for evolutionary approaches. *Journal of Cognition and Culture*, 4(2), 207–262.

Fessler, D.M.T. (2007). From appeasement to conformity: evolutionary and cultural perspectives on shame, competition, and cooperation. In Tracy, J.L, Robins, R. W., & Tangney, J.P. (eds.),*The Self-Conscious Emotions: Theory and Research* (pp. 174–193), Guilford Press.

Fessler, D.M.T. & Haley, K.J. (2004). Strategy of affect: emotions in human cooperation. In Hammerstein, P. (ed.), *The Genetic and Cultural Evolution of Cooperation* (pp. 125–152), Dahlem Workshop Report. MIT Press.

Finney, M.T. (2013). Servile supplicium: shame and the Deuteronomic curse-crucifixion in its cultural context. *Biblical Theology Bulletin*, 43(3), 124–134.

Flannery, M.C. (2012). The concept of shame in late-medieval English literature, *Literature Compass*, 9(2), 166–182.

Flannery, M.C. (2020). *Practising Shame: Female Honour in Later Medieval England*, Manchester University Press.

Fletcher, G.P. (2004). Punishment, guilt, and shame in biblical thought. *Notre Dame Journal of Law, Ethics, and Public Policy*, 18, 343–356.

Frevert, U. (2017). *Die Politik der Demütigung: Schauplätze von Macht und Ohnmacht* (Engl. *The politics of humiliation*, 2020), S. Fischer.

Frevert, U. (2018). Review Peter Stearns: shame: a brief history, *Journal of Interdisciplinary History*, 49(2), 316–318.

Frevert, U. (2020). *The Politics of Humiliation: A Modern History*, Oxford University Press.

Gilby, T. (ed.) (2006). *Thomas Aquinas. Summa Theologiae: Temperance* (2a2æ. 141–154), Latin text, English transl., introd., notes, appendices & glossary by Th. Gilby, Cambridge University Press (first ed. 1968).

Griffin, S. (1995). A Cognitive-Developmental Analysis of Pride, Shame, and Embarrassment in Middle Childhood. In Tangney, J.P. & Fischer, K.W. (eds.), *Self-Conscious Emotions: The Psychology of Shame, Guilt, Embarrassment, and Pride* (pp. 219–236), New York: Guilford.

Gvozdeva, K. & Velten, H.R. (eds.) (2011). *Scham und Schamlosigkeit: Grenzverletzungen in Literatur und Kultur der Vormoderne* (Trends in medieval philology; 21). De Gruyter.

Harper, K. (2013). *From Shame to Sin: The Christian Transformation of Sexual Morality in Late Antiquity*, Harvard University Press.
Harré, R. (1986). *The social construction of emotions*, Basil Blackwell.
Harré, R. & Parrott, W.G. (eds.) (1996). *Emotions: Social, Cultural and Biological Dimensions*, Sage.
Hobbs, T.R. (1997). Reflections on honor, shame, and covenant relations, *Journal of Biblical Literature*, 116(3), 501–503.
Hurtado-de-Mendoza, A., Molina, C., & Fernández-Dols, J.-M. (2012). The archeology of emotion concepts: a lexicographic analysis of the concepts shame and Vergüenza, *Journal of Language and Social Psychology*, 32, 272–290.
Jacquet, J. (2015). *Is Shame Necessary? New Uses for an Old Tool*, Knopf Doubleday Publishing.
Jaffe, K., Flórez, A., Gomes, C. M., Rodríguez, D., & Achury C. (2014). On the biological and cultural evolution of shame: using internet search tools to weight values in many cultures, *Computers and Societies*. https://arxiv.org/pdf/1401.1100.
Johnston, A.J. (2005). The secret of the sacred: confession and the self in Sir Garwein and the Green knight. In Rupp, S. & Döring, T. (eds.), *Performances of the Sacred in Late Medieval and Early Modern England* (pp. 45–64), Rodopi.
Jorgensen, A. (2012). It shames me to say it: Ælfric and the concept and vocabulary of shame, *Anglo-Saxon England*, 41, 249–276.
Kahan, D. (2006). What's really wrong with shaming sanctions, *Texas Law Review*, 84, 2075–2095.
Kaster, R.A. (2005). *Emotion, Restraint and Community in Ancient Rome*, Oxford University Press.
Katchadourian, H.A. (2009). *Guilt: The Bite of Conscience*, Stanford University Press.
Kazen, Th. (2019). Viewing oneself through others' eyes: shame between biology and culture in biblical texts, *Svensk Exegetisk Årsbok*, 84, 51–80.
Kollareth, D., Kitkutani, M. & Russel, J.A. (2019). Shame is a folk term unsuitable as a technical term in science. In Mun, C. (ed.), *Interdisciplinary Perspectives on Shame: Methods, Theories, Norms, Cultures, and Politics* (pp. 3–26), Lexington Books.
Kollmann, S. (2009). "Si suln bêde schamec sîn, juncherre unde vröuwelîn". Emotionsgeschichtliche Ansätze zur Scham im Mittelalter, Diplomarbeit Univ. Wien.
Krause, B. (2006). Scham(e), schande und êre. Selbstwahrnehmung - zwischen Affekt und Tugend. In Krause, B. & Schenk, U. (eds.), *Emotions and cultural change, Gefühle und kultureller Wandel* (pp. 21–75), Stauffenburg.
Krawczak, K. (2014). Shame and its near-synonyms in English: a Multivariate Corpus-driven Approach to Social Emotions. In Blumenthal, P., Novakova, I. & Siepmann, D. (eds.), *Les émotions dans le discours = Emotions in discourse* (pp. 83–94), Peter Lang.
Lawrence, L.J. (2003). *An Ethnography of the Gospel of Matthew: A Critical Assessment of the Use of the Honour and Shame Model in New Testament Studies*, Mohr Siebeck.
Lemos, T.M. (2006). Shame and mutilation of enemies in the Hebrew Bible, *Journal of Biblical Literature*, 125(2), 225–241.
Lewis, M. (1992). *Shame: the exposed self*, Free Press.
Maresca, S.J. (2006). Aidos. http://www.elsigma.com/site/detalle.asp?IdContenido= 10949 / 14.01.2009

Mariauzouls, C. (1996). Psychophysiologie von Scham und Erröten. Diss. Univ. München.

Markel, D. (2001). Are shaming punishments beautifully retributive? Retributivism and the implications for the alternative sanctions debate. *Vanderbilt Law Review*, 54, 2157–2242.

Mascolo, M., Fischer, K.W., & Li, J. (2003). Dynamic development of component systems of emotions: pride, shame, and guilt in China and the United States. In Davidson, R.J., Scherer, K.R., & Goldsmith, H.H. (eds.), *Handbook of Affective Sciences* (pp. 375–408), Oxford University Press.

Massaro, T. (1991). Shame, culture and American criminal law. *Michigan Law Review*, 89(5), 1880–1944.

Matthews, H. & Benjamin, D.C. (eds.) (1996). Honor and shame in the world of the Bible, *Semeia*, 68. Scholars Press.

Mecklenburg, M. (2007). Evolution - Emotion - Literatur. Studien zur Scham in mittelhochdeutschen Erzähldichtungen. Unpublished habilitation thesis, Berlin.

Michl, P., Meindl, T., Meister, F., Born, C., Engel, R.R., Reiser, M., Hennig-Fast, K. (2014). Neurobiological underpinnings of shame and guilt: a pilot fMRI study. *Social Cognitive and AffectiveNeuroscience*, 9(2), 150–157.

Miller, W.I. (1993). *Humiliation: And Other Essays on Honor, Social Discomfort and Violence*, Cornell University Press.

Miner, R. (2009). *Thomas Aquinas on the passions: a study of Summa Theologiae: 1a2ae 22–48*, Cambridge University Press.

Moxnes, H. (1996). Honor and shame, In Rohrbaugh, R.L. (ed.). *The Social Sciences and New Testament Interpretation* (pp. 19–40), Hendrickson.

Nash, D.S. & Kilday A.M. (2010a). *Cultures of shame: exploring crime and morality in Britain 1600–1900*, Palgrave Macmillan.

Nash, D.S. (2007). *Blasphemy in the Christian World: A History*, Oxford University Press.

Nash, D.S. & A.M. Kilday (2010b). *Histories of cCime: Britain 1600–2000*, Palgrave Macmillan.

Neckel, S. (1991). *Status und Scham: zur symbolischen Reproduktion sozialer Ungleichheit*, Campus.

Nisbett, R.E. & Cohen, D. (1996). *Culture of Honor: The Psychology of Violence in the South*. Westview Press.

Nojima, K. (2011). *Ehre und Schande in Kulturanthropologie und biblischer Theologie*, Arco-Verlag.

Nussbaum, M.C. (2004). *Hiding from Humanity: Disgust, Shame and the Law*, Princeton University Press.

Owen, M.E. (1980). Shame and reparation: woman's place in the kin. In Jenkins, D. & Owen, M.E. (eds.), *The Welsh Law of Women: Studies Presented to Prof. Daniel A. Binchy on His Eightieth Birthday* (pp. 40–68), University of Wales Press.

Palmer, N.F. (1993). The middle high German vocabulary of shame in its literary context, In Flood, J.F., Salmon, P., Sayce, O., Wells, C. (eds.), *Das unsichtbare Band der Sprache. Studies in German Language and Linguistic History in Memory of Leslie Seiffert* (pp. 57–84), [Stuttgarter Arbeiten zur Germanistik, Nr. 280], Hans-Dieter Heinz Verlag.

Paul, A.T. (2007). Die Gewalt der Scham: Elias, Duerr und das Problem der Historizität menschlicher Gefühle, *Mittelweg 36, Zeitschrift des Hamburger Instituts für Sozialforschung* 16(2), 77–98.

Payer, P.J. (2009). *Sex and New Medieval Literature of Confession: 1150–1300*, Pontifical Institute of Mediaeval Studies.

Peristiany, J.G. (ed.) (1964): *Honour and Shame: The Values of Mediterranean Society*. Weidenfeld & Nicolson.

Röttger-Rössler, B. (2020). Kulturelle Facetten der Scham. In Kappelhoff, H. et al. (eds.), *Emotionen: Ein Interdisziplinäres Handbuch* (pp. 230–235), J.B. Metzler'sche Verlagsbuchhandlung & Carl Ernst Poeschel.

Rowbotham, J., Muravyeva, M., & Nash, D.S. (eds.) (2013). *Shame, Blame and Culpability: Crime and Violence in the Modern State*, Routledge.

Rusch, C.D. (2004). Cross-cultural variability of the semantic domain of emotion terms: an examination of English shame and embarrassment with Japanese Hazukashii. *Cross-Cultural Research*, 38, 236–248.

Scheler, M. (1913/1957). *Schriften aus dem Nachlaß, Bd. 1: Zur Ethik und Erkenntnislehre, Über Scham und Schamgefühl* (1913) (pp. 67–154), Franke.

Schore, A.N. (1998). Early shame experiences and infant brain development. In Gilbert, P. & Andrews, B. (eds.), *Shame – Interpersonal Behavior, Psychopathology, and Culture* (pp. 57–77), Oxford University Press.

Schwerhoff, G. (2005). *Zungen wie Schwerter. Blasphemie in alteuropäischen Gesellschaften*, [Konflikte und Kultur - Historische Perspektiven 12], Universitätsverlag Konstanz.

Shryock, A. & Smail, D.L. (2011). *Deep History: The Architecture of Past and Present*, University of California Press.

Smail, D.L. (2007). *Deep History and the Brain*, University of California Press.

Stiebert, J. (2000): Shame and prophecy: approaches past and present, *Biblical Interpretation*, 8 (3), 255–275.

Stiebert, J. (2002): *The Construction of Shame in the Hebrew Bible: The Prophetic Contribution*, Sheffield Academic Press.

Stipek, D. (1995). The development of pride and shame in toddlers. In Tangney, J.P. & Fischer, K.W. (eds.), *Self-Conscious Emotions: The Psychology of Shame, Guilt, Embarrassment, and Pride* (pp. 237–252), Guilford Press.

Svindseth, M.F. & Crawford, P. (eds.) (2019). *Humiliation: Mental Health and Public Shame*, Lexington Books.

Takahashi, H., Yahata, N., Koeda, M., Matsuda, T., Asai, K., & Okubo, Y. (2004). Brain activation associated with evaluative processes of guilt and embarrassment: an fMRI study. *Neuroimage*, 23, 967–974.

Tangney, J.P. & Fischer, K.W. (eds.) (1995). *Self-Conscious Emotions: The Psychology of Shame, Guilt, Embarrassment, and Pride*, Guilford Press.

Teetaert, A. (1926). *La confession aux laïques dans l'église latine depuis le VIIe jusqu'au XIVe siècle, Étude de Théologie positive*, J. de Meester et fils et al.

Thomas, J.-F. (2007). *Déshonneur et honte en Latin: étude sémantique* [Bibliothèque d'Études Classiques, 50]. Peeters.

Tissari, H. (2006). Conceptualizing shame: investigating uses of the English word shame, 1418–1991. In McConchie, R.W., Timofeeva, O., Tissari, H. & Säily, T. (eds.), *Selected Proceedings of the 2005 Symposium on New Approaches in English Historical Lexis (HEL-LEX)*, Cascadilla Proceedings Projects, 143–154.

Vaubel, E. (1969). Pudor, Verecundia, Reverentia. Untersuchungen zur Psychologie von Scham und Ehrfurcht bei den Römern bis Augustin, Diss. Univ. Münster.

Vila B. (2004). Where there is no shame, there is no honor (Ethiopian proverb). *Pediatrics*, 114(3), 897. https://doi.org/10.1542/peds.2004-0972.

Voland, E. & Voland, R. (1993). *Schuld, Scham und Schande: Zur Evolution des Gewissens*. In Voland, E. (ed.), *Evolution und Anpassung. Warum die Vergangenheit die Gegenwart erklärt* (pp. 211–228), Hirzel.

Voland, E. & Voland, R. (2014). *Evolution des Gewissens*, Hirzel.

Wagner, K. (1995). *De vera et falsa penitentia: An Edition and Study*, Ph.D. diss., University of Toronto.

Wettlaufer, J. (2008). The evolution of shame as a prosocial emotion: a cross-cultural study on conflict and cooperation in historical societies. Unpublished paper at EHBE conference at Montpellier, 02.04.–04.04.2008 [doi:10.13140/2.1.1337.3767].

Wettlaufer, J. (2011). Beschämende Strafen in Westeuropa und Ostasien. Zwischenbericht zu einem kulturvergleichenden Forschungsprojekt zum Spätmittelalter und der Frühen Neuzeit. In Kesper-Biermann, S., Ludwig, U., & Ortmann, A. (eds.), *Ehre und Recht – Ehrkonzepte, Ehrverletzungen und Ehrverteidigungen vom späten Mittelalter bis zur Moderne* (pp. 139–156), Meine.

Wettlaufer, J. (2015). Evolutionäre Geschichtswissenschaft: Menschliches Handeln zwischen Natur und Kultur in der Vergangenheit. In Lange, B. & Schwarz, S. (eds.), *Die menschliche Psyche zwischen Natur und Kultur* (pp. 83–93), Pabst.

Wettlaufer, J. (2016a). Shame and cooperation, *The RSA Journal*, January, 36–39.

Wettlaufer, J. (2016b). Beschämung und Kooperation in historischen Gesellschaften. Eine evolutionäre Perspektive auf den sozialen Gebrauch moralischer Emotionen im Mittelalter und in der frühen Neuzeit. In C. Hennighausen, B.P. Lange, & F. Schwab (eds.), *Evolution des Sozialen* (pp. 25–40), Pabst.

Wettlaufer, J. (2021). Review of Ute Frevert, The Politics of Humiliation: A Modern History (tr. Adam Bresnahan, Oxford: Oxford University Press 2020). In The English Historical Review, ceab171, https://doi.org/10.1093/ehr/ceab171.

Wettlaufer, J. & Nishimura, Y. (2013). The history of shaming punishments and public exposure in penal law in comparative perspective: Western Europe and East Asia. In Sère, B. & Wettlaufer, J. (eds.), *Shame between Punishment and Penance: The Social Usages of Shame in the Middle-Ages and Early Modern Times* (pp. 197–228), SISMEL – Edizioni del Galluzo.

Wierzbicka, A. (1999). *Emotions Across Languages and Cultures: Diversity and Universals*, Cambridge University Press.

Yeandle, D.N. (2001). *"Schame" im Alt- und Mittelhochdeutschen bis um 1210: Eine sprach- und literaturgeschichtliche Untersuchung unter besonderer Berücksichtigung der Herausbildung einer ethischen Bedeutung*. [Beiträge zur älteren Literaturgeschichte]. Winter.

Zahavi, D. (2020). Shame. In Landweer, H. & Szanto, T. (eds.), *The Routledge Handbook of Phenomenology of Emotions* (pp. 349–357), Routledge.

Zhao, H. (2016). Cultures of shame in Britain, c. 1650–1800. Ph.D. thesis, University of Warwick.

Zink, M. (2017). *L'humiliation, le Moyen Âge et nous*, Albin Michel.

3 Zero-Sum Emotions and Shame–Honor Dynamics

Richard Landes

Tribal and Aristocratic Honor

Monitum: The following exploration of a mindset quite at odds with the (post-)modern one which we academics largely share may well strike some readers as jarring, even on occasion offensive. This will most likely happen when I "speak" with the voice of the subjects of this chapter, summarizing their attitudes towards "others," in particular towards those "others" systemically disempowered by that mindset, like women, Jews, the poor, or men who don't kill. I wish to make clear at the outset that I do not endorse such views, but only report them. The evidence upon which I base my remarks is plentiful, however, and I do not think I do injustice to the temper of the "primary" or warrior's shame–honor value system I describe. I personally am glad I do not live in such societies and am grateful for the opportunity to freely pursue accurate knowledge about any important subject, a privilege that modern democracies alone offer.

***

We Westerners, especially intellectuals, tend to take our social environments, largely urban, civic "safe" spaces, abundant with food and goods, for granted. But evolutionarily speaking, humankind spent much more time under conditions of scarcity, duress, and often violent competition with other humans for those scarce resources. In the more hostile environments, a different evolutionary dynamic prevailed with a different set of life experiences, rules, and attitudes.

Take, for example, the problem of the in-group and the out-group, us–them. In contemporary public discourse, "us–them" stands for unacceptable tribalism, xenophobia, and even racism. And yet, in earlier periods of human history, and for much longer than any modern cosmopolitan discourse, the basic structure of social reality (i.e., survival) gravitated around a sharp dichotomy between us (band, clan, village, tribe), on whom we depend, and others (strangers whom we, on principle, mistrust, oppose), in order to survive.

In other words, what some of us today dismiss contemptuously was the overriding and necessary *norm* for most of human experience: "moral tribalism" (Banfield, 1958; Greene, 2013). Similarly, whereas today we consider

DOI: 10.4324/9781003022916-5

anger management and conflict-aversion praiseworthy especially among men, in a different environment, it was a matter of survival for societies to produce warriors, men who would police all insults to their or their clan's honor, lest the insulter get the idea he could add the injury of rustling livestock and women to an unpunished insult. All of this looks not only foreign to moderns, but even morally offensive.

In the fourteenth century CE (8th century AH), however, the North African social historian Ibn Khaldun argued just the opposite: that this tribal solidarity—*assabiya*—was the most important moral value that Allah gave to man (Ibn Khaldun, 1987: 105–106). Societies follow cycles from the desert to the town, from the egalitarian warriors with their tribal solidarity, Spartan lifestyle, and predatory ways, to "civilized" urban empire dwellers who share opulent space with outsiders and strangers and therefore lack the overriding commitment to kin and tribe necessary to survive over time. According to his reckoning, in four generations societies go from battle-hardened men with life and death commitments to each other, who successfully invade and conquer cities, to indulgent weaklings, incapable of defending themselves from the next invading wave of hungry, privation-disciplined, mutually committed, desert-dwellers.

The following discussion does not pretend to describe all tribal behavior the world over; nor does it speculate on what was the honor code that dominated the very long period of deep history, the 150,000 years of homo sapiens in traveling in bands (Boehm, 1999; Smail, 2008). It, therefore, makes few claims to specific biological impulses that drive our individual and collective behavior. It does, however, describe the patterns of behavior and the dominant values characteristic of the tribal warrior societies that, from the Bronze Age onward, gave rise to more stratified aristocratic empires (Kautsky, 1982). This *primary honor code* is shared with some variants, among Celts, Greeks, Romans, Germans, Scandinavians, Slavs—all contributors to the cultural and ethnic gene-pool of Western civilization.

This essay hopes to lay out the main contours of this tribal, *primary* honor code, and then follow its mutations as they play out in the more stratified civilizations that at once modified those codes (more hierarchy) and accommodated to them (male dominance). NB: I refer to such primary-code cultures as *shame–honor* both in order to avoid the original term, honor–shame, which has fallen into disrepute (see Conclusion below), and because shame is the prior and more fundamental emotion. And I define those cultures in which the primary honor code dominates as those in which it is *accepted, expected, required to shed blood for the sake of honor*, preferably the "other's" blood.

Self-Help Justice: Revenge, Feud, Vendetta

The man of honor owes overriding loyalty to his clan. If someone kills his kin, whether intentionally or not, he *must* retaliate in blood (Miller, 1983;

Boehm, 1984; Griswold, 2013). The earliest written Germanic law codes identify the *wergild* (man-money), the price of all the various groups within society—men, women, high-born, king's companion, warrior, commoner, German, Roman. They do not replace but provide an outlet for the basic system: clan retributive justice, feud (Wormald, 2003; Esders, 2014). For if the warrior upon whom the burden of vengeance falls accepts blood-money (*wergild*) without first "giving his lance blood to drink," he brings everlasting shame upon himself and his clan (Stetkevych, 1993: 60).

This loss of honor has terrible consequences (Colson, 1953; Gluckman, 1955; Miller, 1983). For the warrior, it can be fatal: blood in the water to his fellow sharks. A man without honor is a sterile woman, contemptible, despised, useless. The Bedouin male who has lost his honor only approaches the oasis last, after the women have washed off their menses (Stetkevych, 1993: 174f.). He cannot speak in public for no one will heed his words; no one will defend him or his family when hostile forces gather. To avoid shame's living death, a warrior's woman will urge her husband to defend his (their) honor, even in the face of certain death. Sooner be the widow of an honorable man than the wife of a cowardly "woman." Many, today, might find such a notion inappropriately misogynistic; for those who considered a man "womanly" for refusing to avenge his honor by the primary code, it was the worst and most painful insult.

Violence and Honor

Warrior alpha males and their honor code dominate social dynamics in these cultures. For them, bravery, indomitability, and the readiness to avenge insults or injuries stand out as the greatest of traits (Bowman, 2006: ch. 2; Nesbitt & Cohen, 1996). Such codes *accept, expect, even require, that the man shed blood for the sake of honor*. This blood could be that of a foe, a neighbor, a family member, or—all else failing—one's own. These are evolutionary developments adapted to environments of scarcity—of food, of women, of resources—that have governed most human life for hundreds of thousands of years (Bennett, 2018).

Nothing, in principle, differs more fundamentally from modern, civic polities and demotic values in which courts mete out justice than this tribal morality, with its self-help justice.

> The ethos of honour is fundamentally opposed to a universal and formal morality, which affirms the equality in dignity of all men and consequently the equality of their rights and duties. Not only do the rules imposed upon men differ from those imposed upon women, and the duties towards men differ from those towards women, but also the dictates of honour, directly applied to the individual case and varying according to the situation, are in no way capable of being made universal.
>
> (Bourdieu, 1966: 15)

The warrior inhabits a world of recurring violence. Shedding blood enforces justice; it defines the parameters of power and prestige; it punishes with mutilation, shame, and death. A male who has not killed is not a man (and not a reliable defender of his clan); a true warrior, a man of respect, has killed many.[1] There are interesting intermediary cases, a form of civic honor arises from risking one's life without necessarily killing anyone. In the South, over time, dueling became a test of one's courage in the face of death, and the duelists who survived often emerged from their mutual opportunity to prove their courage, joining together in an adrenaline-born friendship (Greenberg, 1994: 64f.).

Whereas for the Western progressive, the expression "senseless violence" approaches the status of a tautology—all violence is irrational if not senseless; for the warrior, "senseless violence" is an oxymoron—all violence is meaningful (Blok, 2001; Chagnon et al., 2002; Sapolsky, 2017). The mafia expression "he made his bones" refers specifically to establishing "credibility" (seriousness), by having killed someone: people, especially those afraid of dying, fear those who kill and those who kill have contempt for those afraid of dying.[2]

And alongside "respect" from other lethal males comes access to females:

> Conflicts over the possession of nubile females have probably been the main reason for fights and killings throughout most of human history: the original human societal rules emerged, in all probability, to regulate male access to females and prevent the social chaos attendant on fighting over women.
>
> (Chagnon, 2014: 316)[3]

One can imagine the psycho-pharmacology of the victor's charismatic appeal. The very fact that life is on the line testifies to the weighty nature of honor. Hence, this exchange from the movie *In Bruges* (2008): Natalie: "Will it be dangerous?" Harry Waters: "Of course it'll be dangerous. It's a matter of fucking honor!"

When his drinking mate reminds Chramnesind that it was a good thing that he, Sichar, had killed his relatives (hence they had all this money for drinking from a *wergild* settlement paid by the church), Chramnesind suddenly realizes: "If I don't avenge my relatives, they will say that I am as weak as a woman for I no longer have the right to be called a man" (Landes, Chapter 5 in this volume). So he smashes in his drinking buddy's skull and hangs his body out for all to see that he had washed his honor with blood. In such a world, men who didn't kill, like Jews, were not really men; indeed in the later Middle Ages, the belief circulated among Christians that Jewish men menstruated (Johnson, 1998). Some, today, might consider that a (queer) merit; but to those spreading this rumor, it was a humiliating accusation.

Tribal cultures expend huge social capital on developing warriors, men capable domestically, at the level of clan, of taking vengeance for wrongs (self-help justice), and in relationship with the outside, of at least defending against invaders, and at best, invading and plundering them. Survival depends on it. Warriors therefore have special status (honor) privilege (right to anger and violence) and power (few if any can resist their will). Their peer-enforced (primary) values of valor cater to their needs and desires.

The Proverbs of Tribal Warrior Honor

Every aspect of this warrior tribal code contradicts Jesus' Sermon on the Mount in fundamental ways. To illustrate this, George Jones, scholar of German sagas, produced a collection of pithy, shame–honor apothegms, a parody of Jesus' Sermon on the Mount, itself the extreme articulation of an "anti-honor" code (Jones, 1959). The list below begins with his, to which I add some.

> *Blessed are those with strong kinsmen, for they shall find help.*

One is only protected when outsiders know that one has a strong contingent of backers who will take vengeance for any attack. Ibn Khaldun called this solidarity *Asabiyya*, and considered it the most basic social tie and the highest, God-given morality. Any failure to support a clan member weakens one's ability to call on help in time of need. As societies become more complex, the range of people one can call on to help take vengeance—"friends," household, lords, patrons—widens even as the certainty of the help may weaken. In rare cases, one can disown certain relatives whose indiscretions consistently upset public peace and violate communal norms. In Scandinavian countries, rowdy kin might be repudiated or encouraged to *go viking* "in order to take out their excesses on people too far away to demand wergeld or take vengeance" (Miller, 1983: 91).

> *Blessed are those who keep faith, for they shall be honoured.*

Solidarity must override all other concerns. If someone kills my brother in a fair fight, or worse, my brother behaved badly and started the fight, I still must side with my brother. My side, right or wrong. Few attitudes are more problematic than this "us–them" mentality for moral reasoning. Plato has Polemarchus represent this attitude as a political principle in book II of *The Republic*: Justice is "rewarding your friends and harming your enemies." This attitude holds in contempt sentiments such as empathy for "the other," or siding, when justice calls for it, with outsiders against your own people. In a world of self-help justice, such moral scruples and generosity are a recipe for self-destruction.

> *Blessed are they who take vengeance, for they shall be offended no more, and they shall have honor and glory all the days of their life and eternal fame in ages to come.*

The desire for vengeance seems hard-wired in humans, part of our evolutionary development, and self-help justice demands that it dominate any countervailing force of either justice (the other guy was right, or not guilty) or mercy (Singer, 2006). The warrior dreams of vengeance; he savors accomplishing it (Diamond, 2010; cf. Sillitoe & Kuwimb, 2010). Mercy, in this context, often registers as weakness and invites further aggression. In his saint's life of the lay lord, Gerald of Aurillac, the hagiographer noted that his own people complained that Gerald was too mild with people who plundered his goods, and "when they discovered that he did not wish to take vengeance, they devoured the more greedily that which was rightfully his."[4] Chagnon observed among the Yanomamo that,

> when members of a group acquire a reputation of timidity and cowardice, their neighbors take ruthless advantage of them, push them around, insult them publicly, and take their women. Thus, it is strategically important to react decisively to any affront, no matter how trivial.
>
> (Chagnon, 2014: 86)

For the tribal man of honor, there can be no distinction between accidental and deliberate murder: limbic captivity, the hot emotion of vengeance, cannot make provisions for such a distinction (Radding, 1985: 92–95). To do so would take courts with the power to intervene immediately in the process, and, according to their findings, frustrate hot-blooded seekers of justice (cf. *Deuteronomy*, 19:6). With self-help justice (personal revenge), everyone was "served" with an implacable warning that even accidental injury carried with it the sure promise of retaliation (Salzman, 2008). Tribal warriors surely recognize the difference between involuntary homicide and murder, but given the need for a sure deterrent, for vengeance, and the fear that they might seem weak, avengers often deem the distinction dysfunctional.

But vengeance goes well beyond this logic: its driving force, as in so many other forms of violent aggression, is anger. Despite the "reasons" for vengeance, the drive is primal. We see it in its rawest form in a mid-eleventh-century account, in which the hagiographer described how monks, bearing relics, bringing crowds, and making peace, trapped a vengeance seeker in a church and demanded that he forgive his mortal enemy who lay prostrate before him in repentance. He refused despite their escalating pressure which had him writhing on the ground. "The youth began to cry, to turn different colors, now red, now pale, to gnash is teeth, nearly to go insane" (Koziol, 1986; cf. similar case, Barthelemy 2010: 74). Letting go of the need to bleach the soul with blood does not come easily to those caught up in the talons of honor–shame.

> *Blessed is he who has his enemy for lunch before his enemy has him for supper.*[5]

The tribal warrior, faced with a world of scarce resources—"limited good"—views every exchange as a zero-sum game in which when someone else wins, he loses, and in order for him to win, someone else must lose (Foster, 1965; Salzman, 2008, ch. 2). Honor demands it. Tribal warriors rejoice in seeing their enemies suffer. They torture, humiliate, degrade, and kill with gusto. *Schadenfreude* defines the nature of us–them mentalities: suffering by "us" inspires hatred and desire for revenge; suffering by "them" inspires joy and celebration (White, 2003, 142f.). It is a marker of a great victory to drink from the skull of a slain enemy. As Attila the Hun put it so delicately, "To the strong man, nothing is sweeter than seeking vengeance with his own hand" (Jordanes, *Gettica*, 59, ed. *MGH, AA*, V: 1, p. 110). Joy (at victory) and pain (at loss) are a dyad; like honor and shame they are two faces of the same coin: without the pain of the foe, the victor feels no joy.

> *Those who can, do what they will; those who cannot, suffer what they must. Pillage or be pillaged.*

The Man of Honor's Religion: Triumphalist Religiosity

The warrior's religion is above all one of victory: he seeks the gods' favor so that they will strengthen his sword arm and guide him to glory. His heaven is a great banquet hall for fallen heroes. At a basic level, this alpha triumphalism is a natural human, indeed mammalian drive. All the ancient imperial gods—including their (semi-)divine earthly rulers—reflected this triumphalism: Scandinavians, Germans, Romans, Celts, Greeks, Aryans. Men of honor aspire to glory, or what Fukuyama calls *megalothymia*, the desire to be recognized as superior to everyone else (Fukuyama, 1992: 182). The *Song of Roland* at once critiques and glorifies Roland's *megalothymia*.

Warriors are impervious to the appeal of ethical religions, especially those that preach not to resist evil. When Clovis, Frankish warlord extraordinaire, first heard about the Crucifixion, how Jesus told Peter to put up his sword, and then went unresisting to a painful and humiliating death, he allegedly exclaimed: "If I had been there with my Franks, we would have revenged this injury" (Pseudo-Fredegar 3.21; ed. *MGH Scriptores Rerum Merovingicarum*, 2, p. 101). Half a millennium later, Frankish warriors on the way to liberate Jerusalem from the Muslims slaughtered Jewish communities along the Rhine in order to avenge what "the Jews" had done to the Lord, a desire they now, at long last, were fulfilling (Cohen, 2004; Throop 2021, 43–72).

Triumphalism is the religion of honor-empires (Lendon, 1997). The rulers say, "We rule because our God is the most powerful," although one might rephrase as, "Our God(s) is(are) the true God(s) because we rule—and impose our superiority, our honor on you who must defer by accepting degradation." If "religiosity" designates a religious style, a way of "living" one's religious beliefs, then "triumphalist religiosity" designates believers who assert their own dominance as a *visible* sign of their superiority, as a *proof* of the "favor" of the god(s). Legal privilege, like a double *wergild* for one's ethnic group, or the laws of the *dhimma*, represents just that advantage.

Honor demands public transcripts of submission, of visible signs and rituals of hierarchy, of deference by outsiders paid to true believers. It both demands that others pay it respect and, to varying degrees depending on circumstances, it disrespects others as a matter of principle (Landes, 2016). Historically, triumphalists exercise power in an authoritarian manner; at their harshest, they tend domestically towards inquisitorial persecution of dissent (heretics, apostates) and humiliation of non-believers (*Judensau* ceremonies, *dhimmi* regulations), while in relations with other nations, these attitudes produce holy wars (Jihads, Crusades) and the massacre of resisting unbelievers.

Triumphalists find public challenge intolerably disrespectful and interpret blasphemy laws aggressively in order to silence not merely dissent but disrespect. The last victim of the Inquisition in France was the Chevalier de la Barre in 1766 for not doffing his hat before a solemn procession of clergy (Bringuier, 2018; cf. Geisel, 1938). Intolerance, disdain, violence, repression, intimidation—all of these attitudes reflect triumphalist religiosity in its crudest (most insecure) forms. Not for them the modesty of letting an invisible God decide in an invisible world who is deserving and who not.

From Tribal Warrior to Monarchical Subject: Aristocracy, Honor, and the Prime Divider

Tribal warriors are fiercely independent and, among peers, egalitarian. They resist the rule of kings, the social hierarchies of courts, the social stratification of society (Boehm, 1999; Salzman, 2009). When egalitarian balanced opposition fails, however, when a strong horse gains a decisive advantage over the others, and draws a following, when warlords can, with the help of metal weapons, conquer large areas, including agricultural lands that produce surplus, and, with administrative record keeping (clerics), store vast amounts of wealth ... a new zero-sum dynamic arises within the heart of the free (warrior) population (Gellner, 1990). Under these Neolithic conditions, powerful men can consolidate conquests over vulnerable peasant labor, at once tied to the land and consistently productive far beyond the capacities of nomadic cultures. (The positive-sum payoff to the loss of the honor.)

At that point, we find arising what Ernst Gellner calls "agro-literate" societies, or John Kautsky calls "aristocratic empires" (Kautsky, 1982; Hall, 1985; Gellner, 1986; Crone, 1989). Here rough egalitarianism cedes to hierarchies, monarchies, empires: within the framework of a state, everyone, no matter how powerful and protected, is someone else's "man." The higher up the social ladder one goes (aristocratic elites), the more people one commands and the fewer one has to obey. Indeed, one might even sketch an honor hierarchy in terms of "those whose noble status entitles them to express anger," and against whom (White, 1998: 139). Nothing bespeaks the meaning of honor more clearly than the right to anger and violence.

Ancient tales of the rise of kingship involve clashes between egalitarian warriors and the emerging king (I *Samuel,* 8). Gregory of Tours, a late sixth-century ecclesiastical historian, tells how the warrior-king Clovis handled a power-challenge from a warrior at Soissons (Gregory of Tours, *History of the Franks,* II.27). When Clovis broke the rules of sharing plunder and asked for a most valuable vase (silver?) over and above what he should get (the lion's share anyway), a warrior smashed the vase in protest. Clovis said nothing. Waiting his year allotted for taking vengeance, he martialed his troops, Roman style. When he came to this soldier, he threw his weapons on the ground, and when the man bent down to pick them up, Clovis smashed his head in, crying, "That's for the vase of Soissons!"

In this world, the clan has been folded into a larger hierarchy of power and solidarities, including loyalty to princes who did not always, by the warrior's honor code, deserve it. The success of the Carolingian war machine to conquer most of northwestern Europe, including places even the Romans had not reached, drove a strong internal cleavage between the weapons-bearing men of honor on the one hand, and the agrarian commoners who came to the *mallus* (tribal court and assembly of the host), only to have their staffs broken on their back and sent home degraded. Correspondingly, by the same logic, those who came with weapons, the warrior class, was elevated: *potentes* vs. *impotentes.*

Even within the elite where honor and honors abounded, the hierarchy, the drive to dominate, to have everyone else defer, even bow down, could become an obsession. When Theodora demanded that Justinian hold his ground against the Nike rioters, she framed it in terms of her absolute horror that everyone *not* be subordinated to her, a kind of feminist *megalothymia*: "for one who has reigned it is intolerable to be a fugitive. May I never be deprived of this purple robe, and may I never see the day when those who meet me do not call me empress" (Procopius, *Wars,* I, 24, 33f.). The royal purple as a shroud was preferable to the shameful existence of a life that was not of absolute dominion.

Aristocrats have privileges and rights to a lifestyle that disgraced commoners do not, cannot. Honor—who gets it and what deference they command—is the "animating principle in the nobleman's society" (Kautsky, 1982: 115). In time of peace, the honor-driven hunt, the more dangerous the prey, the more honor. Commoners who hunt violate social order, often a capital crime. The steady erosion of warrior autonomy as aristocratic empires develop, goes hand in hand with rendering commoners servile. One can see the emerging hierarchies in the early barbarian law codes (writing down and organizing the oral), listing rates of exchange for various populations: a Frank (warrior) is worth twice a Roman (literate). Franks bore their swords and axes in public and picked fights with virtual impunity

(Landes, Chapter 5), and (mistakenly perhaps) looked down on those who read and wrote as effeminate. "Violence was built into the very texture of aristocratic life" (Kautsky, 1982: 72).

Compensations of Conquest Hierarchy: The Honor of "Those who can"

> Those who can, do what they will; those who cannot, suffer what they must.
> (Athenian proverb, Thucydides)

Under conditions of imperial stratification, castes or orders emerge defining a series of statuses of descending prestige, unto the water carriers and the wood gatherers. More or less rigid, these statuses allowed for little movement between levels. In medieval Europe, an early eleventh-century conceptual scheme spoke of fighters, prayers, and workers (Duby, 1978). But broadly speaking, the greatest cleavage between various groups was that between the powerful and the powerless, between ruling elites and the working, commoner population, in the medieval European case, between the fighters and prayers above (however they may have fought each other), and the laborers (of varying degrees of servility) below (Duby, 1978). Here we find the crucial division, a cleavage between those with public honor and those with much less or none, those who speak in public councils, and those without voice, between those who walk with their heads high, and those who walk hunched, eyes on the ground, doffing their cap to those above the prime divider. The workings of this world are wonderfully described by James Scott in terms of public transcripts of deference and private transcripts of resentment (1992): "When the great lord passes, the wise peasant bows low and silently farts."

This visible superiority, however great and gratifying, was the compensation for the loss of the status, the dignity, of a free man. Graeber comments on the difference between dignity and honor in the context of zero-sum relations:

> Honor is not the same as dignity. One might even say: honor is surplus dignity. It is that heightened consciousness of power, and its dangers, that comes from having stripped away the power and dignity of others; or at the very least, from the knowledge that one is capable of doing so. At its simplest, honor is that excess dignity that must be defended with the knife or sword.
> (Graeber, 2011: 170)

The free warrior had to choose hierarchical honor—his dominion over the many and subordination to the few, over the dignified egalitarianism of the tribe. Those in the lower ranges of the elite suffered considerably from the now uninhibited arrogance of their superiors, and gave to those below as good as they got. This pattern of discharging humiliation from those above on those below is found everywhere, from children giving their younger siblings a taste of the humiliations they have experienced at school, to the authoritarian personality (Adorno, 1950).

This stigmatization of labor, especially manual labor, lies at the center of the divide. For those above the prime divider, manual labor was a curse that they, by the grace of their god(s) and their virtue, had escaped. As the chronicler Robert d'Auxerre wrote about some uppity peasants who dared challenge the aristocracy's arbitrary exactions of the products of their labor in the 1180s:

> The league of the sworn peace of Puy (*Capucciati*) was a diabolic and pernicious invention. There was *no longer fear or respect for superiors.* All strove to acquire liberty, saying that it belonged to them from the time of Adam and Eve, from the very day of creation. They did not understand that *serfdom is the punishment of the sin.* The result was that there was *no longer any distinction between the great and the small, but a fatal confusion* tending to ruin the *institutions which rule us all, through the will of God and the agency of the powerful of this earth.*
>
> (Luchaire, 1957: 17)

One of the immediate and existential consequences of this divide meant that whenever there was a famine, the poor starved first; they were the ones who had to choose which of their children would die so that the rest of the family might live (Ebert, 2018). You knew how bad a famine it was if the lords could not drink their grains and even starved (Glaber, *Quinque libri* IV.iv.11). No wonder the *pauperes*, the *impotentes*, had an apocalyptic dream that when Jesus returned,

> then will end the tyranny of kings and the injustice and rapine of reeves and their cunning and unjust judgments and wiles. Then shall those who rejoiced and were glad in this life groan and lament. Then shall their mead, wine and beer be turned into thirst for them.
> (*Byrhtferth's Manual* ca. 1012, 1972, p. 242, lines 3–9)

Key to the effectiveness of this split, was a kind of "us–them" thinking that normally differentiates *between* tribes, but here becomes internalized, differentiating between those with and those without power, what medieval commentators referred to as the distinction between *potentes* and *pauperes* or *impotentes* (Bosl, 1964). Warriors rarely felt empathy for commoners whom they often viewed as another, lower race.

Take, for example, this case, written about the year 859:

> The Danes devastated the area beyond the Scheldt (to the north). The mixed multitude (*vulgus promiscuum*) between the Seine and the Loire, taking a collective oath together, vigorously resisted the Danes camped

in the Seine. But, because they had imprudently undertaken their collective oath, they were easily massacred (*facile interficiuntur*) by our more powerful ones (*a potentioribus nostris*).

(*Annals of Saint Bertin, ad an.* 859; Martin (tr.), 1992: 199)

When these *pauperes* took an oath and armed themselves, they violated their condition. Even though the *potentes* had neglected their duties to defend them (they were off rebelling against King Charles the Bald and often in league with their fellow [pagan] Viking warriors), the rabble had no right to take their place. Nor is this just a feature of "Dark Ages barbarianism." Scenes of armed *potentes* slaughtering *impotentes* occur every month and year around the world even today. In parts of Africa (and beyond), life is about the four Ws: "wine, women, wealth, and weapons" (Ellis, 2006: 283). In authoritarian societies such massacres are part of the business of state, Napoleon's "whiff of grapeshot" (Wolin, 1960: ch. 7).

The more pervasive this hierarchical world becomes, the more social relations become matters—games, performances—of dominance and submission. This honor dynamic reinforces the basic hard zero-sum axiom described by the Athenians. This *Realpolitik* proverb, this triumphalist cognitive egocentrism, expresses the outlook of authoritarian dominion from the earliest "civilizations" right up to the advent of modern democracies. The rare exceptions—ancient Israel and Greece, medieval European communes—do not last long, partly because in the dominant political environment, the annual business of the warrior aristocracy is plundering neighbors and exploiting commoners.

In one form or another, prime dividers have dominated most "states" for over five millennia, from the Bronze Age (fourth millennium BCE) until the last couple of centuries, from the earliest empires in ancient times (Egyptian, Assyrian, Chinese) to the great cultures of later antiquity (Greek, Roman) and their Christian and Islamic successor states (Kautsky, 1982: 49–78). These cultures all exhibit the single most characteristic mark of such thinking, a social *prime divider* between those who have power and those who work. On one side of this divider, we find a small group (about 2–10 per cent of the population) of aristocratic elites (sword and pen) who enjoy privilege, power, and wealth. On the other, we find a vast majority of the population living off the land, often at the margins of subsistence (famines are a common feature of life). The elites dominate public life from which they ban the commoners (except under certain carefully choreographed occasions).

This "prime divider" between powerful elites and producing commoners changes the dynamic of shame–honor decisively. While on the one hand, prime-divider societies are much more productive than tribal groups, and mobilize extensive positive-sum interactions, on the other, by making the split visible—honor above, shame below the prime divider—the new arrangement made the disgrace all the more painful. In a more tribal setting, one could treat everyone with respect and dignity; with a prime divider, certain public behaviors (including sumptuary laws) urged deference to superiors, respect for one's peers, and contempt for those below. This pattern survives directly in many places and it reappears in many avatars among those cultures that think they've got it under control: today's global capitalists replicate the patterns of exploitation of (now out-of-country) laborers, while European Union technocrats and ideocrats identify more with their fellow transnational elites than their own country's commoners.

Onēidophobia: *The Overriding Fear of Losing Face*

> Face is to a man is what bark is to a tree.
>
> (Chinese proverb)

Lying silently beneath the turbulent surface of honor lies the fear of losing face. No one wants to be humiliated in public. The issue, then, with *onēidophobia*—the intense fear of public disgrace—concerns just what triggers that fear, and to what lengths will one go to avoid it; put more bluntly, how violent, how quickly? Some of this depends on the peer group: What do they consider losing face? What price will they extract from those who lose that face? How long will they allow a passive response to challenge to go on without loss of face? The answers to these issues depend both on the peer group, and on the individual: how viscerally do they react to the possibility of losing face (limbic captivity), and to what ends will they go in order to avoid (imagined) public disgrace?

Indeed, in some cases the imperative to save face overrides every other "value" of the culture: loyalty, solidarity, truth. US military counter-intelligence agent Jennifer Dunham speaks of her experience in Afghanistan as an encounter with a very different mindset: "Pashtuns appear fiercely loyal to one another, but, in a heartbeat, will betray their own family members just to save face" (Dunham, 2013: 10). Partly it is self-preservation: losing face in some cultures can bring on terrible, even fatal consequences.

Westerners underestimate these matters partly because our culture does not view so many things as forms of public disgrace, nor does it punish those who lose face so severely, partly because much of the lying we do to save face remains petty and largely invisible, like lying about how much one paid for a car so as not to seem a sucker (Smith, 2004). In "primary" honor–shame cultures, in which honor/face is the fundamental unit of social status, the dynamics differ significantly. Tribal warrior cultures, in particular, operate within the limbic confines of two overwhelming needs: for favor in the eyes of one's honor group—honor gained, preserved, recovered—and the even greater dread of public shame and disgrace, *onēidophobia*.

In medieval documents, the term anger appears often in the context of loss (or fear of loss) of face. Damage done—relative killed, property destroyed, insult proffered in public—elicits (or should elicit) anger. Anger then spurs the shamed to an action, often violent, not infrequently very violent, to restore his honor, at which point, the angered can be appeased without loss to his reputation (Rosenwein, 1998). The most uncontrolled expressions of anger come from this fear, not from the (righteous) desire for vengeance.

The Man and His Women: Patriarchal Codes of Honor

The role of women in prime-divider shame–honor cultures constitutes perhaps the single most visible difference between these primary shame–honor cultures and modern ones. Most cultures, historically, have followed a particular public dynamic also characteristic of most primate groupings, where alpha males get first access to food and mating (Ghiglieri, 1999: ch. 1; Wrangham and Peterson, 1996: ch. 7). This has played out differently among many peoples, but in many cases, such as the "Mediterranean," men *gain* honor for their sexual prowess and dominant behavior, and women *preserve* honor by maintaining their sexual fidelity and fertility (Pitt-Rivers, 1966; Stewart, 1994: chs. 6–9).

Men of honor and power find women deeply problematic; indeed, even as they can inspire *megalothymia*, they can trigger equal amounts of *onēidophobia*, the fear of losing control of one's women, of public shame. Men understand the terrifying reality that their women can, at any time, shame them in public, by words or by deeds. And so they punish such breaches severely. Any woman who wants to shame her man does so despite the blows and abuse and even death that such a behavior will rain down upon her. Honor killings (from the perspective of guilt–integrity cultures: "shame murders") represent the farthest extreme of this honor-preserving (shame-averting) violence (Chesler, 2018; Heydari, Teymoori, & Trappes, 2021).[6]

In prime-divider aristocracies, the man's honor trumps women's autonomy: a man is responsible for his women's honor, his wives and daughters; his honor intact when they behave, his honor damaged if they break the codes. In some cases, the forces pushing towards this behavior can be elemental (jealousy and sexual betrayal); in others, they reflect an elaborate social construct of the man's honor defined specifically in sexual matters.

In such cultures for the manly man, womanly ways are cowardly, yielding, effeminate. They flee death. To call a man a woman was an affront to his honor (McGrath, 2010: 56). To call a man's daughter a whore is an assault on anyone's (family's) honor; to a warrior, it is a deadly assault. In some shame–honor cultures, the insulter must die; in others the daughter must die. Thus, warriors have deep ambivalence about, on the one hand, "womanly" talents (discussion, forbearance, forgiveness, compromise); and on the other, need women as sexual objects of desire and procreators of the next generation of warriors. In his warrior peer group, where raping defenseless women is a benefit of membership, he follows the code that says a real man takes as many women as he can. The phallic intrusive notion that men are virile because they penetrate, and that to be penetrated was a sign of a feminine (and hence dishonorable) nature, gave rise to the Greek and Roman homosexual ideal of the "impenetrable penetrator" (McLaren, 2007: 1–23).

Rare in the history of mankind have there been warriors ready to allow their women the same sexual promiscuity they assume for themselves. On the contrary, aristocratic honor groups in prime-divider societies the world over favor the polygamous pattern of male sexuality, where the man has multiple women of all statuses, and women deviate from a procrustean bed of the warrior's honor, at risk of their lives. The body of warrior love poems has a modest place in world literature, at least until the early second millennium CE. There results a zero-sum sexual dynamic between men of honor and their women: men copulate as much as they can with as many desirable mates as possible, acquiring honor (*sharaf*) with every conquest, while women protect their virginity/purity, i.e., their man's honor (*'ird*).

Whenever a man and a woman meet together, their third is always Satan.

Tribal warriors expect deference from others: their prowess accords them singular privileges, including sexual ones, and their psychological needs take priority over those of women and less powerful males, from cradle to (often premature) grave. The warrior's honor entitles him to impose his insecurities on his women, to execute women who damage his honor. In some cases, this is unwritten but understood practice; in other, more anxious cases, this can become an elaborate system of cultural and patriarchal enforcement.

Warriors rejoice over the birth of a son—another warrior!—and frown, or worse, at the birth of a daughter—another mouth to feed. In Arabic, to be an *abu banat*, a father of (only) daughters is a humiliation. Men of honor favor boys over girls: killing, abandoning, or selling baby girls, feeding them less than boys, giving boys arbitrary power over their sisters.

And of course, the more adolescent the girl, the more the sexual danger. Their anxious men make widespread efforts to control the presence of women, secluding them, allowing them into public space only with escorts, covered, in the most extreme cases, from head to toe. "O Prophet! Tell your wives and your daughters and the women of the believers to draw their cloaks all over their bodies that they may thus be distinguished and not molested" (*Qur'ran* 33:59). The logic here takes phallo-centrism to its conclusion: the man of honor's sexuality, including preying on defenseless women, is a force of nature (i.e., men are its limbic captives); women who arouse them with provocative dress are guilty for anything that ensues (Shariff, 2006).

All of this anxiety climaxes in the marriage bed, where the virgin is pierced by the penetrator and bleeds as proof of her purity. Until sexual consummation, the honor of everyone involved—bride, groom, their families—is in danger. Only after their family displays the bloody sheet that attests at once to the bride's previous virginity and the groom's virility, to the satisfaction of all, are the challenges over (Shehadeh, 1982: 78–80).

> Brutally and swiftly deflowering his bride, the husband is responding to a social criterion of virility, which is still very widespread. Deflowering is not a means leading to the consummation of the sexual act, but a proof of power to engender, to be given to friends grouped around the bedroom. Above all, here is a matter of male pride whose consequences may well be disastrous for the couple's future harmony.
> (Pryce-Jones, 2009:131)

William Blake may have had this in mind when he spoke of "the marriage hearse".
("London," 1794).

We sorely dread evil days, a multitude of violent deaths, public panic, humiliation and captivity.
(Women at the death of Beowulf, l. 3136).

Again, warriors tend to replicate the patterns of the primate alpha males:

> In primates, pronounced dimorphism [difference in physical size and strength between male and female] like that of Australopithecines is associated with either harem arrangements or with open, promiscuous mating competition by males, as opposed to permanent pair bonding.
> (Boehm, 1999: 174, paraphrasing Dunbar (1996: 71)

Just as orangutans take advantage of their greater strength to rape as a strategy of reproduction, so do men take advantage of their greater size and strength to force themselves on women (Ghiglieri, 1999: ch. 4; Thornhill & Palmer, 2000; cf. Drea & Wallen, 2003: 29–60). Rape, of course, is not only about reproduction, but about domination, which in most cases involves the ability to humiliate (Scully & Marolla, 2004: 15–30, at 17; Wrangham & Peterson, 1996: 127–152; Smuts, 1993: 1–63). In raping another man's woman, a man at once aggrandizes his own manhood and destroys that of another man (Scully and Marolla, 2004: 20). As far as some men's honor was concerned, the raped wife is a secondary consideration (Johnson, 1988: 147–148).

Where rape is common, so is wife- and child-beating, stretching back, too, to deep history (Tracy & Crawford, 1999: 27–42). The notion of "rule of thumb" allegedly comes from an English legal ruling (1782) that one should not use a stick thicker than one's thumb with which to beat one's wife (Kelly, 1994: 341–365). The Qur'an (4:34) prescribes beating for wayward wives; a hadith assures men they will not be called to task (on Judgment Day) for beating their wives; and the legal commentators elaborate when, where, and how hard (Darwish, 2008: ch. 3–4).

In the most extreme cases, where a community enforces a code that demands the death of females who have besmirched the family honor, there are shame murders, aka, honor killings. One can view these as part of a continuum of male violence, all manifestations of the drive to avoid humiliation in the eyes of others. Certain matters, however, place these shame-murders in a special category. These cases involve explicit public opinion much more than do crimes of passion or wife and child abuse: they are deliberate and collective acts of the entire family performing for the entire community; the family must accede to the pressure of their peers, and if not they risk an informal excommunication (Emery, 2003). They receive widespread approval for deeds that can involve levels of "barbaric ferocity" and ritual mutilation rare in crimes of passion (Chesler, 2009: 61–69; Wikan, 2008).

Moreover, since they are based on collective opinion, it matters less whether the "guilty" party had actually done what she (or he, in the case of homosexuals) was accused of; rather, the mere rumor, the mere suspicion, can be enough to execute sentence. Speaking of Palestinian girls so executed, Robin Morgan notes:

> Whether or not these young women have actually done so is irrelevant; the mere suspicion was sufficient to justify one young man slitting his sister's throat in Nazareth, and another in Gaza's Maghazi Camp, locking his sister inside a large freezer for five hours while he sat outside and waited for her to die.
> (Morgan, 1989: 347)

Where "honor" is at stake among *onēidophobes*, the stakes are fierce, the rage at shame immense, the vengeance, sadistic.

> *I against my brother, I and my brother against our cousin, my brother and our cousin against the neighbors, all of us against the foreigner.*
> (Bedouin proverb)

For tribal warriors, trust is a rare commodity, and generally only to be found in the confines of the family/clan, if that. In prime-divider societies, both the range of those to trust, and the opportunities for betrayal, grow, making these matters increasingly personal, individual. The mistrust of the "other" creates a cycle of suspicion and projection—"they want to do to me what I want to do to them"—that can only be broken with great difficulty. When the Melians complained that the Athenians' offer—join our side or we kill the men and sell the women and children into slavery—was unfair, the Athenians responded, "You plead for fairness only because you are weak. Were you in our place you would be doing the same thing" (Thucydides, *Peloponnesian Wars*, 5:85–116). On a political plane, this means that political initiatives and conspiracies are virtually identical. As Thomas Friedman put it, "Don't try to explain anything in the Middle East if you can't explain it with a conspiracy story" (Friedman, 2006).

> *At the hour of trial, a man is either honored or humiliated.*
> (Arab proverb)

In such a zero-sum world of constant competition, one's honor comes from dishonoring another (Leconte, 1996). Alpha males are on the constant lookout for rivals whom they assume plot zero-sum outcomes that will benefit "them" and harm "us," a system of "ascendancy through aggression" (Kressel, 1996). For such men of honor, every public discussion becomes a potential battlefield for honor, every exchange a "power challenge" (Pryce-Jones, 2009: ch. 4). "Honor is easily challenged and easily lost" (Salzman, 2008: 107). Indeed, people in power can expect at any time—and especially when they show signs of weakness—challenges to their authority, attempts to blacken their face, if not with blood, then with ridicule. Many a "civilizational edifice" aims at making sure such challenges do not happen to those who represent the social order. Cultures of consensus, like imperial China, mobilize huge social capital to avoid public discord.

Under all but the most dire conditions, men of honor consider public criticism a blackening of their face, a deliberate dishonor that must be washed in blood. Public admission of blame is like blood in the water. "No one in France will admit to having made a mistake. It means you're weak, and it's the beginning of the end of your political career," noted one twenty-first-century observer, bearing witness to the *longue durée* of this complex. Rare are the cultures in which public admission of fault redounds to the credit of the confessor. Rather, most people try to blame, and, in some cases, scapegoat a designated victim as "guilty." The "other" *must* be wrong in order to save face.

> *If you don't stop a man who is lying within the day, the lies turn into facts.*
> (Arab proverb)

If it is legitimate to shed blood to save face, *a fortiori* it's legitimate to lie (Smith, 2004). Lying to strangers is particularly easy, since there are no consequences and they are, as outsiders, suspect anyway. The mark of a high-level "honor–shame" culture is how low the barrier to either lies or violence in order to "save face." Warriors lie, then kill other men for calling them liars. Lancelot loudly insisted on his innocence, and as long as no one living could contradict him, he felt no guilt: "Those who told you such tales [of my adultery] were liars, which was proved by their deaths ... in their challenge to me they were not able to prove themselves the stronger, nor in the right" (Bowman, 2006: 42–45). Literally, in an honor–shame culture, where public knowledge is the only measure of truth, *might often makes right*.

Lying aims primarily at concealing weakness; in such cultures showing weakness sends out signals to predators to attack. Jennifer Dunham noted the connection. Among the hundreds of Pashtun men she interviewed, she found:

> an unwillingness to admit fault or bring any negativity towards oneself ... I spoke with some men so unwilling to show any sign of vulnerability, they would craft ridiculous lies in an attempt to portray themselves in a better light.
>
> (Dunham, 2013: 16)

Lying happens everywhere and is often linked to scapegoating, saving face by blaming someone else for failure. In more positive-sum cultures, however, where predators are fewer, showing vulnerability and conceding/accepting some responsibility for the problem can actually advance the collective (and even the personal) efforts of the larger group. One can gently urge the one pointing the finger to show a little self-awareness. "So, it's all the other guy's fault?" is a rhetorical question meant to be answered in the West by, "Of course not."

In *onēidophobic* cultures, by contrast, lying can actually become a game strategy (Jebens, 2002), whereby the liar tests both the intelligence of his interlocutor (how quickly does he or she catch on?) and tests that interlocutor's courage to call him on his lies, thereby risking an escalation of verbal and even physical violence. The interlocutor who does not challenge lies, whether he likes it or not, is thereby tagged as weak.

The advantages of successfully lying are impressive: one can manipulate the unsuspecting and the cowardly, deceive them or maneuver their fear of embarrassment so that they take positions that benefit the liar. In warrior cultures, lying well can be admirable. "You Americans never lie," one Afghan informant told his anthropologist. Being the good earnest, self-critical American anthropologist, he objected: "That's not true, Americans lie often." Then he realized—his Afghani friend meant it as an insult, not a compliment.

Lying is an evolutionary defense mechanism. Signaling theory deals with the ways in which both in body language and in words, both honestly and dishonestly, we signal impressions to others of fierceness or fitness meant to deter predators (Zahavi & Zahavi, 1997; Miller, 2010). For years Saddam Hussein endured crippling sanctions that immiserated his people rather than let Western inspectors come and verify that he did not have weapons of mass destruction. Western cognitive egocentrists, assuming that he would not make his own people suffer and cripple his (impressive) abilities to make his economy work, concluded that he had something to hide, namely weapons. Citing all the evidence available from a distance, the US made the case for invading Iraq in significant part on his claim to have WMD. Much to the chagrin of the Bush administration, and the triumphant acclamations of the anti-war movement, when the invaders got inside Iraq, there was nary a WMD to be found.

Recently released FBI interrogation tapes with Saddam Hussein shed important light on the subject.[7] He pretended to have WMDs because they gave him status—nuclear weapons as hyper-masculinity—and provided a deterrent to Iran, his neighbor whom he had invaded with catastrophic results for both sides, only a year after Ayatollah Khomeini's "revolution" (1980–1988). In other words, being able to posture internationally—signaling threat—that one was someone capable of unleashing WMD on enemies was worth the massive cost to his own people.

Self-Criticism and Secondary Codes

The discussion of lying brings up the allied issue of controlling public discourse, i.e., public lies, imposed by people/groups with power on the public. As the Chinese version of the Emperor's New Clothes runs:

EMPEROR: What do you see?
CHAMBERLAIN: A horse.
EMPEROR: I see a deer.
CHAMBERLAIN: I see a deer.

Perhaps the single most public manifestation of honor–shame culture is the politics of public criticism. We should never underestimate the lengths to which *onēidophobes* will go in order to suppress speech that threatens their honor. Indeed, one could do an extensive analysis of any given society based on what may and must be said openly (public transcripts), and what may only be uttered in secret (private transcripts), and under what circumstances and with what effects, the hidden becomes public (Scott, 1992).

For all but the most self-assured men of honor, public criticism, even subtle, is anathema. The truth of the criticism, if it matters at all, works negatively: an assault on the man's very person that he must resist or lose his honor. Hence, in primary code shame–honor cultures, a "free press" is impossible. In late nineteenth-century Europe, journalists had to know how to fence in order to survive the response of those they dishonored with their criticism. In the Dreyfus Affair, 37 journalists died in duels (Forth, 2004). Those who admit to fault publicly become targets of rivals, and the higher they climb, the more those who envy them will bring them down.

The basic dynamics of one of democracy's most critical freedoms—speech—revolve around shame–honor issues, and on the degree of violence those criticized are willing to bring to bear in order to prevent public loss of face. Without an appreciation of how powerfully we avoid criticism—otherwise stated, how difficult are introspection and self-criticism—we cannot understand the massive psychological and social changes that had to occur in order to make freedom of speech a deed protected by law (Saxonhouse, 2005).

In some sense, modern psychology, starting with Freud, is an exploration, on the one hand, of our own dark side and, on the other, how to build a sufficiently robust ego, so that we can handle the blows to ego inflicted by bad news about ourselves. As Freud liked to put it (*Introductory Lectures on Psychoanalysis*, ch. 18), all knowledge of the real world (science) involved accepting blows to the ego (i.e., blows to one's honor), and Freud stood as third in delivering such blows to the Western psyche: Copernicus (the sun does not revolve around us), Darwin (we are descended from apes), and Freud (we are not even masters in our own psyche).

A third of people die from war, a third from disease, and a third from the evil eye.

(North African proverb)

Zero-sum attitudes have a close relationship to envy: if someone's success necessarily diminishes others in the eyes of the public, then any success will elicit envy, and, in many cases, mobilize forces to bring down the haughty ones. Envy, like shame and vengeance, may be peculiarly human, and play a key role in our evolution. As an individual phenomenon, it is hard to track since, being an admission of inadequacy in relationship to the person envied, few people want to admit to feeling envy (Schoeck, 1987: 1–15; Dumouchel, 2014). As a social phenomenon—i.e., collective envy—it may play an important role in distribution of wealth by forcing those with a great deal to share. In some tribes, hunter-gatherers hide food and eat it alone at night in order not to lose the "lion's share" to envious neighbors who demand theirs. This is the world of the one-eyed peasant-king.

Envy is a pervasive element of the human psyche and of human societies (Schoeck, 1987: 33–56). The expression "crabs in the basket" refers to the way if one crab tries to escape the basket, the others will pull him down, hence, the tendency of people in poverty to show hostility to someone who, by dint of effort, rises above the collective condition and, *by implication*, sheds an unflattering light on those he or she leaves behind. As we have seen, this is not always negative, but can also serve as a strong anti-monarchical force, a contribution to egalitarian, even "democratic" culture (Lindholm, 2002: 13–15; Salzman, 2008: 199–202).

Hans Schoeck argues that cultures that take envy as an inevitable and pervasive part of their lives produce societies of "limited good," and by contrast cultures that resist envy, even in relatively small but significant amounts, become wealth-producing nations (Schoeck, 1987: 57–76). When envy dominates a culture, its members mobilize against success. As the saying goes, "the higher up the pole you get, the more your ass is visible."

If in tribal conditions this envy prevents the emergence of kings, in civil societies it depresses economic growth. When people can tolerate the success of others conditions favor enterprise. Similarly for family dynamics: monogamy, as painful as it is for alpha males who want to (are genetically programmed to?) spread their seed, controls the terrible conflicts of envy between multiple wives, not only for their own status, but for the status of their children. Polygamy gives full range to both the alpha male's power, and to a "family life" brimming with the ferocious competitions at every level.

The notion of the evil eye, the idea that a malevolent gaze can harm the recipient, appears, developed to various degrees, in most cultures (Aquaro, 2004). Where the belief prevails, the members of the society take a wide variety of actions to ward off the evil eye, some magical (talismans), some preventive measures (hiding wealth, disguising good fortune, avoiding any public display of success). Much "black magic" aims at harming others invisibly, and the notion that some people can cast an "evil eye" on another and thereby curse them is widespread (Evans-Pritchard, 1976).

Conclusion

When framed as I have in terms of the primacy of certain emotions, primary honor codes appear to be the antithesis of contemporary progressive values. Not only are many features precisely what progressives reject—cruelty, violence, misogyny, racism, xenophobia, destructive envy—but the very foundational attitude toward the "other" cannot differ more between the primary code I've depicted and the current code. For the shame–honor, zero-sum player, the difference between "us" and "them" is radical and by default negative. "They" register primarily as foe, even deadly foe. Their gain is our loss; we can only win if they lose.

For contemporary progressives, however, it's the opposite: the "other" is to be embraced, made welcome, accepted. Tribalism is a dirty word, along with xenophobia. One might even formulate a progressive outlook as one characterized by the pursuit of precisely the opposite set of emotions— empathy for the "other" (Rifkin, 2009), embracing the "vulnerability" of mutual trust, rooting for the success of others rather than feeling diminished by it, sympathizing with other's pain rather than rejoicing in it. In this sense, one might speak of an alternative honor code, one that systematically switches the valence of key elements from the zero-sum mindset to a positive-sum one.

The very things that the zero-sum players honor, the positive-sum players condemn: holding slaves (coerced dominion), dueling (killing for the sake of honor), taking vengeance (private justice), racism (viewing others as inferior)—all these deeds and attitudes that once brought honor now bring shame (Appiah, 2010). And, whether we like it or not, this shift demands an exceptional level of self-control, especially among the alpha males, whose dominance where shame–honor prevails, matters so. The fight against the honors and liberties waged by the Enlightenment and the French Revolution tried to deny the last remnant of the honor-aristocracies, the "right" to these passions (Hirschman, 1977).

Much of the so-called "Eurocentric" output of scholars in the twentieth century viewed this shift as unquestionably "good" and sought to trace how it came about, how to explain the *European Miracle* (Jones, 2003). For Elias, and independently, for Lucien Febvre, this long process of subduing raw emotions plays a key role in the grand narrative of Western civility (Elias, 1939; Febvre, 1941). Over the course of centuries, according to this view, Westerners—especially men—matured, and learned to control/repress their visceral emotions with much greater consistency than their medieval forbears. When, in the deceptively civil years between the two World Wars, Marc Bloch surveyed the medieval sources in search of a medieval *mentalité*, he was struck by the emotional lability of the times:

> The despairs, the rages, the impulsive acts, the sudden revulsions of feeling, present great difficulties to historians who are instinctively disposed to reconstruct that past in terms of the rational. But the irrational is an important element in all history and only a sort of false shame could allow its effects on the course of political events in feudal Europe to be passed over in silence.
> (Bloch, 1964: 71)

And yet, under Bloch's very nose, France's neighbor, Germany, was about to engage in a sudden revulsion and collective rage such as the world had never before witnessed.

Not inappropriately, then, postwar historians objected to the assumptions of both rational and moral superiority of the West (Duerr, 1988–2002). In the study of the Middle Ages, for example, historians rejected the characterization of medieval actors as "emotionally unstable or caught in a primitive stage of arrested cognitive development, incapable of controlling their emotions" (White, 1998, 151). In fact, often these explosions of revenge indicate that this behavior, including displays of anger, fury, and violence, were neither uncontrolled nor irrational, but directed, often ritualized forms of negotiation and maneuver, a "technology of power" (White, 1998). To describe conditions as "anarchic," for example, projected a Weberian modernist expectation onto a complex web of conflicts and techniques of conflict resolution (Roche, 2010, 116).

And yet, at the heart of the attempt to understand these issues lies a conundrum. In a zero-sum, shame–honor driven world, *all* comparisons are invidious, and those who come out on the short end of the comparison experience them as insulting, degrading, and shameful. If *you* win, *we lose*; and any such negative comparisons blacken *our* "face." Hence the "losing" zero-sum players react with great hostility to any humiliating comparisons between their culture and more productive (in zero-sum terms: powerful) ones. From the point of view of the primary code players in prime-divider societies, such comparisons must *not* be voiced. Edward Saïd's attack on discussions of shame–honor issues as the worst kind of "racist … Orientalism" has been widely accepted in post-colonial studies (Landes, 2007b).

And, ironically, players in a positive-sum world that prizes self-criticism and empathy (modern and postmodern academia), that self-consciously *rejects* such mean-spirited, invidious thinking, come to the same conclusion about this demand for silence. *Not* vaunting one's merits, even (especially) when they are substantial, is dignified behavior; one furthers serious discussion by *not* provoking envy. Drop the discussion.

Hence, for opposite reasons—zero-sum shame, on the one hand, and positive-sum therapy, on the other—"everyone" can agree on *not* discussing shame–honor dynamics, since such comparisons inevitably highlight the West's talents according to these very progressive, positive-sum standards. The result is a cognitive Moebius strip in which two divergent mentalities, product of opposing attitudes towards zero-sum emotions, share the same surface terrain, the contrast eliminated by what Bloch called "false shame." Faced with this demand of silence, some Western positive-sum players, having freed themselves from the grip of *onēidophobia* and, placing a high value on "self-"criticism, even prefer to flip the discussion, making comparisons unflattering to the *self* (the West as a uniquely evil form of imperialism), rather than those that insult "other," more sensitive (if also imperialist) players.

The scholarly results have been problematic. Some politically relevant fields like Middle Eastern Studies have been crippled by the inability to discuss these matters openly (Kramer, 2000; Landes, 2021). In a relative backwater like Medieval Studies, where discussions of honor and shame and its attendant emotions concerns make up so much of the mental furniture of the age, the effect has been less drastic (Rosenwein, 1998; Barthélemy, Le Jan & Bougard, 2006; Tuten & Billado, 2010; Throop & Hyams, 2016; Gilbert & White, 2018). Ironically, however, some of the efforts to avoid the implicit value judgments from a progressive point of view end up replicating the positivist historiography of the early twentieth century that Bloch criticized: "instinctively disposed to reconstruct that past in terms of the rational."

But whether one rejects the notion of a more primitive, labile emotional condition as a case of "arrested cognitive development" or just an alternative way of processing emotions, the case remains that whatever "logic" one finds in medieval displays of anger and rage, that logic only makes sense in a world where, as I have defined shame–honor cultures, it is *accepted, expected, required to shed blood for the sake of honor*, preferably the "other's" blood. Eurocentric Westerners traditionally viewed the difference between what I have described as the primary code and more modern attitudes in terms of irrational and rational behaviors. But this approach underestimates the rationality *within* the primary codes. Hence, taking vengeance not only feels good, it "makes sense" in a world where *not* taking vengeance has seriously negative consequences including inviting further attacks. Hence if one cares about one's children, it "makes sense" to kill a daughter for being raped if the rest of the community members refuse to let their children marry yours as long as she lives. Hence, Saddam Hussein "signaled threat" that he had a nuclear bomb to frighten his Iranian enemy, even though doing so brought devastating sanctions on his own people. The logic may, in the circumstances, be "rational," even as, from a "progressive" perspective, it partakes of a world of arrested cognitive development.

In the final analysis, I think, this is a matter of *mentalités* (or the overlapping term *habitus*); that is, collective modes of perception and feelings, the culture "from the inside," a unique shared blend of moral values, public opinion, deep-felt emotions, and social dynamics that in many ways cut across all social, ethnic, and economic divides (including the prime divider, Freedman, 1998), standing "at the junction point of the individual and the collective" (Le Goff, 1974). Indeed, what better example of a *mentalité* than attitudes that literally exist only in collective form, exclusively concerned with an imagined and deeply felt collective community. And in the case of shame–honor dynamics, we are dealing with *une mentalité de longue durée*. If the neurophysicists (Sapolsky, 2017; Merlin, 2001) are right that these emotions and reactions have deep roots in our physical (evolutionary) makeup, this dynamic will exist and exert its gravitational pull on people as long as there are people.

Hence, I have attempted to describe that *mentalité* in terms of three overlapping issue—*primary honor codes* (warrior and aristocratic), *zero-sum relations* (I/we only win if you lose), and a range of feelings and desires that are by their very nature zero-sum: anger, hatred, vengeance, *libido dominandi*, the invidious pleasures of demeaning "others," *onēidophobia* and *megalothymia*. These emotions (which every human being has had and will feel) drive an elective affinity between honor–shame dynamics and the prevalence of zero-sum relations, especially in aristocratic empires (Kautsky, 1982), in prime-divider societies.

Has the West truly escaped the draw of this mentality? Only a millenarian could imagine such a possibility for any society. Recent disturbing feedback shows how easily the desire to shame and even destroy others' lives can appear in the most technologically "advanced" circles, like social media (Ronson, 2016). The desire for honor and the fear of shame are permanent elements of the human condition, and key elements in both socialization and economic productivity. The appeal of zero-sum contests lies at the heart of most interesting competition. "Without the '*yetzer harah*' [the selfish gene, Dawkins, 1976]," said the third-century CE rabbis, "a man would not build a home or marry a woman or have children or build a business. As Solomon noted, 'It is the envy of man for his neighbor' (Ecclesiastes, 4:4)."[8]

To have a society entirely governed by integrity–guilt/positive-sum commitments is like having literacy without orality. It could not possibly work. The best humans can hope to do is manage the more violent zero-sum tendencies of shame–honor, a struggle that occurs in every individual, in every generation, and it is in the combination of suppression of, and engagement with, these drives that societies distinguish themselves from the primary code described here.

There is certainly a payoff to restraining these emotions, a success that is painfully obvious to all pre- and post-moderns, the shameful fact of the

West's overwhelming military and wealth advantage. Certain institutions, for example, which could not arise in a shame–honor culture as I have described it, have emerged in the West over the last millennium, in particular, in the information professions. Modern academia, with its open culture of dispute and its scientific prowess,[9] and independent journalism, for example, are both unthinkable developments in a world governed by zero-sum, shame–honor rules.

This hardly means that academia and journalism are not in very significant ways, animated by the zero-sum dynamics of shame–honor, that it's an eternally recurring battle to prevent those predilections from overcoming the sense of equity that makes such institutions, and the reliability of the information they produce, possible. Certainly, studying these ubiquitous dynamics is hardly confined to those societies whose public sphere is dominated by the primary code. On the contrary, studying these dynamics in cultures that openly embrace such values and emotions offers good clues to their working in societies where they are largely repressed and concealed.

Notes

1 "Margaret Mead described the Chambri of New Guinea as a sex-reversed culture because the men were adorned with makeup and curls, omitting the fact that they had to earn the right to these supposedly effeminate decorations by killing a member of an enemy tribe" (Pinker, 2002: 43, citing Daly and Wilson, 1998: 149–152). Chagnon estimated that almost half of the Yanomami men had killed someone and a third of men met "untimely" deaths in feuds (Chagnon, 1984).
2 Mario Puzzi introduced this expression in his novel *The Godfather*. Chagnon noted that the *unokais* (i.e., those participating in killing expeditions) had three times as many offspring as those men who did not (Chagnon, 1984). Cf. Adam Smith's "rational" analysis of division of labor, in which the talented flint chipper stays home to make arrow and spear heads, while the others share with him their hunt (Wealth of Nations, I, 2, p. 31). On the role of deception in giving the impression of fierceness see the discussion of signaling theory (Zahavi & Zahavi, 1997; Miller, 2010) and below.
3 There is a significant literature on Chagnon, whose work got caught in a fierce debate within anthropology, between the peace-studies school and the innate-belligerence school. He himself wrote about it (2014); there is a good summary of the conflict in Pinker (2002: 121–135).
4 Odo of Cluny, Vita Geraldi, 7; Kuefler (2014), identifies this passage as the work of Ademar of Chabannes, historian of the turn of the millennium and witness to the efforts of the Peace movement to outlaw feud and inaugurate the principles of a civil society (Landes, 2007).
5 This was not part of Jones' original list. It is my rephrasing of the Arab proverb, "Have him for lunch before he has you for supper."
6 The issue of "honor killings" (or, rather, "shame-murders") has become a major area of contention that colors relationships between cultures (Welchman and Hossain, 2005; Terman, 2010).
7 National Security Archive Electronic Briefing Book No. 279; ed. Joyce Battle. Assisted by Brendan McQuade, July 1, 2009; Saddam Hussein Talks to the FBI: Twenty Interviews and Five Conversations with "High Value Detainee # 1" in 2004. http://nsarchive.gwu.edu/NSAEBB/NSAEBB279/index.htm.

8 Bereshit Rabbah, 9.7: https://www.sefaria.org/Bereishit_Rabbah.9.7?lang=en& with=all&lang2=en.
9 The medieval universities arose within a culture of dispute already in the eleventh century, but by the thirteenth century triumphalist religiosity imposed inquisitorial restraints. Today's academia is seriously challenged by both politicization and the honor–shame dynamics of cancel culture.

References

Adorno, Th. et al. (1950). *The Authoritarian Personality*. HarperRow.
Appiah, A.K. (2010). *The Honor Code: How Moral Revolutions Happen*. Norton.
Aquaro, G. (2004). *Death by Envy: The Evil Eye and Envy in the Christian Tradition*. Universe.
Banfield, E. (1958). *The Moral Basis of a Backward Society*. Free Press.
Barthélemy, D. (2010). Devils in the Sanctuary: Violence in the Miracles of Saint Benedict. In Belle S.Tuten & Tracey L.Billado (Eds.), *Feud, Violence and Practice: Essays in Medieval Studies in Honor of Stephen D. White* (pp. 71–94). Ashgate.
Barthélemy, D., Le Jan, R., & Bougard, R. (2006). *La Vengeance, 400–1200*. Ecole française de Rome.
Bennett, K. (2018). Environment of Evolutionary Adaptedness (EEA). In *Encyclopedia of Personality and Individual Differences*. ed. Zeigler-Hill and Shackelford. Springer. https://doi.org/10.1007/978-3-319-28099-8_1627-1.
Bloch, M. (1964). *Feudal Society*. University of Chicago Press.
Blok, A. (2001). *Honour and Violence*. Polity Press.
Boehm, C. (1984). *Blood Revenge: The Enactment and Management of Conflict in Montenegro and Other Tribal Societies*. University of Pennsylvania Press.
Boehm, C. (1999). *Hierarchy in the Forest: The Evolution of Egalitarian Behavior*. Harvard University Press.
Bosl, K. (1964). Potens und Pauper: Begriffsgeschichtliche Studien zur gesellschaftlichen Differenzierung im frühen Mittelalter und zum "Pauperismus" des Hochmittelalters. In *Frühformen der Gesellschaft im mittelalterlichen Europa: Ausgewählte Beiträge zu einer Strukturanalyse der mittelalterlichen Welt*. R. Oldenbourg, pp. 106–134.
Bourdieu, P. (1966). The Sentiment of Honour in Kabyle Society. In J.G. Peristiany (Ed.), *Honour and Shame: The Values of Mediterranean Society* (pp. 191–124). Weidenfeld & Nicolson.
Bowman, J. (2006). *Honor: A History*. Encounter Books.
Bringuier, G. (2018). Le chevalier de la Barre: un symbole de la liberté de pensée. *Franc-maçonnerie magazine*, July, HS 5.
Cash, W.J. (1991). *Mind of the South*. Vintage.
Chagnon, N. (1984). *Yanomamo: The Fierce People*. Holt McDougal.
Chagnon, N. (2014). *Noble Savages: My Life Among Two Dangerous Tribes—the Yanomamo and the Anthropologists*. Simon & Schuster.
Chagnon, N., Cronk, L., & Irons, W. (2002). *Adaptation and Human Behavior: An Anthropological Perspective*. Aldine de Gruyter.
Chesler, P. (2009). Are Honor Killings Simply Domestic Violence? *Middle East Quarterly*, 61–69. http://www.meforum.org/2067/are-honor-killings-simply-domestic-violence.
Chesler, P. (2018). *A Family Conspiracy: Honor Killings*. New English Review Press.

Cobley, B. (2018). *The Tribe: The Liberal-Left and the System of Diversity*. Societas.

Cohen, J. (2004). *Sanctifying the Name of God: Jewish Martyrs and Jewish Memories of the First Crusade*. University of Pennsylvania Press.

Colson, E. (1953). Social Control and Vengeance in Plateau Tonga Society. *Africa* 23, 199–212.

Crawford, S.J. (Ed.). (1972). *Byrhtferth's Manual*. Early English Text Society, Original Series, 177.

Crone, P. (1989). *Preindustrial Societies: Anatomy of the Pre-Modern World*. OneWorldPublications.

Daly, M. & Wilson, M. (1998). *Homicide*. Transaction.

Darwish, N. (2008). *Cruel and Unusual Punishment*. Thomas Nelson.

Dawkins, R. (1976). *The Selfish Gene*. Oxford University Press.

Diamond, J. (2010). Vengeance Is Ours. *New Yorker*, April 26. http://www.unl.edu/rhames/courses/war/diamond-vengeance.pdf.

DiAngelo, R. (2018). *White Fragility: Why It's So Hard for White People to Talk About Racism*. Beacon Press.

Drea, C. & Wallen, K. (2003). Female Sexuality and the Myth of Male Control. In Cheryl Brown Travis (Ed.), *Evolution, Gender and Rape* (pp. 29–60). MIT Press.

Duby, G. (1978). *Les trois ordres ou l'imaginaire du féodalisme*. Gallimard.

Duerr, H.P. (1988). *Der Mythos vom Zivilisationsprozeß*. Band 1: *Nacktheit und Scham*. Suhrkamp.

Duerr, H.P. (1990). *Der Mythos vom Zivilisationsprozeß*. Band 2: *Intimität*. Suhrkamp.

Duerr, H.P. (1993). *Der Mythos vom Zivilisationsprozeß*. Band 3: *Obszönität und Gewalt*. Suhrkamp.

Duerr, H.P. (1997). *Der Mythos vom Zivilisationsprozeß*. Band 4: *Der erotische Leib*. Suhrkamp.

Duerr, H.P. (2002). *Der Mythos vom Zivilisationsprozeß*. Band 5: *Die Tatsachen des Lebens*. Suhrkamp.

Dumouchel, P. (2014). A Mimetic Rereading of Helmut Schoeck's *Envy: A Theory of Social Behaviour*. In *The Ambivalence of Scarcity and Other Essays*. Michigan State University Press.

Dunbar, R. (1996). *Grooming, Gossip and the Evolution of Language*. Faber and Faber.

Dunham, J. (2013). *There Is No Goat: A Collection of Insights into the Afghan Mind*. CreateSpace Independent Publishing Platform.

Ebert, S. (2018). Starvation Under Carolingian Rule: The Famine of 779 and the *Annales Regni Francorum*. In D. Collet & M. Schuh (Eds.), *Famines during the 'Little Ice Age' (1300–1800)* (pp. 211–230). Springer.

Elias, N. (1939). *Über den Prozeß der Zivilisation*. Verlag Haus zum Falken.

Ellis, S. (2006). *The Mask of Anarchy Updated Edition: The Destruction of Liberia and the Religious Dimension of an African Civil War*. New York University Press.

Emery, J. (2003). Reputation is Everything: Honor-Killing among the Palestinians. *The World and I*. https://anthropologist.livejournal.com/1080941.html.

Esders, S. (2014). Wergeld und soziale Netzwerke im Frankenreich. In S. Patzold & K. Ubl (Eds.), *Verwandtschaft, Name und soziale Ordnung (300–1100)* (pp. 141–160). De Gruyter.

Evans-Pritchard, E.E. (1976). *Witchcraft, Oracles and Magic among the Azande*. Clarendon Press.

Febvre, L. (1941). La sensibilité et l'histoire: Comment reconstituer la vie affective d'autrefois? *Annales d'histoire sociale* 3, 5–20.
Forth, C. (2004). *The Dreyfus Affair and the Crisis of French Manhood*. Johns Hopkins University Press.
Foster, G.M. (1965). Peasant Society and the Image of Limited Good. *American Anthropologist* 67(2): 293–315. doi:doi:10.1525/aa.1965.67.2.02a00010.
Freedman, P. (1998). Peasant Anger in the Late Middle Ages. In B. Rosenwein (Ed.), *Anger's Past* (pp. 171–188). Cornell University Press.
Freedman, P. (1999). *Images of the Medieval Peasant*. Stanford University Press.
Friedman, T. (1989). *From Beirut to Jerusalem*. Farrar, Strauss, Giroux.
Friedman, T. (2006). Mideast Rules to Live by. *New York Times*, December 20.
Freud, S. (1930). *Das Unbehagen in der Kultur*. Internationaler psychoanalytischer Verlag.
Fukuyama, F. (1992). *The End of History and the Last Man*. Free Press.
Fulton, R. (2015). Talking Points: Three Cheers for White Men, *Fencing Bear at Prayer*. https://fencingbearatprayer.blogspot.com/2015/06/talking-points-three-cheers-for-white.html.
Geisel, T. aka Dr. Seuss. (1938). *The 500 Hats of Bartholomew Cubbins*.
Gellner, E. (1986, 2006). *Nations and Nationalism*. Blackwell.
Gellner, E. (1990). *Plough, Sword and Book: The Structure of Human History*. University of Chicago Press.
Ghiglieri, M. (1999). *Dark Side of Man: Tracing the Origins of Male Violence*. Perseus.
Gilbert, K., & White, S. (Eds.) (2018). *Emotion, Violence, Vengeance and Law in the Middle Ages: Essays in Honour of William Ian Miller*. Brill.
Girard, R. (1978). Des choses cachées depuis la foundation du monde. Grasset & Fasquelle; (1987). *Things Hidden since the Foundation of the World*. Stanford University Press.
Gluckman, M. (1955). The Peace in the Feud. *Past and Present* 7, 1–14.
Graeber, D. (2011). *Debt: The First 5,000 Years*. Melville House.
Greenberg, K. (1994). *Honor and Slavery*. Princeton University Press.
Greene, J. (2013). *Moral Tribes: Emotion, Reason, and the Gap between Us and Them*. Penguin.
Griswold, C.L. (2013). The Nature and Ethics of Vengeful Anger. *Nomos*, 53, 77–124.
Hall, John (1985). *Powers and Liberties: The Causes and Consequences of the Rise of the West*. University of California Press.
Hawley, J.S. (1994). *Sati, the Blessing and the Curse: The Burning of Wives in India*. Oxford University Press.
Heydari, A., Teymoori, A., & Trappes, R. (2021). Honor killing as a dark side of modernity: Prevalence, Common Discourses, and a Critical View. *Social Science Information* 60:1, 86–106.
Hirschman, A. (1977). *The Passions and the Interests: Political Arguments for Capitalism before its Triumph*. Princeton University Press.
Hoebel, E.A. (1954). *The Law of Primitive Man*. Harvard University Press.
Ibn Khaldun (1987). *The Muqaddimah: An Introduction to History*. Princeton University Press.
Jebens, H. (2002). Trickery or Secrecy? On Andrew Lattas's Interpretation of "Bush Kaliai Cargo Cults. *Anthropos* 97, 181–199. http://anthropology.uwaterloo.ca/WNB/Trickery or Secrecy.html.

Johnson, L. (1988). Dangerous Words, Provocative Gestures, and Violent Acts. In L. Johnson and S. Lipsett-Rivera (Eds.), *The Faces of Honor: Sex, Shame, and Violence in Latin America* (pp. 127–151). University of New Mexico Press.

Johnson, W. (1998). The myth of Jewish male menses. *Journal of Medieval History*, 24:3; http://www.medievalists.net/2012/11/25/the-myth-of-jewish-male-menses/.

Jones, E. (2003). *The European Miracle: Environments, Economies and Geopolitics in the History of Europe and Asia*. Cambridge University Press.

Jones, G.F. (1959). *Honor in German Literature*. University North Carolina Press.

Kautsky, J. (1982, 2017). *The Politics of Aristocratic Empires*. University of North Carolina Press, Routledge.

Kelly, H.A. (1994). Rule of Thumb and the Folklaw of the Husband's Stick. *Journal of Legal Education*. 44:3, 341–365.

Koziol, G. (1986). Monks, Feuds, and the Making of Peace in Eleventh-Century Flanders. In T. Head & R. Landes (Eds.), *The Peace of God: Social Violence and Religious Response*. (pp. 239–259). Cornell University Press.

Kramer, M. (2000). *Ivory Towers on Sand: The Failure of Middle Eastern Studies in America*. Washington Institute for Near East Policy.

Kressel, G. (1996). *Ascension through Aggression: The Anatomy of a Blood Feud among Urbanized Bedouins*. Harrassowitz Verlag.

Kuefler, M. (2014). *The Making and Unmaking of a Saint Hagiography and Memory in the Cult of Gerald of Aurillac*. University of Pennsylvania Press.

Landes, D. (1999). *The Wealth and Poverty of Nations: Why Some Are so Rich and Some So Poor*. Norton.

Landes, R. (2007a). Economic Development and Demotic Religiosity: Reflections on the Eleventh-Century Takeoff. In R. Fulton & B. Holsinger (Eds.), *History in the Comic Mode: The New Medieval Cultural History* (pp. 101–116). Columbia University Press.

Landes, R. (2007b). Edward Said and the Culture of Honor and Shame: *Orientalism* and Our Misperceptions of the Arab-Israeli Conflict. *Israel Affairs*, 13:4, 844–858.

Landes, R. (2011). *Heaven on Earth: The Varieties of the Millennial Experience*. Oxford University Press.

Landes, R. (2016). Triumphalist Religiosity: The Unanticipated Problem of the 21st Century. *Tablet*. February 10. https://www.tabletmag.com/sections/israel-middle-east/articles/triumphalist-religiosity.

Landes, R. (2019). Oslo's Misreading of an Honor-Shame Culture. *Israel Journal of Foreign Affairs*. https://www.academia.edu/41012401/Oslos_Misreading_of_an_Honor_Shame_Culture.

Landes, R. (2021). Orientalism as Caliphator Cognitive Warfare: The (Unintended?) Consequences of Edward Saïd's Defense of the Arab World. In G. Sarı & I. Tombul (Eds.), *Contemporary Approaches to Orientalism in Media and Beyond*. ICI Global.

Le Goff, J. (1974). Mentalities: A New Field for Historians. *Social Science Information* 13: 81–97.

LeConte, P. (1996). Ridicule. Polygram Film Distribution.

Lendon, J.E. (1997). *Empire of Honour: The Art of Government in the Roman World*. Clarendon Press.

Lewis, B. (2001). *What Went Wrong: Western Impact and Middle Eastern Response*. Oxford University Press.

Lindholm, C. (2002). *Islamic Middle East*. Blackwell.

Luchaire, A. (1957). *Social France at the Time of Philip Augustus*. Harper Torchbooks.
Martin, J. (Ed. and tr.). (1992). *The Annals of Saint Bertin*. University of Manchester Press.
Matusitz, J. (2012). *Terrorism and Communication: A Critical Introduction*. Sage Publications.
McGrath, K. (2010). The Politics of Chivalry: The Function of Anger and Shame in Eleventh- and Twelfth- Century Anglo-Norman Historical Narratives. In B.S. Tuten & T.L. Billado (Eds.), *Feud, Violence and Practice: Essays in Medieval Studies in Honor of Stephen D. White* (pp. 55–70). Ashgate.
McLaren, A. (2007). *Impotence: A Cultural History*. University of Chicago Press.
Meens, R. (2021). Penance and Satisfaction: Conflict Settlement and Penitential Practices in the Frankish World in the Early Middle Ages. In L. Bothe, S. Esders, and H. Nijdam (Eds.), *Wergild, Compensation and Penance: The Monetary Logic of Early Medieval Conflict Resolution*. Brill.
Merlin, D. (2001). *A Mind so Rare: The Evolution of Human Consciousness*. W.W. Norton.
Miller, W. (1983). Choosing the Avenger: Some Aspects of the Bloodfeud in Medieval Iceland and England. *Law and History Review*, 1:2.
Miller, W. (2010). Threat. In B.S. Tuten & T.L. Billado (Eds.), *Feud, Violence and Practice: Essays in Medieval Studies in Honor of Stephen D. White* (pp. 5–29). Ashgate.
Moore, R.I. (1987). *Formation of a Persecuting Society: Authority and Deviance in Western Europe 950–1250*. Blackwell.
Morgan, R. (1989). *Palestinian Women of Gaza and the West Bank*. Indiana University Press.
Murawiecz, L. (2008). *The Mind of Jihad*. Cambridge University Press.
Nesbitt, R. & Cohen, D. (1996). Insult, Anger and Aggression: An Experimental Ethnography of the Culture of Honor. In R. Nesbitt and D. Cohen (Eds.), *Culture of Honor: Psychology of Violence in the South* (pp. 41–54). Westview Press.
Palestine Royal [Peel] Commission Report (1937). His Majesty's Stationery Office. http://unispal.un.org/pdfs/Cmd5479.pdf.
Patai, R. (1973, 2007). *The Arab Mind*. Charles Scribner's Sons.
Peristiany, J.G.. (1965). *Honor and Shame: The Values of Mediterranean Society*. Weidenfeld & Nicolson.
Pinker, S. (2002). *The Blank Slate: A Modern Denial of Human Nature*. Penguin.
Pinker, S. (2012). *The Better Angels of Our Nature: Why Violence Has Declined*. Penguin.
Pitt-Rivers, J. (1966). Honour and Social Status. In J.G. Peristiany (Ed.), *Honour and Shame: The Values of Mediterranean Society* (pp. 21–77). Weidenfeld & Nicolson.
Pryce-Jones, D. (2009). *Closed Circle: An Interpretation of the Arabs*. Ivan R. Dee.
Radding, C. (1985). *A World Made by Men: Cognition and Society*. University of North Carolina Press.
Rifkin, J. (2009). *The Empathic Civilization: The Race to Global Consciousness in a World in Crisis*. Penguin.
Roche, T. (2010). The Way Vengeance Comes: Rancorous Deeds and Words in the World of Orderic Vitalis. In B.S. Tuten and T.L. Billado (Eds.), *Feud, Violence and Practice: Essays in Medieval Studies in Honor of Stephen D. White*. Ashgate.
Roll, N. 2017. A Schism in Medieval Studies, for All to See. *Inside Higher Ed*. https://www.insidehighered.com/news/2017/09/19/one-professors-critique-another-divides-medieval-studies.

Ronson, J. (2016). *So You've Been Publicly Shamed*. Riverhead Books.
Rosenwein, B. (1998). *Anger's Past: The Social Uses of Emption in the Middle Ages*. Cornell University Press.
Sagan, E. (1991). *The Honey and the Hemlock: Democracy and Paranoia in Ancient Athens and Modern America*. Basic Books.
Salzman, P.C. (2008). *Culture and Conflict in the Middle East*. Humanity Books.
Salzman, P.C. (2009). *Pastoralists: Equality, Hierarchy, and the State*. Westview Press.
Sapolsky, R. (2017). *Behave: The Biology of Humans at Our Best and Worst*. Penguin.
Saxonhouse, A. (2005). *Free Speech and Democracy in Ancient Athens*. Cambridge University Press.
Schoeck, H. (1987). *Envy: A Theory of Social Behavior*. Liberty Fund.
Scott, J.C. (1992). *Domination and the Arts of Resistance: Hidden Transcripts*. Yale University Press.
Scully, D. & Marolla, J. (2004). "Riding the Bull at Gilley's": Convicted Rapists Describe the Rewards of Rape. In C.M. Renzetti and R.K. Bergen (Eds.), *Violence Against Women*. Rowman & Littlefield.
Shariff, S. (2006). *Le voile de la peur*. Editions JCL.
Shehadeh, R. (1982). *The Third Way*. Quartet Books.
Sillitoe, P. & Kuwimb, M.J. (2010). Rebutting Jared Diamond's Savage Portrait. *iMediaEthics*; https://www.imediaethics.org/rebutting-jared-diamonds-savage-portrait/view-all//.
Singer, T., et al. (2006). Empathic neural responses are modulated by the perceived fairness of others. *Nature* 439, 466–469.
Smail, D.L. (2008). *Deep History and the Brain*. University of California Press.
Smith, A. (1776, 1994). *Wealth of Nations*. Modern Library.
Smith, D.L. (2004). *Why We Lie: The Evolutionary Roots of Deception and the Unconscious Mind*. St. Martin's Press.
Smuts, B. & R. (1993). Male Aggression and Sexual Coercion of Females in Non-human Primates and Other Animals: Evidence and Theoretical Implications. *Advances in the Study of Behavior*, 22, 1–63.
Stetkevych, S.P. (1993). *The Mute Immortals Speak: Pre-Islamic Poetry and the Poetics of Ritual*. Cornell University Press.
Stewart, F.H. (1994). *Honor*. University of Chicago Press.
Terman, R.L. (2010). To Specify or Single Out: Should We Use the Term "Honor Killing"? *Muslim World Journal of Human Rights*, 7:1, 1–39.
Thornhill, R. & Palmer, C. (2000). *A Natural History of Rape: Biological Bases of Sexual Coercion*. MIT Press.
Throop, S.A. (2021). *Crusading as an Act of Vengeance, 1095–1216*. Routledge.
Throop, S., Hyams, P. (Eds.) (2016). *Vengeance in the Middle Ages: Emotion, Religion and Feud*. Ashgate.
Tracy, K.K. & Crawford, C.B. (1999). Wife Abuse: Does it have an Evolutionary Origin? In D. Counts, J. Brown, & J. Campbell (Eds.), *To Have and to Hit* (pp. 27–42). University of Illinois Press.
Tuten, B. & Billado, T. (Eds.) (2010). *Feud, Violence and Practice: Essays in Medieval Studies in Honor of S.D. White*. Ashgate.
Waleed, Abu. (2016). British Islamist: Muslims Should Humiliate Christians in Order to Make Them Convert to Islam. MEMRI, Clip #4263, January 16, 2016. https://

www.memri.org/tv/british-islamist-abu-waleed-muslims-should-humiliate-christians-order-make-them-convert-islam.

Welchman, L. & Hossain, S. (Eds). (2005). *'Honour': Crimes, Paradigms, and Violence Against Women*. Zed Books.

White, S. (1998). The Politics of Anger. In B. Rosenwein (Ed.), *Anger's Past* (pp. 130–152). Cornell University Press.

Wikan, U. (2008). *In Honor of Fadime: Murder and Shame*. University of Chicago Press.

Wolin, S. (1960). *Politics and Vision*. Little, Brown and Company.

Wormald, P. (2003). The *Leges barbarorum*: Law and Ethnicity in the Post-Roman West. In H.-W. Goetz, J. Jarnut, W. Pohl, and S. Kaschke (Eds.), *Regna and Gentes: The Relationship Between Late Antique and Early Medieval Peoples and Kingdoms in the Transformation of the Roman World* (pp. 21–54). Brill.

Wrangham, R. & Peterson, D. (1996). *Demonic Males: Apes and the Origins of Human Violence*. Houghton Mifflin.

Zahavi, A., & Zahavi, A. (1997). *The Handicap Principle*. Oxford University Press.

Part II
Honor and Shame in Traditional European Societies

4 Honor–Shame Dynamics in Late Antiquity
Balance and Control

Jan Frode Hatlen[1]

Introduction

Gendered honor may be said to revolve around balance and control, and social dynamics in honor societies are often preoccupied with conserving a balance. If honor is lost, the order of the whole community is threatened. The feelings that arise with those who are responsible for keeping order may be intense: fear, anxiety, and anger. One might think that the social codes that dictate order in society would be strong if they are so important, but they are in fact fragile and debatable.

In order to illustrate the social dynamics of honor and shame, and how fragile the codes of conduct in honor societies are, this essay explores three aspects of honor in Late Antiquity: a) the threat posed by having rumors circulating about oneself; b) how the idea of "henpecked men" was part of persuading men to enforce gender ideals on their wives; and c) how expectations might create an obligation to use violence in order to protect the honor culture. Honor and shame are complex social emotions that rely on a sharing of cultural codes and expectations. Honor especially requires a lot of knowledge about how one should appear and how to act. Expectations around this may be extremely strong. It may, for instance, push people to do things they would prefer not to do. At the same time, such codes and expectations may be ignored, intentionally or unintentionally. When people ignore them, it becomes apparent how vulnerable the honor culture is. The guardians of the honor culture might feel provoked or enraged. They will act to protect the honor system, especially when the person ignoring the code does not appear to feel shame.

Gendered Honor Cultures

As this volume illustrates, honor comes in different forms. The following discussion deals with a specific gendered aspect of honor and shame. I concentrate on honor and shame in connection with gender, families' internal relations, and the interaction between families and their communities. The relationship between honor and shame are complex; they depend on each

DOI: 10.4324/9781003022916-7

other, but are opposites. Honor, on the one hand, is not something that is felt in the same sense as pride or feeling ashamed. Engelen et al. argued that we should distinguish between basic emotions, complex emotions, and what they see as "dispositional states."

> These enduring states are a kind of background feeling, background disposition (love), or in some cases background knowledge (honor, disgrace) that provide a framework within which emotions such as an acute feeling of love, pride, or shame are staged. [...] Although these background states are shaped by social and symbolic categories, they nonetheless have natural, biological foundations.
> (Engelen et al., 2009: 48)

In their understanding, honor is a part of background knowledge that provides a framework, where shame may be staged. Honor as a framework of knowledge has a number of social and symbolic categories, and these may "include an affective disposition facilitating the context-dependent occurrence of specific emotions." Some of the emotions connected to honor are basic emotions, such as fear and anger, but they often arise within specific contexts (Engelen et al., 2009: 42–43; Stephan, 2009: 18). Being convinced of the framework is, however, key to the release of emotional reactions. Honor issues will only be at stake for a person if the people involved share the same understandings of values, ideas and tradition, and we could therefore easily talk about "honor ideologies" rather than "honor cultures" (Ouis, 2009: 452–453).

Some cultures are more permeated by honor codes than others are, and the variations among such societies are great. Nevertheless, honor societies share some common traits that the Late Ancient society also displays. Such societies associate the honor of a family or clan with the perceived sexual purity of the women within that family or clan. This comes from an idea of gendered order, a strict binary view of gender where masculinity is preferred over femininity, and where males dominate and protect their female family members (Faqir, 2005: 109–111). Within this order, women have to be passive, deferential, and, most importantly, chaste and sexually pure. Women's sexuality becomes a capital good, and is objectified into what David Gilmore has referred to as a "contentious and arbitrating social index for masculine reputation" (Gilmore, 1987: 4–5). As we shall see, rumors revolving around families, especially when women in families are the subjects of the gossip, may be dangerous to the family. In honor societies, honor is typically associated with a woman's chastity, which reflects upon the whole honor group, most commonly her family, clan, or tribe (Wikan, 2008a: 58).

Honor societies tend to put special emphasis on paternity, and the measures taken to secure that paternity are equally stressed (Delaney, 1991: 39). Protecting honor has the highest priority, and so any action taken to secure the wife's fidelity, and hence his paternity of the children, is considered legitimate because they are taken to protect his honor. Membership of a descendent group is not only patrilineally determined, but is legitimized through so-called patrogenerative theories of procreation; that is, theories of conception where the male contributes more to the conception of life than the female. Fatherhood is, in other words, considered more important than motherhood. Although the woman is reduced to a vessel for the man's offspring, she still is crucial for his lineage.

The protection of the lineage therefore circles around abiding to honor codes, rules for correct gender behavior. If women follow these rules, they are likely to be considered sexually pure. Hence, the credibility of a family has a lot to do with how well they appear to follow general rules (see, e.g., Wikan, 2008a: 58). In these circumstances, families will be very vulnerable to rumors. Women's behavior may make or unmake honor and is therefore under constant scrutiny (Faqir, 2005: 110; Wikan, 2008a: 58; Wikan, 2008b: 190–191). Consequently, family honor is a fragile thing. Rumors of women not adhering to gender norms, such as dressing or speaking correctly, may lead to questions about how much control the men have over their women—and thereby also how certain they can be of their children's paternity.

Shame is often regarded as a complex or secondary emotion. As such, it is an example of social emotions, which are culturally dependent, but virtually omnipresent. Basic emotions, such as fear, can be felt by all species with a functioning amygdala (as well as a functioning memory) (Casimir, 2009). Shame, however, cannot be experienced without an image of the self and expectations by others. It is therefore not a basic emotion, but a complex, or non-basic emotion. After assessment, the feeling of shame or similar emotions (such as anxiety, pride, or jealousy) arises (Engelen et al., 2009: 40–41). Shame is a cross-cultural phenomenon and is key to how communities preserve cultural standards and facilitate cooperation (Stearns, 2016: 199). Being a part of our neural wiring, it is both cultural, since what creates shame varies, and biological, as it leads to roughly the same physiological sensations and reactions across cultures (Sère & Wettlaufer, 2012: xxxi; Wettlaufer, 2015: 36–37). A major factor in understanding the function of shame bio-culturally is that the people within a community, in order to feel shame, have to identify with the group's norms (Wettlaufer, 2015: 37–38). Even though honor and shame are not opposites, this shows that they do rely on each other, and they will intersect at times.

Family Life and Rumors in the Fourth Century

The Roman family was a fusion of Mediterranean family systems, especially through the impact of Christianity. What we consider today the typical nuclear family, with two or three children, was the traditional and pagan Roman family structure. This old family structure faced new ideas and morals in the fourth century. How quickly this happened may be illustrated by the life of the Church Father St. Jerome. He was born in the year 341, in other words, 16 years after Constantine's council at Nicea. He died about 80 years later, and he was among the most influential Christians authorities of his time. During his lifetime, almost the entire Roman aristocracy converted to Christianity. Before Constantine, Christians who belonged to the aristocracy were probably not numerous, perhaps numbering 10 percent of the population, and they were mainly grouped together in the Eastern provinces (Brown, 2003: 64). This changed abruptly when Constantine came to power, and the conversions changed the Roman way of life entirely. From the time of Constantine onwards, Imperial policies were often also Christian policies.

With Christianity, the Roman family, which was already influenced by the Greeks, received ideas from Jewish family life, wrapped in Christian belief. To some extent, we may say that the European family came of age during Jerome's lifetime. As opposed to the family in Classical Rome, serial monogamy came gradually to an end, partially because of new divorce laws. One consequence of this was that the family to a much larger extent became subject to public scrutiny (Nathan, 2000: 75).

The Late Roman household was a continuation of its classical predecessor, and much of family life centered around the house of the paterfamilias. Private houses were used for business and public duties, and Jerome's letters show that the houses of widows, too, were vibrant places full of activity. The Roman house, *domus*, was hence both a public and domestic space, and was also closely watched by the other families, who were keen to see if the family lived up to the expected standards (Cooper, 1992, 2005, 2007). Such scrutiny of family behavior is common in many honor societies, where rumors about women are hazardous for the family. Women's behavior may make or unmake honor, and is therefore under constant scrutiny (Faqir 2005: 110; Wikan 2008a: 58; 2008b: 190–191). The intensity of the scrutiny families were put under may have increased in Late Antiquity, but the idea that the behavior of wives could bring dishonor to the family was not novel.

Notions of family honor as a reflection of women's chastity are easily found in Roman and Late Roman evidence as well. In Justinian's Digest, a "husband is understood to have some regard for his wife's reputation for chastity" and "a father is considered to sustain damage when the character of his children is assailed" (*Codex Iustiniani* 9.35.2).

> It is the saying of a very learned man, that chastity must be preserved at all costs, and that when it is lost all virtue falls to the ground. This holds the primacy of all virtues in woman. This it is that makes up for a wife's poverty, enhances her riches, redeems her deformity, gives grace to her beauty; it makes her act in a way worthy of her forefathers whose blood it does not taint with bastard offspring; of her children, who through it have no need to blush for their mother, or to be in doubt about their father; and above all, of herself, since it defends her

from external violation. There is no greater calamity connected with captivity than to be the victim of another's lust.

(St. Jerome, *Against Jovinianus*, 49)

Some scholars have argued that Roman men's reputation did not depend on their wives' sexual behavior (Evans-Grubbs, 1995: 212–213; Treggiari, 1991: 233, 312–313; Dossey, 2008: 31). However, several sources suggest otherwise. During the Republic, immoral marriages and the sexual transgressions of a Roman woman were considered to have "constituted a dishonor to her family as a whole" (Cic. *Clu.* 15.188). One late ancient law text, a Visigoth interpretation of the Theodosian Code, stated that a woman's adultery pertains to her kinsmen on her father's side (*Codex Theodosiani* 9.7.2). Furthermore, an abusive husband called Eulalius considered a lawsuit against his wife for leaving him. However, the word had gotten around and he was subject to so much ridicule and humiliation that he decided to remain silent (Greg. T. *Hist.* 8.27). Such examples show that men's reputation in both Roman and post-Roman culture did in fact depend on how women behaved. The text passages discussed below also support this claim.

St. Jerome's letters reveal the anxiety Roman noble families felt for their family honor. Appearance was extremely important for their honor, and so was avoiding gossip. The Late Roman ideal for women was in essence to be invisible, and certainly not to be talked about. One way to avoid gossip is to admonish people not to engage in it. Jerome's approach, on the other hand, was that it was women's responsibility not to become subject to gossip. In other words, shame was put on the person subject to gossip, not on those doing the gossiping. If women behaved properly, dressed properly, and did not socialize with the wrong people, gossip would not arise in the first case. Jerome believed that following these codes would make old rumors disappear (Hier. *Ep.* 54.13). He offered guidance to women on how to avoid gossip, which implies that the honor code could be complicated and not self-explanatory. Among this advice, we find the idea that women have to take care whom they associate with:

Let your house never see beneath its roof wanton long-haired dandies. Repel a singer like the plague. [...] Let no curled steward or handsome foster-brother or fair ruddy footman stand continuously by your side. [...] if you are obliged to talk with men, do not refuse to have other people present. Let your conversation be so sure of itself that the entry of a third person will neither make you start nor blush.

(Hier. *Ep.* 54.13)

Daughters were not to appear unattended in public, so that "no youth or curled dandy [could] ogle her" (Hier. *Ep.* 107.9). Appearing moderate and not flamboyant was equally important, and "young persons of the frailer sex" were expected not to confuse freedom with the possibility to do as they pleased (Hier. *Ep.* 54.13).

A well-known irony with Jerome is the anxiety he expressed about rumors, while he himself willingly engaged in gossip about others (which may explain why he did not emphasize the shame of gossiping, as opposed being the subject of it). In his view, Rome was an especially "slander-loving community." It is perhaps his own fascination for gossip that led him to see gossip all around him, but if we are to believe him, gossip flourished everywhere. Jerome is, however, but one of many sources that show how damaging rumors of women could be. Augustine, too, observed that rumors, whether true or false, could spread fast. He described how rumors were constructed to damage reputations, and spread until they were "universally believed." (Aug. *Ep*.78.6). Another bishop from North Africa also complained that people in Church acted as if they were meeting in the baths, and gossiped as if the Church was a fair (Commodianus, *Instructions*, 76).[2]

Rumors and reputations were dangerous to Roman men because they could question the "purity" of the girls and women in the family. Roman men sought chaste wives, and hence "unpolluted" virgins were the most desired brides (Aug. *Serm*. 132.2). This may be compared with contemporary honor cultures, where women may lose their lives simply by being rumored to be flirtatious (Faqir, 2005: 104–124; on rumors, p. 110).

In Late Antiquity, both Augustine and Jerome created rhetorical cases where honor was portrayed as threatened by unchaste behavior. Augustine told a story (on two occasions) of an astrologer who had a wife who appeared in the window of their house. Appearing in windows was associated with prostitutes, and so the imagined astrologer would have to beat his wife to show that he was still in command of her. Jerome, too, created a story who has a similar point. His story was about a mother and daughter who took in two monks, apparently only for religious reasons, but in his rhetorical exercise, Jerome admonishes the women to take into account what people would have thought in such a case:

> I wish you to know that I am writing not because I suspect anything evil of you, but that I am begging you to live in harmony *to prevent other people becoming suspicious* [my italics]. [...] Lastly I say this: even if your own conscience is unhurt, scandal brings disgrace.
> (Hier. *ep*. 117.2)

These passages show signs of collective shame, a sense of worthlessness, although there is no individual being portrayed as feeling ashamed. Rather, it is perhaps the women's lack of shame that provokes the emotional response of their families. Their fears probably went further, to prospects of complete dishonor. Dishonor affects not only one person, but the whole family, or lineage. It is "the demon, the ultimate disgrace, the point of no return" (Wikan, 2008a: 3). The reason for this is that the family who loses honor loses their place in society (cf. above). The cause of dishonor is not the true issue. It is when the dishonor becomes public that it becomes a problem, precisely because of the severe repercussions it has for all of the family members (Wikan, 2008a: 6). Rumors, in the extreme theoretical case, could therefore have the power to threaten the social existence of a person or a family. Reputation matters more than truth and one's reputation thus correlates with one's honor (Wikan, 2008a: 17).

Preserving the Gender Order

The symbolic protection of female chastity was not the only display of family honor. Honor and shame dynamics in Late Antiquity were also influenced by adherence to gender expectations. Roman gender norms in Late Antiquity were to a great extent typical for patriarchal societies, as described above. Adhering to norms and expectations helped keep the order of the world in place. The polarized view of gender was part of a general worldview based on binary pairs, or antitheses. According to Peter Brown, the Romans considered these antitheses absolute. If one of the absolute boundaries in their minds (such as Christian/pagan, Bible truth/"worldly guesswork," soul/body) was stretched or breached, the whole world would be "set vibrating" (Brown, 2008: 347). This world of absolutes makes out the context for women's roles and their place.

This is probably also why Augustine did not praise a wife who complained about her adulterous husband, despite Augustine's views on adultery and his complaints about double standards. Even if her intentions were good, like protecting her family's reputation, it was not a wife's place, as a woman, to either refuse or correct her husband. Even though Augustine argued strongly for sexual moderation and criticized adultery, and despite his habit of shaming those who were not sexually moderate, he still did not consider it proper for women to confront their adulterous husbands (Aug. *ep.* 262). If a wife behaved contrary to expectations, she did not only shame herself, but her actions would hurt the prestige and manhood of her husband. In a letter to Paulinus of Nola, Augustine praised Therasia, Paulinus' wife, for supporting her husband, but without taking control: "In [Paulinus' letter] one beholds a wife who does not bring her husband to effeminacy, but by union to him is brought herself to share the strength of his nature" (Aug. *ep.* 27). According to Augustine, then, Therasia was worthy of praise because she did not put shame on her husband by taking a man's role, which would lead Paulinus to appear like a woman. If that had taken place, that would have been shameful. According to their ideas of order, control was to be in the hands of the men.

If we were to rely only on Christian authors and read them at face value, we might get an erroneous image of Late Roman views on gender, where patriarchal opinions were shared by everyone. Although there is reason to think that most men of stature did have views of women as weaker and more incomplete as men, there are examples of men who did not share this view of women. One such example was Volusianus, who was depicted as a henpecked man, of which Romans had numerous examples throughout their history. The following quote is from a heated letter between bishop Ruricius and bishop Volusianus (c. 495 AD). Ruricius argued that shame fell upon men if their wives dominated them. The letter concerns the treatment Ruricius' letter carriers had received from Volusianus' wife. Replying to what seems to have been a condescending tone in the letter from Volusianus, Ruricius writes:

> For this reason, if I had not taken heed of my status and office, I would have sent back to you the bearer of your letter in such a state as my men were rendered not by your wife, but by an excessively forward and unrestrained governess, whose manners—even if you tolerate them for so long, either voluntarily or with compulsion, to the diminution of your reputation—you should know that others neither wish nor are content to bear. For—because you write that you are rendered stupefied by fear of the enemy—he who is accustomed to a domestic enemy ought not—to fear a foreign one.
>
> (Ruricius, *ep*. 2.65)

According to Leslie Dossey, we can here observe how a wife's behavior affected the husband's reputation (Dossey, 2008: 18, n. 69). Volusianus ought to be worried about his reputation for being unable to control his wife—he should have felt ashamed. His domineering wife could question both his authority and his masculinity. We have no evidence indicating that Volusianus sought to correct her behavior, quite the opposite; Ruricius' letter indicates that Volusianus condoned it. This shows that even though silence and deference generally appear to be considered the most important female virtues, women could end up with husbands like Volusianus, who seem to have been much more lenient and accepting of a strong wife.

The willful wife could be shameful to the husband, but mostly because it implied that the husband failed as a man. In the Late Roman binary worldview, there were just as many and clear norms and expectations around men. Late Roman masculinity was in part typical for patriarchal societies. For instance, St. Ambrose (ca. 340–397), described the virtues of Abraham, and among them were Abraham's bravery, his faithfulness and his righteousness (Ambr., *de Abraham* 1.2.4). Rationality, wisdom and judgment were equally qualities that were attributed to male role models, whether they appeared in the Bible or they were qualities exhibited by contemporary emperors (Ambr. *De Abraham*, 1.3.12. 1.3.19. 1.9.85, 2.5.20, 2.10.68; Eusebius, *De Vita Constantini*, 1.19.).

The Romans' obsessiveness with masculine control changed in Late Antiquity, when the Roman Empire's political control of the world was threatened. The focal point of the masculine control, or domination, was among many in the elite turned inwards. As Erin Sawyer has pointed out, for a man who wished for a world without sexuality, Augustine appears to have been almost obsessed with the concept of desire. He turned chastity, which could be viewed as a passive refraining from intercourse, into an active battle against dangerous desires. To win such a battle demanded strength and courage (Sawyer, 1995). For Ambrose, too, chastity is a victory of the mind and the rational over the body and irrational passions (Ambr. *De Abraham*, 1.2.4.). The manliest thing, then, was control. In a binary worldview, the loss of control implied loss of manhood, which in an honor society is the same as losing one's place in society.

Some scholars have, for instance, argued that the new masculinity implied that men adapted some feminine traits while distancing themselves from others. This "new man" of Late Antiquity was a man of continence and discipline (Burrus, 2000; Kuefler, 2001; Brown, 2003, 2008). Late ancient masculinity was, in other words, fixated on concepts of control, but in a world with political and religious turmoil, that control was directed more inwards. By bringing self-discipline, asceticism and sexual abstinence into the discourse of manhood, it emphasized more than ever in Roman history the need to be in control over oneself.

"Forced" Violence

Late ancient authors such as Augustine considered the paterfamilias a king in his household. Hence, the father was still considered a source of authority at this time, although Augustine also emphasized that the power of a paterfamilias was a burden. The following passage from Augustine's *De Civitate Dei* illustrates the notion of the father as a ruler of the household. This notion represents a continuation of the unique power Roman fathers were considered to have in the classical era. The passage also illustrates the moral obligation that followed becoming a paterfamilias. *Patria potestas* implied a duty to ensure that the family members followed moral codes and were obedient and pious. It is this obligation that Augustine considered to be a burden on the paterfamilias:

> And therefore, although our righteous fathers had slaves, and administered their domestic affairs so as to distinguish between the condition of slaves and the heirship of sons in regard to the blessings of this life, yet in regard to the worship of God, in whom we hope for eternal blessings, they took an equally loving oversight of all the members of their household. And this is so much in accordance with the natural order, that the head of the household was called paterfamilias; and this name has been so generally accepted, that even those whose rule is unrighteous are glad to apply it to themselves. But those who are true fathers of their households desire and endeavor that all the members of their household, equally with their own children, should worship and win God, and should come to that heavenly home in which the duty of ruling men is no longer necessary, because the duty of caring for their

> everlasting happiness has also ceased; but, until they reach that home, masters ought to feel their position of authority a greater burden than servants their service.
>
> (Aug. *Civ. Dei.* 19.16)

According to Augustine, there are those who can rightly call themselves a paterfamilias and those who do so without deserving it. The difference between the two is of course one between those who follow (Augustine's) morals are good Christians. Augustine's description fits a pattern we find in areas where honor often is considered highly important, where men compete in who best can fulfil the expectations in a male head of family. Marcia Inhorn has, for instance, pointed out that Middle Eastern men often compete for social success, which also includes competition to demonstrate one's piety more fervently than men from other regions do. This is done, for instance, by attending the mosque more frequently than others, or through external appearance (e.g., an untrimmed beard) (Inhorn, 2012: 49–50).

Augustine continues by addressing the consequences if the family members do not live up to the standards expected of them. In such cases, because of the obligation Augustine considers a burden, as mentioned above, the paterfamilias has a duty to punish them for their transgressions:

> And if any member of the family interrupts the domestic peace by disobedience, he is corrected either by word or blow, or some kind of just and legitimate punishment, such as society permits, that he may himself be the better for it, and be readjusted to the family harmony from which he had dislocated himself. For as it is not benevolent to give a man help at the expense of some greater benefit he might receive, so it is not innocent to spare a man at the risk of his falling into graver sin. To be innocent, we must not only do harm to no man, but also restrain him from sin or punish his sin, so that either the man himself who is punished may profit by his experience, or others be warned by his example. Since, then, the house ought to be the beginning or element of the city, and every beginning bears reference to some end of its own kind, and every element to the integrity of the whole of which it is an element, it follows plainly enough that domestic peace has a relation to civic peace—in other words, that the well-ordered concord of domestic obedience and domestic rule has a relation to the well-ordered concord of civic obedience and civic rule. And therefore it follows, further, that the father of the family ought to frame his domestic rule in accordance with the law of the city, so that the household may be in harmony with the civic order.
>
> (Aug. *Civ. Dei.* 19.16)

In other words, a paterfamilias was characterized by his obligations to his household. This implied mainly that he had to make sure that its members behaved correctly. If they did not, they were considered to be breaking the peace. Such behavior could not pass without consequences. Therefore, a good paterfamilias punished disobedience by words or corporal punishment, but within what society considered reasonable. If the paterfamilias did not fulfill his obligations, it seems the fear was that the family, and hence society, would fall into chaos. It was the paterfamilias who brought peace and order to the household, an order that relied on everyone knowing their place and obeying their superiors.

When the order between genders was disturbed, men were expected to restore it, by force if necessary. A lack of response could be provocative. The historian Gregory of Tours (sixth century) told a story about a family who forced a husband to act on rumors about his wife committing adultery. When the family heard this, the kinsmen approached her father, stating: "Either make your daughter behave properly or she shall surely die, lest her wantonness lay a disgrace on our family" (Greg. T. *Hist.* 5.32). Here, the community was clear to state that the father was responsible for forcing the daughter to comply with gender standards. The three alternatives were that the daughter complied, that she was killed to restore honor, or the whole family and relatives were disgraced and lost their place in the community.

Lactantius was a fourth-century author who associated and identified the role of a paterfamilias with control and punishment. He explained that God is to be Father because he indulges and bestows many great things upon us, but also Lord because "he has the greatest power of chastising and punishing" (Lactantius, *Div. Inst.* 4.3.). A paterfamilias was, of course, both master and father. Authors would often use the ruling of a household as a metaphor for power in public life, and this was not only typical of North African authors. Ambrose's explanation of how sermons needed to be powerful suggests that a similar manner of thinking existed in North Italy as well:

> Just as a paterfamilias namely dwells in his house, and has in power and rules his household, just so reason dwells in our sermons, governs our words, and force and discipline is manifested in sermons. As a good paterfamilias is assessed by the excellent entrance of the house, thus our reason also is carefully assessed by our sermons.
>
> (Ambr., *De Abraham*, 2.1.2)

The idea that a paterfamilias was responsible for presenting an impeccable and well-managed household therefore appears to have been common. There were of course differences between how a master exercised authority over slaves and a father exercised authority over his household, and we must take into account that women also punished slaves, for instance. However, Christian authors were clear that being a proper paterfamilias implied strict discipline, and the threat of violence had to appear credible. The power the authors wrote about could not have existed if sons thought they could get away with everything, and hence corporal punishment was likely to be used.

Punishment and discipline permeated the Roman world, and was regarded as a duty that followed possessing power. According to Augustine,

> All discipline is exerted for this purpose, just as fitting and suitable for anyone who rules, not only for a bishop ruling his congregation, but also a pauper ruling his household, a husband ruling his wife, a father ruling his offspring, a judge ruling his province, a king ruling his people.
> (Aug., *Sermo de generalitate eleemosynarum*, PL40, 1229)[3]

The same pattern of power and chastisement was, in other words, common throughout society. Obedience and deference, on the one hand, and punishment and discipline, on the other, may therefore be considered practices supporting male dominance over women. Only the paterfamilias who fulfilled his duties (including devotion to God) could be considered a righteous paterfamilias in Augustine's mind.

Disobedience had to be punished and doing so was part of being a paterfamilias and a man. Based on the reactions observed in the quotes above, we can imagine the dynamics of dishonor and shame that were in play if men did not fulfill their duties to discipline and punish their family members. This is why Romans developed mechanisms for watching and evaluating patresfamilias' exercise of power, as Cooper (2007) has shown. A key component of being a male head was, according to Lactantius, unleashing anger towards dependents who failed to uphold discipline. Anger was therefore considered both appropriate and necessary:

> But I speak of those in particular who are in our own power, as slaves, children, wives and pupils; for when we see these offend, we are incited to restrain them.
>
> For it cannot fail to be, that he who is just and good is displeased with things which are bad, and that he who is displeased with evil is moved when he sees it practiced. Therefore, we arise to take vengeance, not because we have been injured, but that discipline may be preserved, morals may be corrected, and licentiousness be suppressed. This is just anger.
>
> (Lactantius, *Ira dei*, 17)

These words need to be put in context alongside a society permeated with violence. Among his childhood memories, the first-century poet Martial reminisced about how humiliating the beatings from his *paedagogus* Charidemus (the slave escorting children to school and taking care of them at home) had been (Martial, *Epigrammata* 11.39). Early Christian texts show that strict discipline and respect was expected, and that verbal and corporal chastisement was used to maintain that discipline and respect (see, e.g., Horn & Martens 2009: 147–148). Roman law texts show that floggings by teachers and parents were considered legitimate usages of violence, since it was administered in order to correct and improve the child (Dig. 48.19.16.2; see also Hillner, 2013: 25). Corporal punishment of children was, in other words, not only administered by patresfamilias, but also by mothers, possibly even by house slaves (Clark, 1998: 125). At least in the sources discussed here, it is possible to argue that these religious leaders considered the use of violence to correct lack of morals and licentiousness as necessary and normal. Punishments for something as serious as injuring honor would likely be seriously severe.

Conclusion

The Roman world was a fragile order. In the writings of Christian leaders discussed in this contribution, we find evidence suggesting these Roman authors considered *patresfamilias* as essential to stabilizing that order. Preserving the order between the sexes was the responsibility of any true man. If women and children in a household were considered immoral or undisciplined by their community, the father of the household would be dishonored. Honor and shame were part of a system that disciplined the population in order to uphold morals and standards. The case of Volusianus is interesting, because he did not appear to accept being shamed and appeared untouched by mockery for having a willful wife. This demonstrates how honor and shame are always surrounded by an honor code. The honor code cannot function as a disciplinary tool if it is not accepted.

Notes

1 The essay is based on parts of my unpublished dissertation, Honour and Domestic Violence in the Late Roman West, c. 300–600 AD, Thesis for the degree of philosophiae doctor, The Norwegian University of Science and Technology 2015.
2 See also Jörg Wettlaufer, Chapter 8 in this volume, on shaming punishments and his reference to *Decretum Gratiani*.
3 For translation and also the reattribution of the sermon to Augustine, see Leslie Dossey, "Judicial Violence and the Ecclesiastical Courts in Late Antique North Africa" in Ralph W. Mathisen (ed.), *Law, Society, and Authority in Late Antiquity* (Oxford, 2001: 114), where this translation is taken from, and C. Lambot, "Sermon sur l'aumône à restituer à saint Augustin," *Revue Bénédictine* 66 (1956): 149–158.

References

Abraham, M. (2000). *Speaking the Unspeakable: Marital Violence among South Asian Immigrants in the United States*. Rutgers University Press.
Brown, P. (2003). *The Rise of Western Christendom: Triumph and Diversity, A.D. 200–1000*, 2nd ed., Oxford University Press.
Brown, P. (2008). *The Body and Society: Men, Women and Sexual Renunciation In Early Christianity*. Columbia University Press (originally published 1988).
Brown, P. (2012). *Through the Eye of the Needle: Wealth, the Fall of Rome, and the Making of Christianity in the West, 350–550 AD*. Princeton University Press.

Burrus, V. (2000). *Begotten Not Made: Conceiving Manhood in Late Antiquity*. Stanford University Press.

Casimir, M.J. (2009). On the origin and evolution of affective capacities in lower vertebrates. In Markowitsch H. & Röttger-Rössler B. (eds.), *Emotions as Bio-cultural Processes* (pp. 55–85). Springer.

Clark, P. (1998). Women, slaves and the hierarchies of domestic violence: the family of St. Augustine. In Joshel, S.R. & Murnaghan, S. (eds.), *Women and Slaves in Greco-Roman Culture: Differential Equations* (pp. 109–129). Routledge.

Cooper, K. (1992). Insinuations of womanly influence: an aspect of the Christianization of the Roman aristocracy. *Journal of Roman Studies*, 82, 150–164.

Cooper, K. (2005). Household and Empire: the materfamilias as Miles Christi in the anonymous handbook for Gregoria. In Mulder-Bakker, A.B. & Wogan-Browne, J. (eds.), *Household, Women and Christianities in Late Antiquity and the Middle Ages* (pp. 91–107). Brepols.

Cooper, K. (2007). Closely watched households: visibility, exposure and private power in the Roman domus. *Past & Present*, 197, 3–33.

Delaney, C.L. (1991). *The seed and the soil: gender and cosmology in Turkish village Society*. University of California Press.

Dossey, L. (2001). Judicial violence and the ecclesiastical courts in Late Antique North Africa. In Mathisen, R.W. (ed.), *Law, Society, and Authority in Late Antiquity* (pp. 98–114). Oxford University Press.

Dossey, L. (2008). Wife beating and manliness in Late Antiquity. *Past & Present*, 199, 3–40.

Ellis, S. (2007). Late Antique housing and the uses of residential buildings: an overview. In Lavan, L., Özgenel, L., & Sarantis, A. (eds.), *Housing in Late Antiquity: From Palaces to Shops* (pp. 1–22). Brill.

Engelen E.M., Markowitsch, H.J., von Scheve, C., Röttger-Rössler, B., Stephan, A., Holodynski, M., & Vandekerckhove, M. (2009) Emotions as bio-cultural processes: disciplinary debates and an interdisciplinary outlook. In Markowitsch, H. & Röttger-Rössler B. (eds.), *Emotions as Bio-cultural Processes* (pp. 23–53). Springer.

Evans-Grubbs, J. (1995). *Law and family in Late Antiquity: the Emperor Constantine's marriage legislation*. Oxford University Press.

Faqir, F. (2005). Intrafamily femicide in defence of honour. In Moghissi, H. (ed.), *Women in Islam: Critical Concepts in Sociology. Volume 2: Social Conditions, Obstacles and Prospects* (pp. 104–124). Routledge. [Originally published in *Third World Quarterly*, 22 (1) 2001: 65–82.]

Gilmore, D.D. (1987). Introduction: the shame of dishonour. In Gilmore, D.D. (ed.), *Honour and Shame and the Unity of the Mediterranean* (pp. 2–21). American Anthropological Association.

Graham, J. (1998). The woman at the window: observations on the 'Stele from the harbour' of Thasos, *Journal of Hellenistic Studies* 118, 22–40.

Griffin, J. (1977). Propertius and Antony. *Journal of Roman Studies*, 67, 17–26.

Haj-Yahia, M.M. (2000). Wife abuse and battering in the sociocultural context of Arab society. *Family Process*, 39 (2), 237–255.

Herter, H. (1960). Die Soziologie der antiken Prostitution im Lichte des heidnischen und Christlichen Schriftums. *Jahrbuch für Antike und Christentum*, 3, 70–111.

Hillner, J. (2013). Family violence: punishment and abuse in the Late Roman Household. In Brubaker, L. & Tougher, S. (eds.), *Approaches to the Byzantine Family* (pp. 21–45). Ashgate.

Horn, C. & Martens, J. (2009). *"Let the little children come to me." Childhood and children in Early Christianity*. The Catholic University of America Press.
Inhorn, M.C. (2012). *New Arab Man: Emergent Masculinities, Technologies and Islam in the Middle East*. Princeton University Press.
King, D.E. (2008). The Personal is patrilineal: Namus as sovereignty. *Identities*, 15 (3), 317–342.
Kuefler, M. (2001). *The Manly Eunuch: Masculinity, Gender Ambiguity, and Christian Ideology in Late Antiquity*. University of Chicago Press.
Lambot, C. (1956). Sermon sur l'aumône à restituer à saint Augustin. *Revue Bénédictine* 66, 149–158.
Lindisfarne, N. (1994). Variant masculinities, variant virginities. Rethinking "honour and shame." In Cornwall, A. & Lindisfarne, N. (eds.), *Dislocating Masculinity: Comparative Ethnographies* (pp. 82–96). Routledge.
Nathan, G. (2000). *The family in Late Antiquity. The Rise of Christianity and the endurance of tradition*. Routledge.
Ouis, P. (2009). Honourable traditions? Honour violence, early marriage and sexual abuse of teenage girls in Lebanon, and Occupied Palestinian Territories and Yemen. *International Journal of Children's Rights*, 17, 445–474.
Reddy, R. (2014). Domestic violence or cultural tradition? Approaches to 'Honour Killing' as species and subspecies in English. In Gill, A., Strange, C., & Roberts, K. (eds.), *'Honour' killing and violence* (pp. 27–45). Palgrave.
Sawyer, E. (1995). Celibate pleasures: masculinity, desire and asceticism in Augustine. *Journal of the History of Sexuality*, 6 (1), 1–29.
Sère, B. & Wettlaufer, J. (2012). Introduction. In Sère, B. & Wettlaufer, J. (eds.), *Shame Between Punishment and Penance: The Social Usages of Shame in the Middle Ages and Early Modern Times* (pp. xxxi–xliv). Sismel.
Stearns, P. (2016). Shame, and a challenge for Emotions History. *Emotion Review*, 8 (3), 197–206.
Stephan, A. (2009). Homo Sapiens—The Emotional Animal. In Markowitsch, H. & Röttger-Rössler, B. (eds), *Emotions as Bio-cultural Processes* (pp. 11–19). Springer.
Treggiari, S. (1991). *Roman Marriage: Iusti Coniuges from the Time of Cicero to the Time of Ulpian*. Oxford University Press.
Vuolanto, V. (2008). Family and Asceticism. Continuity Strategies in the Late Roman World, Tampere: PhD thesis.
Wettlaufer, J. (2015). The Shame game. *RSA Journal*, 4, 36–40.
Wikan, U. (2008a). *In Honor of Fadime: Murder and Shame*. University of Chicago Press.
Wikan, U. (2008b). Honour, Truth, and Justice. In Wainryb, C., Smetana, J.G., & Turiel, E. (eds.). *Social Development, Social Inequalities and Social Justice* (pp. 185–208). Routledge.
Yarbrough, A. (1976). Christianization in the Fourth Century: The Example of Roman Women. *Church History*, 45 (2), 149–165.

Source Editions

Ambrosius, *De Abraham Libri Duo*, CSEL, 32, 1. Transl. Theodosia Tomkinson, *On Abraham*. Saint Ambrose of Milan, Etna, California, 2000.
Augustinus, *De Civitate Dei*. CCSL 47, 48. Transl., R.W. Dyson, *The city of God against the pagans*, New York, 1998.

Augustinus, *De Excidio Urbis Romae*, CCSL 46. Transl. Edmund Hill, Sermons. III/ 10 (341–400) *On Various Subjects*, New York, 1995.

Augustinus, *De Sermone Domini in Monte*, Transl. Rev. William Findlay, NPNF vol. 6, Augustin: Sermon on the Mount, Harmony of the Gospels, Homilies on the Gospels.

Augustinus, *Epistulae*, CSEL, 34, 1; 34, 2; 44; 57; 58. Transl. Sister Wilfrid Parsons, Letters, vol. 1–3, Washington D.C., 2008 [1951–1953]; James Houston Baxter, St. Augustine. *Select Letters*, Loeb series, Harvard, Mass., 1955.

Cicero, *Pro Cluentio*. Transl. H. Grose Hodge, Pro Lege Manilia. Pro Caecina. Pro Cluentio. Pro Rabirio Perduellionis Reo, Loeb-series, Cambridge, Mass., 1927.

Codex Theodosiani, Transl. Clyde Pharr, The Theodosian code and novels and the Sirmondian constitutions: a translation with commentary, glossary, and bibliography, Princeton, 1952.

Commodianus, *Instructions: Ante-Nicene Fathers*, vol. 4, Christian Literature Publishing, 1885.

Corpus Iuris Civilis, P. Krueger, Corpus iuris civilis, 11th ed., Berlin, 1954. Transl. Samuel P. Scott, The civil law: including the Twelve Tables, the Institutes of Gaius, the Rules of Ulpian, the Opinions of Paulus, the Enactments of Justinian, and the Constitutions of Leo / translated from the original Latin, edited, and compared with all accessible systems of jurisprudence, ancient and modern, vol. 1–17, Union, NJ, 2001 [1932].

Eusebius, *De Vita Constantini*, PL 8. Transl. Rev. Arthur Chushman McGiffert in Eusebius: Church History, Life of Constantine the Great, and Oration in praise of Constantine, NPNF, vol. 1, Buffalo, 1995.

Gregorius episcopus Turonensis (Gregory of Tours), Historiarum libri X, MGH SS 1, 1. Transl. Lewis Thorpe, Gregory of Tours: *The History of the Franks*, Harmondsworth, 1974.

Hieronymus (St. Jerome), Adversus Jovinianum, Patrologia Latina 12. Transl. W.H. Fremantle, Jerome: Letters and select works, Nicene Post-Nicene Fathers, 6, 1995.

Hieronymus (St. Jerome), Epistulae, CSEL, 54; 55; 56; CSEL, 88. Transl. F. A. Wright, *Select letters of Jerome*, Loeb series, Cambridge, Mass., 1963.

Lactantius, *Institutiones divinae*, CSEL 19. Transl. William Fletcher in ANF vol. 7, *Lactantius, Venantius, Asterius, Victorinus, Dionysius, Apostolic teaching and constitutions, 2 Clement, Early Liturgies*, Peabody, Mass., 1995.

Ruricius, *Epistulae*. Mathisen Ralph W.: Ruricius of Limoges and friends: a collection of letters from Visigothic Gaul: letters of Ruricius of Limoges, Caesarius of Arles, Euphrasius of Clermont, Faustus of Riez, Graecus of Marseille, Paulinius of Bordeaux, Sedatus of Nîmes, Sidonius Apollinaris, Taurentius and Victorinus of Fréjus, Liverpool, 1999.

5 Gregory of Tours on Sichar and Chramnesind

Richard Landes

For insights into the dynamics of violent warrior values, few passages offer a thicker description than Gregory of Tours' account of a feud that occurred in his own bishopric at the end of the sixth century CE (Gregory of Tours, 1927). I present the text, with running comments specifically on the shame–honor dynamics:[1]

> VII, 47] A feud [*bella civilia*] now arose between citizens of Tours. While Sichar, the son of one John, deceased, was celebrating the feast of Christmas in the village of Manthelan, with Austregisel and other people of the district, the local priest sent a servant [*puer* = lad] to invite several persons to drink wine with him at his house. When the servant came, one of the invited drew his sword and did not hesitate to strike, so that the lad fell dead upon the spot.

Note the near randomness (and anonymity) of the violence. Gregory does not even try to explain it or identify the killer and we only know from inference that he was one of Austregisel men. Nor does Gregory give a motive was for killing the lad—perhaps because it was all too common: the "gratuitous" violence of bullies (Depreux 2006, 62, n. 22). The slayer, drunk, and rowdy;[2] perhaps the servant was insolent (or insufficiently deferential); perhaps he resisted sexual advances. The drunken companions of the slayer, including Austregisel, may well have thought his "prank" hilarious, thereby, as we shall see, becoming complicit in the insult. Apparently, the difference in status meant that killing the boy *seemed* like a matter of little consequence (which, it turns out, was a mistaken/drunken assessment).

Such—to us, random ("senseless")—violence from weapons-bearers in public suggests that warriors with low triggers to violence dominated public space; their unarmed social inferiors had to tread very carefully, showing all the necessary deference not to provoke their sudden wrath. We might note here that Roman norms and philosophies of anger-management in public space seem to have little influence over the behavior of these tribal warriors, who carry weapons, and—whose *wergild* is often double that of Romans (Esders, 2011).

DOI: 10.4324/9781003022916-8

> Sichar was bound by ties of friendship to the priest; and as soon as he heard of the servant's murder he seized his weapons and went to the church to wait for Austregisel. Austregisel in his turn, hearing of this, took up his arms and equipment and went out against Sichar. There was an encounter between the two parties; in the general confusion Sichar was brought safely away by some clerics, and escaped to his country estate, leaving behind in the priest's house money and raiment, with four wounded servants. After Sichar's flight, Austregisel burst into the house, slew the servants, and carried off the gold and silver and other property.

Sichar's ties of *amicitia* to the priest meant that, out of solidarity, he was/felt obligated to revenge an attack on his "friend's" servant, and the fact that he targets Austregisel suggests that either Austregisel or one of his men killed the servant boy. Gregory tells us nothing of the battle, but that it went badly for the avenger Sichar, whose retreat brings on Austregisel rampage, wherein he breaks into a priest's house, kills his foe's wounded servants, and steals his goods. Plunder or be plundered. Losers continue to lose. The occasion permitting, armed men do not hesitate to kill unarmed men.

> The two parties afterwards appeared before a tribunal of citizens, who found Austregisel guilty as a homicide who had murdered the servants, and without any right or sanction seized the property.

But the excess violence against the unarmed brings in the "tribunal of the citizens" (*in iudicio civium*) that tries to resolve the problem. They find Austregisel guilty of homicide. Since he only killed servants whose *wergild* was low, however, the costs may not have been seriously damaging. But the tribunal also ordered the return of the goods seized without sanction, unjustified plunder from the battle over the dead lad. Indeed, what might have been legitimate for Sichar—seeking recompense—was not legitimate for Austregisel, a homicide who went from successfully fighting off retaliation to plunder further.

> A few days after the case had been before the court, Sichar heard that the stolen goods were in the hands of a man called Auno, his son, and his brother Eberulf. He set the tribunal at naught, and taking Audinus with him, lawlessly attacked these men by night with an armed party. The house where they were sleeping was forced open, the father, brother, and son were slain, the slaves murdered, and the movable property and herds carried off.

The ineffectiveness of the tribunal becomes immediately apparent. It's not clear from Gregory's account, but most likely, the tribunal had commanded Austregisel to return what he had stolen, and rather than transfer the wealth to Sichar, he had moved it to the home of an ally (clan member?). Sichar impatiently dismisses the (impotent) tribunal, takes an ally and band of men and attacks *at night*, kills the ally and his family, all their servants, and plunders everything. Bloodlust and the thirst for revenge leads to deeds that Gregory considers "lawless" and, by most warrior standards, would be considered cowardly (nighttime attack, killing unarmed). And the circle of injured parties seeking revenge widens. As the saying goes, "blood feuds don't die natural deaths."

> The matter coming to my ears, I was sore troubled, and acting in conjunction with the judge, sent messengers bidding them come before us to see if the matter could be reasonably settled so that the parties might separate in amity and the quarrel go no farther. They came, and the citizens assembled, whereupon I said: "Desist, O men, from further crime, lest the evil spread more widely. We have already lost sons of the Church, and now we fear that by this same feud we may be bereft of others. Be ye peacemakers, I beseech you; let him who did the wrong make composition for the sake of brotherly love, that ye be children of peace, and worthy, by the Lord's grace, to possess the kingdom of heaven. For He Himself hath said: '*Blessed are the peacemakers, for they shall be called the children of God.*' And behold, now, if he who is liable to the penalty have not the means of paying, the Church shall redeem the debt from her own moneys; meanwhile let no man's soul perish." Saying thus, I offered money belonging to the Church. But the party of Chramnesind, who demanded justice for the death of his father and his uncle, refused to accept it.

Now even the Bishop intervenes. He makes no effort to punish those guilty of the crimes involved; neither he, nor the tribunal, have the means to do so. Instead, he tries to bribe them, and offers the reader an excerpt from a sermon of exhortation that probably went on for considerably longer. It clearly marks off the immense distance between what the Church preached and what (real) men did and felt—"blessed are the peacemakers" vs. "blessed are those who take vengeance" (Landes, Chapter 3 in this volume). Gregory tries to sweeten the pot by offering to give the guilty party the means to pay the blood money.

Some see in Gregory's somewhat self-congratulatory account evidence of the Church's role in negotiating peaceful resolutions (James, 1983). The same narratives also underline the Church's failure to resolve this or any feuding violence in its "hot" phase, and the futility of their solutions. Gregory's account is studiously, even disquietingly cold, lacking any moralizing about the agonists (Rosenwein, 2006, p. 245). Was this an unspoken acknowledgment on Gregory's part that the kind of violence that men like Austregisel and Sichar and Chramnesind engage in in this tale were quite beyond control?

But the injured party, Chramnesind (a, the? surviving son of Auno), rejects the deal. Obviously. To accept blood money for the vicious death of his father, uncle, and brother would be bad enough, but to have it supplied to Sichar by the Church, so that he didn't even pay from his own estate, would be unbearable. (One can well imagine the sneer on Sichar's face as he handed over *wergild* that was not even his.) Gregory might think himself rendering justice and peacemaking here; from the tribal warrior's viewpoint, he merely offered a contemptible, ineffective bribe.

> When they were gone, Sichar made preparations for a journey, intending to proceed to the king, and with this in mind set out for Poitiers to see his wife first. But while he was there admonishing a slave to work, he struck him several times with a rod, whereupon the man drew the sword from his master's baldric and did not fear to wound him with it. He fell to the ground; but friends ran up and caught the slave, whom they first beat cruelly; then they cut off his hands and feet and condemned him to the gibbet.

The incident with his slaves in Poitiers gives us further insight into Sichar's character. On the run from a deadly enemy, he beats a slave to the point where the slave tries to kill him. The slave's predictable fate—mutilation then execution—illustrates what desperation he must have felt so to act. Sichar's character resembles that of Austregisel: quick to anger and violence. The slave's fate illustrates the abandon with which alpha males inscribed their honor on the body social. Sichar goes to the king to get protection. Belligerent warriors could appeal to Frankish kings to prefer them to public peace. That alone might keep Chramnesind, now clearly bent on revenge, from striking him.

> Meanwhile the rumor reached Tours that Sichar was dead. As soon as Chramnesind heard it, he warned his relations and friends, and went with all speed to Sichar's house. He plundered it and slew some of the slaves, burned down all the houses, not only that of Sichar, but also those belonging to other landholders on the estate. He then took off with him the cattle, and all the movable effects.

As we already saw with Austregisel's attack on the priest's house, weakness invites aggression. Chramnesind takes his family and friends to avenge his father's death by plundering Sichar's (and his neighbors') cattle, burning their buildings, killing their slaves. Chramnesind and his party had now drawn blood and acquired booty. Was it enough?

> The parties were now summoned by the count to the city and pleaded their own causes. The judges decided that he who had already refused a composition and then burned houses down should forfeit half of the sum formerly awarded to him, wherein they acted illegally, to ensure the restoration of peace; they further ordered that Sichar should pay the other half of the composition. The Church then provided the sum named in the judgment; the parties gave security, and the composition was paid, both

sides promising each other upon oath that they would never make further trouble against each other. So the feud came to an end.

Apparently, the thirst for blood revenge had been slacked by the raid. Granted, it cost Chramnesind and his clan half of the blood money awarded to them in the earlier settlement, but a small price to pay for honor. The church then supplies Sichar with the money; the two parties swear oaths to put an end to the spiraling violence, thus restoring peace—or so Gregory thought. From the warrior's perspective, however, there is something unsettling about taking money provided by a third party from the murderer of one's father, uncle, and brother ... The feud was not over. A few years later, Gregory returns to the unfinished tale.

> [IX, 19] The feud between the citizens of Tours, which I above described as ended, broke out afresh with revived fury. After the murder of the kinsfolk of Chramnesind, Sichar formed a great friendship with him; so fond of one another did they grow that often they shared each other's meals and slept in the same bed.

It's not clear how seriously to take this account of reconciliation. Gregory would probably like us to think that his mediation and earnest exhortations, and the men's love of Christ brought them together. An alternate explanation comes from the American South where quite often, after duels, the two antagonists become good friends (Greenberg, 1996: 53–62). Wallace-Hadrill (1962: 141) invokes a seemingly similar case in eleventh-century England between Uhtred's son Ealdred and Thurbrand's son Carl who carried on their fathers' feud (Hudson, 2010: 30). "Indeed, they were so united in mutual love that they set out for Rome together as sworn brothers."[3] But that was, apparently, never sincere (although for the dupe, Ealdred, believable).

It may, on the other hand, have been the wealth—and boozy lifestyle it supported—that overrode the code of a warrior's honor. As the Arab poetess commented derisively: "You have been diverted from avenging your brother by a bite of minced meat, a lick of meager milk" (Stetkevych, 1993: 196). That they shared meals together, and collapsed in a drunken stupor on occasion, perhaps. Possibly they became devoted and affectionate friends. In any case, they were close enough so that, with the help of some heavy drinking, Sichar let his guard down.

> One evening Chramnesind made ready a supper, and invited Sichar. His friend, came, and they sat down together to the feast. But Sichar, letting the wine go to his head, kept making boastful remarks against Chramnesind, and is reported at last to have said: "Sweet brother, you owe me great thanks for the slaying of thy relations; for the composition made to you for their death has caused gold and silver to abound in your house. But for this cause, which established you not a little, you, would this day be poor and destitute."

Did Sichar just drop that bombshell out of nowhere, or had he been needling Chramnesind for a while? Was he humiliating Chramnesind … to complete his mastery over the man whose father, uncle, and brother he had killed? Or was an inebriated and overconfident Sichar jokingly insulting Chramnesind's honor? (As we know from other details, Sichar has a mean character.) In any case, *in vino veritas*; this remark brought to the surface the unspoken tension of the feud's "resolution." If, in taking blood money, Chramnesind had dishonored himself, then all the more did he further dishonor himself by sharing that blood money with the murderer of his kin, who hadn't even paid the money in the first place.

> Chramnesind heard these words with bitterness of heart and said within himself: "If I avenge not the death of my kinsmen, I deserve to lose the name of man, and to be called weak woman." And straightway he put out the lights and cleft the head of Sichar with his dagger. The man fell and died, uttering but a faint sound as the last breath left him. The servants who had accompanied him fled away. Chramnesind stripped the body of its garments and hung it from a post of his fence; he then rode away to the king.

The comment breaks the spell of the negotiated resolution and the feasting it had allowed. All of a sudden, inside his head, Chramnesind hears the voices of his fellow citizens of Tours, imagines their contemptuous remarks about his behavior—not taking vengeance, indeed befriending his family's murderer, makes him a weak woman (*mulier infirma*)!—and realizes that, in the eyes of his peers, he has lost all honor. So he cleaves Sichar's head with his dagger, strips his body, and hangs it on the fence for all to see that he has indeed accomplished the vengeance required (Wallace-Hadrill, 1962: 141), and goes to seek protection from the king, who always had need of violent men in his debt and service.

Note here how the motive is not vengeance but reputation: others see him as a woman because he has not taken vengeance, indeed, has welcomed his mortal enemy into his bosom. Chramnesind doesn't burn with a desire for vengeance on Sichar; that he had given up long ago. But the *onēidophobic* moment, the realization of how his behavior was seen by others, unleashed instant, unhesitating violence.

In a moment, the laborious efforts to get men to transcend the blood feud and resolve disputes in a spirit of fairness and mutuality vanished. Honor and blood trumped civic peace. At least this time, rather than ever widening hostilities, the killing closes them down: Sichar's relatives would feel little need to avenge a clan member who had behaved so disgracefully.

> He entered a church and threw himself at Childebert's feet. "Mighty King!" he said, "I come to plead for my life. I have killed the man who in secret destroyed my relations and then stole all their possessions." He explained what had happened, point by point. Queen Brunhild took it

> very ill that Sichar, who was under her protection, should have been killed in this way, and she began to rage at Chramnesind. When he saw that she was against him, he fled to the village of Bouges in the Bourges area, where his people came from, this being under the jurisdiction of King Guntram.

Chramnesind's appeal to the king is based entirely on his right of revenge. The agreement of the reconciliation has no bearing here: once again, one of those involved in the feud "set the tribunal for naught." Whatever the king might have decided, the enmity of the Queen, not for breaking the law, not for crimes, but because the slain was under her protection, bodes ill for Chramnesind. Weapons-bearing Franks were restrained only by royal protection.

> Tranquilla, Sichar's wife, abandoned her children and her husband's property in Tours and Poitiers, and went off to join her own relations in the village of Pont-sur-Seine. There she married again. Sichar was only about 20 when he died. He was a loose-living young man, drunken and murderous, causing trouble to all sorts of people when he was in liquor.

Sichar's wife takes his disgraceful death as a liberation from any obligation to him and his offspring. Given his youth, they were probably married at a very early age and had little to keep them together, even offspring. Sichar's *mauvais caractère* had no bearing on Brunhild's favoritism, and his drunken violence (the same kind that set off the feud in the first place) had apparently little impact on his ability to have an estate with slaves.

> Chramnesind went to the King a second time. The judgment was that he must prove that he had taken life in order to avenge an affront, and this he did. In view of the fact that she had taken Sichar under her protection, Queen Brunhild ordered Chramnesind's property to be sequestered. Eventually his goods were handed back by Flavinius, one of the Queen's retainers. Chramnesind rushed off to Count Aginus and obtained a letter of restitution from him. It was to Flavinius that the Queen had made over his possessions.

It's not entirely clear why his goods were returned, but it may have something to do with the fact that they were in the hands of a Roman, who had much to fear from the enmity of a weapons-bearing Frank, despite being the Queen's retainer.

Conclusion: What This Incident Tells Us about Late Sixth-Century Western Europe

The current view of many historians is that Rome didn't fall, even in the West (Goffart, 1980; Mathison and Shanzer, 2001). Others disagree, noting that whatever remnants of Roman administration one may find in the documentation (itself obviously favorable to such expressions of literary-based Roman authority), the world of the sixth century is considerably impoverished and localized in comparison with that of even the faltering empire of the fifth century (Ward-Perkins, 2004; Heather, 2006; Goldsworthy, 2009).

This tale of Gregory's about a feud, for which there are ample if not quite as peculiar details for other such ongoing conflicts (Wallace-Hadrill, 1962: 121–47), offers much food for thought. Indeed, its interpretation offers an almost paradigmatic case in historiographical method, starting with the Roman vs. German approach to both historiography and to the period (Geary, 2006). New translations and new readings like this one, continue to flow (Depreux 2006; Wood, 2006; Meens, 2021),

Above all, it makes clear that brawling, drunken, weapons-bearing Franks with royal protection, quick to anger, could carry on their extravagantly violent feuds with near impunity, certainly as far as both municipal and ecclesiastical authorities were concerned. The random nature of the initial violence, which Gregory feels no need to explain, suggests how common such violence—Wallace-Hadrill compares the ensuing feuds to volcanoes, some extinct, most quiescent, but always capable of eruption (1962: 141). Anger, hatred, honor, rage ... all primary emotions among a Frankish elite that had the laws of wergild and the politics of Frankish monarchy on their side (Rosenwein 2003).

This is a society far removed from the Rome where anger was managed and law held a primary place in the resolution of conflict, where this kind of behavior was typical, in the Roman view, of "barbarians" (Harris, 2001: 211–230). Indeed, it is also removed from traditional tribal "feuding societies" in which feuding is closely clan-based as a way to "limit conflict" and its retaliations carefully (Boehm, 1984: 202–7, Wood, 2006). Instead, here in late sixth-century Gaul, municipality, church, and king, where not helpless to intervene, indulged and bribed the belligerents (Wallace-Hadrill, 1962: 143) while the weapons-bearers themselves indulged their profligate anger at the cost of many lives and much property.

Indeed, the graves from the period, with their plethora of warriors killed by weapons, "proves" what the texts suggest (Steuer, 2012): that in times of open warfare or supposed peace, warriors killed each other often. In this case described by Gregory, every side engages in extravagant violence, including deeds that some shame–honor cultures would consider dishonorable behavior—night attacks, killing slaves and children, burning people's houses (Graeber, 2011: 357). The clear message here is the force of the tribal warrior aristocracy, indulging their petty if not capricious ire at will, grafted onto a larger agro-literate society that largely suffered what it must at their hands.

Charlemagne and his ecclesiastical allies tried hard but unsuccessfully to tame this same warrior aristocracy, going so far as to attempt banning the feud. But the warriors' imperious appetites shattered his empire in one generation (Brown, 2014: 31–69). They still rampaged in the eleventh century (White, 1986), despite the efforts of "Peace Councils" to ban homicide (Van Meter, 1996), and a significant shift among some aristocrats from "plunder and distribute" to "exploit and spend" in the first centuries of the millennium (Duby, 1978). These "warriors" were still exercising their right to "private war" in the late Middle Ages (Algazi, 2000). Those proposing a history of the Middle Ages owe it to their readers to trace the impact of this violent, shame–honor-driven, warrior aristocracy in both the fall of the Roman Empire, and the slow, dialectic, millennium-long rise of a culture where self-help justice among the aristocrats had ceded to demotic systems built on dignity and equality before the law (Landes, 2017).

Notes

1 This feud has been studied with much attention to the role of justice and mediation in trying to resolve it, starting in the late nineteenth century (Monod, 1886; Fustel de Coulanges, 1887), right up to the present (Depreux, 2006; Wood, 2006; Meens, 2021).
2 The issue of drunkenness came up in the dispute between Monod (referring to Tacitus on drunk Germans) and Fustel de Coulanges (who claimed there was "no mention" in the text, 1887, 8), echoed by Wood (2006, 496f.). Given the *longue durée* of drinking habits in Germany, it seems strange to take the absence of mention as evidence of absence.
3 *De obsessione Dunelmi*, c. 7, Symeon, *Opera Omnia*, ed. Arnold, vol. 1, p. 219.

References

Algazi, G. (2000). Pruning Peasants: Private War and Maintaining the Lords' Peace. In E. Cohen and M. de Jong (Eds.), *Late Medieval Germany Medieval Transformations: Texts, Power and Gifts in Context* (pp. 245–274). Brill.

Auerbach, E. (1954). *Mimesis: The Representation of Reality in Western Literature*. Princeton University Press.

Boehm, C. (1984). *Blood Revenge: The Enactment and Management of Conflict in Montenegro and Other Tribal Societies*. University of Pennsylvania Press.

Brown, W. (2014). *Violence in the Middle Ages*. Routledge.

Depreux, P. (2006). Une faide exemplaire? À propos des aventures de Sichaire: vengeance et pacification aux temps mérovingiens. In D. Barthelemy, R. Le Jan, & R. Bougard (eds.), *La Vengeance, 400–1200* (pp. 65–85). Ecole française de Rome.

Duby, G. (1978). *Guerriers et Paysans*. Hachette.

Esders, S. (2011). "Eliten" und "Strafrecht" im frühen Mittelalter. In F. Bougard, H.-W. Goetz, & R. Le Jan (eds.), *Überlegungen zu den Bussen- und Wergeldkatalogen der Leges Barbarorum: Théorie et pratiques des élites au Haut Moyen Âge* (pp. 261–282). Turnhout.

Fustel de Coulanges, N.-D. (1887). L'analyse des textes historiques. *Revue des questions historiques*, 41, 5–25.

Geary, P. (2006). Gabriel Monod, Fustel de Coulanges et les aventures de Sichaire: La naissance de l'histoire scientifique au XIXe siècle. In D. Barthélemy, F. Bougard, & R. Le Jan (eds.), *La Vengeance, 400–1200* (pp. 87–99).

Goffart, W. (1980). *Barbarians and Romans, AD 418–584: The Techniques of Accommodation*. Princeton University Press.

Goldsworthy, A. (2009). *The Fall of the West*. Weidenfeld & Nicolson.

Graeber, D. (2011). *Debt: The First 5,000 Years*. Melville House.
Greenberg, K. (1996). *Honor and Slavery*. Princeton University Press.
Gregory of Tours (1927). *History of the Franks*, trans. by O.M. Dalton. Clarendon Press.
Harris, W. (2001). *Restraining Rage: The Ideology of Anger Control in Classical Antiquity*. Harvard University Press.
Heather, P. (2006). *The Fall of the Roman Empire: A New History of Rome and the Barbarians*. Oxford University Press.
Hudson, J. (2010). Feud, Vengeance and Violence in England from the Tenth to the Twelfth Centuries. In B.S. Tuten & T.L. Billado (Eds.), *Feud, Violence and Practice: Essays in Medieval Studies in Honor of Stephen D. White* (pp. 29–54). Ashgate.
James, E. (1983). 'Beati pacifici': Bishops and the Law in Sixth-Century Gaul. In J. Bossy (Ed.), *Dispute Settlements, Law and Human Relations in the West* (pp. 25–46). Cambridge University Press.
Landes, R. (2017). The Peace of God: Demotic Religiosity and the Millennial Dynamics of the Central Middle Ages. In Y. Friedman (Ed.). *Religion and Peace* (pp. 44–66). Taylor & Francis.
Mathison, R. & Shanzer, D. (eds.) (2001). *Society and Culture in Late Antique Gaul: Revisiting the Sources*. Ashgate.
Meens, R. (2021). Penance and Satisfaction: Conflict Settlement and Penitential Practices in the Frankish World in the Early Middle Ages. In L. Bothe, S. Esders, and H. Nijdam (Eds.), *Wergild, Compensation and Penance: The Monetary Logic of Early Medieval Conflict Resolution* (pp. 212–239). Brill.
MGH Scriptores rerum Merovingicarum 1, 1. Latin text. https://www.dmgh.de/mgh_ss_rer_merov_1_1/index.htm#page/(III)/mode/1up.
Monod, G. (1886). Les aventures de Sichaire. *Révue historique*, 31, 259–290.
Rosenwein, B. (2003). Communautés émotionnelles en Francie au VIIe siècle. *Annales. Histoire, Sciences Sociales* 58 (6), 1271–1292.
Rosenwein, B. (2006). Les emotions de la vengeance. In D. Barthelemy, R. Le Jan, & R. Bougard (eds.), *La Vengeance, 400–1200* (pp. 237–257). Ecole française de Rome.
Stetkevych, S.P. (1993). *The Mute Immortals Speak: Pre-Islamic Poetry and the Poetics of Ritual*. Cornell University Press.
Steuer, H. (2012). Fehde und Blutrache bei den Alamannen. *Archäologie in Deutschland* 3, 20–25.
Van Meter, D. (1996). The Peace of Amiens-Corbie and Gerard of Cambrai's Oration on the Three Functional Orders: the Date, the Context, the Rhetoric. *Revue belge de philologie et d'histoire*, 74, 633–657.
Wallace-Hadrill, J.M. (1962). *The Long-Haired Kings*. Methuen and Co.
Ward-Perkins, B. (2004). *The Fall of Rome and the End of Civilization*. Oxford University Press.
White, S. (1986). Feuding and Peace-Making in the Touraine around the Year 1100. *Traditio*, 42, 195–263.
Wood, I. (2006). 'The Bloodfeud of the Franks': a historiographical legend. *Early Medieval Europe*, 14, 489–504.

6 Better to die in honor than to live in shame?

A Comparative Approach to the Literary Dynamics of Honor and Shame in French Chanson de Geste, Romance, and Fabliau (Twelfth to Thirteenth Centuries)

Lisa Sancho[1]

Introduction

Between death in honor or life in shame, which experience is the worst? Given what historical anthropology has uncovered about the ideological conceptions of the Western Middle Ages, the answer seems obvious. In the literary production of that time, this is evidenced by the recurrence of the proverb "Better to die in honor than to live in shame,"[2] which conveys two main pieces of information.

On an ideological level, the proverb draws an axiological scale, where honor and shame are perceived as two sides of the same coin. The first one is elevated to the rank of supreme value and conceived as a capital to be preserved at all costs;[3] on the contrary, the second one is considered as a complete counter-value to the point that, given the choice, even death would be a preferable fate.[4]

On a rhetorical level, the grammatical structure of the sentence combines parallelism of construction, binary rhythm, impersonal turn, use of the infinitive and of the present tense; expressing here a universal truth (both the infinitive and this specific aspect of the present tense connote an ahistorical value). This gives the statement a sentemtious solemnity, an impact that seeks to reach universality and a normative aim all at once. Obviously part of a social and moral code, the phrase becomes a true principle of conduct.

On the basis of these preliminary observations, we can draw the two following deductions: firstly, the well-defined hierarchy established between honor that has to be preserved and shame that must be avoided seems to enshrine the proverb in a shame culture (Benedict, 1946),[5] which is theoretically characteristic of medieval Western society;[6] secondly, the generalizing, normative dimension of the proverb tends to prove that it is intended to innervate the whole community.

However, despite its seemingly crystal-clear, unequivocal meaning, the proverb actually raises more questions than it provides answers. More specifically,

DOI: 10.4324/9781003022916-9

on top of being a dual notion like honor is (see endnote 4), shame is also an ambivalent one.[7] Since the concepts themselves appear to be heterogeneous, doesn't the assumed transparency of the proverb now take on a certain opacity? Is the code of conduct according to which an honorable death is unvaryingly preferable to an existence spent in shame, really relevant in all literary contexts and for all types of characters without distinction? And thus, what about the ideology that establishes honor and shame as separate, hierarchical opposites?

In fact, in spite of its apparently crystal-clear wording, this proverb prompts a broader reflection on the literary representations of the dynamics of honor and shame.

In order to do so, it seems fitting to: first, focus the subject of this essay on a comparison between the discourses of three distinct genres (chanson de geste,[8] romance,[9] fabliau[10]); and, second, to set it in the twelfth and thirteenth centuries.[11]

Death rather Than Dishonor? A Short Handbook for Use by Fictional Characters

The Passing of Roland at Roncevaux Pass: Chanson de Geste as an Illustration of Feudal Honor

The recurrence of the proverb "Better to die in honor than to live in shame" in chanson de geste is undeniable. For the sole *Chanson de Roland*,[12] which is considered the matrix of medieval French epic production (Suard, 2006), it is summoned at a remarkably high frequency (about ten times), albeit with some variants.[13] Already, some facts should be pointed out. One, out of the 4,000 or so verses in the text, the greatest part of the occurrences is clustered in the first half—that is, until the death of the protagonist. Two, grammatically speaking, the proverb undergoes an "integration" (see endnote 13) that results in a rewording which includes personal pronouns. Three, as a direct consequence of the previous point, the sentence—which does not involve an impersonal form anymore—now linguistically applies to at least one character, and although the subjects of the enunciation may be friends as well as foes, the subjects of the utterance inevitably remain the Christian heroes.

These observations speak volumes about the ideology at work here. The personalizing reconfiguration of the proverb reduces its previously extensive nature: it slides from a claim to the universal towards a restriction applying to the Christian heroes and aristocrats only.[14] Far from being trifling, such a movement of concentration aims to isolate the values animating this group from those of the other characters and, in so doing, to underline their exceptional nature. Therefore, the concentration of proverbial occurrences in the first half of the chanson appears as anything but fortuitous. In this section of the text, the key episode of the Battle of Roncevaux, which reaches its climax with the death of the protagonist, epitomizes the opposition between heroes and outcasts. Roland is the exemplary incarnation of the epic hero's idiosyncratic *furor*. Cornered by the heathens, he refuses to flee as much as he rebuffs the idea of sounding the horn in order to call Charlemagne for help. Instead, he purposefully throws himself headlong into the fray. By readily making the ultimate sacrifice for the service of his emperor, the character becomes the paragon of feudal ideology.[15] The Saracens' cowardice draws a striking contrast with Roland's hardline attitude. In addition to already being at fault for ungodliness, they usually run away as soon as death comes too near. This behavior reinforces the hierarchy drawn by the chanson de geste: bound together around Roland's glorifying, sacrificial death, the Christian community asserts its axiological superiority over those who are labelled as "the Other" and deliberately depicted in a dishonorable manner, hence disqualifying conduct.[16]

Thus, in the *Roland* as in many medieval epic texts, honor is simultaneously warlike, religious, ethnic, gendered, social. Its definition is based on a series of oppositions: valiant (vs. coward), Christian (vs. Pagan), Western (vs. Saracen), masculine (vs. feminine), aristocrat (vs. peasant). But above all, it is embodied in the correspondence between gesture and word, seeing that the proverb is here taken literally: dying with weapons in hand is perceived as a supremely eloquent proof of one's absolute commitment to the feudal mission. For the hero of chanson de geste, this is undoubtedly the most honorable escape from shame.

Dying in Honor within Romance? From a Gendered to a Rhetorical Matter

Of all the proverbs in late twelfth-century narrative literature, "*Mius vaut morir a joe que vivre à onte*" is an undisputed favorite (Schulze-Busacker, 1985: 22). Romance was at the time a work in progress, taking on different directions that explain its heterogeneous nature.

As translations-adaptations of the great texts of Ancient Greece and Rome, romances of Antiquity share many features with the epic material, both on a thematic and stylistic level, but above all ideologically. This is evidenced by the *Roman d'Énéas*, which is a translation from Virgil's *Aeneid* into Old French created during the 1160s. As in the Latin version, Queen Didon de Carthage falls in love with young Énéas who survived the fire of Troy, and does so despite the oath she swore to remain faithful all her life to her deceased husband Sychée. Exposed by her guilty love, she finds herself subjected to gossip: rumor has it that she has disgraced herself. Eventually abandoned by her lover, Didon resolves, in the depths of despair, to commit suicide by fire and iron. Like epic heroes, the queen knowingly chooses to walk towards her own death rather than fully face the shame that would irretrievably follow her misfortune. But what strikes readers the most is the discrepancy with the Roland case, starting with the matter of gender. However, the issue here has less to do with the fact that Didon is a woman than with her grasp of honor and shame, which seems really peculiar given her gender. What was expected of her as a female bound to preserve her own honor was to keep the promise made to her late husband, i.e., to adopt the virtuous conduct of chastity.[17] Nevertheless, the romance presents a gendered reversal of the male model spotted in chanson de geste: here, the *"felenie de la dame,"*[18] and consequently the accusations of dishonor weighing on her, arise out of a lack of decency, not out of a cowardly, shameful military withdrawal. As of this point, the character's reputation shifts from virtue to *"putage."*[19] The dread of social judgment plays at least as important a part in the queen's fateful decision as does amorous grief, even more so than in the Latin model.[20] Dishonored from her sexual integrity but above all frightened by the mere potentiality of yet another humiliation—this one inflicted by her former suitors—Didon is caught between the devil and the deep blue sea. She decides to set her destiny on a path resolutely chosen, not imposed. But in electing to die by the sword, she diverts her honor from the sphere of intimacy to that of the battlefield. That way, she enters into a process of cultivating virility that leads to the substitution of a male emotional regime of honor for the female one that was initially assigned to her.[21] Such a feminine conquest of male honor is only made possible for the character by her monarchical status, which allows a transfer of the referential point of honor from gender to rank.

Things are somewhat different in Chrétien de Troyes' chivalric world. On a grammatical level, the proverb is, as for the *Roland*, integrated in a personal form: *"Ne ja Dex n'ait de moi merci, / se jel di mie por orguel, / et s'asez mialz morir ne vuel / a enor que a honte vivre!"*;[22] *"N'ai pas de ma mort tel peeur / Que je mielz ne voille a heneur / La mort soffrir et endurer / Que vivre a honte et perjurer."*[23] In the first quote, the Knight Lancelot questions himself about the shame that would fall upon him were he to turn a blind eye to the rape of a young girl by not rescuing her. Eventually castigating himself for such hesitation, he even goes so far as to say, *"or en ai honte, or en ai duel / tel que je morroie, mon vuel, / quant je ai tant demoré ci."*[24] In the second one, Gauvain, King Arthur's nephew and his best knight after Lancelot, is held captive by the king of Escavalon. Yet he refuses even in exchange for his freedom to find the Bleeding Lance in the name of said king because, according to a prophecy, this spear will destroy Arthur's realm. In both instances, the proverb is spoken by knights, i.e., eminently noble, honor-driven characters. However, unlike Roland or Didon, the statement never reaches the stage of actuality but remains latent, a mere potentiality not to be fulfilled: Lancelot may claim that, were it up to him, he would die of shame for having delayed so much, he never really seeks to commit the ultimate sacrifice; as for Gauvain, the king merely makes him solemnly swear to search for the Lance, thus sparing him the dilemma of whether or not to take his own life.

This is because, from Roland and Didon to Lancelot and Gauvain, romance has set chivalric honor on a decidedly more courtly path. As far as Arthurian knights are concerned, there is no need to meet death just to escape shame, whether it be potential or actual: saying the proverb does not aim at actualization, but has a purely rhetorical value. Several factors can explain such a difference:[25] more specifically, a text like the *Roland* strives to celebrate the necessarily tragic destiny of the hero caught up in a "geopolitical epic"; conversely, Chrétien de Troyes' romances are set in a "fairytale parenthesis" (Chrétien de Troyes, *Œuvres complètes*: XIX) of a 12-year period of peace, during which it is more about showing a slice of the lives of the Knights of the Round Table rather than erecting a symbolic funerary monument to them.

"Fi de L'honneur, Vive la Vie!"[26] *The Pragmatic Logic of Fabliau*

One might as well say it now: the proverb does not appear in the fabliau*x* of the twelfth and thirteenth centuries (Schulze-Busacker, 1985: 335–349). This is surely the most outstanding distinctive feature on this subject between chansons de geste and romances, on the one hand, and fabliau*x*, on the other. Not that proverbs are not favored by fabliau*x*—which, on the contrary, have an irrefutable affinity with them—but their uses differ from the material of epic or romance.

The situations depicted no longer take place on the battlefields of chanson de geste or the paths of Arthurian adventure, but are part of everyday domestic or urban life (Alexandre-Bidon & Lorcin, 2003). Consequently, the topics at play in fabliau*x* as well as the characters involved are thoroughly altered. The same goes for the aims of the genre: "[laughter] being without a doubt the dominant feature" (Boutet, 1985), chivalric and courtly ideologies aren't relevant within fabliaux. Of course, this is not to say that awareness of honor and shame doesn't exist in this genre. But the ideological paradigm underlying these texts originates from a reversal of the scale of values. In the name of a logic of pragmatic efficiency where the goal is to try and get the upper hand over the opponent, life is seen by the characters as a more precious treasure than honor and ought to be protected, without question.[27] As a direct consequence, it is death, and no longer shame, that embodies the absolutely repulsive enemy. That is why characters quite rarely die in fabliau*x*. Moreover, when death does occur, it has neither a tragic dimension nor a heroic aim—which would make it unbearably serious—but is underlain by a comic dimension.[28] Conversely, the choice to flee from humiliation prevails countless times as a means of preserving life, if not honor. For example, in *Le Prestre crucefié*, the eponymous character seduces the wife of a craftsman. In punishment for his crime, he is subjected to being emasculated, beaten, smeared, and ransomed. Significantly, the priest attempts to escape in order to try to save his life after being mutilated by the cuckolded husband.[29] To put it in a nutshell, in fabliau*x* saving one's skin is preferable to saving face.[30]

While the social need to avoid dishonorable shame innervates all three genres, the degree of importance imparted to this requirement as well as the strategies to achieve it differ quite considerably. From chanson de geste to fabliau and to romance, there is a shift from a value system in which honor takes precedence over life, to a strictly opposite conception. Whereas fabliau characters are relieved to run away and escape after having suffered humiliation, epic and romance heroes make it a point of honor to anticipate and ward off shame, in a performative or merely rhetorical logic. Above all, this axiological divergence depending on the literary genre is emblematic of an ideal of civilization built and spread by the ruling classes, where a social and religious hierarchy clearly arises between honorable and shameful characters.

How, then, can it be explained that many texts seem in spite of everything to display shame, whereas the characters, on the contrary, try to avoid it? Such a paradox prompts to study the honor/shame dynamics from the angle of their connection to time and history.

The Literary Honor/Shame Dynamics: The History of Time and the Time of History

Displaying Shame: Between Temporary and Temporal

Contrary to these avoidance strategies, fabliau seems to elevate the display of shame to the rank of a work of art. This is quite surprising, considering the fact that, although they are certainly not inclined to sacrifice their lives for honor, characters in this literary genre are no less aware than others of the omnipresence of public observation. Their taking society's judgment into account explains two of the most specific narrative themes of fabliau: the flight of the humiliated, of course (see above), but also the countless situations of revenge where a deceived, humiliated victim gets back at the offender.[31] In the fabliau *Jouglet*, the eponymous prankster tricks a naive peasant who has just married a young lady to eat a great number of pears and forbids him to relieve himself when he inevitably has diarrhea. On the wedding night, it suddenly dawns on the young bride why her new husband shows so little eagerness to fulfill his marital duties. She then suggests that he defecates on the minstrel's personal belongings, so that when Jouglet wakes up and puts on his clothes, he will be covered in excrement. And now the boot is on the other foot. As a means of pressure to turn the situation around, the use of the counter-ruse aims to level out the playing field by humiliating the prankster. The purpose is therefore less the restoration of the first victim's honor than a playful, constantly renewed illustration of the proverb "there's always somebody smarter than you somewhere." Such a narrative choice is of course related to the comic register inscribed in the genre's horizon of expectations: the plot's goal is always to ridicule the target of the trick, to offer some good comedy, and to make the audience laugh. The aesthetics of brevity is at the heart of the narrative effectiveness of fabliau, which rests on a constant succession of episodes so as to leave no respite to the reader-listener. The triggering of laughter depends on this cumulative logic, which is often overkill and regularly associated with other traits (in the case of *Jouglet*, the scatological vein). Through this concatenation of degrading, comic situations, fabliau tends to shorten the duration of individual shame: at the end of the day, it's always one humiliation after another, the latter erasing the former, to the point that the stories sometimes seem to revolve only around a series of humiliations. As a result, when avenged, one might say that shame has only been temporary. Herein lies the paradox: while the characters do their utmost to try and conceal their own humiliation by bringing another one into the spotlight, the narrative constantly brings shame back to the forefront, by displaying this stream of degrading episodes. *De facto*, shame becomes omnipresent. Fabliaux thus build up an everlasting tension between attempting to make shame temporary (on the diegesis level) and wanting to display it (on the narration level).[32]

As genres much more concerned with the preservation of honor, chansons de geste and romances also occasionally display shame, but in slightly different ways and for quite distinct purposes. In *Le Couronnement de Louis*, a Saracen giant cuts off the tip of Count Guillaume d'Orange's nose with his sword. The gesture naturally brings shame upon the hero. But far from trying to alleviate it, he turns this humiliation into an honorable symbol of his heroism, which he proudly shows off for all to see: the loss of his nasal appendage is incorporated into the character's very name (Guillaume becomes Guillaume au court nez, i.e., Guillaume with the short nose). Through a skillful inversion of signifiers, this incredibly voluntarist approach transforms the accident passively suffered into an actively chosen identity trait: it then becomes a significant part of the Count's personal history and contributes to shape Guillaume's glorious legend (*Le Couronnement de Louis*: XXVIII, v. 1159–1165, p. 37).

With the Arthurian character Lancelot, romance delves a bit deeper into this strategy of reversing concepts and their settling in temporality. In *Le Chevalier de la Charrette*, a chivalric, courtly romance by Chrétien de Troyes, the Knight Lancelot is in love with Queen Guenièvre who has been abducted and volunteers to rescue her from her captor. In order to do so, he agrees to ride in a cart, even if this means of transportation is likened in medieval culture to the pillory of the condemned. He thus knowingly exposes himself to great humiliation. However, the narrator's commentary[33] prevents any misinterpretation as to the cause of Lancelot's emotional distress: the character's subsequent misfortune does not stem from his tarnishing his knightly honor, but from his wavering when getting into the "cart of infamy"—a fault that Queen Guenièvre will explicitly blame him for. As a matter of fact, the courtly ideology sets up a "debate [...] between arms and love" (Chrétien de Troyes, *Œuvres complètes*: XXVI), in which honor is a kind of linchpin: what is dishonorable for the *Knight* Lancelot (riding in the cart of infamy) becomes highly honorable for the *Lover* Lancelot (agreeing to demean himself out of love for the queen).[34] Beyond this romance, Lancelot's literary fortune experiences significant, sometimes contradictory fluctuations on the extra-diegetic level. In the late twelfth century, at the same time as the courtly ideology expanded within romance, a more spiritual, soteriological ideology spread in the first half of the thirteenth century: the specific vein of chivalric romance which focuses on the Grail and matches up with the transition from verse to prose tilts the axiological paradigm from a *terrien* extreme (material, i.e., taken up to feudal-courtly values) to a *celestiel* extreme (spiritual, i.e., turned towards the precepts defended by Christianism). To sum up, yesterday's heroes who used to be praised and honored for their loyalty to chivalrous, courtly ideals become today's reprobates. Lancelot's journey is emblematic of such an ideological mutation. The Lancelot–Grail cycle includes a Cistercian romance, *La Queste del Saint Graal*, which relates an episode that speaks volumes, to say the least: a hermit lectures the knight about his failing not towards chivalrous honor or love, but regarding the honor due to God. By committing adultery with Queen Guenièvre, Lancelot is guilty of a "*pechié*" (sin) against the Almighty. Shame falls upon him and materializes with tears when he becomes aware of his wrongdoing. Yet this feeling of shame has very little to do with feudal dishonor: as a direct consequence of the humiliation of being berated in this way, shame here is above all a vector of humility, which is an eminently Christian virtue considered as a higher form of honor (Zink, 2017: 35 and *passim*). In so doing, this specific form of shame, controlled as it is chosen rather than inflicted, is seen as a transitory but necessary step in the individual journey of the knight who experiences, on the path of *conversion*, a temporal and ideological evolution from the dishonorable, blameworthy service of Love to the honorable, salutary service of God.

On the face of it, one might find rather puzzling such a display of shame within a system of values where steering clear of humiliation is paramount. All things considered, it turns out to be quite coherent. Shame's aesthetic and ideological purposes depend on the literary genre in which it takes place, and are set on both an intra- and extra-diegetic level: on the one hand, displaying shame reveals the tensions existing between various contemporary schools of thought and ideologies, which can be embodied diachronically (between works from different periods) or synchronically (at the same time, or even within the same work); on the other hand, it brings to light the porousness existing between the notions of honor and shame, which appears in the end less clear-cut than it seems, since they are likely to be reversed on the axiological scale depending on the ideological and cultural context.

Literary Honor and Shame through the Prism of Regimes of Historicity

At this point, one might feel inclined to assume that, at the diachronic level of literary history, the corpus mirrors the shift from a shame culture to a guilt culture which supposedly occurred around 1200: firstly, because the first observations inferred from the works themselves seem to reveal an evolution from chansons de geste to courtly romances and then to Grail romances which, beyond the purely chronological and stylistic aspects, would match up with the switch from a feudal ideology to a courtly, and then a spiritual one; secondly, because the epistemological standpoint of certain specialists seems to confirm such an alteration in Western medieval culture.[35] Such an analysis raises a set of issues that echoes the process of civilization (Elias, 1939): one, beyond the criticism that the concept of the "civilizing process" went through (Gauvard, 1991: 868) and the fact that some historians pointed out the misuse of the shame/guilt culture binomial (Creighton, 1990; Boquet, 2019), many medievalists support the idea that the Middle Ages were part of a shame culture. Yet a closer look shows little evidence of such a transition.[36] Since the evolution of literature is anything but linear, neither the transition from a shame to a guilt culture, nor even the unequivocal triumph of one or the other seem really conclusive. Rather than an unambiguous opposition, the generic and ideological fluctuations of the literary corpus reveal a coexistence of distinct, even sometimes contradictory discourses.[37] Therefore, let us formulate the following working hypothesis: that each literary genre develops a relation to time (as we have seen) and to its own historical dimension, that is a specific "regime of historicity."[38]

As it is set within a "tight time frame (the action takes place within a few hours)" and the plot seldom is to "follow a hero for several years, let alone a lifetime" (Ménard, 1983: 28), the corpus of fabliaux is unquestionably the most ahistorical of the three genres. Completely ingrained in the present, it features characters who usually have neither past nor future (Zink, 1999: 617). Such a relation to time is not without consequences for the writing of the honor/shame dynamics within fabliau. The genre stresses more on the shaming than on the feeling of being ashamed since, because of the necessity of narrative effectiveness, humiliation is far more likely to provoke the required laughter than emotion is. However, the near-total silence of the authors regarding the characters' possible shame in fabliau traps them in a temporary frame (see above) and prevents them from entering a temporal one,[39] namely an individual story of continuities and ruptures bound to make them evolve throughout time, and therefore throughout history. Above all, insofar as the plot most often ends with a tale of humiliation, the last victims are generally condemned to remain in disgrace: after the end of the fabliau, they have no possibility of taking revenge on the pranksters; with its closure, the story traps them forever in their humiliation which is thus experienced as an eternal present.[40]

In contrast to this closed structure, chansons de geste and romances develop a pattern that is eminently more tied up to time and history. For the former, the opening is upstream: "this experience of temporality is characterized by the omnipresent reference to the past so as to justify present or future action" (Bonansea, 2018). The chanson de geste *Raoul de Cambrai*, dating back to the very early 1200s, includes the episode of a confrontation between King Louis and the eponymous hero, his vassal. Because the monarch has just unfairly taken away the fief that he inherited, Raoul submits a request and provides evidence for his entitlement to receive his rightful legacy from his father.[41] What is interesting is that the protagonist recalls the military support he provided to his suzerain and for which he was not rewarded in any way. The reference to the past here is twofold: it relates both to the notion of inheritance, which refers to ancestry (and thus echoes the deep connection of chanson de geste to the matter of origins), and to the memory of warlike deeds. Belonging to the "cycle des barons révoltés" (the "rebellious barons' cycle"), this chanson depicts "a decaying universe" (Calin, 1974): in short, this is a time of crisis where feudal values are challenged and where the hero is ashamed at the very thought of giving up his honor (here in the concrete sense of "fief") into the hands of another.[42] For their part, Grail romances are open to the opposite: "this other conception of time is partly detached from the value of anteriority to open up to future plenitude" (Bonansea, 2018). The present is, this time, perceived in relation to an eschatological and soteriological future: History is then considered as a path necessarily leading to redemption. In this respect, the choice of prose, which is characteristic of Grail romances made up within the literary cycles and sums of the thirteenth century, is part of a quest for and writing of the truth. As it is, the dividing line between prose and verse is heightened, seeing verse is confined to the area of fiction and "*mençonge*" (lies, fable, and invention). Thus, when Lancelot renounces his earthly love for Guenièvre in order to devote himself more fully to the spiritual love of God, his perspective, now undeniably imbued with spirituality, casts new light on his assessing the matter of honor: he no longer sees it as the feudal, courtly notion that links him to the *terrien* extreme and to the old world (thus to his original literary identity), but rather embraces the Christian vision of honor which invites him to turn to a salvation inflected future in order to obtain the redemption of his sins. It is this truth that romance in prose claims to transcribe and transmit.

Conclusion

On the question of whether it is better to die in honor or to live in shame, literature seems to agree with the proverb and to recognize the axiological superiority of honor over shame. Consequently, from the characters' point of view, the latter can only be a momentary step on the way to the regaining of honor. In any case, shame cannot last, at the risk of being forever condemned to opprobrium. Seeing this expected answer, this reflection could have been somewhat pointless, had it not led to the opportunity to nuance some pretty important points.

Because they are simultaneously linked to two different but strongly intertwined spheres (feudal and religious), the notions of honor and shame each cover, in absolute terms, two distinct realities. The actualization of one or the other of these realities depends on the context of enunciation and the generic, aesthetic, ideological, cultural background in which honor and shame take place. Both concepts therefore appear to be much more relative than one might have thought. This is evidenced by the fact that if honor is generally conceived of as a value and shame as a counter-value, the axiology can be completely reversed, with shame becoming honorable and vice versa. The relationship of opposition that tradition has established between these two concepts thus conceals in fact their truly porous nature ranging from one to the other. Far from being clear-cut, static and unequivocal, the articulation between honor and shame is therefore highly dynamic, caught in a perpetual reshaping of its modes of expression, between invisibility and visibility.

Such an instability does not spur us on to consider these complex relationships from the perspective of a linear historical evolution (the univocal transition from a shame to a guilt culture), but rather to highlight the competition between distinct, sometimes contradictory discourses. These are contemporary with each other and reflect an era of great upheavals that necessarily give rise to concerns, doubts, and questions. Various scales of values come out from this polyphony, contributing to the construction of different systems of representation. An ideological correspondence emerges within each of these systems, between emotional regimes, regimes of historicity, and regimes of writing. It proves, if such proof were effectively needed, that "representation in the Middle Ages is not only a means of reflecting upon the world, but also of shaping it" (Gauvard, 2015b).

Notes

1 I would like to thank Damien Boquet and Jean-Marie Fritz for their thorough proofreading of the French version of this essay, as well as for their valuable advice and suggestions.
2 This is a modernized translation of what appears as the most emblematic version of this proverb. Many variants exist, the most widespread being undoubtedly "Mius vaut morir a joe que vivre a onte" – "Better to die in joy than to live in shame", no. 1272 (*Proverbes*, 2007 [1925]: 46). This translation in English as well as all the translations from this point forward are mine.
3 Claude Gauvard has extensively developed this idea in her work: "Honor remains a capital that ought not to be diminished" (1991: 701). Proverbs seem to prove her right, as they frequently use an economic reference to signify just how precious honor is: "*Mieux vault tresor d'onneur que d'or*"—"Better wealth of honor than wealth of gold", no. 1295 (*Proverbes*, 2007 [1925]: 47). In this respect, it is quite telling that in Old French, "honor" has, in addition to its symbolic dimension, a very concrete meaning; indeed, the word can designate the office delegated by an overlord to his vassal, and in particular the land granted in fief.
4 Before going any further, it is perhaps worth recalling that honor and shame are defined by an intrinsic duality, which covers "both a subjective feeling and an objective social fact" (Boquet, 2019: 47). Hence, honor is simultaneously "the value that a person has in her own eyes but […] also what she is worth in the

eyes of those who make up her society" (Pitt-Rivers, 1977). As for shame, it refers to "a situation of dishonor, of humiliation resulting from the transgression of a norm produced by a social group," as well as to "the [distressing, painful] emotion that comes from the person's awareness of the transgression, whether it be actual or only dreaded" (Boquet, 2019: 7–8). For the purposes of this essay, I will use the term "shame" in its broad meaning of "act of humiliation" and "emotion." Whenever I refer only to the act of shaming someone, I will use the word "humiliation," and whenever referring solely to the emotion, the expression "feeling of shame."

5 Initially formalized by Ruth Benedict—with the intention of applying it solely to the twentieth century's Japanese and American affective cultures in order to pinpoint "patterns of culture"—the antithetical binary shame culture/guilt culture was later reclaimed by a whole historiographic trend, so as to be extended to other periods and designed as an anthropological paradigm used to single out a society as a whole. Shame-oriented societies would base the social existence of the individual on the (external) judgment of the community, where shame would be considered as a social sanction; guilt-oriented societies would be based on an internalized judgment, which would make shame a valuable instrument for the construction of individual responsibility and consciousness.

6 "The feudal society and the entire medieval world are so clearly part of the 'shame culture' that it seems idle to dwell on it" (Zink, 2017: 34–35).

7 It "takes shape around two quite distinct polarities" since it is as much "related to the morality of honour […], to reputation […] and to their opposites […]", as it is "to sin, to repentance and to contrition, to penance and admission"; it is thus, in short, caught up in a double dynamic, feudal and religious (Sère and Wettlaufer, 2013: XXXII).

8 Emerging towards the end of the eleventh century and declining during the fifteenth, it consists of a long verse poem, akin to Ancient epic poems. It features noble, heroic characters, and recounts past feats and warlike exploits, as a way to unite the community.

9 From the twelfth century onwards, romance gradually developed into a literary genre. Highly disparate, it started in a versified form before being superseded by prose. It is marked by various ideologies, especially the courtly culture.

10 Produced between the twelfth and the fifteenth centuries, fabliaux are defined as comical, sometimes satirical short "tales in verse giving rise to laughter" (Bédier, 1893) intended for an aristocratic public, but depicting a more prosaic reality and giving more room to merchants, craftsmen, clergymen, and *vilains* (peasants) than to nobles.

11 This time period, specifically the turn of the twelfth and thirteenth centuries, is impacted by an upheaval in frames of thought and has proven extremely insightful for studying the uses made of the notions of honor and shame.

12 Dated from the very end of the eleventh century, this epic poem reaches its peak in the episode of the Battle of Roncevaux: the rearguard of Charlemagne's Christian army falls into an ambush set by the Saracens, their Pagan enemies. They were betrayed by Ganelon because of his deep resentment against Roland, the emperor's nephew. Fighting heroically, Roland and his companions sacrifice their lives at the service of Charlemagne's honor and glory.

13 The proverb is actually never quoted as such, but loses some of its lexical or syntactic traits: it is used in a way that comes under the category of "integration" (more often than not, it is incorporated in a direct speech; sometimes, in the narrative), in the form of a "proverbial afterthought," a "proverbial core" or a "proverbial expression" (Schulze-Busacker, 1985: 167–173).

14 That is not to say peasants can never show honor (Gauvard, 2015a). But in addition to being underrepresented in the epic corpus, they rarely distinguish themselves in dignity, let alone in heroism.

15 The highly symbolic meaning of Roland's death keeps fueling the debate about its either profane or sacred interpretation. However, while the text "[indeed] prompts one to equate the emperor's service with the service of God", the fact remains that "the chivalry in the chanson is primarily an instrument in the service of imperial power and the empire's glory, even if a religious atmosphere surrounds it" (Boutet, 2019: 343, 347). Thus, it seems fair to say that Roland's self-abnegation is mainly an illustration of a feudal conception of honor rather than a religious one.
16 "Death is a sign of otherness and it plays a part, in the great sharing always renewed, between the same and the other: it is a distinctive feature, i.e. 'tell me how you die and I'll tell you who you are.' […] It operates as a discriminating trait" (Hartog, 2001 [1980]: 229).
17 Traditionally, the feminine performance of honor is regarded as a kind of passivity, of withdrawal into the interiority that consists in preserving one's sexual purity, while the masculine performance is linked to a more active behavior of projection towards the outside (Pitt-Rivers, 1977).
18 The "betrayal of the lady" (*Le Roman d'Énéas*: v. 1580, pp. 260–261).
19 "Debauchery" (*Le Roman d'Énéas*: v. 1584, pp. 260–261).
20 "*Quant ne m'avra cist a moillier, / Irai ge donques mes oroier / Ças dunt ne voil nul a seignor? / Ferai ge dont tel desenor? / Quant il voltrent, ge ne deignai, / Or de rechief les proierai? / Nel ferai, voir, mialz voil morir, / Quant autrement ne puis garir*" ("Since this one will not have me as his wife, shall I then go and pray to those I did not want as husbands? Shall I then commit such a shameful deed? When they wanted me, I despised them. Now, would I solicit them again? No, in truth I would rather die, for I cannot get away with it," *Le Roman d'Énéas*: v. 2009–2016, pp. 282–285).
21 On the concept of "woman of honor" understood as a masculinization of female honor, see Pitt-Rivers (1977); Gauvard (2001); Boquet (2019: 50–51 and 237).
22 "May God never have mercy on me, if it is true that any sense of pride dictates my words and if I would not rather die with honor than live in shame!" (*Le Chevalier de la Charrette*: v. 1118–1121, pp. 128–129).
23 "I do not have such a fear of my death that I would not rather suffer and endure death in honor than live in shame and perjure myself" (*Le Conte du Graal*: v. 6105–6108, pp. 434–435).
24 "Yes, I am ashamed of it, I am in so much pain that I would die—that is all I want—for having waited so long here!" (*Le Chevalier de la Charrette*: v. 1115–1117, pp. 126–129).
25 The size of this chapter prevents me from detailing them, but I present them in my Ph.D. dissertation which is currently still a work in progress: "'*Mar en ot honte*': Representing shame in French literature of the 12th and 13th centuries" (working title).
26 French poet Clément Marot (1496–1544) is usually considered to be the author of this one-liner. See *Dictionnaire universel, contenant généralement tous les mots françois, tant vieux que modernes, et les termes des sciences et des arts* (1727), entry "Fi."
27 "Who is deceived or beaten is belittled; who deceives and strikes, i.e. who coerces, is valued. […] Thus, […] fabliaux confront neither the reader nor their characters with a 'vertical', traditional scale of values. In a purely 'horizontal' project, they advocate not the fact of outdoing oneself, but practical superiority through violence: rather than adversity, it is the adversary that must be defeated, in a relativistic morality. The hero qualifies himself as such not because he supports well-established, absolute values which are aiming at an ideal, but because of his emerging victorious from the confrontation. Success constitutes the reference value" (Roguet, 1994: 458). This is why it was long thought that fabliaux

fitted in with "amoralism," according to the "materialist vein" at work in most of these laughing tales (Ménard, 1983: 141).
28 "The ludicrous nature of the situations [...] stems from the authors' obvious eagerness to make the anguish that assails every man when facing death disappear. Behind laughter, beneath laughter, there is a whole breeding ground of obscurely buried, temporarily abolished pain" (Ménard, 1983: 220).
29 "*Quant li prestres se sent blecié, / Lors si s'en est tornez fuiant*" ("When the priest realized he was injured, he ran away," in "*Du Prestre crucefié*": 167).
30 Here, "face" means the positive social value that someone claims through their actions, gestures, attitudes. It has much to do with the concepts of self-image and social representation. See Goffman (1967).
31 "Given the number of fabliaux based on the pattern of counter-ruse, one might even wonder if fabliaux might not be a genre against ruse rather than a genre of ruse, after all" (Garnier, 2019: 256).
32 About the difference between diegesis and narrative, see Genette (1972).
33 "*Tantost a sa voie tenue / li chevaliers que il n'i monte. / Mar le fist et mar en ot honte, / que maintenant sus ne sailli, / qu'il s'an tendra por mal bailli! / Mes Reisons, qui d'Amors se part, / li dit que del monter se gart, / si le chastie et si l'anseigne / que rien ne face ne anpreigne / dom il ait honte ne reproche.*" ("At the time, the knight went on his way, without getting on [the cart]. What a misfortune for him, what a misfortune indeed to be ashamed of hopping on at once, because one day he will suffer greatly for it! But Reason who opposes Love tells him not to go up there. She advises him and she recommends him to do nothing, to undertake nothing that could bring shame and reproach upon him.", *Le Chevalier de la Charrette*: v. 360–369, p. 88–89).
34 "Chrétien's text stresses quite explicitly the incompatibility of different value systems. They are often in competition with each other: Reason (and chivalric honor) demands one course of action, Love another. Even within a single system, different values may create incompatible choices" (Bruckner, 1986: 172).
35 "In the 12th century, a revolution of sorts in theology and philosophy took place. At the very moment when the West was moving from a shame culture to a guilt culture, the emphasis was put on individual responsibility and subjectivity," thus on a reflection on fault and sin which are seen as the real causes of shame, as opposed to honor (Payen, 1979).
36 The size of this chapter does not permit detailed explanation of this. Let me simply point out that fabliaux were produced over the entire time period, and that guilt then took a very small place in them (Eaton, 2000). Also, from the middle of the thirteenth century onwards, there was "a return to an ideal that can be described as feudal-courtly" in some epic and romance works, while the great cycles in prose seemed to mark narrative literature with a discourse focusing on sin, guilt, and more generally the evangelical and penitential model (Boutet, 2011: 353). See also footnote 6; Gauvard, 1991.
37 Such an observation is moreover in line with many historians' conclusions: while noticing a paradigm shift at the turn of the twelfth and thirteenth centuries—as the Church gave a much more important place to sin, guilt and the ritual of confession—they do not detect either the evolution of a shame culture towards a guilt culture, or its integration into one or the other. This is why some of these historians question the relevance of the very idea of a shame or a guilt culture (Boquet, 2019).
38 It is a "heuristic tool that helps to better understand [...] moments of crisis in time. [...] Focus is first on [...] the forms or ways of linking together the universal categories or forms that are the past, present and future" (Hartog, 2003: 27).

39 Here, "temporal" must not be understood as "earthly" (as opposed to "spiritual") but as what takes place within time (as opposed to what seems timeless). Temporary and temporal here match up with a conflict between ahistorical and historical.

40 As it is, *Le Prêtre teint* depicts a priest who wishes to seduce the wife of the burgher Picon. When the latter discovers the affair, he prepares to castrate his rival at the end of the fabliau: *"li prestre a la coille empoignïe, / et vet fuiant aval la rue – / et dant Picon aprés li hue. / Dant Picons ne demandoit el / mes que du prestre fust vengié: / or est de li bien estrangié!"* ("the priest grabs his balls and runs off into the street; and he is booed off by Master Picon. Finally, he takes refuge in his house. Master Picon asked for nothing more than to take revenge on the priest: he well got rid of him!" (in *Le Prêtre teint*: v. 435–448, p. 295). The very last image of this churchman ingrained in the reader's mind is his near-castration—from which he could only escape by grabbing his genitals—and his shameful getaway under the booing of his persecutor. No matter how the priest succeeded in taking shelter within the walls of his house, it does not change anything: the touch (bodily lower stratum)/sight (the priest fleeing the scene)/hearing (Picon is booed) triptych condemns the character. The fact that he feels the need to hide in his house only shows that he wishes to shield himself from prying eyes and confirms his shame. And since the fabliau ends there, the character's condemnation to live in this state of shame is somewhat indefinite and, as a result, of a potentially unlimited duration.

41 *"Drois empereres, par le cors saint Amant, / servi vos ai par mes armes portant; / ne m'en donnastes le montant d'un bezant. / Viax de ma terre car me rendez le gant, / si con la tint mes pere(s) au cors vaillant"* ("My fair emperor, on Saint Armand's relics, I served you with my arms, but as a reward you gave me nothing. At least give me back, by the gift of your glove, the land that belonged to my valiant father" (*Raoul de Cambrai*: v. 506–510, pp. 66–67).

42 *"l'onnor del pere, ce sevent li auqant, / doit tot par droit revenir a l'esfant. / [...] me blasmeroient li petit et li grant / se je plus voie ma honte conqerant / qe ma terre voie autre home tenant"* ("the father's fief must rightfully be passed down to his son, it is well known. [...] The nobles and the commoners would also blame me were I to aggravate my shame by accepting that someone else owned my fief") (*id.*: v. 525–530, pp. 66–67).

Sources

Chrétien de Troyes (2006). *Le Chevalier de la Charrette*, ed. Catherine Croizy-Naquet, Paris, Honoré Champion.

Chrétien de Troyes (1990). *Le Conte du Graal*, ed. Charles Méla, Paris, Librairie Générale Française/Le Livre de Poche.

Chrétien de Troyes (1994). *Œuvres completes*, ed. Daniel Poirion, Paris, Gallimard.

Dictionnaire universel, contenant généralement tous les mots françois, tant vieux que modernes, et les termes des sciences et des arts (1727). Ed. Antoine Furetière, II, La Haye, Pierre Husson.

Du Prestre crucefié (1998). In *Fabliaux du Moyen Âge*, ed. Jean Dufournet, Paris, GF Flammarion, 162–167.

Gautier Le Leu (1992). *Le Prêtre teint* in *Fabliaux érotiques: Textes de jongleurs des XIIe et XIIIe siècles*, ed. Luciano Rossi, Paris, Librairie Générale Française/Le Livre de Poche, 266–295.

Jouglet (1983–1998). In *Nouveau Recueil Complet des Fabliaux (NRCF)*, ed. Willem Noomen et Nico van den Boogard, Assen, Van Gorcum (10 vols.), 185–214.

La Chanson de Roland (2003 [1971]). Ed. Cesare Segre, translation Madeleine Tyssens, Genève, Droz.

Le Couronnement de Louis (2013). *Chanson de geste du XIIe siècle*, ed. Ernest Langlois, Paris, Honoré Champion.

Le Roman d'Énéas (2018). Eds. Wilfrid Besnardeau and Francine Mora-Lebrun, Paris, Honoré Champion.

Proverbes français antérieurs au XVe siècle (2007 [1925]). Ed. Joseph Morawski, Paris, Honoré Champion.

Raoul de Cambrai (1996*)*. *Chanson de geste du XIIe siècle*, ed. Sarah Kay and William Kibler, Paris, Librairie Générale Française/Le Livre de Poche.

References

Alexandre-Bidon, D. & Lorcin, M.-Th. (2003). *Le Quotidien au temps des fabliaux*, Paris, Picard.

Bédier, J. (1893). *Les Fabliaux: Étude de littérature populaire et d'histoire littéraire du Moyen Âge*, Paris, Honoré Champion.

Benedict, R. (1946). *The Chrysanthemum and the Sword*, Boston, Houghton Mifflin.

Bonansea, M. (2018). "Le 'futur passé': récit de guerre épique et expérience du temps," in *Les Temps épiques: Structuration, modes d'expression et fonction de la temporalité dans l'épopée*, eds. Claudine Le Blanc and Jean-Pierre Martin, Publications numériques du REARE, 15 November: http://publis-shs.univ-rouen.fr/reare/index.php?id=345.

Boquet, D. (2008). "Introduction. La vergogne historique: éthique d'une émotion sociale," in *Histoire de la vergogne, Rives nord-méditerranéennes* [Online], 31: http://rives.revues.org/2753.

Boquet, D. (2019). Sancta verecundia: Conceptions et usages de la honte dans l'hagiographie féminine au XIIIe siècle, Ph.D. thesis.

Boutet, D. (1985). *Les Fabliaux*, Paris, PUF.

Boutet, D. (2019). "Le sens de la mort de Roland dans la littérature des XIIe et XIIIe siècles (*Chanson de Roland, Chronique de Turpin, Chronique rimée de Philippe Mousket*)," in *L'Épique au Moyen Âge: D'une poétique de l'Histoire à l'historiographie*, Paris, Honoré Champion, 339–353 (1st publication in Chevalerie et christianisme aux XIIe et XIIIe siècles, eds. Martin Aurell and Catalina Gîrbea, Rennes, PUR, 2011, 257–269).

Bruckner, M.T. (1986). "An Interpreter's Dilemma: Why Are There So Many Interpretations of Chrétien's Chevalier de la Charrette?," *Romance Philology*, XL, 2, 159–180.

Calin, W.C. (1974). "*Raoul de Cambrai*: un univers en decomposition," in *Actes du VIe Congrès de la Société Rencesvals*, Aix-en-Provence, CUER MA, 427–438.

Creighton, M.R. (1990). "*Revisiting Shame and Guilt Cultures: A Forty-Year Pilgrimage*," *Ethos*, 18, 3, 279–307.

Elias, N. (1939). *Über den Prozeß der Zivilisation*, Basel, Verlag Haus zum Falken.

Garnier, N. (2019). Dynamiques du récit comique bref: Le Roman de Renart et les fabliaux, Ph.D. thesis.

Gauvard, C. (1991). *"De Grace especial": Crime, État et société en France à la fin du Moyen Âge*, Paris, Publications de la Sorbonne.

Gauvard, C. (2001). "Honneur de femme et femme d'honneur en France à la fin du Moyen Âge," *Francia*, 28, 1, 159–191.

Gauvard, C. (2015a). "*Fama* explicite et *fama* implicite: Les difficultés de l'historien face à l'honneur des petites gens aux derniers siècles du Moyen Âge," in *La Légitimité implicite*, ed. Jean-Philippe Genet, Paris/Rome, Éditions de la Sorbonne/ École française de Rome, 39–55.

Gauvard, C. (2015b). "Les représentations au Moyen Âge: quelques pistes de réflexion," in *Sociétés & Représentations*, 2 (40), 277–287.

Genette, G. (1972). *Figures III*, Paris, Éditions du Seuil.

Goffman, E. (1967). *Interaction Ritual: Essays on Face-to-Face Behavior*, London, Penguin Press.

Hartog, F. (2001 [1980]). *Le Miroir d'Hérodote: Essai sur la représentation de l'autre*, Paris, Gallimard.

Hartog, F. (2003). *Régimes d'historicité: Présentisme et expériences du temps*, Paris, Éditions du Seuil.

Ménard, Ph. (1983). *Les Fabliaux: Contes à rire du Moyen Âge*, Paris, Presses universitaires de France.

Payen, J.-Ch. (1979). "Pour en finir avec le diable médiéval ou pourquoi poètes et théologiens du Moyen Âge ont-ils scrupule à croire au démon?," in *Le Diable du Moyen Âge: Doctrine, problèmes moraux, représentations, Senefiance*, 6, Aix-en-Provence, Presses universitaires de Provence, 401–425: https://books.openedition.org/pup/2675.

Pitt-Rivers, J. (1977). *The Fate of Shechem or The Politics of Sex: Essays in the Anthropology of the Mediterranean*, Cambridge, Cambridge University Press.

Roguet, Y. (1994). "La violence comique des fabliaux", in *La Violence dans le monde médiéval, Senefiance*, 36, Aix-en-Provence, *Presses universitaires de Provence*, 455–458.

Schulze-Busacker, E. (1985). *Proverbes et expressions proverbiales dans la littérature narrative du Moyen Âge français: Recueil et analyse*, Paris, Honoré Champion.

Sère, B. and Wettlaufer, J. (2013). *Shame between punishment and penance. The social usages of shame in the Middle Ages and Early Modern Times*, International Conference, Paris, 21–23 October 2010, Micrologus' Library, 54, Firenze, SISMEL— Edizioni del Galluzzo.

Suard, F. (2006). "La *Chanson de Roland* comme modèle épique," *Olifant*, 25, 401–418.

Wehner Eaton, E. (2000). Shame Culture or Guilt Culture: The Evidence of the Medieval French Fabliaux, Université de Toronto, Ph.D. thesis.

Zink, M. (1999). "Fabliau," in *Dictionnaire du Moyen Âge*, eds. Claude Gauvard, Alain de Libera, and Michel Zink, Paris, PUF.

Zink, M. (2017). *L'Humiliation, le Moyen Âge et nous*, Paris, Albin Michel.

7 The Dynamics of Gender-Specific Honor and Shame in the Middle Ages
The *Nibelungenlied* as Example

Jutta Eming

Introduction

The culture and literature of the Middle Ages offer fertile ground for investigating questions concerning historical change in the social connotations of honor and shame. Unlike the present, during the pre-modern era, honor was a guiding principle in Western cultures for the organization of social relations, political relationships and social communication as well as for the construction of personal identity.[1] Questions as to which behaviors in social contexts were either conducive to one's honor, or in violation of it, were discussed in medieval literary texts and played out in ever new exemplary situations.

Shame plays a less central role in medieval literature than honor, but it is undoubtedly also one of the important emotions that regulate and internalize standards of appropriate social behavior. Since Norbert Elias's *Theory of Civilization*, shame has been seen to be a socio-historically acquired emotion, for which the great feudal courts of the Middle Ages played a decisive role in providing training (Elias, 1981). Today, however, shame is considered to be a basic emotion that is acquired very early by humans, which fundamentally contradicts Elias's assumptions. Nonetheless, it is still considered a social emotion par excellence; an "emotion related to social rules" (Heller, 1981: 111). The "self-bonding" of an individual to social norms, as expressed by the shame emotion (Landweer, 1999: 172), was also a prerequisite in medieval culture. In medieval texts, shame regimes as well as concepts of honor provide excellent insights into changing historical forms of social self-understanding (Eming, 2006).

Honor and shame are considered to be complementary in medieval studies just as frequently (Haferland, 1988: 241–249; Krause, 2006: 55–57; Althoff, 2012: 57) as they are in emotion research (Frevert, 2013: 17–43). The latter, however, also regards pride to be the emotional counterpart of shame (Ben Ze'ev, 2000: 509–529): "a reference to the self" is equally essential for both shame and pride (Ben Ze'ev, 2000: 510). Honor was frequently associated with an *Ehrgefühl* (sense of honor or pride) and a kind of code that the noble society of the Middle Ages developed in relation to its members,

DOI: 10.4324/9781003022916-10

which they would have internalized in the long term (Ehrismann, 1995: 66). Its role in medieval culture and literature is now considered to be primarily a pattern of action and attribution. This was outwardly asserted and became especially clear to its constituents when conflicts arose (Haubrichs, 1996: 43). One could strive to achieve honor, but it was fundamentally a "fortunate gift from God" (Ehrismann, 1995: 66) like noble birth itself.

Revealing insights into the historical understanding of honor may be attained by linking it not only to the issue of shame but also to gender. As Ruth Mazo Karras noted some time ago, "'Honor' in the Middle Ages was a heavily gendered concept. It could have a fairly simple, class-based meaning: the quality of being a member of the aristocracy [...], when applied to women, it referred almost exclusively to sexual behavior. An honorable woman was one who maintained her chastity, either as a virgin or as faithful wife" (Karras, 2003: 60). Under these circumstances, it has also been said that women were "condemned to passivity" with regard to their honor (Ehrismann, 1995: 68).

In the famous love potion episode in Gottfried von Straßburg's *Tristan*, this situation became especially pronounced when the protagonists' adultery was introduced. While the two felt the effects of the potion and with it their incipient love, they put up resistance, for Isolde was Marke's bride, and it was Tristan's duty to bring her to him. In this dilemma, the male protagonist's honor was foremost, while the female character felt mostly shame (Eming, 2015: 77–79). Can we generalize such an attribution of honor to the male character and shame to the female character? How do corresponding assignments of shame and honor in medieval works of poetry play out with respect to the issue of gender?

These relationships are indeed complex and worthy of further intensive investigation. As an example, I would like to use the *Nibelungenlied*, a text that has been researched in medieval studies like few others. It is highly relevant to the subject and especially germane to questions of honor. All conflicts in the *Nibelungenlied* and its much-described final downfall scenario ("endgame") are organized around questions of honor. The spiral of violence is ignited by the revenge Queen Kriemhild takes on Hagen, the murderer of her husband Siegfried. However, this seemingly unambiguous reprisal grew out of a multitude of preceding conflicts and can only be understood in light of them. These conflicts primarily concern differences in rank between two noblemen and the honorary privileges attached to them— but not their gender. It is noteworthy, however, that the conflict between the two main female characters, which involves their husbands, is played out in a highly personalized manner and contoured in gender-specific terms.

Conventions of Gender-Specific Attributions of Honor and Shame in the *Nibelungenlied*

It is difficult to evaluate questions about the role of honor and shame in medieval literature without considering the poem's genre. The *Nibelungenlied* (developed around 1200 from earlier, partially oral narrative traditions) is in this respect a hybrid form. It is broadly classified as a heroic epic, but at the same time it exhibits central elements of the courtly novel, for example through the love theme. Constituents of honor in heroic epics have recently been compiled by Elisabeth Lienert (Lienert, 2019). She emphasizes that especially in the *Nibelungenlied*, *êre* is something external (Lienert, 2019: 172, 176). Honor is identical to the prestige one enjoys in feudal court culture, and it manifests itself accordingly in representative acts (Lienert, 2019: 173) that are often gender-independent. The feudal courtly virtue of *milte* (generosity), for instance, generates *êre* and is practiced by female and male figures alike. The affirmation and negation of honor as power and glory in feudal realms provide a framework for the *Nibelungenlied* (Lienert, 2019: 173). Men's rank, power, and honor, however, are stereotypically correlated with heroic deeds and violence. While even murder can enhance the honor of male characters, as in the case of Hagen (Lienert, 2003: 6), this does not apply to female characters to the same degree.

Even at first glance, the *Nibelungenlied* reveals what a wealth of connotations the lexeme *êre* invokes, and the diverse aspects of the narrative world it can denote. In this context, there are also attributions to gender in different contexts and semantic variants. The first example concerns the tale's heroine, Kriemhild, with whom the poem begins:

> *In disen hôhen êren troumte Kriemhilde / wie sie zuge einen valken* (11,13f.)[2]
> "Living in such magnificence, Kriemhild dreamt she reared a falcon."[3]

This phrase exemplifies a convention described by Otfried Ehrismann in which *êre* in a metonymic usage refers to the magnificence of noble life (Ehrismann, 1995: 69). With regard to the construction of female honor in the feudal noble world, it should be noted that Kriemhild is afforded this status-appropriate power and its resulting prestige by her brothers (Müller, 2007a: 207), who all have the status of kings. The choice of whom she marries, i.e. Siegfried, is also made based on her status:

> *sît wart si mit êren eins vil küenen recken wîp* (16, 4).
> "Accordingly, she later was wed to a very brave warrior."

Siegfried's wooing of women at his parents' court had already been conducted honorably; consequently, an intervening love would have also been honorable:

> *di trûten wol mit êren des küenen Sîvrides lîp* (24, 4).
> "They would have done themselves high honor in loving fearless Siegfried."

Since the era of Old High German, i.e., before the height of courtly culture, honor was also attributed to God (Seidl, 2015, 52):

> *Got man dô ze êren eine messe sanc* (31, 1).
> "Mass was sung to the glory of God."

And it was always an instrument of (self-)reassurance about one's position in society:

> *dar umb ich niht vergezzen mac der êren mîn* (148, 3).
> "This will not let me forget my honor."

Despite the characteristic formality and external effect of honor, its self-reference (or its subjective side, Krause, 2006) must always be taken into consideration as well. These are inseparable. Honor thus denotes the appropriately high standard of living of noble persons, the elaborate rituals attached to it, a respectful personal devotion, reverence to God, and the individual sensibilities of a man or woman of status.

Shame, as a correlative of honor, plays a much smaller role in the heroic epic than in the courtly novel (Mecklenburg, 2009: 74). However, the *Nibelungenlied* also exhibits many traits of courtly storytelling. While emotions such as anger and grief are prominent in the *Nibelungenlied*, there is also *vreude*, which characterizes life at court in a special way. Shame is also explicitly mentioned. What, then, is its relation to honor? In certain contexts, the Middle High German word *scham* can refer to a "sense of honor," meaning the feeling that one's honor has been violated. Clearly, however, *scham* is less correlative to *êre* than *schande*; disgrace is a reason for one to feel ashamed. "Shame is the appropriate reaction to disgrace; disgrace, however, is the antonym of honor" (Müller, 2012: 69). Gestures of shame can also be publicly expressed to compensate for a loss of honor (Althoff, 2012: 57). In part, honor is understood to be a sign of social exclusivity, which means some people are fundamentally incapable of having it, such as a peasant (cf. Dinzelbacher, 2015). But those who have lost honor or do not display it appropriately have *schande* (a feeling of disgrace) or, indeed, *scham* (shame). This is portrayed in many places in the *Nibelungenlied*, for example, after success in battle:

> Dâ kômen die gesunden, die wunden tâten sam,
> si mohten grüezen hœren von friuwenden âne scham (242,1f.)

> "And there came the unscathed, together with the wounded. They could hear their friends' welcome without shame."

To a degree, gender-specific regimes of shame in the *Nibelungenlied* are (stereo)typical in that they follow widespread social norms. We are informed that Kriemhild feels "shame" at her wedding to Siegfried (612, 1); the reason being the wedding itself. This apparently points to the expectation that young women (Frevert, 2013; differentiated Schnell, 2002: 305–318) would feel shame regarding situations related to sexuality, such as the wedding night. During all her preceding encounters with Siegfried, there is no mention of shame. Because he becomes *varwe rôt* (611, 1) during his marriage with Kriemhild, Siegfried also reveals at least some degree of inner tension. Whether this is truly a matter of shame is not clear from his body language. Other examples (153, such as when the Burgundians ask him for support in battle) show that these are polyvalent in his physicality. Corporeal reactions to feelings of shame as well as honor violations are frequently featured (Dinzelbacher, 2015: 106–109).

However, as often as especially the lexeme *êre* is used in the *Nibelungenlied*, the instances in which it is negotiated extend even farther beyond such explicit mentions. I am of the opinion that where, for example, "tears and mourning" are referred to, it is possible to establish a "dingfest" (solid) association to honor (Lienert, 2019: 181). In the *Nibelungenlied*, the narrative employs a noticeable cluster of the same emotion words (in the case of honor and mourning, one speaks rather of conditions). However, this does not imply stereotyping. The corresponding words *zorn, vreude, schame*, etc. are not only applicable to a wide range of emotional states, but also impart their own semantic nuances to the respective contexts, i.e. they are highly flexible. It is similar with the expression of body language (turning pale or red, crying). Emotions cannot be simply substituted for one another. It is part of their dynamics, however, that they refer to each other, compensate for each other (Krause, 2006: 51), and even mask each other (Wurmser, 1998). Shame, for example, is often replaced by anger. The relationship between honor and shame/disgrace itself is similarly dynamic. While a sense of shame can indicate a loss of honor, it can also engender a sense of honor, as in the case of female shame during marriage (see above).

The Antagonism between Kriemhild and Brünhild

The *Nibelungenlied* differs from most other Middle High German novels and heroic epics in that two "strong" women take center stage concurrently (Müller, 2015: 136), and at first glance they even appropriate male behavioral patterns. Kriemhild, for example, takes revenge on her husband's murderer, while Brünhild possesses the explicitly masculine quality of physical strength, which the text accentuates (Schausten, 1999: 36). This could give the impression that they are autonomous characters, but this is precisely not the case.

Instead, the *Nibelungenlied* reveals a patriarchal order within which the honor of the males seems to be challenged by an extraordinarily strong and violent woman (Brünhild) (Lienert, 2003: 8). The fact that her strength is fundamentally measured against that of men establishes her exceptionality (Renz, 2012: 85–94). However, it is all the more significant that this woman can be overpowered by a combination of male collusion, strength, and cunning (Michaelis, 2011: 209–215). Brünhild's strength tellingly disappears in the course of her wedding night, which is sometimes smugly commented on by the narrator and sometimes described with drastic linguistic violence

(Lienert, 2003: 4; Michaelis, 2011: 218). It should also be noted that Kriemhild, in taking (blood) revenge on Hagen and her brothers, claims a right for herself that contemporary legal sources do acknowledge in principle. What is unusual, however, is that a female character becomes the driving force in the extraction of revenge. Furthermore, she is also only able to carry it out after her (re)marriage to Etzel, king of the Huns (Renz, 2012: 194–197). In this respect, the *Nibelungenlied* appears as a text with experimental plot constellations that encourage a discussion of contemporary legal norms. Kriemhild and Brünhild define themselves in relation to their male counterparts, their husbands. While Kriemhild's honor is also dependent on the fact that she is the sister of a king, Brünhild's honor is exclusively tied to that of her husband (Lienert, 2003: 9). Therefore, she wants to marry only the strongest of men. For her, the highest level of violence corresponds to the highest rank (Müller, 2007b).

From an intersectional point of view, female identity, according to the self-image of noble families, is not primarily based on belonging to the gender "woman." Instead, it is about "belonging to a house and clan and having a special position within them" (Klinger, 2014: 266). Gender relations are part of a social structure that is first and foremost established among men, and according to courtly norms, the beauty of male and female bodies is not rooted in their sexual characteristics, but in their membership in the nobility. "The 'bodies that matter' to courtly lovers—the ones that cause them to fall in love—are not marked morphologically by sex. Some are merely said to be beautiful and nothing more. Where additional information is provided, it tends to be very limited, and most commonly is nothing more than red lips, rosy complexion, and general radiance" (Schultz, 2006: 26).

Just as the heroic men of the *Nibelungenlied* are capable of excessive violence, especially Siegfried and Hagen, their female counterparts, Kriemhild and Brünhild, are "excessively beautiful" (Klinger, 2014: 267).[4] In this respect, they surpass all standards of normal measure. Yet a latent competition between the two women is alluded to early in the text. When Brünhild and Kriemhild meet each other for the first time at court, they treat each other in a befittingly friendly and deferential manner. At the same time, however, their beauty is secretly judged and compared by the men of the court. These "look-overs" are certainly about "masculine" regard for "feminine bodies" (Klinger, 2014: 275): "*Vrouwen schouwen* 'looking at the ladies' is one of the pleasures that the court offers to men" (Schultz, 2006: 38). This does not change the fact that a body under scrutiny is fundamentally a member of the nobility. Although some Middle High German poems also refer to females gazing at male bodies, they lack the dimension of comparative appraisal: "Such aggressive, possessive viewing is elicited by the sight of a woman, not of a man" (Schultz, 2006: 38). From the male viewings of Kriemhild and Brünhild, it is initially said that both are incomparably beautiful. But then [...] *sprâchen dâ di wîsen, die heten iz baz gesehen, / man möhte Kriemhilden vor vroun Brünhilden jehen* (590, 3f.): "Those who had looked more discerningly declared Kriemhild to have the advantage." Kriemhild deserves precedence. However, it is possible that there is only a superficial connection to her beauty, and it is instead an expression of her noble rank, which is derived from being the wife of Siegfried with his singular strength.

It is precisely from the "heroic" strength of Siegfried and his position as sovereign ruler that the conflict continued to develop. Kriemhild and all others at her brothers' court were aware of Siegfried's true status. But in the course of Gunther's courtship, Brünhild was told that Siegfried had come to her court as a vassal of Gunther. What neither woman knew was that it was Siegfried, with his invisible cloak, who arranged for Kriemhild's brother, King Gunther, to overcome the strong Queen Brünhild, so that he himself could marry Kriemhild. This "barter" had been agreed between them before the courtship of Brünhild. Both men made it appear to Brünhild that Siegfried was only Gunther's vassal, thus lower in rank, dependent and indebted. Not just a simple deceit, it involved the question as to whether and how two more or less equal-ranking rulers in the Middle Ages could possibly conspire together. However, after Siegfried's first appearance in Worms at the court of King Gunther and his brothers, the men had found a way of dealing with the difficulty of linking courtship, hospitality and a willingness to use violence (Siegfried supported the Worms court in the Saxon War) (according to Müller, 1974; Czerwinski, 1979). Because the women were not included in the agreement, however, the conflict would soon become explosive.

Tears of Shame

It was a fundamental function of medieval courtly ceremony to precisely characterize differences in rank and hierarchies of estates. Seating arrangements at table, the order of precedence upon entering and exiting rooms and buildings, and in general one's "position in space" (Dinzelbacher, 2015: 104), substantiated the level of honor of those involved. This was the reason for many episodes in medieval literature to be concerned with whether and how rituals and unwritten laws were observed or violated. The corresponding evaluations of story lines were then depicted with expressive manifestations of emotion. This is also what happened in the *Nibelungenlied* in a revealing narrative sequence during the double wedding of Kriemhild with Siegfried and Brünhild with Gunther at the court of Worms.

From Brünhild's perspective, it was inappropriate for Kriemhild, as Siegfried's bride, to take a seat at the table next to her and King Gunther during the wedding celebration. For neither the wife of a vassal nor the vassal himself had any right to dine at the same table as the ruler. At the same time, it was an even more grievous problem that Kriemhild, the sister of King Gunther, had not married according to her rank. Brünhild's reaction to this situation is revealing: she began to weep, although the reason for her tears was not immediately clear. Tears are a polyvalent expression of emotion that are both culturally and historically variable, and whose causes cannot be generalized. When asked the reason why by her husband Gunter, Brünhild stated: *umb dîne swester ist mir von herzen leit. / die sihe ich nâhen sitzen dem eigenholden dîn. / daz muoz ich imer weinen, sol si alsô verderbet sîn* (617, 2–4). "My heart aches to see your sister sitting next to a vassal, and I will always have to cry because of her disgrace."

Brünhild's reaction was not due to personal dismay, or a sign of sympathy, helplessness, or bewilderment. Her tears were an expression of solidarity of rank, which was considered a typical sign of honorable chivalric behavior (Dinzelbacher, 2015: 112), and which here has been transposed to a female character. Therefore, Brünhild's solidarity with Kriemhild did not arise out of personal sympathy. Rather, it indicates that "crying can be initiated by an appraisal of one's environment" (Lutz, 1999: 147), and Brünhild's tears signaled a condition in her environment that alarmed her. In this sense, they also amounted to a "political protest" (Schausten, 1999: 41). It threatened her own honor to such a degree that she feared Kriemhild should *verderben* (see above), meaning harmed or disgraced. As she saw it, Kriemhild's disgrace was generating Brünhild's shame. The emotion would have been the reason for her weeping without having to be labeled as such. At the same time, it was about Kriemhild's loss of honor, which was also a threat to Brünhild herself that struck her to the core. She found herself at a court where the relationships of political power seemed to be out of kilter, or at the very least, opaque (see below). It is not explicitly addressed whether she also feared having possibly failed to marry the most powerful king, which up to that point had been her assumption. In any case, her tears express what Siegfried Christoph has noted about reactions to shame in the courtly novel: "The reference to shame [...] is not to point out fault, but rather to show that the characters [...] seek to avoid unnecessary peril to their own or others' honor" (Christoph, 1995: 30).

When King Gunther tried to convince her that everything was in order, Brünhild was not assuaged. Instead, she felt that a constellation in which female honor seemed inadequately protected meant that her bond with Gunther and thus her further existence were actually at stake:

> Si sprach: "mich jâmert immer ir schœne unt ouch ir zuht.
> wess ich, war ich mohte, ich hete gerne fluht,
> daz ich iu nimmer wolde geligen nâhen bî,
> irn saget mir, wâ von Kriemhilt diu Sîfrides wine sî." (629)

> "She said: 'I regret her beauty and fine breeding. If I could, I would gladly take refuge, if only I knew where, so as not to share your bed, unless you told me why Kriemhild should be Siegfried's spouse.'"

The question of whether Siegfried was a sovereign ruler or a vassal of King Gunther created an unsolvable problem. Ultimately, Gunther was unable to explain to his wife Brünhild why he gave his sister in marriage to a man of lower rank. In order to find out after all, Brünhild refused to consummate the marriage (635, 3f.). Keeping the women uninformed was unsuccessful, and over time their being disallowed this knowledge led to the downfall of the Nibelungian world (Robles, 2005: 361).[5]

Wounded Honor

Open confrontation between the two central female characters of the *Nibelungenlied* was ignited at the moment when the issue of Siegfried's rank was raised between them. The dispute reached its climax with the much-discussed, so-called "quarrel of the queens." What was it about? Brünhild believed that she held a higher rank over Kriemhild and that she should enter the cathedral first to hear mass since, according to Brünhild's husband Gunther, Kriemhild was married to one of his vassals.

Brünhild clearly stated that this was a matter of honor. The argument was then conducted in terms of honor relative to the female body. Kriemhild claimed more of it for herself than she seemed to be entitled to:

> "Du ziuhest dich ze hôhe", sprach des küniges wîp.
> "nu wil ich sehen gerne, op man den dînen lip
> habe ze solchen êren, sô man den mînen tuot."
> di vrouwen wurden beide vil sêre zornec gemuot. (823)

> "'You are getting above yourself,' replied the Queen, 'and I should like to see whether you are held in such esteem as I.' The ladies were growing very angry."

The close relationship between a person's identity and their body (= *den dînen lîp*), which Middle High German conveys, cannot be adequately reflected in the modern translation in which the simple personal pronoun (= you) is used. In context, the attribution of the emotion *zorn* is also of interest, since *zorn* is above all an emotion typical of a ruler. In medieval literature, crises were induced (and in some cases even settled again, Rosenwein, 1998) by means of a king's anger. At the same time, its extent was evaluated by means of a matching vocabulary of body language (Freienhofer, 2016). One can question with some justification whether this is a gender-specific emotion, since it is expressed by women in medieval literature primarily when they are ruling. Angry heroines can be explicitly described as unfeminine (Eming, 2015: 123–125). The attribution of this emotion to Brünhild and Kriemhild is considered unusual (Briški, 2012: 94), which perhaps indicates that their disagreement was actually about a conflict in the ranking of men. Furthermore, anger is viewed as a typical emotion for averting and transforming shame—an emotion that is also physically stressful (Eming, 2006: 207–209; Krause, 2006: 51). Therefore, this means that in the situation described here, we are witnessing a dynamic of honor and anger and thus implicitly also of shame.

Kriemhild accepts the challenge by making clear that she wants to defend her honor: *ez muoz âne schande belîben hie mîn lîp*, "I must not be put to shame" (828, 2). She strikes the heaviest blow against Brünhild when she accuses her—as she thinks, correctly—of having brought the greatest shame upon herself on her wedding night, *du hâst geschendet selbe den dînen schœnen lîp* (836, 3), "You yourself have brought shame to yourself" by having been deflowered by the "vassal" Siegfried: [...] *den dînen schœnen lîp, / den minnet êrste Sîfrit, der mîn vil lieber man* (840, 3f.), "my dear husband Siegfried was the first to enjoy your lovely body."

This astonishing assertion has the even more astounding background of Brünhild's and Gunter's first conjugal intercourse. This could only have occurred with the help of the extremely powerful Siegfried, and his assistance to Gunter from behind a cloak of invisibility. However, as expressly agreed, he only physically subdued Brünhild, but did not sleep with her. Kriemhild apparently knows enough about the incident to be able to lord it over Brünhild, even though her claim is not true. In this context, it is revealing with regard to the historicity of gender-based honor that the "quarrel of the queens" is initiated by the question of the sexual integrity of a woman, namely Brünhild, which is at the same time inextricably intertwined with her status-related identity. It is also revealing that Kriemhild herself does not seem to be bothered by her own husband's alleged transgressions, which allegedly involved a double adultery. It is not by chance that the female body is the *locus* of the negotiation of validity, but it is not a matter of sexual integrity per se. Such an act of absolution was not applicable until the bourgeois era. This is about control over accessibility to one's own body, which in principle a noble woman grants to one who is of equal rank, and that was continually the subject of "homosocial arrangements between men" (Michaelis, 2011: 217). For this, the purity of the noble female body was identified with the security of rulership (Dohmen, 2017). The reports of conflicts found in early medieval sources that related to married noble women almost always concerned their (alleged) adultery, which was generally punished by death (Haubrichs, 1996: 51).

Brünhild's reaction to Kriemhild's insulting comments mirrored her behavior during the wedding feast; she "began to weep" (840). She cried even more when Kriemhild appeared to substantiate her claim with a belt and a ring that Siegfried stole from Brünhild on their wedding night and later gave to his own wife Kriemhild as a kind of trophy (*dô den gesach vrou Brünhilt, weinen si began*, "Brunhild burst into tears when she saw it," 847, 3). Nonetheless, after being presented with this evidence, the fact that she initially "remained weeping in front of the cathedral" (Michaelis, 2011: 220) should again not be understood as helplessness, nor as an admission of defeat. Even when seen as an objective sign of the disruption of the social order (Lienert, 2019: 181), this is not an adequate interpretation of

Brünhild's tears. It obscures the subjective side of the honor violation as well as the performative and appellative character inherent in weeping. Brünhild's tears signified that a violation of honor had taken place, and she sought allies to help restore it (Briški, 2012: 91). Her weeping thus set the dynamics of shame and honor forcefully in motion. Brünhild turned to Gunther and demanded an explanation. She felt insulted and expected her husband to relieve her of the *vil grôzen schande* (very great disgrace) (851), which had arisen because Kriemhild wished to "rob me of my honor" (850) ([v]*on allen mînen êren* [...] *scheiden*). The correlation between Brünhild's honor and Brünhild's shame is evident. Siegfried also felt *scham* because of Kriemhild's *ungefüege* (lack of empathy), i.e., because of her scandalous public behavior, which reaffirmed the extent of the honor violation. For this reason, Siegfried then physically beat his wife, about which the text raises no questions (Lienert, 2003: 14).

Lienert attaches great importance to the fact that, in her view, Brünhild is explicitly not credited with any honor violation in the course of the Queen's quarrel: "An irreversible objectification of Brünhild's insult is thus avoided [without calling it a loss of honor], which potentially precludes the option of settling the conflict" (Lienert, 2019: 181). She thus joins a recent trend in scholarship to view the text's downward spiral of violence into doom as less of an inevitability than was previously thought. Today, the discussion refers to alternative possibilities in the text (Toepfer, 2012) and to varying views in evaluating plot elements (Renz, 2012: 297–330) that make clear attributions of guilt impossible.

To a great degree, however, the impression of inevitability and the pall of death is produced rhetorically with a view to the female character(s). We are told again and again from the very first stanzas that they are responsible for the death of many heroes. Even in the very first stanzas of the text, the rhyme describes Kriemhild as: [...] *ein schœne wîp. / dar umbe muosen degene vil verliesen den lîp*, "a beautiful woman, causing many knights to lose their lives" (1, 3f.). In the context of the "queens' quarrel," the responsibility is attributed to both female protagonists, for example: *daz si bî ein ander niht giengen alsam ê. / dâ von wart manigem degene sît vil sorclîchen wê*; "They no longer went together as before. In the end, many brave knights had to suffer gravely for that" (831, 3f.). Assuming a reciprocity between honor and disgrace, this joint participation of Kriemhild and Brünhild in the conflict is clearly and explicitly realized through the dynamics of honor and shame/disgrace. Brünhild demands that Gunther resolve the disgraceful situation in order to effectively save her honor. Therefore, contrary to what Lienert argues, the issue of honor can frequently be at the core of a textual passage without the term honor itself being specifically mentioned.

Whether the issue has been successfully resolved and Brünhild's disgrace has been eradicated depends fundamentally on how one gauges issues of honor (Czerwinski, 1979: 61–62). According to Lienert, it is logical for Brünhild to have Siegfried eliminated in order to fulfill "her" personal standard of marrying the strongest man. It is noteworthy that her aggressions are never directed against Gunther, but only toward Siegfried and Kriemhild (Lienert, 2003: 13). Her vexations revolve exclusively around questions of power and rank, not around the issue of possible infidelity by her husband Gunther, Siegfried, or both (Lienert, 2003: 13). Thus, even after she has been "conquered" and "normalized" (Renz, 2012: 94–109), Brünhild remains effective in the text as a particularly complex gender construction and an outstanding example of an *agonal habitus* who only accepts hierarchical power relations (Klinger, 2014: 277). She puts up resistance whenever these power relations become ambiguous (Klinger, 2014: 281).

The motivation for the act of revenge that Hagen finally executed on Brünhild's behalf is, however, like much of the text, ambiguous. It was Brünhild's tears which finally motivated Hagen to murder Siegfried just at the point when Siegfried had already publicly asked for his wife's forgiveness (870). Due to Hagen compensating for the violation of her honor, Brünhild became the first "avenger" of the *Nibelungenlied* (Lienert, 2003: 14).

Assigning Honor and Narrating

The *Nibelungenlied* tells of perhaps the best-known conflict concerning honor in German literature, one with catastrophic consequences. While this was primarily about the honor of men, a (related or married) woman was also fully capable of being involved in this issue by claiming honor for herself, representing it to the outside world and defending it. Thus, in medieval literature, a woman was less condemned to "passivity" (see above) than is sometimes stated. When her honor was threatened, a cluster of different emotions became virulent, which could include shame, anger, and *leit* (suffering). These additional emotions make it clear that honor itself need not always be explicitly mentioned when questions of honor are part of the narrative. Men also felt shame, especially in the context of conflicts concerning honor (Siegfried). Apart from a few gender-specific attributions such as shame before the wedding night (Kriemhild), no gender-specific qualities of shame can be observed. However, the exercise of violence did not affect men's honor anywhere near as much as it did the honor of women.

Nevertheless, what makes the conflict surrounding honor in the *Nibelungenlied* exceptional in gender-specific terms is the vehemence with which the two women defend their honor (which is derived from the honor of their husbands). This is further marked by their insistence on the importance of rank and power (based on the hierarchy between their husbands), and the extent to which they see themselves injured and subsequently exact revenge. As is well known, Kriemhild's alleged "transformation" from gentle royal sister to *vâlandinne*, devil-woman, especially represents perhaps the greatest peculiarity in this difficult text (Müller, 2007a: XI–XV). On the other hand, in his research Jan-Dirk Müller in particular has worked out the nature of the consistencies and inevitabilities that underlie Kriemhild's actions as well as those of the other characters (Müller, 2007a). That which distinguished both Kriemhild and Brünhild in equal measure, however, was their stubbornness and the unconditional defense of their positions, despite all male attempts at deception, compensation, and appeasement. And this was even in the face of male violence. Thus, on the one hand, they exhibited exemplary behavior with regard to asserting their right to maintain their honor in medieval society and, on the other hand, they behaved transgressively. There are probably few literary conflicts which involve such a relentless rejection of shame as well as an energetic defense of honor as that in the *Nibelungenlied*. There are even fewer with female protagonists.

Notably, there is yet another fact that stands out. Among the men involved, especially King Gunther and his supposed vassal Siegfried, their purported disparity in status never developed into a lasting problem.[6] Siegfried was not abashed to conceal his status and to appear as Gunther's vassal. Conversely, Gunther did not feel that his reputation or honor were threatened by Siegfried's great strength. Through the agreed "barter," which amounted to "traffic in women" (Rubin, 1975), and through their shared knowledge about the real circumstances, the men's equality was preserved. Only when appearances at court could no longer be maintained and Brünhild's violation of honor could not be satisfied without extreme measures (in Hagen's opinion) was Gunther ready to sacrifice Siegfried, i.e., to have him murdered. The latter is expressed in the *triuwe*, the (political) bond of loyalty, to which Siegfried adhered, while ultimately, Gunther did not (Müller, 2005: 100). Thus, a revelation of the truth was sidestepped, and in the end this caused the conflict to spread from the men to the women (Grimstad & Wakefield, 2007). The latent competition between the two beauties that runs through the narrative is not enough to justify this shift. Nor can the actual lines of conflict be camouflaged by the rhetorically repeated reminder since the first *aventiure* that strong genders will perish because of one or two women and their quarrel. Finally, Hagen remained heroic even after murdering Siegfried; Kriemhild became the much-described she-devil; Brünhild was also considered to be one due to her premarital strength (Grimstad & Wakefield, 2007). It is difficult not to see a gender-based textual strategy in this. The dynamics of honor and shame apply to both sexes, but when explaining the bitter consequences of hard-fought honor conflicts, the relationships become asymmetrical.[7]

Notes

1 An overview is provided in Frevert (2013).
2 The manuscript tradition of the *Nibelungenlied* is relatively broad and complex. I follow a widespread convention and use manuscript B in the edition by Ursula Schulze (2010).
3 The translations adhere to Hatto (1965) except for some deviations.
4 This designation is from Peter Czerwinski.

5 This is true not only for Brünhild, but for Kriemhild as well. If indeed she fully shares the secret of Brünhild's courtship with her husband Siegfried, as Schnyder assumes (Schnyder, 2003: 382), the rest of the text only reveals how much the personal bond is overburdened with such knowledge when trying to maintain a public sense of êre.
6 This is true after Siegfried's aggressive first appearance at the court of Worms, where the balance of power could be offset by Gunther's generous invitation to Siegfried.
7 The quotations come from both German and English sources. The German quotations have been translated.

References

Althoff, G. (2012). Kulturen der Ehre—Kulturen der Scham. In Gvozdeva, K., & Velten, H. (eds.). *Scham und Schamlosigkeit. Grenzverletzungen in Literatur und Kultur der Vormoderne* (pp. 47–60). De Gruyter.

Ben-Ze'ev, A. (2000). *The Subtlety of Emotions*. MIT Press.

Briški, M.J. (2012). Angst—Trauer—Zorn. "Emotionen" im Nibelungenlied. *Acta Neophilologica*, 45, 87–96.

Christoph, S. (1995). Honor, Shame and Gender. In Wolfzettel, F. (ed.), *Arthurian Romance and Gender: Masculin / Féminin dans le roman arthurien médiéval / Geschlechterrollen im mittelalterlichen Artusroman* (pp. 26–33). Brill.

Czerwinski, P. (1979). Das Nibelungenlied: Widersprüche höfischer Gewaltreglementierung. In Frey, W., Raitz, W., & Seitz, D. (eds.), *Einführung in die deutsche Literatur des 12. bis 16. Jahrhunderts. Band 1: Adel und Hof—12./13. Jahrhundert* (pp. 49–87). Springer.

Dinzelbacher, P. (2015). "strîtes êre." Über die Verflechtung von Ehre, Schande, Scham und Aggressivität in der mittelalterlichen Mentalität. *Mediävistik*, 28, 99–140.

Dohmen, L. (2017). *Die Ursache allen Übels: Untersuchungen zu den Unzuchtsvorwürfen gegen die Gemahlinnen der Karolinger*. Jan Thorbecke.

Ehrismann, O. (1995). *Ehre und Mut, Aventiure und Minne: Höfische Wortgeschichten aus dem Mittelalter*. Beck.

Elias, N. (1981). *Über den Prozeß der Zivilisation: Soziogenetische und psychogenetische Untersuchungen*. Suhrkamp.

Eming, J. (2006). *Emotion und Expression: Untersuchungen zu deutschen und französischen Liebes- und Abenteuerromanen des 12.–16. Jahrhunderts*. De Gruyter.

Eming, J. (2015). *Emotionen im 'Tristan': Untersuchungen zu ihrer Paradigmatik*. V&R unipress.

Freienhofer, E. (2016). *Verkörperungen von Herrschaft: Zorn und Macht in Texten des 12. Jahrhunderts*. De Gruyter.

Frevert, U. (2013). *Vergängliche Gefühle*. Wallstein.

Grimstad, K., & Wakefield, R. (2007). Monstrous Mates: The Leading Ladies of the Nibelungenlied and Völsunga Sage. In Poor, S.S., & Schulman, J.K. (eds.), *Women and Medieval Epic. Gender, Genre, and the Limits of Epic Masculinity* (pp. 35–58). Palgrave.

Haferland, H. (1988). *Höfische Interaktion: Interpretationen zur höfischen Epik und Didaktik um 1200*. Fink.

Hatto, A.T. (1965). *The Nibelungenlied*. A new translation. Penguin.

Haubrichs, W. (1996). Ehre und Konflik: Zur intersubjektiven Konstitution der adligen Persönlichkeit im früheren Mittelalter. In Gärtner, K., Kasten, I., & Shaw, F. (eds.), *Spannungen und Konflikte menschlichen Zusammenlebens in der deutschen Literatur des Mittelalters* (pp. 35–58). De Gruyter.

Heller, A. (1981). *Theorie der Gefühle*. VSA.

Karras, R.M. (2003). *From Boys to Men: Formations of Masculinity in Late Medieval Europe*. Pennsylvania Press.

Klinger, J. (2014). Ent/Fesselung des fremden Heros: Sîvrit zwischen Exorbitanz und Assimilation. In Bedeković, N., Kraß, A., & Lembke, A. (eds.), *Durchkreuzte Helden: Das »Nibelungenlied« und Fritz Langs Film "Die Nibelungen" im Licht der Intersektionalitätsforschung* (pp. 259–318). De Gruyter.

Krause, B. (2006). Scham(e), schande und êre: Selbstwahrnehmung—zwischen Affekt und Tugend. In Krause, B., & Scheck, U. (eds.), *Emotions and Cultural Change: Gefühle und kultureller Wandel* (pp. 22–75). Stauffenburg colloquium.

Landweer, H. (1999). *Scham und Macht: Phänomenologische Untersuchungen zur Sozialität eines Gefühls*. Mohr Siebeck.

Lienert, E. (2003). Geschlecht und Gewalt im "Nibelungenlied". *Zeitschrift für deutsches Altertum und deutsche Literatur*, 132 (1), 3–23.

Lienert, E. (2019). Heldenepische êre. In Klein, D. (ed.), *Ehre. Teilband I: Fallstudien zu einem anthropologischen Phänomen in der Vormoderne* (pp. 171–185). Königshausen & Neumann.

Lutz, T. (1999). *Crying: The Natural and Cultural History of Tears*. Norton.

Mecklenburg, M. (2009). Erecs Scham: Kulturelle Umbesetzung einer Emotion im mittelhochdeutschen höfischen Roman. *Arcadia*, 44, 73–92.

Michaelis, B. (2011). *(Dis-)Artikulationen von Begehren: Schweigeeffekte in wissenschaftlichen und literarischen Texten*. De Gruyter.

Müller, J.-D. (1974). SIVRIT: künec—man—eigenholt. Zur sozialen Problematik des Nibelungenliedes. *Amsterdamer Beiträge zur Älteren Germanistik*, 7, 85–124.

Müller, J.-D. (2005). *Das Nibelungenlied*. Klassiker-Lektüren, Bd. 5 (2, neu bearbeitete Auflage). Die Bibliothek Konrad Peutingers.

Müller, J.-D. (2007a). *Rules for the Endgame: The World of the Nibelungenlied*. Translated by William T. Whobrey. Johns Hopkins University Press.

Müller, J.-D. (2007b). Circa 1200: Contagious Violence. In Wellbery, D.E. (ed.), *A New History of German Literature* (pp. 87–91). Belknapp Press.

Müller, J.-D. (2012). Scham und Ehre. Zu einem asymmetrischen Verhältnis in der höfischen Epik. In Gvozdeva, K., & Velten, H. (eds.), *Scham und Schamlosigkeit. Grenzverletzungen in Literatur und Kultur der Vormoderne* (pp. 61–96). De Gruyter.

Müller, J.-D. (2015). *Das Nibelungenlied*. 4. neu bearbeitete Auflage. Schmidt.

Renz, T. (2012). *Um Leib und Leben: Das Wissen von Geschlecht, Körper und Recht im Nibelungenlied*. De Gruyter.

Robles, I. (2005). Subversives weibliches Verhalten im "Nibelungenlied". *Zeitschrift für deutsche Philologie*, 124, 360–374.

Rosenwein, B.H. (1998). *Anger's Past: The Social Uses of an Emotion in the Middle Ages*. Cornell University Press.

Rubin, G. (1975). The Traffic in Women: Notes on the 'Political Economy' of Sex. In R. Reiter (ed.), *Toward an Anthropology of Women* (pp. 157–210). Monthly Review Press.

Schausten, M. (1999). Der Körper des Helden und das "Leben" der Königin. Geschlechter- und Machtkonstellationen im "Nibelungenlied". *Zeitschrift für deutsche Philologie*, 118, 27–49.

Schnell, R. (2002). *Sexualität und Emotionalität in der vormodernen Ehe.* Böhlau.

Schnyder, M. (2003). *Topographie des Schweigens: Untersuchungen zum deutschen höfischen Roman um 1200.* Vandenhoeck & Ruprecht.

Schultz, J.A. (2006). *Courtly Love, the Love of Courtliness, and the History of Sexuality.* University of Chicago Press.

Schulze, U. (2010). *Das Nibelungenlied: Mittelhochdeutsch / Neuhochdeutsch. Nach der Handschrift B herausgegeben. Ins Neuhochdeutsche übersetzt und kommentiert von Siegfried Grosse.* Reclam.

Seidl, S. (2015). Eine kleine Geschichte der êre: Thesen zur historischen Semantik von Ehre und zu ihrer Narrativierung in höfischen und legendarischen Texten des hohen Mittelalters. In Kellner, B., Lieb, L., & Müller, S. (eds.), *Höfische Textualität: Festschrift für Peter Strohschneider* (pp. 45–63). Universitätsverlag Winter GmbH Heidelberg.

Toepfer, R. (2012). Spielregeln für das Überleben: Dietrich von Bern im 'Nibelungenlied' und in der 'Nibelungenklage'. *Zeitschrift für deutsches Altertum und deutsche Literatur*, 141, 310–334.

Wurmser, L. (1998). *Die Maske der Scham: Die Psychoanalyse von Schamaffekten und Schamkonflikten.* Springer.

8 The Emergence and Social Usage of Shaming Punishments in the Twelfth and Thirteenth Centuries in Northwest European Cities

Jörg Wettlaufer

Introduction and Method

Honor and shame have been important constituents in medieval social life. Villages, towns, and urban spaces entailed intensive social interactions between numerous persons of different status and gender. Mutual trust in economic interactions was equally important as peacekeeping and maintaining moral standards. In this situation, the rulers of the emerging towns looked out for possibilities to grant peace, law, and order for all members of the community. They found alternative sanctions inspired by the theology of penance and confession, building on the social usage of shame and the loss of honor, of being an honorable member of these emerging civil communities. This chapter explores the emergence of shaming punishments in the twelfth and thirteenth centuries in Northwest European cities as they appear in charters, franchises, and privileges issued by the lord of these communities or their legal bodies. Within the struggle for freedom and independence from their noble or ecclesiastical overlords, the right to punish misdeeds within the cities' walls and correct wrongdoing became a significant privilege, indicating sovereignty.

This essay builds on comparative research on the social and cultural history of emotions, namely the moral emotion shame and its counterpart honor in relation to the penal customs in different regions of the world. This interest is inspired by the idea that, although all humans are capable of feeling shame, this capacity is exploited very differently in human cultures. An evolutionary-inspired cultural history or historical anthropology gives us an idea of the flexibility of culture in an anthropological perspective by looking at adaptive traits in their cultural variability over time and space, allowing for a better understanding of the historicity of culture itself (Wettlaufer, 2015).

On the methodological level, digital and analogue collections of material are used through a kind of distant reading from the already published (and often digitized) sources throughout Europe and coded information is stored in a research database on shaming punishments.[1] Data- and text-mining methods are applied to the material to find relevant pieces of information, and statistical analysis is used for pattern recognition and theory building.

DOI: 10.4324/9781003022916-11

The advantage of the comparative method, taking into account material from different European regions, is that we are able to observe historical, social behavior in more detail and from complementing viewpoints from a time of few surviving sources under changing circumstances, but in the context of very similar material and social conditions. From this, we can gain better insights into the performance of morality and law and observe the social usage of honor and shame within these groups.

Maybe the most interesting aspect of research on the conception of honor and shame concerning shaming punishments is that shame is an emotion that only works in a social context. For effective shaming, a person must feel as a member of a group or community and share that group's moral norms and values. This is mandatory to trigger the physiological reaction of shame that consists in the confusion of mind, a lowered posture and in general opens up the possibility to re-evaluate one's actions in the light of the shared norms and values of the group.[2] Today one might ask if setting somebody on the pillory on market day for three hours really elicits this physiological reaction or rather evokes contradiction and rage. The answer to this question is that at least in the high and later Middle Ages, in the tradition of confession of sins and public penance, a feeling of being ashamed seemed to be an expected outcome beside other essential effects, mainly the publication of the perpetrator, the prevention of repetition of the offense, and deterrence. We have to consider the vital role ecclesiastical justice for laymen still played in those days and how deeply the emerging jurisdictional autonomy of elite groups in the cities has been influenced and shaped by examples from Christian legislation, namely the court jurisdiction of the "Send."[3]

Therefore, we have to understand normative regulations on penal shaming as mentioned in city charters and franchises in a Christian theological context located precisely in the intersection between punishment and penance with a strong emphasis on reformation as a purpose of punishment. The shaming punishments in the high Middle Ages were applied in general as an alternative to a monetary fine or added to other, more severe punishments. The typical offenses that were punished by those rather complicated punitive measures include ignominious words (*verbis contumeliosis*), scolding, gossip, fraud, theft, and adultery. They were applied in particular in the context of moral failure against the community bound by oath (*verschworene Bürgergemeinde*) in case of repetition of an offense and have a strong relationship to the marketplace that also often served as a stage for the execution of public shaming. In detailed statutes, we can see how these punishments applied differently to social groups (e.g., Speyer, 1230) and how far gender was an essential distinctive criterion.

In many cases, families of town charters and privileges are related and similar to each other.[4] However, some particular developments and traditions cannot be found in all parts of the growing network of towns in Western Europe, which make every case somehow individual. Embracing this space and more than 300 years means that developments and processes only can be sketched on a very broad level and with the help of exemplary spotlights on particular charters and franchises. A more complete picture is neither intended nor would it be possible within the boundaries of this volume. Therefore, generalization should be undertaken with caution, and one has to be aware of the possibility of local traditions and regional particularities while sketching broader lines of developments based on the available material.

Current State of Research

For the observation of the regime of honor and shame in social groups in the light of medieval criminal justice we can build on some solid research that has already been carried out more than a decade ago. For the Holy Empire I will refer especially to the work of Barbara Frenz on peace, infringement of law and sanction in German towns before 1300, which also provides a catalogue of statutes and franchises ordered by offense.[5] Another author that has to be mentioned in this context is Paul de Win, who presented mostly in the 1990s his findings on shaming punishments (*schandstraffen*) from a perspective of archaeology of law (*Rechtsarchäologie*). Although he concentrated on the southern Low Countries, his very detailed work is well informed about other European regions and he was the first that consistently categorized the different types of punishments from a functional point of view (De Win, 1991). Finally, I can build on my own research on this topic and a research database that has been already introduced. First results have been presented in various articles and a volume with the title "Shame between punishment and penance," published together with Bénédicte Sèrè (Paris) in 2013 (Sère & Wettlaufer, 2013).

The curious interweaving of secular and ecclesiastical justice in the high Middle Ages has already been described by some scholars in the first half of the twentieth century (e.g., Oakley, 1932). Later on, Winfrid Trusen and Lotte Kery emphasized the influence of the *forum internum* (confession and penance) on the *forum externum* (ecclesiastical law and justice) (Trusen, 1971; Kéry, 2006a/b; Kéry, 2007). Furthermore, the intrusion of shame into ecclesiastical and secular penal justice has been stressed by Georg Gromer and Amédée Teetaert in their work about the confession to laypersons during the eleventh and twelfth centuries (Gromer, 1909; Teetaert, 1926). They refer to the anonymous eleventh-century treatise "De vera ac falsa penitentia" and the idea that in confession the shame about the committed sins is already part of the penance.[6] This new theological doctrine (and only this!) qualified shame as a formal measure of punishment in ecclesiastical and secular justice, although it seems artificial to separate both spheres in this period and can only be justified from a post hoc position that we take today.

A general overview on the social development in the cities and towns of the twelfth and thirteenth century in the Holy Empire can be found in the informative volume edited by Karsten Igel and colleagues about the emerging towns around 1200 and the exhaustive work of Frank Hirschmann about the episcopal centers in the high Middle Ages, published in 2011 and 2012 in three volumes (Igel et al., 2013: 31–46; Hirschmann, 2011/2012). The legal background of the new town charters in the Holy Empire can be found in Gerhard Dilchers work (Dilcher, 1996). Material on the crucial role played by honor in the late medieval and early modern town is available in Eberhard Isenmanns volume titled "Ehre" published in 2019 (Isenmann 2019).

Evidence

With a focus on the evidence east of the Rhine before 1300, the following will concentrate on early normative examples of shaming at the pillory, carrying the stones of shame (*Schandsteine*) and other humiliating processions through the city as well as the custom of dunking offenders in water or mud. In this early period, shaming punishments were already customary in many European regions. Typical shaming in the urban setting was, beside the examples already given, to whip offenders through the streets of a town or display them in a public space, attached to the stocks or a ladder.[7] From the Italian charters we have early testimony of such punishments, although the earliest examples are from franchises in lower Lotharingia, Flanders, and Northern France.[8]

I intend to start with evidence from a pictorial source, related to the punishment of fraudulent bakers and other misdemeanors related to weights and measures.

We have an excellent picture of the custom from the so-called Nequam-book (literally the book of useless bunglers). It got its title from the fact that it chiefly consists of a list of banished people from the city of Soest in Westphalia from between 1309 to 1412. The pictures in the books are exceptional for the time and in the context of such a book, which has been in general not usually been decorated with these kinds of high-quality drawings (Wilkes, 1976; Pieper, 1980; His, 1980). Soest possesses one of the oldest German town charters that have come down to us. It dates back to the first half of the twelfth century and served as a model for Lübeck (1160), Korbach (1188), Rostock (1218), and many other towns in Westphalia and through Lübeck also in the Baltic Sea region.

Taking a closer look at the picture, the reddish color on the cheeks of the culprit may indicate the shame he is feeling (or ought to feel) while undergoing the punishment. There is no question that this man is bald (and not just accidentally), he suffers a punishment of skin and hair (Haut und Haar), so his head has most probably been shaved before he has been put on this special "seesaw." Very similar instruments have been in use in France and especially in England. There are also traces of this custom in the town privileges of South-Western Germany. The oldest notices are from Strasburg.

144 Jörg Wettlaufer

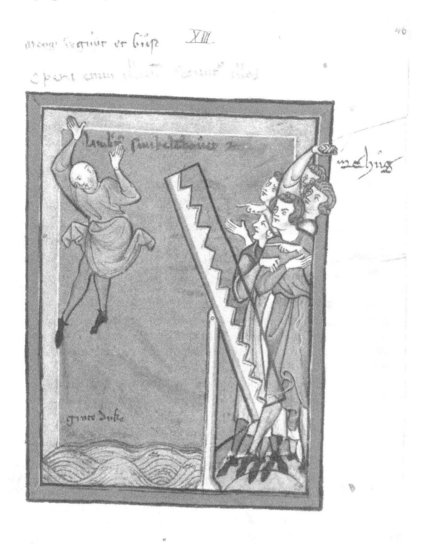

Figure 8.1 Soester "Nequam"-book, early fourteenth century. Das Soester Nequambuch, hrsg. v. d. Historischen Kommission für die Provinz Westfalen, Leipzig 1924, Fig. XIII, fol. 46r. in the original Ms.

The charter that has been promulgated between 1214 and 1219 stipulated: "Art. 44: … quicunque etiam vina injuste mensuraverit, de scupha cadet in merdam" (Frensdorff, 1874: 30). The franchise of Freiburg im Breisgau from 1275 prescribes this punishment for merchants who do not respect the prohibition of cattle-trade before and after St. Martins Day.[9] It is also mentioned by Berthold von Regensburg (1220–1272).[10]

We have a fine monograph on this custom by John W. Spargo, who already observed the uniformity of the custom in different European regions:

> Yet more striking is the uniformity, in England and Germany, during some centuries from about 1100, of punishing violations of the assizes of weights and measures by "balancers." Is it possible that we have here one of those "spiegelnde Strafen," as German historians of the law call them, one of those punishments which reflect as in a mirror the nature of the crime punished?
>
> (Spargo, 1944: 147)

It is likely that his supposition is correct.

One general feature of shaming punishments is the visible marking of people (using symbols like a mitre or signs indicating the offense) and a tendency to avoid measures that leave irreversible damage to the body. Maybe the oldest and most widespread custom was the cutting or shaving of the hair combined with corporal punishment for the unfree. The famous illuminated manuscripts of the mirror of the Saxons illustrates the custom of cutting the hair and beating the culprit *ad palum*, attached to a pillar that might be the precursor of the later continental pillory. These punishments probably date back to the earlier Middle Ages and bear universal character because of their simplicity.[11]

The blueprint of the correctional punishments can be found in the episcopal judicial regime of "Sendgerichte."[12] In the "Lex familiae Wormatiensis" (around 1024) is demonstrated how a bishop dealt with the judicial challenges of a town in this intermediate time between the composition system and the emerging public criminal law: shaving the head and burning through the cheeks are mentioned already, but the pillory is still absent and public penance is treated in Burchards' other book, the "*Decretum*."[13]

Another custom that appears quite early in the sources and has a strong relation to the emerging towns in Western Europe was the so-called "*currant nudi*" of adulterous couples. It belongs to the type of infamous processions that can be found in many cultures of the world. In an illustration of the custom passed down in a manuscript of the customs of Toulouse (between 1300 and 1325),[14] "the guilty couple are exposed to the derision of the townsfolk, who are probably also permitted to beat them with clubs; they are preceded by two men blowing trumpets. In this way, the couple is shamed" (Akehurst, 2005: 7; Carbasse, 1987; Winkler, 2009). It is well known for Southern France from the Coutumes de Toulouse (between 1300 and 1325) and Agen (between 1250 and 1275),[15] but it is also practiced (and this is less known),[16] at Lübeck in Northern Germany. In a document about legal customs, which also contains extracts from the privilege of the town from between 1220 and 1226, we read that "If a man is taken with the legitimate wife of somebody (in adultery), it is legal (*ius est*) that he himself is drawn up and down by her through the villages or the town."[17] Later, in

Figure 8.2 Herzog August Bibliothek Wolfenbüttel, Cod. Guelf. Aug. 3.1 2, fol. 42v. Last quarter of the fourteenth century. The content refers back to the thirteenth century (Scheele, 1998). © Herzog August Bibliothek Wolfenbüttel: http://diglib.hab.de/?db=mss&list=ms&id=3-1-aug-2f

1243 (for Tønder, Denmark, an exact copy of the statutes of Lübeck): "If a man is found in adultery with the lawful wife of someone, it is the law of the state to be dragged up and down by him through the streets through his penis, and thus he will be free for that cause."[18] The fact that the custom was not only flourishing in Gascony and Catalonia, but also in the very north of Germany at about the same time is curious at least. The similarities are too obvious to be only incidental—it is definitely worth considering this from a broader perspective than has been done so far.[19]

Some scholars have characterized the social function of these particular punishments for sexual crimes as collective humiliation.[20] Shame was the foremost and predominant means of punishment in this particular case, because of the prescribed nudity and, even more dishonorable, the cord fixed at the male genital that connected the couple. From Southern France we know that this type of punishment was carried out rather often (although it was initially limited to adultery that was discovered *in flagrante*).[21]

The townsfolk are presented as a community that condemns the breach of communal peace committed by the adulterers. The almost ridiculous (but also painful, we may suspect) procession through the town chases the sinful couple through the streets. This recompenses somehow for the breach of the peace. Supplementary banishment seems to be an exception, but the loss of social status must have been enormous and the sources report about the loss of the capacity for public office. The social and moral identity of the community was strengthened through this kind of ritual performance, very similar to what is achieved by the *charivaris* better known from later centuries. Nevertheless, we can also think about models for this custom from the practice of public penance and humiliating rituals of the earlier Middle Ages (cf. Moeglin, 1996).

The two most common shaming punishments in high medieval towns were the pillory in its manifold forms and the stones of shame (*Schandsteine*), a punishment in particular for slander and quarrels between women. Their application to particular groups of the townsfolk allows us to observe the interaction of honor and shame within the community in greater detail.

In fact we do not know very well how the early pillories east of the Rhine may have looked like in the twelfth and thirteenth century, but they may have developed from a simple pillar as shown in the mirror of the Saxons (Figure 8.2) or the stocks that have been in use already in the early Middle Ages (cippus, cep).[22] Those devices, including the iron collar and the French *carcan*, are all used for changing purposes of punishment and it seems impossible to establish a general distinction of lesser and higher justice between them for the total period of their usage (cf. Bader-Weiß & Bader, 1935; De Win, 1991: 96–189; Preu, 1949). We know about their existence not only from statutes and franchises, but also from financial documents and conflicts about the sovereignty over these instruments. In Cologne a quarrel between the bishop and the town council about the lesser and intermediate criminal jurisdiction of the town that was never really settled during the following centuries reveals some interesting details. In the center of the dispute is the *cyppus*, the stocks that obviously also were used for punishment and display and not only for detention. In the arbitration the protagonists refer to another paragraph where they are expressing the opinion that the criminal jurisdiction of skin and hair should be in the hands of the city of Cologne and not only at the court of the bishop.[23] This is a typical topic and development for the second half of the thirteenth century, when more and more towns strived for emancipation from their ecclesiastical overlord.

Another interesting reference to the punishment of the pillory can be found at Speyer in an article of the town charter that outlaws ignominious words, pugnacity, or brawl. The text explicitly relates to "poor or impious people" who cannot pay the fine. The pillory is described as the "common column," no vernacular word like *schreiat* (southern Germany and Austria) or *ka(a)k* (Northern Germany) is used.[24] We find this pattern in several other charters and statutes, e.g., at Passau at around 1300. Here the offense is ignominious words again and the punishment of the pillory is prescribed if the fine cannot be paid.[25] At Lübeck (charter of 1294), the punishment of carrying the stones of shame (*Schandsteine*) for women was combined with the pillory (called *kaak* in lower German and Dutch) for dishonorable women in the context of perjury and slitting the ears as a permanent mark plus banishment where added.[26]

At Brünn, today Brno in the Czech Republic, the pillory (*schreiat*) is used in 1243 as a place for supplementary punishment like burning and marking with a hot iron for lesser theft.[27] Going back west, we have a very telling example for the punishment of the ladder from the town charter of Aardenburg (Sluis Municipality, province of Zeeland) from the middle of the thirteenth century and Schlettstadt near Strasburg from the second half of the fourteenth century.[28] The ladder is a typical custom of Western Europe (France) and seems to have been primarily used by ecclesiastical courts. It was sometimes accompanied by signs or objects to communicate the offense to the onlookers. But the ladder was not only used as a pillory in ecclesiastical law; we have also sources for the usage in the secular context for high treason and on the marketplace for fraud and forgery.[29] A miniature from a moralizing bible of the fourteenth century depicts the punishment with two culprits attached to the latter and the bishop pointing at them.[30]

The most telling sources about the social usage of pillories in the emerging towns of Northwestern Europe are from the west of the Rhine. In fact, the intended usage of pillories in the early statutes was, beside publication of the offense and deterrence, really about doing penance by feeling shame for the sins committed. The *Etablissements* of Rouen are an influential family of city charters from the second half of the twelfth century. Paragraph 15 reads as follows:

> If somebody has stood in the pillory, not because of theft, but because he has offended the statutes of the community, and if somebody else reproaches this to him later to make him feel ashamed in front of his *conjurates* or other men, he shall pay 20 solidi, of which the man who was shamed shall have 5 and the city shall have 15. And if he does not want to pay or cannot pay the 20 solidi, he himself shall stand in the pillory.[31]

It is quite significant that the pillory has elicited, from the very beginning, narratives of exclusion and infamy, although the charter explicitly orders that the penitential shaming should be terminated after the punishment. Other sources insist that the execution of the punishments should take place in a decent manner, referring to the origin and purpose of shaming (that was not ridicule, of course) (De Win, 1991: 75; Wettlaufer, 2011: 360, note 44).

To conclude this section, I shall provide some examples for the custom of carrying the stones of shame (*Schandsteine*), a widespread custom typical for the German speaking regions. The punishment itself is quite curious and although some people, including myself, have devoted some effort to understand the logic behind it, we still cannot be sure how the custom really came into use and why it originally only applied to women who spoke ignominious words with each other, breaking the peace of the town through slander and gossip (see above and Künssberg, 1907). The custom puts some symbolic meaning in the stones that is not easy to unveil today. My own reasoning goes in two directions: There is of course the model of public penance and especially penitential pilgrimage with iron collars and heavy stones.[32] The other direction is even more abstract, but fits very well in both chronology and context: The *Decretum Gratiani* has a chapter about the unrighteous exclusion of others and combines two biblical sayings and thereby establishes a connection between stones, penance and maledictions:

> Stone diminishes or absorbs the sin, and stone forgives the sin, the dove diminishes and forgives the sin. And like a bird is flying without purpose and a sparrow goes everywhere it wants, an unjust *maledictum* (an invective word) without reason spreads above those who pronounced it (this means spreading uncontrolled like the flying birds).[33]

As already said, the most telling examples are not from the towns in the Holy Empire but from Northern France in the second half of the twelfth century. In fact, it seems that the customs originate in this region and did spread eastwards. A classic example from Beaumont-en-Argonne stipulates: "The woman who said *convitia* to another woman in the presence of witnesses, shall pay to the lord and the majores of the city, but if she does not want to pay she shall carry the stones at the procession on Sunday in a shirt. If a man does commit the same misdemeanor, he also pays the fine but there is no option to carry the stones."[34] We find an early adaptation of the custom at Dortmund from 1275. The weight of the stones is specified and in this case, it is in fact quite heavy: 50 kg for both stones together in modern measurement. The course of the infamous procession is also specified very detailed and leads from one gate to another—quite a distance at Dortmund even at that time.[35] The punishment of the stones of shame can also be found in the statues of Güstrow (1270), Hamburg (1292), Lübeck (1294), Speyer (1328), and Berlin at the end of the fourteenth century.[36] It was in usage throughout the late Middle Ages up to the early modern period, when it was at least partially replaced by the punishment of the fiddle.

Conclusion

To recall the questions posed by the editors of this volume: What can the observation of shaming punishments tell us about how honor and shame dynamics have been implemented in Western history, especially on how they became part of medieval culture and identity? What types of behavior and cultural expressions described in our sources signaled the importance of honor and shame and how were they perceived in jurisdictional and extraordinary conflicts? The latter question can be partially answered by the evidence presented in town charters and statutes. Men and women appear in quite different and separated juridical spheres of criminal law. For the same offenses, different types of punishment are scheduled (prescribed). In the statutes and franchises we also encounter the poor, the honorless people who cannot pay the fine and are subjected to harsh shaming punishments, in other words to "secular public penitence." It is interesting to observe how the lesser jurisdiction, also touching the moral failure of people (the church would call it sin), is taken over (at least at some places) from the (often ecclesiastical) lord of the town and is organized around the actual problems that the town council faced in the emerging cities. Through their integration as jurors in the episcopal lesser justice the magistrates and members of the council learned and imitated to control unwanted and peace breaking behavior, but they forgot sometimes quite rapidly the grace and mercy that inspired the ecclesiastical idea of justice in the *forum externum* (at least in principle).[37] The market, which brings together different social groups, challenges the idea of Christian justice and moral integrity of the members of the parish. Feeling shame for one's actions is doing penance—at least in the Christian doctrine of the twelfth and thirteenth century. This formula from the penitential theology of the high Middle Ages was happily integrated in secular criminal justice of the towns and practiced by the ruling groups with the aim to build a better community. In the later Middle Ages, shaming punishments were not (primarily) any longer about doing penance and the possibility of reintegration, but about stigmatization and exclusion of subjects that did not meet the moral standards of an honorable burgher. Banishment became, from the thirteenth century onwards, the probate measure to solve all kind of problems, often combined with previous shaming through public exposure and corporal punishment (cf. Halba, 2006; Zaremska, 1996).

Regarding the offenses that have been punished with shaming penalties we can notice that the early sources from the twelfth to the fourteenth century put an emphasis on breaking the peace of the city by ignominious words (*verbis contumeliosis*), scolding, gossip, fraud, perjury, theft, and adultery. Peace-keeping was one of the fundamental issues that faced the emerging communities (Frenz, 2002; Jansen, 2002). Assembling many people on a relatively small spot called for potential conflict situations, especially in the context of commerce and intensified division of labor. This shaped the identities of particular subgroups within the town (Gilden, Zünfte), but at the same time the community of the members, the *conjuratores*, is striking. I add to these observations some more general thoughts about the role of shame and honor in social groups, and put forward some arguments why both have been important for the establishment and function of these communities.

Shame and honor seem to play a special role in the maintenance of human cooperation. Although this idea is not very new, this link has explicitly only been established by evolutionary studies, using anthropological observations and game theoretical models, trying to solve the puzzle of cooperation in social groups.[38] Of course, cooperation yields some advantages for those who engage in it, but the problems come with free riders, who cheat on the common good and abuse the mutual trust that is crucial for effective cooperation. Applying these findings of evolutionary anthropology and game theory to the medieval town sheds some new light on already established knowledge about the core values of these communities. There is abundant material about the notion of honor for the identity of burghers in medieval towns (e.g., Isenmann 2012: 711). The often-repeated self-description of being an honorable person only makes sense when interpreted in the context of the central goal to establish and maintain cooperation within these communities. Honor supports cooperation even more than shame and being labeled as honorable is valuable information about the prospective value and trustworthiness of a person in future cooperation (Jacquet et al. 2012). Losing honor and being shamed in public was like a warning to the other members of the community: look, this person has morally failed and committed fraud, perjury, adultery, or blasphemy and might be therefore a dangerous partner in future interactions! This is, from a functional point of view, in fact the background of why shaming punishments became so popular and were so easily adopted from penitential customs. Their potential for reforming people and curing their moral failures was very attractive for this community of tradesmen and merchants. Trust was the basic value for prosperous mercantile trade and keeping up the peace of the town served to establish this precondition of cooperative engagement for both the common and the individual good.

Notes

1 See www.shamestudies.de. The internal functions provide maps of shaming punishments and allow aggregations and analysis for offenses and types of punishments.
2 See for definitions of shame from the psychology of emotions with comprehensive reference to further literature: Tangney & Fischer (1995); Robins, Robins, & Tangney (2007).
3 The "Sendgericht" was a church court that tried cases of sins and vice. See footnote 23. Cf. Pahud de-Mortanges (1992); Wettlaufer (2010); Schulze et al. (2008); Hermann (2012: 484–496).
4 See the fine example of Soest treated by Dusil (2007).
5 Frenz (2003). The shamestudies database (https://shamestudies.de) annotates the data in a similar manner. Sources were collected in Keutgen (1901).
6 De vera et falsa poenitentia, caput X. 25. (eleventh century?): "Erubescentia enim ipsa partem habet remissionis: ex misericordia enim hoc praecepit Dominus, ut neminem poeniteret in occulto. In hoc enim quod per seipsum dicit sacerdoti, et erubescentiam vincit timore Dei offensi, fit venia criminis: fit enim per confessionem veniale, quod commiserat mortale. Multum enim satisfactionis obtulit, qui erubescentiae dominans, nichil eorum quae commissit, nuntio Dei denegavit … Laborat enim mens patiendo erubescentiam. Et quoniam verecundia magna

est poena, qui erubescit pro Christo, fit dignus misericordia. Unde patet quod quanto pluribus confitebitur in spe veniae turpitudinem criminis, tanto facilius consequetur gratiam remissionis" (Migne: Patrologia Latina (PL), 40: 1113–1130). Cf. Wagner (1995).

7 For the most complete catalog of European shaming punishments during the Middle Ages see De Win (1991).
8 Some early examples can be found in chronicles and annals in this period, but those exceptional and politically motivated trials and executions do not reflect properly the intended usage of these instruments. Cf. MGH SS 7, p. 495; 298; MGH SS 26, p. 543. Cf. ibid. p. 471. For Italy see Gatti (1933: 693–696).
9 Blattmann, 1991: 667, art. 67; cited also by Frenz, 2003: 645.
10 "projicitur pistor in lutum" (Schönbach, 1900: 117).
11 Nevertheless, some cultural variations exist. In Edo Japan the penal shaving of hair has been problematic, because the result resembled the customary hairstyle of monks. So here the solution was to shave only one half of the head. See Wettlaufer & Nishimura (2013: 215).
12 For examples of the (later) usage of shaming punishments at the "Send" see Koeniger (1910: 70–71, 91, 109); Koeniger (1931); Dusil (2012).
13 "Cap. XXX: constituimus, ut ei tollantur corium et capilli et in utraque maxilla ferro ad hoc facto comburatur," *Lex familiae Wormatiensis ecclesiae*, Weinrich (1977: 100). Cf. Dilcher (1993); Frenz (2003: 43–45; 196–197).
14 BNF ms lat. 9187, f. 30v. See L'Engle (2002) about why the pictures have been inserted into the manuscript. For a pictorial representation of the punishment see https://gallica.bnf.fr/ark:/12148/btv1b105090434/f66.item.
15 Costuma d'Agen, Agen, Archives departementales du Lot-et-Garonne, MS 42, folios 42r–43r. Akehurst (2005: 6–7). See also: Tropamer (1911); Akehurst (2010: 40–41, chap. 19).
16 But De Win (1991: 33, note 2) does mention it for Lübeck with reference to Ebel (1968: 72).
17 Codex diplomaticus Lubecensis (1843: 42); Hach, 1839: 198: "De comprehenso cum muliere legitima. Si vir cum legitima alicuius deprehenditur, iuris est ut ipse ab ea per vicos civitatis sursum et deorsum trahatur per veretrum. Sed non debet deprehendi nisi sint presentes amici viri vel mulieris & postea iudicium advocabitur." See also: Frensdorff (1918: 29–33).
18 Ernst Joachim von Westphalen, Monumenta inedita rerum Germanicarum praecipue Cimbricarum et Megapolensium 3 (Lipsiae: Joh. Chr. Martini, 1737): 626: "Si aliquis vir cum legitima alicuius uxore in adulterio deprehendatur, iuris est civitatis, ut ipse ab ea per plateas per veretrum suum sursum et deorsum trahatur, et sic de illa causa liber erit."
19 The stunning similarity has been observed already by Frensdorff (1918: 33–35). He expressed hope that comparative historical research might shed some light on this in the future. The same punishment can be found in the affiliated charters for Riga (1201) and Ripen (1269), equally for Riom (1270) and Figeac in Auvergne. The earliest traces stem from Catalonia. For the most recent synopsis, see Winkler (2009: 364–369).
20 Trexler (1984). On humiliation: Miller (1993).
21 Gilles (1969: 256, note 2).
22 The earliest picture of a stock-device can be found in illustrated Psalters from the middle of the eleventh century (Thomson, 1972: 21, Figure 4).
23 "I. 37. Item quod magistri civium per iniuriam de novo cyppum fecerunt et aliquibus pollices amputaverunt, cum tamen de hoc minime valeant iudicare. III. ad I. 37: Item ad hoc, quod magistri civium per iniuriam de novo cyppum fecerunt et aliquibus pollices amputaverunt etc. dicimus, quod superius diffinivimus" (Strauch, 2008: 91).

24 Speyer 1230, Art. 9: "ist aber, das eyn arme persone oder eyn unfrume mensche (der die pene, die er darumb verschuldigt, nicht mag gegeben) yemant schiltet, reufft oder schlecht, den sal man vast slahen an der gemeynen seile und darnach uß der stad werfen und uß der stetde banfriede, numer nie wieder yne zu komen, die rate heren erleubens jme dan" (Frenz, 2003: 505).

25 Passau 1299: "swen man verbotniu wort ... der sol dem Rihtaer ein phunt geben und des chlagaers huld gewinnen; hat er sin niht ze pezzaern, so sol man in bei der schraiat an slahen." Frenz (2003: 505). Iglau 1249, § 46. "Item wann ayn snoder mensch ymand schendt. Ist aber, das ayn lekker ader ayn loter ymande sulche scheltrede tüt smeheleich, den schol man czü der sewl pinden vnd geisseln vnd von der Stat vnd von yren greniczen vnd gemerken treiben" (Tomaschek, 1859: 240).

26 "Is ok dat en man dre mene ede sweret den mach me bauen ander deue henghen deyt id ok ene vrouwe de is erlos de schalme to deme kake slan unde sniden er en ore af unde late et den sten dreghen ze schal de stadt vorschweren X mile lank unde bred nicht na to kamende" (Hach, 1839: 372).

27 Brünn, 1243, § 19. (48.): "Um deube. Ist daz iemand an deube begriffen wiert, daz vierczig phenning wert ist, den schol man hahen; wiert er awer an minner begriffen, so schol man in nicht hahen: man schol in vuren czu der schraiat und schol in merchen mit eim gluenden eysen" (Rössler, 1852: 349).

28 Aardenburg 1250: § 109. "So wie die wort bedraghen van valscher wareden, verbuert L libra, ende men salne setten drie daghe in die ladere of in den stoc; ende dan sel men hem gheven een teeken en sijn lier, ende men salne bannen VI jaer uter casselrie van Brugghe up zine oghen." Vorsterman van Oyen 1892: 108; Schlettstadt 1374, § 26: "Von meyneides wegen. [...] und bessert vorhin IIII libra, [...] Het aber er nút der iiii libra ze gebende, so sol man ein leiter binden an den diepstogk und sol in daruff binden und im drige vinger ufbinden an der rehten hande und uf sin houbt einen geschriben brieff setzen, wie er meynedyig si, und sol uff der leytern sitzen ..., untz daz in der meister oder der rat ab der leitern heissent gan" (Gény, 1902: 281).

29 Varin (1843: 156–159, 1243); Verriest (1905: 12, 56, 106); De Win (1991: 118).

30 BNF ms. fr. 167, fol. 301v. Bible moralisée (1345–1355). See https://gallica.bnf.fr/ark:/12148/btv1b8447300c/f610.item for a picture of the punishment.

31 "§ 15. Si quis in pillorico fuerit, non propter furtum set quia egerit contra statutum communie aliquid et aliquis ei exprobraverit ut faciat ei verecundiam coram conjuratis vel coram aliis hominibus, paccabit viginti solidos, quorum is cui exprobracio facta est habebit quinque solidos, et quindecim erunt ad negotia civitatis Rothomagi. Et si ille qui exprobraverit non velit vel non possit pagare viginti solidos, ponetur in pillorico" (Giry, 1885: 22).

32 Miracula S. Walburgis Tilae facta (ca. 1025): "In confinio Gallorum & Aquitanorum Episcopis ea consuetudo est, vt ad poenitentiam vocatis lapides magni ponderis cum circulis ferreis ad collum suspendant: [cuidā ferreum brachij vinculum soluitur:] vt ventrem hominis ferro circumdent, siue brachia itidem ferreis circulis circumligent: & litteris, facinore eorum commendato, per diuersa mittant loca, vt per hanc poenam erubescendo grauius affligantur, & ad perpetrandum tale scelus, terrorem ceteris incutiant: parricidarum, vel aliorum horum similium ea poena est" (Platelle, 2004: 75).

33 *Decretum Gratiani*, 1140: "C. LXXXVII. Iniuste aliquem anathematizans sibi, non alii nocet [...]. Pax ecclesiae dimittit peccata, et ab ecclesiae pace alienis tenet peccata non secundum arbitrium hominum, sed secundum arbitrium Dei. Petra tenet, petra dimittit; columba tenet, columba dimittit. [Gratian.] Item Salomon: "Sicut auis in incertum uolans, et passer quolibet uadens, sic maledictum frustra prolatum uenit super eum, qui misit illud" (Friedberg, 1879).

34 Beaumont-en-Argonne, circa 1182: "§43. Mulier que mulieri convitia dixerit duorum vel duarum testimonio convicta V solidos solvet, Domino IV solidos, Majori VI denarios et ei cui convitia dixerit VI et si nummos solvere noluerit, lapides portabit ad processionem die dominica in camisia et si viro dixerit convitia testibus convicta V solidos solvet, et si vir convitia dixerit mulieri X solidos reddet simili modo dividendos" (Arbois de Jubainville, 1851: 254; cf. Collin, 1977).

35 "De libertate opidi nostri: [...] Si due mulieres rixantur ad invicem, percutiendo se vel verbis contumeliosis, quod Verkorne Wort dicuntur, portabunt duos lapides per cathenam coherentes, qui ambo ponderabunt unum centenarium, quod teutonice dicitur enen Cyntener, per longitudinem civitatis in communi via. Una primo portabit eos de orientali porta civitatis ad occidentalem portam, et alia stimulabit eam stimulo ferreo, fixo in baculo, et ambe ibunt in camisiis suis. Alia tunc assumet eos in humeros suos et reportabit eos ad orientalem portam et prima e converso stimulabit eam" (Frensdorff, 1882: 34–35).

36 Güstrow: "iuris vel emende de rixis seu contencionibus mulierum emerserit, que debent ferre lapides pro excessu," Mecklenburgisches Urkundenbuch (Schwerin: Stillersche Hofbuchhandlung 1864): 37, nr. 1.182; Hamburg (statutes from 1497, identical with the statutes of 1292): "der schalme by dem kake hangen an eren halß twe stene de dar tho denen, vnde schal van dm fronen apenbar dorch de stadt gheleyt werden, Vnnde de fronen scholen er myth hornen vor vnd achter blaßenn, er tho hone vnnd schmaheyt vnnde scholen se alßo vther stadt bringen, vnd se scal de stadt vorsweren" (Preu, 1949: 101). For more examples see Neumann (2002: 170–172).

37 Cf. for this process Anton & Haverkamp (1996: 264–266).

38 To support this argument in the case of the nascent towns in the European high Middle Ages, I refer to some selected publications and my own work in evolutionary history. See Wettlaufer (2016a/b). See also: Fessler & Haley (2004); Gächter (2014); Tangney (2013).

References

Akehurst, F.R.P. (2005). Adultery in Gascony. In Busby, K. et al. (eds.). *"De sens rassis": essays in honor of Rupert T. Pickens* (pp. 1–15). Rodopi.

Akehurst, F.R.P. (2010). *The Costuma d'Agen: A Thirteenth-Century Customary Compilation in Old Occitan Transcribed From The Livre Juratoire*. Brepols.

Anton, H.H. & Haverkamp, A. (eds.) (1996). *Trier im Mittelalter* 2. Spee Verlag.

Bader-Weiß, G. & Bader, K.S. (1935). *Der Pranger: Ein Strafwerkzeug und Rechtswahrzeichen des Mittelalters*. Jos. Waibel'sche Verlagsbuchhandlung.

Blattmann, M. (1991). *Die Freiburger Stadtrechte zur Zeit der Zähringer. Rekonstruktion der verlorenen Urkunden und Aufzeichnungen des 12. und 13. Jahrhunderts*. Vol. 2. Ploetz.

Carbasse, J.-M. (1987). Currant nudi: La répression de l'adultère dans le midi médiéval. In Poumarède, J. & Royer, J.-P. (eds.), *Droit, Histoire et Séxualité* (pp. 83–102). Espace juridique.

Codex diplomaticus Lubecensis. Urkundenbuch der Stadt Lübeck, 1 (Lübeck, 1843).

Collin, H. (1977). La charte de Beaumont-en-Argonne (1182), *Revue historique ardennaise*, 12, 133–141.

D'Arbois de Jubainville, H. (1851). Le Loi de Beaumont, *Bibliothèque d'Ecole des Chartes*, 2, 3rd series, 248–256.

De Win, P. (1991). *De schandstraffen in het wereldlijk strafrecht in de Zuidelijke Nederlanden van de Middeleeuwen tod de Franse Tijd bestudeerd in Europees perspective*. WLSK.

Dilcher, G. (1993). Mord und Totschlag im alten Worms: Zu Fehde, Sühne und Strafe im Hofrecht Bischof Burchards (AD 1023/25). In Buchholz, S. et al. (eds.), *Überlieferung, Bewahrung und Gestaltung in der rechtsgeschichtlichen Forschung: Festschrift für Ekkehard Kaufmann* (pp. 91–104). Schöningh.

Dilcher, G. (1996). *Bürgerrecht und Stadtverfassung im europäischen Mittelalter*. Böhlau.

Dusil, S. (2007). *Die Soester Stadtrechtsfamilie: mittelalterliche Quellen und neuzeitliche Historiographie*. Böhlau.

Dusil, S. (2012). Zur Entstehung und Funktion von Sendgerichten. Beobachtungen bei Regino von Prüm und in seinem Umfeld, In Schmoeckel, M. et al. (eds.), *Der Einfluss der Kanonistik auf die europäische Rechtskultur Bd. 3: Straf- und Strafprozessrecht* (pp. 369–409). Böhlau.

Ebel, W. (1968). *Curiosa juris Germanici*. Vandenhoeck & Ruprecht.

Fessler, D.M.T. & Haley, K.J. (2004). Strategy of Affect: Emotions in Human Cooperation. In Hammerstein, P. (ed.), *The Genetic and Cultural Evolution of Cooperation, Dahlem Workshop Report* (pp. 125–152). MIT Press.

Frensdorff, F. (1874). Die beiden ältesten hansischen Recesse, *Hansische Geschichtsblätter*, 1, 9–53.

Frensdorff, F. (1882). *Dortmunder Statuten und Urtheile*. Verlag der Buchhandlung des Waisenhauses.

Frensdorff, F. (1918). Verlöbnis und Eheschließung nach hansischen Rechts- und Geschichtsquellen, *Hansische Geschichtsblätter*, 24, 1–126.

Frenz, B. (2002). "Si convinci potest ydoneis testibus, eadem pena ac si in civitate contigisset puniatur": Konzeptionen der Beweisführung und Sanktionierung beklagter Friedensverletzungen in Stadtrechten des 12. und 13. Jahrhunderts. In Schlosser, H. Sprandel, R. & Willoweit, D. (eds.), *Herrschaftliches Strafen seit dem Hochmittelalter: Formen und Entwicklungsstufen* (pp. 133–156). Böhlau.

Frenz, B. (2003). *Frieden, Rechtsbruch und Sanktion in deutschen Städten vor 1300: mit einer tabellarischen Quellenübersicht nach Delikten und Deliktgruppen*. Böhlau.

Friedberg, A. (ed.) (1879). *Decretum magistri Gratiani. Ed. Lipsiensis secunda post Aemilii Ludovici Richteri curas ad librorum manu scriptorum et editionis Romanae fidem recognovit et adnotatione critica instruxit Aemilius Friedberg, Corpus iuris canonici* 1. Bernhard Tauchnitz.

Gächter, S. (2014). Human Pro-Social Motivation and the Maintenance of Social Order. In Teichman, D. & Zamir, E. (eds.), *The Oxford Handbook of Behavioral Economics and the Law* (pp. 28–60). Oxford University Press.

Gatti, T. (1933). L'imputabilità, i movimenti del reato e la prevenzione criminale ngeli statuti italiani dei secoli XII–XVI, *CEDAM*, 693–696.

Gény, J. (1902). *Elsässische Stadtrechte I, Schlettstadter Stadrechte*. Winter.

Gilles, H. (1969). *Les Coutumes de Toulouse (1286) et leur première commentaire (1296)*. CNRS.

Giry, A. (1885). *Les établissements de Rouen: études sur l'histoire des institutions municipales de Rouen, Falaise, … etc.* Vieweg.

Gromer, G. (1909). *Die Laienbeicht im Mittelalter: ein Beitrag zu ihrer Geschichte*. Verlag der J.J. Lentnerschen Buchhandlung.

Hach, J.F. (1839). *Das alte Lübische Recht*. Rohdensche Buchhandlung.

Halba, E.-M. (2006). Le vocabulaire du bannissement aux XIIe et XIIIe siècles. In Gonthier, N. (ed.), *L'Exclusion au Moyen Âge* (pp. 347–372). Cahiers du centre d'histoire de Lyon III, n° 4. Aprime.

Hermann, H.G. (2012). Kanonistische Kapitel in der Geschichte der Freiheitsstrafe: "Ut Episcopi suos carceres habeant." In Schmoeckel, M. et al. (eds.), *Der Einfluss der Kanonistik auf die europäische Rechtskultur* (pp. 457–496). Vol. 3: *Straf- und Strafprozessrecht*. Böhlau.

Hirschmann, F.G. (2011/2012). *Die Anfänge des Städtewesens in Mitteleuropa: die Bischofssitze des Reiches bis ins 12. Jahrhundert*. Vol. 1–3, Anton Hiersemann.

His, R. (1980). Die Rechtsgeschichtliche Beurteilung des Nequambuches, In Kohl, W. (ed.), *Das Soester Nequambuch: Neuausgabe des Acht- und Schwurbuchs der Stadt Soest* (pp. 80–88). Dr. Ludwig Reichert Verlag.

Igel, K. et al. (2013). Gesellschaftlicher Wandel—städtischer Wandel? Zur Formierung urbaner Gesellschaften im 12. Jahrhundert. In Igel, K. et al. (eds.), *Wandel der Stadt um 1200: die bauliche und gesellschaftliche Transformation der Stadt im Hochmittelalter* (pp. 31–46). Theis.

Isenmann, E. (2012). *Die deutsche Stadt im Mittelalter 1150–1550: Stadtgestalt, Recht, Verfassung, Stadtregiment, Kirche, Gesellschaft, Wirtschaft*. Böhlau.

Isenmann, E. (2019): *Ehre. Teilband II: Die Ehre und die Stadt im Spätmittelalter und zu Beginn der Frühen Neuzeit. Publikation aus dem Kolleg Mittelalter und Frühe Neuzeit, Bd. 5/2, hg.* von Dorothea Klein, Königshausen & Neumann.

Jacquet, J. et al. (2012). Could Shame and Honor Save Cooperation? *Communicative & Integrative Biology*, 5(2), 209–213.

Jansen, S. (2002). Der gestörte Friede: Konfliktwahrnehmung und Konfliktregelung in Stadtrechtsquellen des 12. und 13. Jahrhunderts. In Schlosser, H., Sprandel, R., & Willoweit, D. (eds.), *Herrschaftliches Strafen seit dem Hochmittelalter: Formen und Entwicklungsstufen* (pp. 83–131). Böhlau.

Kéry, L. (2006a). Canonica severitas und amor correctioni:. Zur Ausbildung des kirchlichen Strafrechts im Spannungsfeld zwischen Strafanspruch und Besserungsverlangen. In Müller, L. et al. (eds.), *Strafrecht in einer Kirche der Liebe—Notwendigkeit oder Widerspruch?* (pp. 23–44). LIT.

Kéry, L. (2006b). *Gottesfurcht und irdische Strafe: der Beitrag des mittelalterlichen Kirchenrechts zur Entstehung des öffentlichen Strafrechts*. Böhlau.

Kéry, L. (2007). Verbrechen und Strafen im kanonischen Recht des Mittelalters. In Kesper-Biermann, S. & Klippel, D. (eds.), *Kriminalität in Mittelalter und Früher Neuzeit. Soziale, rechtliche, philosophische und literarische Aspekte* (pp. 13–33). Harrassowitz.

Keutgen, F. (1901). *Urkunden zur Städtischen Verfassungsgeschichte*, 1. Emil Felber.

Koeniger, A.M. (1910). *Quellen zur Geschichte der Sendgerichte in Deutschland*, J.J. Lentnersche Buchhandlung.

Koeniger, A.M. (1931). Die Sendgerichte: Eine Übersicht, *Bonner Zeitschrift für Theologie und Seelsorge*, 8, 34–40.

Künssberg, E.F.v. (1907). *Über die Strafe des Steintragens*. M. & H. Marcus.

L'Engle, S. (2002). Justice in the Margins: Punishment in Medieval Toulous, *Viator*, 33, 133–165.

Migne, J.-P. (ed.) (1865). *Patrologia Latina (PL)*, 40. Garnier fratres.

Miller, W.I. (1993). *Humiliation: and Other Essays on Honor, Social Discomfort and Violence*. Cornell University Press.

Moeglin, J.-M. (1996). Harmiscara / Harmschar / Hachée - Le dossier des rituels d'humiliation et de soumission au Moyen Age, *Archivum latinitatis medii Aevi, Bulletin Du Cange LIV*, 11–65.

Neumann, F. (2002). Von Kirchenbuße und öffentlicher Strafe. Öffentliche Sanktionsformen aus der Sendgerichtsbarkeit in städtischem und landesherrlichem Recht. In Schlosser, H., Sprandel, R., & Willoweit, D. (eds.), *Herrschaftliches Strafen seit dem Hochmittelalter: Formen und Entwicklungsstufen* (pp. 159–187). Böhlau.

Pahud de-Mortanges, R. (1992). Strafzwecke bei Gratian und den Dekretisten, *Zeitschrift der Savigny-Stiftung für Rechtsgeschichte, Kanonistische Abteilung*, 78, 121–158.

Pieper, P. (1980). Die Miniaturen des Nequambuches. In Kohl, W. (ed.), *Das Soester Nequambuch: Neuausgabe des Acht- und Schwurbuchs der Stadt Soest* (pp. 17–79). Dr. Ludwig Reichert Verlag.

Platelle, H. (2004). Pratiques pénitentielles et pratiques religieuses au moyen-âge: la pénitence des parricide et l'esprit de l'ordalie. In Platelle, H. (ed.), *Présence de l'Au-delà* (pp. 73–94). Presses Universitaires du Septentrion.

Pollack Oakley, T. (1932). The Cooperation of Medieval Penance and Secular Law, *Speculum*, 7, 515–524.

Preu, A. (1949). Pranger und Halseisen. Diss. jur., Univ. Erlangen.

Robins, J., Robins, R.W., Tangney, J.P. (2007). *The Self-Conscious Emotions: Theory and Research*. Guilford Press.

Rössler, E.F. (1852). *Die Stadtrechte von Brünn aus dem XIII. und XIV. Jahrhundert, nach bisher ungedruckten Handschriften herausgegeben*. J.G. Calve'sche Buchhandlung.

Scheele, F. (1998). Strafvollzug und Illustration: das Beispiel der Strafe zu Haut und Haar, *Hildesheimer Jahrbuch für Stadt und Stift Hildesheim*, 69, 89–116.

Schönbach, A.E. (1900). Studien zur Geschichte der altdeutschen Predigt. 2. Stück: Zeugnisse Bertholds von Regensburg zur Volkskunde, *Sitzungsberichte der Philosophisch-Historischen Klasse der Kaiserlichen Akademie der Wissenschaften in Wien*. A. Hölder.

Schulze, R. et al. (eds.) (2008). *Strafzweck und Strafform zwischen religiöser und weltlicher Wertevermittlung*. Rhema.

Sère, B., Wettlaufer, J. (eds.) (2013). *Shame between Punishment and Penance: The Social Usages of Shame in the Middle-Ages and Early Modern Times*. SISMEL—Edizioni del Galluzo.

Spargo, J.W. (1944). *Juridical Folklore in England Illustrated by the Cucking-Stool*. Duke University Press.

Strauch, D. (2008). *Der grosse Schied von 1258: Erzbischof und Bürger im Kampf um die Kölner Stadtverfassung*. Böhlau.

Tangney, J.P. & Fischer, K.W. (eds.) (1995). *Self-Conscious Emotions: The Psychology of Shame, Guilt, Embarrassment, and Pride*. Guilford Press.

Tangney, J.P. et al. (2013). Communicative Functions of Shame and Guilt. In Sterelny, K. et al. (Eds.) *Cooperation and its Evolution* (pp. 485–502). MIT Press.

Teetaert, A. (1926). *La confession aux laïques dans l'église latine depuis le VIIe jusqu'au XIVe siècle, Étude de Théologie positive*. J. de Meester et Fils, Ch. Beyaert, Éditeur pontifical, J. Gabalda.

Thomson, A. (1972). *I stocken: studier i stockstraffets historia*. Carl Bloms Boktryckeri A.-B.

Tomaschek, J.A. (1859). *Deutsches Recht in Österreich im 13. Jahrhundert, auf Grundlage des Stadtrechts von Iglau*, Tendler & Comp.

Trexler, R. (1984). Correre la terra: Collective Insults in the Late Middle Ages, *Mélanges de l'Ecole française de Rome (Moyen Age - Temps Modernes)* 96, 845–902.
Tropamer, H. (1911). La coutume d'Agen. Thèse en droit, Univ. Bordeaux.
Trusen, W. (1971). Forum internum und gelehrtes Recht im Spätmittelalter. Summae confessorum und Traktate als Wegbereiter der Rezeption. *Zeitschrift der Savigny Stiftung für Rechtsgeschichte, Kanonistische Abt.* 57, 83–126.
Varin, P. (1843). *Archives administratives de la ville de Reims: collection de pièces inédites pouvant servir à l'histoire des institutions dans l'intérieur de la cité*, 2:2. Crapelet.
Verein für mecklenburgische Geschichte und Altertumskunde (ed.) (1864). *Mecklenburgisches Urkundenbuch*. Stillersche Hofbuchhandlung.
Verriest, L. (1905). *Institutions judiciaires de Tournai au XIIIe siècle: Les registres de la justice dits Registres de la Loi.* H. & L. Casterman.
Vorsterman van Oyen, G.A. (1892). *Rechtsbronnen der Stad Aardenburg*. Nijhoff.
Wagner, K. (1995). De vera et falsa penitentia: An Edition and Study. Ph.D. diss., University of Toronto.
Weinrich, L. (Ed.). Lex familiae Wormatiensis ecclesiae. In *Quellen zur deutschen Verfassungs-, Wirtschafts- und Sozialgeschichte bis 1250* (pp. 88–105). Wissenschaftliche Buchgesellschaft.
Westphalen, E.J. von (1773). *Monumenta inedita rerum Germanicarum praecipue Cimbricarum et Megapolensium* 3. Joh. Chr. Martini.
Wettlaufer, J. (2010). Schand- und Ehrenstrafen des Spätmittelalters und der Frühneuzeit—Erforschung der Strafformen und Strafzwecke anhand von DRW-Belegen. In Deutsch, A. (ed.), *Das Deutsche Rechtswörterbuch—Perspektiven* (pp. 265–280). Winter.
Wettlaufer, J. (2011). Über den Ursprung der Strafe des Steintragens, *Zeitschrift der Savigny Stiftung für Rechtsgeschichte, Germanistische Abteilung*, 128, 348–360.
Wettlaufer, J. (2015). Evolutionäre Geschichtswissenschaft: Menschliches Handeln zwischen Natur und Kultur in der Vergangenheit. In Lange, B.P. & Schwarz, S. (eds.), *Die menschliche Psyche zwischen Natur und Kultur* (pp. 83–93). Pabst.
Wettlaufer, J. (2016a). Beschämung und Kooperation in historischen Gesellschaften: Eine evolutionäre Perspektive auf den sozialen Gebrauch moralischer Emotionen im Mittelalter und in der frühen Neuzeit. In Hennighausen, C., Lange, B.P., & Schwab, F. (eds.). *Evolution des Sozialen* (pp. 25–40). Pabst.
Wettlaufer, J. (2016b). Shame and Cooperation, *The RSA Journal*, Jan. 36–39.
Wettlaufer, J. & Nishimura, Y. (2013). The History of Shaming Punishments and Public Exposure in Penal Law in Comparative Perspective: Western Europe and East Asia. In Sère, B. & Wettlaufer, J. (eds.), *Shame between Punishment and Penance: The Social Usages of Shame in the Middle-Ages and Early Modern Times* (pp. 197–228). SISMEL—Edizioni del Galluzo.
Wilkes, W. (1976). *Die Miniaturen des Soester Nequambuches von 1315. Mit stadtgeschichtlichen Erläuterungen von Gerhard Köhn.* Technische Hochschule.
Winkler, N. (2009). In Flagranti: Zur Bestrafung eines Sittlichkeitsdelikts in der mittelalterlichen Gascogne. In Bandini, D. & Kronauer, U. (eds.), *Früchte vom Baum des Wissens. Eine Festschrift der wissenschaftlichen Mitarbeiter* (pp. 353–369). Winter.
Zaremska, H. (1996). *Les bannis au Moyen Âge*. Aubier.

9 Christian Humility, Papal Humiliations

An Honor-and-Shame Criterion in the Church's History Grand Narratives

Bénédicte Sère

The Impossible Humility of the Pontiff

Can the Pope be humble? This is the starting question, to answer which it is necessary to examine the sources of the time. Since the eleventh century, rhetorical constructions have endeavored to shape the figure of a Pope of power. In this regard, the Decree of Gratien played a vital role and the so-called "Gregorian reform" movement was an affirmation of a pontifical authority of the sovereign type. As advances were made in theorization, the majesty of the pontiff fed on exchanges with models of secular sovereigns as much as it inspired them.

From then on, the difficulty of thinking of the Pope's humility in relation to the question of his authority is based on the Augustinian reference as much as on the Thomasian reference. Saint Augustine, quoted by Saint Thomas Aquinas, raises the aporia. In question 161 of the *Summa Theologiae*, IIa IIae, article 3 explicitly deals with the problem: "Should we, out of humility, put ourselves below all?" Augustine is invoked in the preliminary arguments contradicting the thesis:

> According to St Augustine, "humility must be placed on the side of truth, not on the side of falsehood." Now, some men occupy a very high position: if they placed themselves below their inferiors, this could not be done without falsehood.[2]

Then Thomas responds in a rebuttal to the preliminary arguments by distinguishing between the inner act of humility, proper to the soul, and the outer act of humility that must be measured in order not to impair the authority of the superior:

> Humility, like the other virtues, resides mainly within the soul. One can thus, according to the inner act of the soul, put oneself below another, without allowing what might be at the expense of his salvation. It is in this sense that Augustine says in his "Rule": "Let the superior, by a feeling of fear of God, put himself under your feet." However, in the

DOI: 10.4324/9781003022916-12

external acts of humility, as also in the acts of other virtues, it is necessary to use the appropriate moderation, so that they cannot be turned at the expense of the other.

(Ibid., p. 915)

Humility, therefore, as well as affability or friendship elsewhere, threatens to tarnish and tarnishes the presence of pontifical authority. The *plenitudo potestatis* cannot be encumbered by a virtue which, as a result, is somewhat repressed in the religious field of monasteries, models of holiness and mysticism, before being gradually extended to the field of the laity.

As virulent as the attacks on the pontiff were at the time of the great invectives around the Schism, in the context of acute polemics, no text contains the reproach of a lack of humility against the pontiff. Pride and *superbia* are never invoked to demolish the pontiff, a visible sign that humility is not an expected virtue of the Pope. The evils with which the pontiff is charged are more stereotyped: he is accused of bad manners, of ambition, above all of lousy will, of infamy, of being a source of scandal, obstinacy, and pertinacity. He must be the good shepherd who gives his life for his sheep, and not the mercenary who flees his flock upon the arrival of the wolf or who sheds his sheep or abandons them to be dispersed. He is expected to be selfless, not humble. The example we are talking about does not contain the ingredient of humility.

Indeed the polemical context insists, as early as 1394, on the resignation of the Pope. Opponents of Benedict XIII proposed the way of surrender or abdication, or even resignation, of the two pontiffs, and first of all that of their obedience, Benedict XIII. To invite the pontiff to resign, the argument is not that of reasonable humility that would allow laying without charge despite an attack on his honor. The argument is instead that of the gift of oneself in the image of the Good Shepherd who gives his life for his sheep. If the Pope as a good shepherd must be ready to give his life for his sheep, how much more is owed to lay down his tiara and clothes for the cause of the unity of the Church?

> For this consideration, this memorable and truly worthy word of the Supreme Pontiff is founded, words that these ears have often heard from the mouth of our Lord: "I am ready," he said, "to bring about the union of the Church, even to the point of death or even the immolation of my own body, if necessary." How much more until the abdication of his status, for, by giving his life, who would not leave his garment, his crown or his miter?[3]

There is indeed one Pope, *apax* in the history of the Church up to the Great Schism, who lays down his functions out of humility. This was Pope

Celestine V, who resigned on December 10, 1294. He invoked humility, his lack of physical and intellectual strength in the face of his office. Aside from Pierre d'Ailly no one talked about this "angelic" Pope, this former hermit-monk, who confirmed more with the canons of holiness than with authority. Dante, moreover, placed him in hell for having shown cowardice (*viltade*) by his great refusal—*che fece per viltade il gran rifiuto*—a position refuted by Petrarch who deemed Celestine V a saint and his renunciation an act of courage.[4]

It is therefore certain that humility of the Pope was not apparent at the time of the Great Schism. Its impossibility comes from a distant construction of the *potestatis plenitudo* as a source of sovereignty, sublimity, and authority made of majesty. Moreover, the figure of a humble Saint Louis remains problematic, as Jacques Le Goff clearly showed: "A passage by Geoffroy de Beaulieu shows how Saint Louis' humility led him to perform acts deemed incompatible with royal dignity."[5]

The Great Schism: A Time of Humiliation for Popes

In Anagni, in October 1303, the Pope had already been humiliated. The episode is famous and dated. At the time of the Great Schism, the humiliation of the Pope was more structural. It touched the two bodies of the Pope: his political body and his personal body.

The political humiliations of the Pope were part of the ecclesiology of the moment, or rather the ecclesiological debates and experimentations of the moment. Indeed, the time had come to challenge the monarchical authority of the Pope. After having proposed several options (*via cessionis*, withdrawal of obedience, neutrality), theoreticians in the years 1407–1408 turned to the conciliar solution whereby a Council was proposed as the governmental alternative in the Church. It was a question of thinking differently about the distribution of power; no longer in a monarchical way, that is to say with a pyramidal head, but in a more collegial manner organized on the oligarchic principle, dear to Aristotle, of representativeness, delegation and mandate. Thus the Council, assisted by the Holy Spirit and *representans ecclesiam*, became the governing body of the Church, as proclaimed by the Decree *Haec Sancta* and ratified by the Decree *Frequens*, codifying the regularity of meetings. Of course, most actors of the time who agreed with the so-called "conciliarist" theses or at least conciliar theories were often counted among the ranks of the first opponents of the pontiff—the cessionists or the subtractionists—but also among all those who had distanced themselves from Benedict XIII out of spite, disappointment or weariness. In any case, conciliar theorization advanced from 1407–1408 to its implementation at the Council of Constance (1414–1418) and ultimately making the Council the body to resolve the Schism. In 1417, having deposed three Popes, it duly elected Martin V as the sole Pope of Christianity. By the Decree *Frequens*, regular meetings consecrated the idea of a Council as an ecclesial governing body and, in Basel, it became radicalized to the point of challenging again, with violence and radicalism, the monarchical supremacy of the pontiff until the end of the 1440s (1449). During this first half of the fifteenth century, consecrated as the "golden age of conciliarism," the Pope's authority was thus fully shaped by the progress and vitality of conciliar ideas. His authority was undermined, his legitimacy discussed by a powerful counter-power and the fullness of his power questioned.

However, the humiliations of this era of unrest also concerned the Pope's personal body. The ups and downs and vicissitudes of the moment were so many trials for a Pope already weakened in political charisma. First of all, the imprisonment of the Pope in Avignon for five years followed his unlikely escape, on March 11, 1403, were as much attacks on the dignity of his person as on his function (Valois, 1901: 189). The Pope suffered material deprivation, surveillance, boredom, and isolation. His fundamental rights were violated. On June 11, he was forced to consent to surrender. Pierre Le Roy and Gilles des Champs had threatened, in the case of his refusal, to suspend the entry of food supplies and cause the invasion of the palace. Then came the escape. The episode, worthy of a cape and sword novel, was potentially a source of desecration of the Pope's person.

> It was March 11, 1403. [...] At night he took a disguise, placed a consecrated host on his chest, and put a consecrated host under his clothes and put a letter from Charles VI under his clothes [...]. The removal of a few rubble blocks is enough to open a passage through a solid door that had once been used to communicate the Palace with the house of the dean of Notre-Dame-des-Doms. Benedict XIII slipped through this opening, accompanied by his doctor, one of his cameramen and an Aragonese lord [...]. During his captivity, Benedict XIII had allowed not only his hair to grow, but also his beard, which now two palms long, did so, according to a columnist (Martin d'Alpartil), resembling Patriarch Abraham. This was a severe departure from the habits of the Latin Church.
>
> (Valois, 1901: 325–328)

Likewise, when on March 20, 1415, the anti-Pope John XXIII fled Constance, in the middle of the Council, to go to Schaffhouse, stupor quickly gave way to insubordination and emancipation. The Council Fathers subsequently decided to maintain conciliar authority without the presence of the Pope, believing that the Council was sufficient on its own as it was the *Congregatio fidelium universalium.*

Besides the significant events of this desacralization of the two bodies of the Pope, it must also be said that the period was one of invectives and pamphlets against the Pope. The Pope was defamed, attacked, and accused in multiple treatises and polemical writings intended to make him yield.[6] The settlement of personal accounts were numerous, like that of Simon de

Cramaud with Benedict XIII (Sère, 2019), the invectives violent,[7] the grievances numerous,[8] and the attacks had various edges.[9] At the time of the Council of Basel, Pope Eugene IV even underwent two legal trials, during which many judgments condemned him. Émilie Rosenblieh, a specialist in the Council of Basel and judicial procedures of that conciliar period, unearthed a little-known manuscript: Paris, BnF, lat. 1511 (Rosenblieh, 2009). This manuscript holds the records of the hearing and the evidence produced against the Pope from July 26, 1437 to October 17, 1438, making it possible to understand how the Council of Basel instructed the second trial of Pope Eugene IV, from July 1437. In order to assert its judicial primacy over the papacy, the Council had developed a new conception of pontifical heresy based on violation of the canons and decrees of the Council. The Pope, on the testimony of 29 witnesses and a series of proofs, was accused of violating the ancient canons; in particular, those of the Council of Chalcedon whose sacredness had long been admitted, and especially those of Constance, including *Haec Sancta* on the front line. He was declared "an assiduous violator and contemplative of the sacred synodal canons."[10] Embodying the sacred authority of the assembly, the Basel Council justified its primacy at the top of the ecclesiastical hierarchy (Rosenblieh, 2019).

Indeed, previous epochs had been able to distinguish the two bodies of the Pope, to insist perhaps on the humanity of the body *ex natura* and the sublimity of the body *ex gratia* (see Paravicini-Bagliani, 1997: 85). The sovereign was God and Christ by the effect of grace; what is needed, he does not do "in any way as a man" (Pellens, 1966: 135). The contrast between person and function was pushed to the extreme. Some authors even claimed that Christ himself was "weak" (Pellens, 1966: 144–145) in his humanity; as they insisted: it is not as a man that we must obey him, because one cannot have such obedience to a man. If one owes obedience to the Pope, it is as an apostolic, that is, sent from Christ. The author Anonymous of York defined the *geminata persona* of the sovereign prince around the 1100s. However, the significant difference from the late-medieval period is precisely that the fictional person of the Pope is attacked. The mystical nature of the Pope in his authority and the fullness of the pontifical powers is no longer evident. A Paulinist theory has besides emerged to defend the idea that Paul is the peer of Peter, who had erred and has been rebuked by Paul. All the opponents of the Pope had excavated this verse of the *Acts of Apostles*.[11] Franciscus Zabarella is one of the rare individuals who commented on the text insisting on the humility of Peter: When Cornelius the Centurion (Act 10) fell at his feet, Peter had raised this convert up and reminded him of their shared humanity. Zabarella used Peter as an example of humility for the claimants to the papacy.[12]

In short, during the period of the Great Schism the Pope in his dual body was somehow desecrated. He lost the presence that the Gregorian movement had patiently built. He saw himself weakened and fragile. The proof appears in the theoretical construction at this time around the precept of fraternal correction: the Pope could be corrected under cover of the precept of fraternal correction, precisely because he was no longer the father but was the brother of the cardinals and bishops. He was brought back to the rank of peer among others. There was no longer a pontifical primacy.

Church Memory Faced with the Weakness of the Papacy during the Great Schism

The episode was therefore, for the memory of the Roman Church, painful because it was humiliating. It was, therefore, a question of erasing this memory by rewriting official accounts. As early as the fifteenth century, Juan de Torquemada became the appointed historiographer of pontifical centralization and thus founded the great narrative of what conciliarism would be: an accident in the history of the Church, a fatal revolution, a movement with heretical origins (Marsile of Padoue and Guillaume of Ockham), a happily definitive death thanks to the Lateran Council V, and also an unnamed plague, a heresy.[13] From this point on, all the stories extend and repeat the litany of anti-conciliarist arguments to the point that the official discourse runs until the 1960s of the contemporary era. At this time, following the announcement by John XXIII of the meeting of the Second Vatican Council for the year 1960, the studies on the Councils reflected. This was called *New Conciliarism*. Francis Oakley, among others, stressed the persistence of the conciliarist movement from the fifteenth century until the twentieth century, thus refuting the idea of a death of conciliarism in 1511 in Pisa II.[14] For the British historian teaching in the United States, the conciliarist movement remained alive, albeit underground, in the North of the Alps and allowed the emergence of the political parliamentarism of the seventeenth century in northern Europe. By reconstructing these discursive teleologies, whether they fell under anti-conciliar memory or conciliar counter-memory, one could say that the narrative rewrote history. On the one hand, it is a question of reaffirming the power and honor of the pontiff by erasing the dark episodes. On the other, it is a question of thinking about the constitutionality of a pontifical monarchy, the sole guarantor of the proper functioning of the Church.

To this double discursive plot, initiated by the Church and fought by historians of the twentieth century, is added the narrative resulting from the infallibilist movement of the end of the nineteenth century. When the protagonists of papal infallibility demanded a dogma eventually consecrated to the first Vatican Council in July 1870, they too worked, not surprisingly, to set aside the elements of every pontifical weakness that the Council had brought about in the history of the fifteenth century.[15] In the same vein as the discursive construction of the impossible humility of the Pope, it was necessary to consider the honor and power of the pontiff in the light of tradition. Historiography can thus be read only in the context of a history of ecclesial passions, made of honor and shame, between history and memory.

Notes

1 For higher periods, see for instance Kaufman (2012).
2 Thomas Aquinas, *Somme théologique*, IIa IIae, qu. 161, art. 3, Paris, éd. Cerf, 1985: 914. Among many titles on humility by Aquinas, see for instance Tarasievitch (1935).
3 Jean Gerson, *Sermo habitus Tarascone coram Benedicto XIII, inc.*: "Apparuit gratia Dei..." (January 1, 1404), éd. Glorieux, V, § 212, pp. 64–90, here p. 86: "Fundatur in hac consideratione dictum illud memorabile et vere dignum summo pontifice quod his auribus pluries accepti ab ore Domini nostri [...]: 'Paratus sum, inquit, etiam usque ad mortem vel immolationem corporis proprii si ita res exigat, ecclesiasticam unionem procurare'; quanto amplius usque ad proprii status abdicationem, nam quando daret vitam qui non desereret vestem aut coronam seu mitram?" See Roth (2018: 632).
4 Quoted by Mandelbaum, Oldcorn, & Ross (1999: 44).
5 Le Goff (1996: 610): "Ce souci hagiographique a parfois permis cependant de souligner, au niveau de la gestualité, certaines tensions entre les modèles incarnés par Saint Louis, le laïc qu'il était le clerc, le régulier qu'il a peut-être voulu être, le roi qu'il devait et voulait être, exposé par sa fonction sinon à tomber dans l'orgueil, la *superbia*, du moins à se montrer plus ou moins souvent 'en majesté', et le saint qu'il voulait être aussi et plus encore, un saint fortement marqué par les idéaux de sainteté du XIIIe siècle et d'abord par l'humilité."
6 See for instance Dietrich von Niehem, *Invectiva in diffugientem*, (March 22, 1415), *inc.*: "Alma mater catholica et apostolica ecclesia, unica et virgo sine ruga ...," éd. Von der Hardt, II, pp. 296–330. B. Sère, Les débats d'opinion à l'heure du Grand Schisme. Ecclésiologie et politique, Turnhout, Brepols, 2016.
7 E.g., Jean Courtecuisse in Di Stefano 1967: 317–333 or Pierre Plaoul, *Discours de clôture des débats avant le vote* (juin 7, 1398), éd. Du Boulay, IV, pp. 835–843, p. 837: "Item probatur per dictum Christi, *Omne Regnum in se divisum desolabitur*. Ex qua conclusione sequitur collorarie quod schisma est aeque mala aut peiora dispositio in Ecclesia ..."
8 Some examples out of many: Université de Paris, *Narratio et gravamina: (I) Narratio, inc.*: "Primo recommendetur Ecclesia in brevibus ..." (janvier 1396), Paris, BnF, lat. 14643, fol. 306r-308v; éd. Du Boulay, IV, pp. 799–803; (II) *Prima appellatio Universitatis a Benedicto XIII* (21 mars 1396 contre Benoît XIII), *inc.*: "Si tramitem veritatis vas electionis beatissimus Paulus judeorum ...," Paris, BnF, lat. 14643, fol. 309r-315v; éd. Du Boulay, IV, pp. 803–820.
9 Université de Paris, *Novem questiones, inc.*: "Utrum papa teneatur acceptare viam cessionis ..." (Fin août 1395), Paris, BnF, lat. 14643, fol. 71r; éd. Du Boulay, IV, pp. 753–753 bis; Université de Paris, *Requeste Universitatis facte Regi Francie* (programme de l'université au Grand Conseil), *inc.*: "Primo quod placeat prefato domino nostro regi ..." (août 31, 1395), Paris, BnF, lat. 14643, fol. 52v; *Thesaurus*, II, c. 1135–1136.
10 Décret *Prospexit Dominus*, edited in *AC*, t. 29, col. 180: "violatorem assiduum atque contemporanem sacrorum canonum synodalium ..."
11 On this point, see Izbicki (2009); Posthumus Meyjes, 1967, 1978. See also Posthumus Meyjes, 1968 [not seen]. Froehlich (1980, 2010).
12 Franciscus Zabarella, *Tractatus de Schismate*, in *De jurisdictione, autoritate, et praeeminentia imperiali ac potestate ecclesiastica ...*, ed. Simon Schard, Basel, 1566, p. 704.
13 See Izbicki (1986: 14). See also Pope Eugene IV's bull *Etsi non dubitemus*, dans *Concilium Florentinum, Ep. Pont.* I, pp. 7–9 n. 248. The bull quotes Torquemada's text, *Summa*, c. C, II, Venise, M. Tramezinum, 1561. On this bull Bäumer (1964).
14 For the bibliography see with a complete list Oakley (2003).
15 See, in particular, Sesboüé (2013) or Thils (1963, 1969, 1972).

References

Bäumer, R. (1964). Die Stellungnahme Eugens IV: Zum Konstanzer Superioritätsdekret in der Bulle "Etsi non dubitemus." In Franzen, A. & Müller, W. (eds.), *Das Konzil von Konstanz. Beiträge zu seiner Geschichte und Theologie* (pp. 337–354). Herder.

Di Stefano, G. (1967). *L'œuvre oratoire française de Jean Courtecuisse*, G. Giappichelli.

Froehlich, K. (1980). Fallibility Instead of Infallibility? A Brief History of the Interpretation of Ga. 2, 11–14. In Empie, P. & Murphy, A. (eds.), *Teaching Authority and Infallibility in the Church* (pp. 259–269, 351–357) Minneapolis, Augsburg.

Froehlich, K. (2010). *Biblical Interpretation from the Church Fathers to the Reformation*, Ashgate.

Izbicki, Th.M. (1986). Papalist Reaction to the Council of Constance: Juan de Torquemada to the Present, *Church History*, 55, 7–20,

Izbicki, Th.M. (2009). The Authority of Peter and Paul: the Use of Biblical Authority during the Great Schism. In Rollo-Koster, J. & Izbicki, Th.M. (eds.), *A Companion to the Great Western Schism (1378–1417)* (pp. 375–393). Brill.

Kaufman, P.I. (2012). Humility, Civility, and Vitality: Papal Leadership at the Turn of the Seventh Century, *Leadership*, 8 (3), 245–256.

Le Goff, J. (1996). *Saint Louis*, Gallimard.

Mandelbaum, A., Oldcorn, A. & Ross, C. (eds.) (1999). *Lectura Dantis: Inferno. A Canto-by-Canto Commentary*, University of California Press.

Oakley, F. (2003). *The Conciliarist Tradition: Constitutionalism in the Catholic Church, 1300–1870*, Oxford University Press.

Paravicini-Bagliani, A. (1997). *Le corps du pape*. Seuil.

Pellens, K. (1966). *Die Texte des Normannischen Anonymus*, Steiner.

Posthumus Meyjes, G.H.M. (1967). *De controverse tussen Petrus en Paulus. Galaten 2:11 in de historie*, M. Nijhoff.

Posthumus Meyjes, G.H.M. (1968). Iconografie en Primaat: Petrus en Paulus op het pauselijk zegel, *Nederlands Archief voor Kerkgeschiedenis*, 49, 4–36.

Posthumus Meyjes, G.H.M. (1978). *Jean Gerson et l'assemblée de Vincennes (1329). Ses conceptions de la juridiction temporelle de l'Église*, Brill.

Rosenblieh, É. (2009). La violation des décrets conciliaires ou l'hérésie du pape: le procès d'Eugène IV (1431–1447) au concile de Bâle d'après le manuscrit latin 1511 de la Bibliothèque nationale de France, *Revue belge de philologie et d'histoire*, 86 (3–4),245–268.

Rosenblieh, É. (2019). L'Esprit saint, ou la légitimation de l'autorité conciliaire: le procès du pape Eugène IV au concile de Bâle (1431–1439). In Cuchet G. & Mériaux, Ch. (eds.), *La dramatique conciliaire de l'Antiquité à Vatican II* (pp. 219–238). Presses universitaires du Septentrion.

Roth, C. (2018). Irrtum und Wahrheit: Die Auseinandersetzung Johannes Gersons mit wahren und falschen Visionen und Lehren. Versuch einer Kriteriologie, In Speer, A. & Mauriège, M. *Irrtum, Error, Erreur* (pp. 627–636). De Gruyter.

Sère, B. (2019). Haïr le pape: Les antécédents médiévaux d'une émotion moderne. In Andurand, O., Deniel-Ternant, M., Galland, C., & Guitienne-Mürger, C. (eds.), *Histoires croisées. Politique, religion et culture du Moyen Âge aux Lumières; études offertes à Monique Cottret* (pp. 165–178). Presses Universitaires de Paris Nanterre.

B. Sère, L'invention de l'Eglise. Essai sur la genèse médiévale de la modernité politique, Paris, PUF, 2019, English translation forthcoming, 2023.

Sesboüé, B. (1913). *Histoire et théologie de l'infaillibilité de l'Église*. Lessius.

Tarasievitch, J. (1935). Humility in the Light of St. Thomas, Diss. Theol., Fribourg University, Switzerland.

Thils, G. (1963). *L'Infaillibilité du peuple chrétien "in credendo": Notes de théologie post-tridentine*, Bibliotheca Ephemeridum Theologicarum Lovaniensium.

Thils, G. (1969). *L'Infaillibilité pontificale: source, conditions, limites*, Duculot.

Thils, G. (1972). *La Primauté pontificale: la doctrine de Vatican I, les voies d'une révision*, Duculot.

Valois, N. (1901). *La France et le Grand Schisme*. Picard & fils.

Part III
Honor and Shame in Modernity

10 Collective Shame in the Modern World

The Case of Blasphemy Laws and Tolerant Sensibilities

David Nash

Blasphemy has been a fault line lying between the sacred and secular since comparatively modern times. Before this date the offense was characterized by those whose attitudes or behavior indicated a complicated response to the idea, and often the reality, of authority. In more modern times it has been characterized as an assault upon the religious feelings and identities of others. Both the past and contemporary history of interactions around blasphemy have displayed ideas of shame and shaming as an integral part of its mechanism. Despite calls to abolish blasphemy laws some modern states have retained and even enhanced them as a species of protection for government and its agendas associated with managing its populations.

This chapter investigates how the peculiar nature of blasphemy laws have regularly utilized the concept of shame as a psychological lever to achieve aspirations and ends. In the medieval world communities acted against the blasphemer because they brought the specter of providential judgment and shame down upon such a community. As Jörg Wettlaufer's Chapter 8 indicates, such individuals were ostracized and comfort was offered to such a society by seeing perpetrators punished in shame-orientated spectacles. In more modern times some blasphemers in the West have utilized shame as a method of indicting forms of religion for their poor treatment of minorities. The survival of these motifs is notable in many modern episodes of blasphemy in both East and West. Modern conceptions of shame, as expressions of the collective will, are utilized to describe breaches of multiculturalism, of tolerance, of laws against incitement, and generally as breaches of more civilized taste. This chapter investigates the endurance of shame phenomenon within societal confrontations with blasphemy. It also asks what shame strategies mean within modernity for the concept of censorship, and indeed free speech, alongside their respective mechanisms and purposes.

The Medieval and Early Modern Origins of the Blasphemer and Their Treatment Invoking Shame

The offense of blasphemy in the medieval and early modern period was extremely gendered and was very often characterized as a wholly male offense. The

DOI: 10.4324/9781003022916-14

blasphemer of the early modern period was an emphatically solitary figure. Indeed they were made so by Western culture's construction of the offense as a clear and intolerable aberration, one induced by the individual's effect upon the community. This marginality could be attained through transgressive thought manifesting itself in errant behavior. In the first of these instances we frequently encounter individuals who were drunk, were cursing their ill luck at the gambling den or were overcome with anger for some very unusual reason (Villa Flores, 2007). Many contemporaries, and some historians, were conscious that blasphemy could be a characteristic which was identified specifically with some occupations and lifestyles. This was regularly thought to have been associated especially with itinerancy. This meant traders and carters were associated with "bringing" blasphemy from outside into stable communities. Occupational characteristics associated with both danger and itinerancy were also a prominent feature with sailors and soldiers regularly suspected, accused, and prosecuted for blasphemy. To an extent marginality attracted elements of shame. This stemmed from a belief that this characteristic was an intrinsic threat to stable communities—much in the manner that many early modern historians have established around the accusation of witchcraft in various contexts (Cabantous, 2002). It was also the case that the religious and ethnic marginality of some individuals and groups made them vulnerable to accusations of blasphemy, especially when religious conversion to the preferred faith of a confessional state was involved. This was a particular feature of blasphemy's history within the Iberian Peninsula (Flynn, 1995).

When such individuals perpetrated blasphemy societies would regularly react with horror, but this would be very often tinged with responses that sought species of marginalization of the culprit in answer to blasphemy. This characteristic often featured explicitly in punishment for it as a crime (van Dülmen, 1990: 56, 142–143 and 156; Schwerhoff, 2005). The blasphemer could also, whilst exhibiting the aforementioned characteristics, still be the victim of providential judgment made by rulers of cities states and territories. It was often the case that blasphemy would be at the center of pogroms that rulers decided to enact, or were persuaded to do so, as a prelude to war as a means of pacifying the almighty and actively seeking providential help (Belmas, 1989).

The blasphemer was considered shameful and the marginalization of blasphemers was completed by the numerous shame punishments which were enacted against blasphemers in the early modern period. Many of these were closely linked to their transgression against religion and the community by containing obviously religious content and were frequently linked to sites of communal religious worship. In parts of Europe (notably the Netherlands) and colonial America it was commonplace for individuals to be dressed in a white sheet and to process to the church, chapel, or cathedral. Sometimes they would be forced to wait outside during divine service, at other times they would be admitted to the building. In parts of Germany and the Netherlands a large barrel-type jacket, often reserved for drunkards, would be prescribed wear to the place of worship for such an offense, perhaps further indicating the perceived link between drunkenness and blasphemy (Nash, 2007a: 153–155).

In the Iberian Peninsula, notably Spain, those convicted of low-level blasphemy were made to ride backwards upon a donkey (Nash, 2007a: 154). Sweden prescribed a ritual in which blasphemers were forced to run down a local thoroughfare to be greeted by the whole community lined up to beat such miscreants with wooden sticks. In other instances individuals were made to ritually kiss the earth (Nash, 2007a: 154). In several of the American colonies there were some quite extremely demonstrative shame punishments such as being made to witness oneself being executed in effigy by hanging (Nash, 2007a: 166).

These were relatively unusual and notable punishments for blasphemy. The far more commonplace occurrence was a series of progressive punishments which created stigma which, if the code was known widely enough, would actively mark out recidivists and place a marker upon the severity and frequency of their crimes of blasphemy. These punishments involved disfigurement of the face with branding being used as a primary element in this. Progressive punishment showcasing disfigurement centered around stapling or cutting of the lip. This could occur to a number of different degrees signifying first, second, and indeed subsequent offenses (Nash, 2007a). Alternatives to this were mutilations of the tongue which were similarly deemed appropriate for speech crimes. Several of these punishments were augmented by others such as public whipping and imprisonment. On occasions individuals were also subject to the death penalty for the perpetration of such crimes.

So what are we to make of this catalogue of punishments and their implications for the societies which dispensed them, and what do they similarly tell us about the crime of blasphemy and its relationship to shame? What we might first notice about the crime of blasphemy is there is not a great deal of uniformity to how the crime was punished. There are progressive punishments for minor transgressions involving mutilation for likely successive infractions. This indicates low-level offense that fits in with the subculture marginality idea alluded to by contemporaries and some historians (Cabantous, 2002). However, there are also some cases where there is no mention of lower-level punishments and merely a capital sentence is recorded. But equally there are others where a multitude of punishments, including an eventual capital option, are applied.

This inconsistency might suggest that punishment for the crime of blasphemy in this period is, at least, sometimes related to context. This element in particular would conceivably have been exacerbated by the fear such blasphemers generated within individual contexts. As already suggested periods of strain and trauma served to psychologically heighten the potential threat blasphemers posed, a phenomenon linked to providentialism. Certainly in looking at England and Scotland the threat posed by some individuals suggests this. In Scotland, Thomas Aikenhead, a humble Edinburgh student was executed for blaspheming amidst a series of dangerous events that overtook the city and country also ravaged by foreboding created by rumors and fears (Graham, 2013; Nash, 2016). In England the Quaker James Nayler's entry into the city of Bristol on a donkey in 1656 in imitation of Christ was an equally inflammatory gesture. This was perpetrated during a period of political turmoil when the stability of government was in question, following the upheaval of the War of Three Kingdoms (Civil War). Nayler was dangerous for the government because his actions, and those of Quakers generally, tested the limits of religious toleration, because they sought to disrupt existing religious practice. Although Nayler's case provoked discussion about Parliament's right to try him for a capital offense, he was nonetheless eventually exposed to serial shame punishments in three separate localities. (Nash, 2007a: 119–122 and 159–160)

We have to acknowledge that both types of blasphemer, the casual drunk or itinerant and the religious/political threat were dangers to social stability and constituted a form of violence upon this. If we genuinely consider errant behavior to be a form of violence it is worth considering how far shaming such individuals constitutes evidence of the working of an Eliasian "civilizing process." Blasphemers were sometimes dangerous and sometimes uncouth others which a confessionalizing society would seek to marginalize and exclude. It is also noteworthy that the protection of oaths and their binding power was one of the aims of early European statutes limiting blasphemy. Oaths and agreements binding individuals in the sight of God were essential for the wellbeing of commerce (Nash, 2007a: 47). This would certainly fit with the Eliasian idea that the plutocratic urge amongst early European urban elites was a determining factor in the creation of codes of conduct which marginalized errant behavior. Around blasphemy this suggests a nexus of tighter knit, God-fearing parvenus that identified their prosperity with divine providence and favor, or at least did not wish to contemplate its destabilization by tolerating the improvident blasphemer. Thus, we might legitimately add careless "improvidence" to the litany of the uncouth and unacceptable that Elias identified as the wholesale targets of a commercial, modernizing, and improving urban Europe.

Such a conscious move against blasphemy from the world of commerce and improvement-minded elites might also put us in mind of the ideas of Tawney and Weber (Tawney, 1926; Weber, 2004). Realigning and streamlining religious belief was instrumental to both these thinkers for the rise and consolidation of commercial capitalism. The use of shame punishments against blasphemers is also a characteristic of what I have identified elsewhere as "passive" blasphemy. This is effectively the suggestion that in the medieval and early modern periods individuals stood passive, relying upon forms of authority to take action against the crime of blasphemy (Nash, 2007b). In thinking about the function of shame punishments, dispensed for the crime of blasphemy, these exhibit significant elements of the prolonged and targeted display of authority and power. They enabled forms of authority to take action that is highly visible, sometimes in different dimensions of this facet. The visibility of shame punishments, as we are well aware, have important spatial and temporal qualities. Punishing an individual in a well-noted and recognized public place, often one specifically identified with the offense, maximized the visibility of the criminal and of the exercise of power. This also had temporal dimensions since many sentences had the provision that the punishment be repeated on subsequent well-publicized occasions. There was also another temporal dimension in the visibility of disfiguring punishments which displayed the miscreants' individual or serial offenses for many years to come. Thus authority was exhibited to reassure, as shame punishments worked as an antidote seeking to rob blasphemers of their episodic power. They also had an obvious capacity to ostracize and reintegrate, serving to further confirm the suggestion that shame was (and is) an emphatically social emotion. Many of these elements can be observed in looking at the pronouncements of organizations that set themselves up as moral authorities seeking to police behavioral nuisances. Evidence of this comes through in records concerning medieval confraternities which sought to save from error and indeed into later attempts to suppress vice in seventeenth- and eighteenth-century societies (Housley, 1982).

The waning of shame punishments served to forget this power when the punishment for the blasphemer gradually moved from shaming to incarceration. By the end of the eighteenth century and into the nineteenth the identity of blasphemers had also importantly shifted to embrace writers, artists, and the sporadic outbreak of political/anti-religious dissidents. These individuals remained marginal to mainstream society and, unlike the blasphemers of earlier epoch, their offense was frequently to take critiques of religion too far into the realm of scurrility.

However we should also notice that these new blasphemers, in their creation of critique, were themselves individuals who organized and very often actively dealt in the currency of shame. Having acquired psychological independence from religion their emotions were often employed in developing and framing their critiques of it. Shame was a frequent candidate enlisted for an assault of this nature. In the nineteenth century the quest to embrace the enlightenment amongst the liberal and secular minded would often provoke an accusation that religion itself was an anachronism, something that clearly had not earned a legitimate place within modern society upon merit. Frequently invoked was the idea of the "spirit of the age" which was deemed to be progressive, secular, and beyond the religious (Nash 2007a).

In the nineteenth century some works of anticlericalism and what came to be prosecuted as blasphemy sought to shame the church for the poverty of irrational belief it clung to in the face of all the empirical evidence beloved of modernity. Biblical criticism could be merged with rational moral indignation when confronted with the apparent barbarity of a number of biblical episodes. Attacking these was the stock in trade of freethought writers and publishers such as Léo Taxil and George William Foote (Marsh, 1998; Nash, 1999). The latter in particular regularly offered cartoon depictions of embarrassing episodes from the Old Testament. Occasionally they would be even harder-hitting assaults on Christian doctrines, such as forgiveness, where Christianity could be shamed for demonstrating that faith in its doctrines and tenets could trump and circumvent natural justice and morality (Nash, 1999: 133). Where secular society could be arguing for degrees of tolerance and equality, religion's attempt to fight back and reassert itself could be seen as an attempt to re-establish spurious control over behavior and conscience. This critique was also transported to the contemporary world of Europe's colonial present in the nineteenth century. Secularists readily critiqued Christianity's especially poor record in seeking to convert colonial indigenous populations. The British establishment's condescending view of the indigenous populations of the Indian subcontinent drew critiques into other territory, as its credibility was swiftly compared with that of the religious traditions of India itself and quite regularly found to be wanting (Nash, 2000). Quite often Christianity itself would be seen as encouraging the colonial enterprise and the resulting critique, at least in England, would shame the aristocracy's attitude to the Indian subcontinent as a playground ripe for material despoliation.

In this period the artists and writers, individuals capable of exploring shame within the imaginary, also frequently created and inhabited outsider status. This status and the assaults upon conventional society and morality itself fueled shame-filled responses from the conservatively minded who saw the outsider as an intrinsic betrayer.

Together these responses point to how we might seek to uncover and explore how shame might be a central component of how blasphemy and the depth of feeling it conveys could be experienced and communicated to the contemporary world of the offended. But also, importantly, this might help historians uncover vital information about, and recover, the precise contexts of blasphemous incidents. This is to judge the whole effect of feelings around blasphemous words or actions, rather than maintaining a concentration upon laws and the content of utterances. In turn this offers to show to wider society both how and why blasphemy can become important at particular historical junctures. As such it potentially also further builds upon the work of Ute Frevert's enterprise of investigating shame and emotion in macro-political events and its use as a tool of negotiation and international diplomacy (Frevert, 2020).

Blasphemy appears here in the nexus of fear and shame. We might first ask the question about whether this is a key genuine reaction to the real fear that is individual and visceral, or how far this is fear generated by an abstract concept. If it is the latter, then the history of blasphemy ought to appreciate the history of how individuals organized themselves to overcome such fears and ultimately to remove these from the cultural makeup of many modern societies. After all those who rejected secular liberalizing tendencies referred to themselves as "God fearing." This project would also enable the history of emotions like approach, since emotions like shame become a way into what it means, or was like, to feel blasphemy—a project unpicking a past emotion. But this also intersects with the earlier mentioned project considering the relationship between blasphemy and Norbert Elias's "civilizing process." This is relevant because this is supposed to be an emotion or emotional reaction which our modern selves have learned to forget.

I have already discussed elsewhere that the crime of blasphemy is the one offense containing a component of violence whose historical trajectory runs emphatically counter to the modernizing teleology of the "civilizing process" (Nash, 2007c). Forms of government grow in sophistication and gather to themselves progressively enhanced responsibilities for policing a range of serious offenses against peace and order, thereby guaranteeing the safety of their citizens, the trajectory for the offense of blasphemy is very different. The nineteenth/early twentieth century produces an overall trend where societies actually seek to shed and step back from providing protection and restitution to the injured party. Indeed the state itself in many noted pronouncements, and case law, gives significant notice to societies that the state no longer considers itself to be such an injured party in instances where blasphemy becomes an accusation or indictment. This coincides with the same period's flowering conception of human rights and the primacy of individual beliefs and feelings which come to take center stage.

Whilst this history, thus far, is one revolving around liberal modernizing and secular progress, such an outlook needs to appreciate the backlash-inspired history of refusenik ideas that failed to embrace this. Within the historiography of blasphemy I have labeled this transition the movement to "active blasphemy," a period in which the individual becomes responsible for processing policing and prosecuting the offense, where once they relied upon other forms of institutional authority to do so (Nash 2007b). This was, as far as blasphemy was concerned, the culmination of the Enlightenment's argument for autonomous individual religious conscience. Indeed the anti-Eliasian withdrawal of the state from legislation and policing in this seems to have actually fed free-speech narratives and tropes.

Ironically for Eliasian theory what society saw as policing devolved to the conscience of the individual relied precisely upon the outcome of the civilizing process. In English law this turned on conceptions of what became known as "manner" which governed the conduct of the criticism of religion. Judges and Home Office civil servants frequently alluded to this idea which meant temperate and reasoned criticism was effectively permitted by law and could not, within the modern world, be legitimately productive of offense or attract the opprobrium of others. In its own way this described the culmination of the civilizing process around the offense of blasphemy, at least as far as its conception of a teleological model of human development was concerned. Within this vision humankind would have evolved away from civil strife around religion to have reached a plateau of tolerance, whereby Christianity had civilized itself away from the caricatures of inquisitorial torture beloved of anticlericalists. Likewise modern society had seemingly made the "required" concession to the conscience of the agnostic, laodicean, or outright atheist. This is as long as such individuals exhibited thought and decorum and themselves to have banished the uncouth debasement of religion. Alongside such restraint the attitudes of government and law enforcement persuaded writers and artists into the culture of the "chilling effect" which potentially removed from them the capacity and desire to explore the outer reaches of religious themes, and more importantly to publish upon these. Seemingly, with a cursory glance, this looks like the fulfillment of the civilizing process banishing the blasphemous tendency and the religiously dogmatic tendency to the margins of a modern civilized society—both seemingly uncouth remnants of an earlier age.

But this analysis does not account for the stubborn resistance put up by some elements within organized Christianity which fought a rearguard action to somehow preserve the components of confessional society. In retrospect these refuseniks of secular society seek to attain this through foregrounding the idea of community and the communitarian impulse. They cling to the past in a self-conscious creation of imagined communities of the offended. Certainly within English society these have a resonance for moral guardians and politicians. The myriad generations of apparently honest church goers and believers whose faith led them to exercise restraint and decorum, are regularly invoked as betrayed by the new and the shocking. This is an attempt to narrativize and give voice to a collection of ideas about morality and prosperity being utterly contingent upon maintaining the state as a confessionalizing entity.

Any tolerationist weakening of this smacked of betrayal. Liberalizing terms and processes were deemed to be denying the importance of conventional morality, tradition and the power of providentialism which had itself a dual importance. Firstly, God-fearing morality could be invoked as having preserved society from the worst excesses of allowing blasphemy to prevail. But equally, within this narrative, providentialism could yet permit forms of divine judgment to cause damage to the society that had been so fortuitously preserved from harm. This latter attitude has been surprisingly enduring (Nash, 2008).

It is important that one of the tools of narration and persuasion within this narrative is the use of shame. Those who flout such providence and those who permit such flouting are equally indicted as having shamed their society. Within the context of assaults upon Christianity this could range from those with a permissive mindset, to those perpetrators of artistic blasphemy that cared little for religion and wanted to peddle their godlessness at the supreme cost of morality. Likewise, those who stood by and permitted this were similarly shamed. Custodians of cultural institutions could equally be accused of permitting the deluge to overtake a previously benevolent society that had extended effective prosperity and psychological peace to all (Nash, 1999).[1] Also indicted were apparent quisling members of the clergy who had embraced degrees of permissive liberalism in pursuit of popularity, or an illusory relevance in an age dangerously tilted away from its God-fearing equilibrium. Again the language of shame was part of the indictment for such betrayal. In England this is especially visible in the rhetoric of moral-majority groups in the 1970s and the language of their de facto leader Mary Whitehouse (Thompson, 2012; Whitehouse, 1993). This lay-inspired moral majority became self-appointed custodians of religious feeling and became vigilant around any cultural challenges to Christianity that threatened to render it unstable in the minds of the easily influenced. It was no surprise to see within a few short years of each other complaints about the West End musicals *Jesus Christ Superstar and Godspell*; these were followed by complaints about the Danish filmmaker Jens-Jorgen Thorsen's proposed *Sex-Life of Christ*; swiftly followed by complaints about *Monty Python's Life of Brian*; reaching court eventually in the *Gay News* case (Nash, 1999: 239–257; Nash 2007a: 211–219).

Within the last thirty years we have also witnessed the use of blasphemy to shame religions and the ideas that they ferment. This was clearly the motivation behind the illustrations that were central to both the *Charlie Hebdo* and *Jyllands-Posten* Danish cartoon incidents. This motive might also be ascribed to Michel Houlebeque whose pronouncements upon the nature of Islam stemmed from external contempt for the ideas it promoted (Dacey, 2012: 88–89). Free-speech ripostes to this view arguing for the value of society enriching social change echoed the age-old attitude of the shamed who perhaps see themselves as the trailblazers of better societies and moralities. However the situation becomes more complicated when we consider the Salman Rushdie affair. It was obvious that what was written by Rushdie in *The Satanic Verses* was construed as an insult, although intention to do so was manifestly less than clear. Some sidestepped the issue of intention by suggesting Rushdie had showed a distinct lack of respect for the norms and values represented by Islam and its communities (Gubo, 2015: 47–49). These examples also opened the door to views which argued that defamation of other religions was a cloak for racism (Gubo, 2015: 69). In the eyes of Rushdie's critics tension appeared irrelevant since Rushdie had "failed" to police himself. He had engaged upon "offending conduct" and was no longer in control of the thoughts and attitudes of respondents. As Joel Feinberg notes, such conduct "produces unpleasant or uncomfortable experiences—affronts to the sense or sensibility, disgust, shock, shame embarrassment, annoyance, boredom, anger, fear, or humiliation—from which one cannot escape without unreasonable inconvenience or even harm" (Dacey, 2012: 78).

Shame on the Grand Scale: The Politics of National and Supranational Blasphemy Law Making

Ute Frevert has pioneered the investigation of shame as a component of international relations and diplomacy and has cited an important range of examples from the nineteenth and twentieth centuries as well as from the contemporary world. These clearly indicate that the whole panoply of emotions and responses that we are used to seeing in action in microencounters around shame are also substantially in play when we consider human interactions at the macro level of the national and international context (Frevert, 2020). In her analysis we discover the opening exchanges between individual nations, often of vastly different cultures, retain the desire to maintain and certainly not lose face. This loss of face is conceived of as surrendering power and initiative within the dynamic of exchanges that are central to the phenomenon of diplomatic relations. From here we can speculate that many other of the theoretical approaches to contemporary performance and a history of shame may also usefully be applied in these particular circumstances. Here we might think of Irving Goffman's idea of "frames" and of life constituting a series of performances that the individual has to prepare for, negotiate whilst in progress, and forensically dissect upon their inevitable conclusion (Goffman, 1959; Goffman, 1963a; Goffman, 1963b; Goffman, 1971). Shame, in these encounters outlined by Frevert, is a tool in a series of battles between individual nations with each seeking establish some form of hegemony over other nations; often this is with the particular aim of selling the achievement of such triumphs to their own populace. Although democracies appeared to be marginally less prone to such actions the fit with such a conclusion is scarcely complete.

We might now, however, contrast this with the recent history of blasphemy which has some different dynamics at work. The nation state, as constructed by Frevert's schema and with reference to minorities within it appealing to the imagined communities of offense, remains an important factor. However, we also need to note that there is now a significant third player at work within the dynamics of these interactions around blasphemy upon the international stage. The modern history of the offense has actually moved to a macro level beyond the national whereby supranational agencies become involved. In most of these instances there are presumptions about the nature of law, of human rights, and of freedom of expression. In contrast to the exceptionalism that narratives of the providential create within the context of the nation state, such narratives of laws and rights seek to be umbrella standards formulated by supranational bodies with the intention of being applicable to all.

These organizations range from regulatory and legislative bodies who oversee the creation and promulgation of laws to watchdogs constituted by official organizations and NGOS. In this we might count organizations such as the European Court of Human Rights, the European Commission, and various bodies established by the United Nations. Darara Gubo notes that the imperative for toleration has been present in multinational prescriptions for treaties and the establishment since the treaty of Westphalia of 1648. Nations refusing to conform have been censured in subsequent twentieth-century documents such as the Covenant of the League of Nations and the

Charter of the United Nations; indeed, the latter of these actively pledges to take action in the event of detecting such breaches of rights (Gubo, 2015: 5).

This last document also contains a pre-prepared shaming admonishment about how errant behaviors produce wars, suffering, interference in the internal affairs of other nations, and kindle hatred between peoples and nations.[2] This was subsequently augmented by the Universal Declaration of Human Rights (UDHR), the International Covenant on Civil and Political Rights (ICCPR), and the Declaration on the Elimination of All Forms of Intolerance and of Discrimination Based on Religion or Belief. This described actions against its provisions as "an affront to human dignity." Similarly declarations on behalf of individual religious groupings, such as the Universal Declaration of Islamic Human Rights, contain similar prohibitions (Gubo 2015: 9, 10). The universalism of such declarations and their intended provisions would be frequently cast into stark relief, especially since they also protected the right for individuals to change their religion, and for all religions to manifest themselves. This ran against the grain of some religious groups and their identity as communities. Occasionally there are mutually binding agreements that are either yet to be enforced or ratified (Limon, Ghanea, and Power, 2018). Together all of these amounted to a complex and self-reinforcing web of Eliasian civilizing sanctions against the tendencies that a wider (international) society had pronounced as barbarous and beyond acceptance in a polite and civilized world. Critiques of the language of cultural universalism would frequently equate this with civilizing colonial projects of the past.

In many respects these organizations described above delegate work to some individuals such as the United Nations creation of a "Special Rapporteur on Religious Intolerance." This office interestingly in recent years (2000) changed its name to Special Rapporteur on Freedom of Religion and Belief (Limon, Ghanea, and Power, 2018). The work of the UN and its appointees can also be seen as supplemented by the work of ad hoc and single-purpose commissions. These tend to be convened at specific moments to address immediate problems and, occasionally, to pronounce further and actively make policy and recommendations that intend to be inclusive and far reaching. Frequently their conclusions have resonance that is often referred to, actively quoted, and recapitulated. In this category we might class the convention and reports emanating from the Venice Commission. This foregrounded the principle that citizens of European countries had a duty to accept freedom of expression as essential to debate in democratic societies.[3]

There is also a network of national nongovernmental organizations (NGOs) and pressure groups (both religious and secular) that operate both within their own country and sphere of influence, as well as seeking to be foci of the efforts to showcase and alter religious laws which operate to the detriment of individuals and their freedoms. Members of these networks are frequently galvanized into action by the appearance of an emotive challenge to religious freedom or free speech infraction, often resulting in detention or the imprisonment of individuals. This group of disparate forces are the agents in the modern world of critiquing and narrating the effects of blasphemy laws on contemporary societies. These organizations and individuals by and large oppose blasphemy laws as forms of legislation on behalf of state religions and frequently use each other's pronouncements as justification for such sustained criticism.[4] They also see such laws as potential incitement and trigger for extra-judicial activity including clandestine murder (Gubo, 2015: 41). Such ideas are often indicted by cultural relativists as stemming from species of universalism that were coined and shepherded by Western liberalizing influences (Gubo, 2015: 20–22).

What is striking here is the use of shame within so many of these interactions. For individual states, so frequently cornered by the pressure exerted by these supranational organizations, the traditional protection for their populations remains the goal in view. Miscreants from the country's population are frequently considered to have damaged the religious peace and their activities are considered shameful. Such instances are, to a great extent, not a significant departure from the religious history described in this chapter up to this point.

What is, however, new and innovative in our history is the use of shame by the supranational bodies described. This indicts countries for departing from, or not adhering to in the first place, many of these international protocols. In many of these tabled criticisms shame is reached for as an emotive language to defend international standards which are seen to be self-evidently superior, modern, and more civilized. When such narratives are created with reference to Muslim countries—the most frequent refuseniks who resist the clarion calls for stringent and defensible international standards—they can be especially sharp. Indeed, many of these criticisms regularly attract the accusation of Orientalism in seeking to present the liberal ire of the West as a superficially agreed international standard of religio/legal conduct and behavior. Occasionally this is countered in the West by fears expressed around a potential backlash that would damage the identity and rights of Muslim citizens in European countries (Gubo, 2015; 42: Jenkins, 2007).

Dialogues from supranational organizations seek to shame individual countries for their intransigence and obscurantism in failing to accept the language and logic of human rights. Such countries reply with arguments centered upon cultural relativism—the live and let live approach of dissidents and individual blasphemers for many centuries. The difference here is that liberal societies who claim to have transcended shame seek human rights conformity and denounce heterogeneous cultural relativism. This looks especially stark in the eyes of Eastern European societies which do not have recent social democratic traditions and, in part, explains their ambivalence about the universalism of human rights when it comes to votes within supranational organizations (Gubo, 2015: 22).

Occasionally this "shaming lobby" can have an impact upon countries in the West who have revisited their blasphemy laws and produced solutions which contravene international standards. Ireland's creation of a new blasphemy law in 2008 was an interesting case in point. This law was formulated as an attempt to respond to the pressures exerted by supranational organizations that sought to offer universal protection to religious beliefs. Ireland's existing law had been formulated in the 1930s as a protection for Christianity within a majority Christian country (Nash, 2020).[5] The new law enacted in 2008 sought to extend this protection to all religions, in the manner of many attempts to embrace the agenda of creating incitement to religious hatred laws, which had been an agenda pressed forward by agencies such as the European Court of Human Rights.

This extension of the law in Ireland met with opposition from a number of different groups. Many of the standard arguments, which saw the law as an anachronism, were dusted down and rebooted for the twenty-first century. However, what became an especially potent argument for the Irish government was how the law it had framed had an influential existence beyond Ireland's shores. Having expressed its opposition to the danger and "chilling effect" of blasphemy laws within the United Nations context, the country had seemed to some to now be led into an embarrassing *volte face*. The existence of a new, and apparently viable, new blasphemy law in a Western country changed the dynamic of international thinking around such legislation. When it became obvious that the wording of Ireland's new law was being expressly used by other countries seeking to enact more stringent laws of their own this became deeply problematic. Organizations in Ireland had begun to suggest that the liberal community should feel a degree of shame associated with how its government was justifying the creation of such a law, urging other countries, supranational agencies, and individuals to join in this clamor. As Gubo suggested:

> The ripple effect of Ireland's blasphemy law has been felt around the world ... Ireland, perhaps unwittingly, has complicated the fight for religious freedom, freedom of expression, even the right to life because its actions had given legitimacy to blasphemy laws in some repressive states.
> (Gubo, 2015: 93)

It is slightly ironic that here we have an almost classical instance of the use of shame albeit on the grand scale. However, it is interesting because this occurred as the very result of the triumph of Western forms of liberalism. This had ignited human rights as the intrinsic currency of the law and would do much to protect these. As one individual in Ireland's opposition to blasphemy suggested around issues of religious freedom, "you have rights, your beliefs do not."[6] Yet the appearance of individuals feeling ashamed of their government's stance indicated a new international dimension for shame. Liberal social democracies would fight hard to protect individual citizens from harm and discrimination, even if they occasionally created heavy-handed laws to do so, such as the 2008 blasphemy law in Ireland. Yet this episode also showed that the actions of an individual nation on the world stage could activate and weaponize shame within its own population. Shame directed against an inanimate entity could be embraced by the liberalism that had marginalized shame. In this particular instance, shame was permissible as a weapon because it was used to further the empowerment of liberalism and its agendas—protecting individuals from the crude power of non-liberal states elsewhere. In other words, liberal societies had digested the necessity to publically shame transgressors in the name of legally and morally established norms.

Conclusion

The presence of shame in and around the offense of blasphemy has been central to the functioning of the offense's effects upon societies and populations. In particular, its use has shifted from what it has been intended to protect narratives about its precise purpose as a legal and cultural form over several centuries. What appears crucial for studying blasphemy is to note that it has never disappeared completely. In the medieval and early modern world the blasphemous individuals were shamed because they transgressed norms that Christian societies believed kept them safe, protecting them from the providential judgment of a God who intervened in the world. The public display of such shaming reassured those in passive blasphemy-dominated societies that equilibrium could be restored. Societies themselves gradually withdrew from the act of shaming and indeed the act of prosecuting those who transgressed the idea of the polite religious encounter with others. This gave the power of shame to lay persons and concerned individuals who often continued to indulge a providentialism about the society they cherished. This frequently enabled them to see blasphemous threats in everyday life, and more importantly in the notion of "advanced," "experimental" and "artistic" sensibilities.

Shame survived in the realm of blasphemy to become important in twenty-first-century international and diplomatic exchanges, especially where Western liberal social democracies created and sustained standards of human rights that they hoped were protecting individuals. These weaponized shame as a tool to try and bring errant and refusenik societies into line. That these attempts have been successful in the West is quite evident. Their impact on non-Western nations, unable to subscribe to what is perceived shameful by Western liberalism, indicates that shame in these societies operates differently to the West, and that its attempts to promote and police supposed universal norms of behavior will founder. The connection with shame-regulating behavior in this area might best be appreciated by noting the argument of the secularist Keith Porteus-Wood who has noted that blasphemy's new guise is evident in the idea of "respect." Whilst this is an unequivocal indictment of reverence shown to religious feelings, the message of this chapter is that it will be met with suggestions that Western universalism consistently demands respect for its prescriptions around human rights and free expression. We should also not be surprised to notice the language and attitudes of shame used to discredit the opponent in such encounters. Thus shame in this area of human encounters has not ended with modern societies. Instead these societies (and supranational organizations that embody their ideals) have civilized and modernized their outlooks. The process of doing so has meant these societies have recast their norms to make a greater number of different things shameful. Standards of behavior have apparently "improved," but identifying and calling out the transgressor has also become increasingly frequent.

Notes

1 Complaints to the Home Office concerning the Godless Congress of 1938 contained some quite formulaic providential fears about a moral consensus becoming endangered. This formulation survived long enough to be reiterated by written correspondents to the House of Lords Select Committee on Religious Offences in 2003.
2 Declaration on the Elimination of All Forms of Intolerance and of Discrimination Based on Religion or Belief, G.A. res 36/55, 36 U.N. GAOR Supp. (No.51 at 171, U.N. Doc. A/36/684, pmbl (November 25, 1981 quoted in Gubo (2015: 6; see also 28).
3 https://www.venice.coe.int/webforms/documents/?pdf=CDL-STD(2010)047-e (accessed April 8, 2021).
4 One such organization (International Christian Concern) produced, in 2011, a *Hall of Shame* report which outlined the persecution of Christians in Muslim countries. See Gubo (2015: 62).
5 The final chapter of this book covers the law of 2009 and the campaign towards its subsequent repeal.
6 This phrase was frequently used by Atheist Ireland in its campaigning against the Irish blasphemy law.

References

Belmas, É. (1989). La Monteé des blasphèmes. In J. Delumeau (ed.), *Injures et blasphèmes: Mentalités*, II (pp. 13–33). Paris, Imago.
Cabantous, A. (2002). *Blasphemy: Impious Speech in the West from the Seventeenth to the Nineteenth Century*. New York, Columbia University Press.
Dacey, A. (2012). *The Future of Blasphemy: Speaking of the Sacred in an Age of Human Rights*. London, Continuum.
Flynn, M. (1995). Blasphemy and the Play of Anger in Sixteenth Century Spain. *Past & Present*, 149 (1), 29–56.
Frevert, U. (2020). *The Politics of Humiliation*, trans. A. Bresnahan. Oxford, Oxford University Press.
Goffman, I. (1959). *The Presentation of Self in Everyday Life*. London, Penguin.
Goffman, I. (1963a). *Behaviour in Public Places: Notes on the Social Organisation of Gatherings*. New York, Free Press.
Goffman, I. (1963b). *Stigma: Notes on the Management of Sploiled Identity*. Harmondsworth, Penguin.
Goffman, I. (1971). *Relations in Public: Micro-studies of the Public Order*. Harmondsworth, Penguin.

Graham, M. (2013). *The Blasphemies of Thomas Aikenhead: Boundaries of Belief on the Eve of the Enlightenment*. Edinburgh, Edinburgh University Press.

Gubo, D.T. (2015). *Blasphemy and Defamation of Religions in a Polarised World*. London, Lexington Books.

Housley, N. (1982). Politics and Heresy in Italy: Anti-heretical Crusades, Orders and Confraternities, 1200–1500. *Journal of Ecclesiastical History*, 33 (2), 193–208.

Jenkins, P. (2007). *God's Continent: Christianity, Islam, and Europe's Religious Crisis*. Oxford, Oxford University Press.

Limon, M., Ghanea, N., & Power, H. (2018). Freedom of Expression and Religions, the United Nations and the "16–18 Process." In J. Temerman and A. Koltay (eds), *Blasphemy and Freedom of Expression: Comparative, Theoretical and Historical Reflections after the Charlie Hebdo Massacre* (pp. 645–680). Cambridge: Cambridge University Press.

Marsh, J.L. (1998). *Word Crimes: Blasphemy, Culture and Literature in Nineteenth Century England*. Chicago, Chicago University Press.

Nash, D. (1999). *Blasphemy in Modern Britain 1789- to the Present*. Aldershot, Ashgate.

Nash, D. (2000). Charles Bradlaugh, India and the Many Chameleon Destinations of Republicanism. In D. Nash and A. Taylor (eds.), *Republicanism in Victorian Society* (pp. 106–124). Stroud, Sutton.

Nash, D. (2007a). *Blasphemy in the Christian World: A History*. Oxford, Oxford University Press.

Nash, D. (2007b). Analyzing the History of Religious Crime. Models of "Passive" and "Active" Blasphemy since the Medieval Period. *Journal of Social History*, 41 (1), 5–29.

Nash, D. (2007c). Blasphemy and the Anti-Civilising Process. In K. Watson (ed.), *Assaulting the Past: Violence and Civilisation in Historical Context*. Newcastle, Cambridge Scholars Press.

Nash, D. (2008). "To Prostitute Morality, Libel Religion and Undermine Government." Blasphemy and the Strange Persistence of Providence in Britain since the 17th Century. *Journal of Religious History*, 32(4), 439–456.

Nash, D. (2016). The Uses of a Martyred Blasphemer's Death: The Execution of Thomas Aikenhead, Scotland's Religion, the Enlightenment and Contemporary Activism. In D. Nash and A.-M. Kilday eds., *Law Crime and Deviance since 1700: Microstudies in the History of Crime* (pp. 19–36). London, Bloomsbury.

Nash, D. (2020). *Acts Against God: A Short History of Blasphemy*. London, Reaktion Books.

Schwerhoff, G. (2005). *Zungen wie Schwerter: Blasphemie in alteuropäischen Gesellschaften 1200–1650*. Konstanz, UVK Verlagsgesellschaft.

Tawney, R.H. (1926. 2015 edition). *Religion and the Rise of Capitalism*. London, Verso.

Thompson, B. (2012). *Ban this Filth: Mary Whitehouse and the Battle to Keep Britain Innocent*. London: Faber and Faber.

Van Dülmen, R. (1990). *Theatre of Horror: Crime and Punishment in Early Modern Germany*. Trans. E. Neu. Cambridge, Cambridge University Press.

Villa Flores, J. (2007). *Dangerous Speech*. Tucson, AZ, University of Arizona Press.

Weber, M. (2004). *The Protestant Ethic and Other Writings*. London, Penguin.

Whitehouse, M. (1993). *Quite Contrary: An Autobiography by Mary Whitehouse*. London, Sidgwick & Jackson.

11 The Culture of American Dueling under Attack

The 1856 Public Beating of an Abolitionist Massachusetts Senator by a South Carolina Congressman

Kenneth S. Greenberg

On May 22, 1856, pro-slavery South Carolina Congressman Preston S. Brooks brutally assaulted Massachusetts abolitionist Senator Charles Sumner in the chamber of the United States Senate. The Senate was already adjourned for the day, but Sumner had chosen to continue working at his desk. He seemed genuinely surprised as the attack began. He certainly understood that many people in Washington were angry at him—in general for his abolitionist beliefs and specifically for the speech he had recently delivered aggressively attacking slavery and the South. He knew that as a result of that speech, various Southerners hoped to confront him in some way. But he was not expecting physical violence at that moment—and not from this member of Congress. At the commencement of the assault, Sumner was focused on his work. He had never met Congressman Brooks and did not recognize him as he approached (Benson, 2004: 136–137; Donald, 1960: 294; Hoffer, 2010: 8).

Brooks's weapon of choice was what he later characterized as "an ordinary cane" (Benson, 2004: 151–152). The confrontation ended quickly, within a minute—with Sumner receiving between twenty and thirty blows to his head, shoulders, and arms. By the end of the encounter, the cane used by Brooks had shattered into fragments; and Sumner lay unconscious on the floor, his shirt and jacket soaked with blood (Benson, 2004: 137). Due to his physical and psychological injuries, Sumner would not return to the Senate for over three years. His seat remained vacant during this absence, a visual void that served as a reminder of the deep divide that separated the nation's pro-slavery and anti-slavery forces. Immediately after the attack, many in the press, as well as political leaders and ordinary citizens, understood the "caning" of Charles Sumner as an important marker that portended additional future sectional violence.

As one would expect, the attack by Congressman Brooks on Senator Sumner immediately generated strong reaction from large segments of the American public. Cities all over the nation erupted in public gatherings of outrage or admiration—outrage in the North and admiration all over the

DOI: 10.4324/9781003022916-15

South (Benson, 2004: 175–186). Since then, virtually every historian who has told the story of the coming of the Civil War includes the assault as an important element of their narrative—along with other significant examples of sectional conflict such as the battle against enslaved people who liberated themselves by leaving their home plantations; the fight over the extension of slavery into the territories; the triumph of the anti-slavery Republican party; the Supreme Court's Dred Scott decision denying African Americans the possibility of citizenship; and abolitionist John Brown's attack on the Federal arsenal at Harper's Ferry.

However, the central purpose of this essay is not to discuss the caning in the context of the coming of the Civil War, but to consider it as part of the comparatively neglected history of honor, shame, and dueling in America. The Sumner/Brooks encounter occurred at a critical moment in that history. Although most Americans during the antebellum period would have been surprised to hear it, we can see in retrospect that the formal duel among national political leaders, as well as related assaults, would soon become less common and then fade away during and after the Civil War, although they lingered longer on the local level (Ayers, 1984: 266–276; Bruce, 1979: 42–43; Freeman, 2018: 268–274).

This is not to suggest that violence connected with issues of honor diminished after 1861. By almost any measure, the Civil War was the most destructive war in the nation's history—and it centrally involved issues of honor. The bloodshed continued into the Reconstruction period as part of the turmoil in the South created by the end of slavery—including the collapse and reconstruction of the justice system, as well as the struggles over the new racial, social, economic, and political order. Moreover, this was the era in which parts of the South were under military occupation; and it was an age of widespread vigilante terror orchestrated by groups like the Ku Klux Klan. Not only did bloodshed increase in America during and after the Civil War, but it was violence often connected to issues of honor and shame. The dominant class of whites in the South felt deeply humiliated by their defeat in the war, the destruction of their property, the liberation of the people they once enslaved, and the loss of their economic and political dominance. Honor did not die in America with the coming of the Civil War. It simply underwent a radical transformation. It was only the duel that died.

Before the Civil War, battles for honor among political leaders typically took place within the structure of values and behaviors associated with the culture of dueling. Especially in the Southern states, this culture prevailed during the antebellum period. But it was not confined to the South. It was nationalized under strong Southern influence and functioned as a central part of life in the nation's capital. Historian Joanne B. Freeman has counted over 70 violent clashes involving issues of personal honor among political leaders in Washington between 1830 and 1860 (Freeman, 2018: 5). Elected political leaders physically attacked each other with surprising frequency in formal and informal ways—with fists, bowie knives, bricks, canes, and pistols. Some of the confrontations occurred within the legislative chambers of the Capitol, others in the immediate vicinity, and still others on nearby dueling grounds. But to focus narrowly on those 70 violent confrontations is to underestimate significantly both the actual number of people in public life involved in violent conflicts over honor and the significance of the culture of dueling in the life of the nation.

Consider the following. Every duel that ended in an exchange of shots involved large numbers of people other than the principals. In formal duels, each party needed a second, charged first with negotiating a proposed resolution of the dispute to prevent the exchange of shots. If that negotiation failed, the seconds then became responsible for determining the weapons to be used, the timing and location of the encounter, the positions on the ground, and a host of other details. Duels also included doctors who cared for the wounded or the dead, as well as witnesses who wrote about the confrontation after it was completed. Beyond those directly involved, duels also touched friends and family who offered advice and sometimes mourned; fellow members of the legislature who commented publicly and privately on the proper response to inflammatory words used in speeches; as well as the broader public who read about and discussed the meaning of each violent encounter. The most common visual depiction of a duel—two men facing each other armed with pistols and surrounded by a handful of other participants—is misleading. It misses the connection of the duel to the larger society that surrounded it (Bruce, 1979: 21–43; Freeman, 2001: 170–180; Freeman, 2018: 91–103; Wyatt-Brown, 1982: 350–361).

While the formal duel that included notes, seconds, and the exchange of pistol shots represented an "ideal" violent encounter involving honor, most such conflicts never assumed that form. The culture of the duel shaped many confrontations that never proceeded to the level of pistols being discharged. Everyone who rose to speak in the nation's legislative chambers needed to pay careful attention to their choice of words or they might trigger an immediate violent assault or a challenge to a duel. In other words, the threat of violence, not just the violence itself, significantly shaped the public language of the era. It also shaped behavior. As sectional tensions increased during the late antebellum period, many Congressmen and Senators began to bring weapons into the legislative chambers. At any given moment, scores of legislators carried guns, knives, and canes as they conducted the business of the nation. Any formal speech or even a casual remark could suddenly erupt in violence. Men who valued honor and dueling created a world where the threat of death became a central feature of democratic governance (Freeman, 2018; Greenberg, 1996).

The culture of the duel also extended well beyond formal duels into confrontations like the caning of Charles Sumner. If we examine closely the Sumner caning, we can get a good sense of the major elements of the culture of dueling at its most influential moment, and at the same time gain insight into why that culture disappeared so quickly after the Civil War. The caning allows us to appreciate just how central dueling culture had become to American political life on the brink of the Civil War, and enables us to understand the major vulnerabilities of that culture on the eve of its destruction. The Civil War transformed American life in countless ways during the nineteenth century. Among the most neglected changes caused by that war was the "moral revolution" in ideas and practices related to honor (Appiah, 2010). The caning of Charles Sumner gives us important clues about the nature of that moral revolution.

It is important to recognize that although the Sumner/Brooks caning was not a duel, it was connected to the set of values and practices associated with dueling. Of course, it was also part of the larger sectional conflict over slavery in America. However, for the sectional conflict to move into the culture of dueling, it had to involve a "personal" insult. The most common insult associated with American duels and other honor conflicts of this era involved one man calling another man a "liar"—the accusation that what a man seemed to be or to say did not represent his true self (Greenberg, 1996: 3–50). One common implication of such an accusation was that the accused was a coward, that he distorted the truth to protect his life and that he lacked the courage to defend his version of truth with his life. Another implication was that if a man's projections of himself or his version of the truth could not command respect then he should be ostracized from the group of honorable gentlemen, becoming "socially dead" to them—shamed, dishonored, disgraced, and disrespected (Bruce, 1979: 21–43; Patterson, 1982). There were many variations of these "personal insults," but in one way or another they all involved an accusation of inferiority or deficiency associated with lying and its implication of cowardice, fear of death, lack of power, and lack of manhood. They all involved the threat of losing an honored place among the recognized group of "gentlemen." If a man received an insult without "resenting" it in some way, either through a challenge to a duel, a physical assault, or "posting" a note in a public place denouncing the offending party as a coward or liar, then he acknowledged his inferiority and tacitly admitted that he no longer merited membership in the group of honorable gentlemen.

The immediate verbal assault and insults that led to the caning of Charles Sumner were included in an extraordinary speech he delivered in the Senate on May 19 and 20, 1856. He entitled his remarks "The Crime Against Kansas," and it was an all-out, unrestrained attack on the efforts of Southerners and pro-slavery sympathizers to legalize slavery in the territory of Kansas as it transitioned to statehood (Benson, 2004: 94–156). The controversy over slavery in Kansas was complex and played out over a period of years, but Sumner sought in this speech to summarize what he understood as the history of the conflict, to describe the nature of the dispute in 1856, to attack the position of Southerners and pro-slavery apologists, to chastise leading politicians and members of the Senate who defended the extension of slavery into Kansas, and to denounce the use of violence by those supporting the spread of slavery.

The speech had long been anticipated as a major event. Sumner already had a reputation as a powerful speaker and the Senate galleries were filled with an audience anticipating a display of eloquence by a great orator. Sumner himself understood the speech as a key moment in his career and his battle against slavery—preparing it with great care, rehearsing it aloud repeatedly, committing it to memory, and printing many copies in advance so that he could mail them out immediately to newspapers, constituents, and others. He delivered the speech over a period of two days—three hours on the first day and two on the second. When it was printed, it filled 112 pages. Most of the speech focused on the substance of the Kansas controversy, but it also included several personal insults that a man living in the culture of dueling would have recognized immediately.

For example, when Sumner discussed the "crime" that had been committed in Kansas, he described it as the "rape of a virgin Territory, compelling it to the hateful embrace of Slavery" (Benson, 2004: 97). Who were the rapists and what was the nature of their assault? They involved, Sumner argued,

> a control of public opinion, through venal pens and a prostituted press; an ability to subsidize crowds in every vocation of life—the politician with his local importance, the lawyer with his subtile [sic] tongue, and even the authority of the judge on the bench, and a familiar use of men in places high and low, so that none, from the President to the lowest border postmaster, should decline to be its tool; all these things and more were needed; and they were found in the slave power of our Republic. There, sir, stands the criminal—all unmasked before you....
> (Benson, 2004: 98)

Southern men who were part of the culture of honor and dueling would have understood immediately the nature of such a verbal attack. Sumner had exposed the group he and others labeled the "slave power" as the "rapists" of Kansas and he had "unmasked" them before the world. "Unmasking" was the equivalent of calling someone a liar (Greenberg, 1996: 24–50). It was a way of accusing a man of presenting a false image of himself to the world. Of course, Sumner's verbal assault in this section of his speech was a generalized accusation and, other than the President, he singled out no individual. In the context of the culture of dueling, it would not have been clear to the substantial number of people he attacked who was responsible for "resenting" such an insult.

Sumner's speech included many other attacks on those who supported slavery and acted in its interests. He singled out for special assault the group of Southerners who had flocked to Kansas to participate in the formation of a pro-slavery state government, especially those from Missouri under the direction of former Senator David R. Atchison. He labeled them "Hirelings, picked from the drunken spew and vomit of an uneasy civilization—in the form of men" (Benson, 2004: 104). Sumner's wrath also included insulting references to Senator Stephen A. Douglas of Illinois, at one point labeling him "the squire of slavery, its very Sancho Panza, ready to do all its humiliating offices" (Benson, 2004: 100). In the end, there were more than enough insults of both a general and a specific personal nature in Sumner's speech to prompt Senator Stephen A. Douglas at one point to leave his seat and to pace at the rear of the Senate chamber, muttering to himself, "That damn fool will get himself killed by some other damn fool" (Freeman, 2018: 219).

However, the specific verbal attack that generated the chain of events leading to the caning were the words Sumner directed at Senator Andrew Pickens Butler of South Carolina—an elderly colleague who was not even present during the delivery of any portion of the speech. Sumner asserted that he considered Stephen A. Douglas to be the Sancho Panza of slavery, but he regarded Butler as its Don Quixote—a man who

> has read many books of chivalry, and believes himself a chivalrous knight with sentiments of honor and courage. Of course he has chosen a mistress to whom he has made his vows, and who, though ugly to others, is always lovely to him; though polluted in the sight of the world, is chaste in his sight—… the harlot, slavery.
>
> (Benson, 2004: 99)

Sumner saved his harshest words about Butler for a section near the end of the speech. Here, he made an insulting reference to Butler's partial facial paralysis which sometimes caused him to spit while speaking. Sumner noted that when Kansas applied for admission to the union, Butler spoke "with incoherent phrases [as he] discharged the loose expectoration of his speech.…" Most notably, he also described Butler as a man whose words could not be believed. Butler was a liar. "[T]he senator," Sumner claimed, "touches nothing which he does not disfigure—with error, sometimes of principles, sometimes of fact. He shows an incapacity of accuracy … He cannot open his mouth, but out there flies a blunder" (Benson, 2004: 117).

Finally, Sumner extended his verbal assault to include Butler's own state of South Carolina. He objected to Butler treating Kansas and its people with disrespect and felt compelled to call the Senator's attention to the serious defects in his own community. Sumner noted that during the Revolution, South Carolina showed a "shameful imbecility from slavery." This was a reference to a frequently made accusation that South Carolina did not contribute its fair share to the Revolutionary struggle because it needed to devote some portion of its resources to defending slavery and to protecting itself from the possibility of rebellions of enslaved people. Sumner also criticized South Carolina for its persistent involvement in the slave trade, and for having created a republican government that placed dominant political power in the hands of those who enslaved people. In the end, Sumner contended,

Were the whole history of South Carolina blotted out of existence, from its very beginning down to the day of the last election of the senator to his present seat on this floor, civilization might lose—I do not say how little, but surely less than it has already gained by the example of Kansas, in its valiant struggle against oppression....

(Benson, 2004: 118)

What did all this have to do with Congressman Preston S. Brooks, the man who would assault Sumner? Brooks was certainly from the state of South Carolina, but he was not personally named by Sumner in "The Crime Against Kansas" speech. In fact, as already noted, the two had never met. The link between Sumner and Brooks came through Senator Andrew Pickens Butler. Brooks and Butler were cousins. Brooks had attended a portion of the opening day of the speech and had heard some of the insults directed at his relative. In the culture of dueling, an insult to a member of a family was considered an insult to the entire family. Brooks also read the Sumner speech as soon as it was printed, and he noted additional insults to his cousin as well as to their state of South Carolina. Brooks understood, as would any man who was embedded in the culture of dueling, that such insults required a response. It was reported by Andrew Pickens Butler himself that after the Sumner speech, Brooks "could not go into a parlor, or drawing-room, or to a dinner party, where he did not find an implied reproach that there was an unmanly submission to an insult to his State and his countrymen" (Benson, 2004: 144).

Brooks believed that his cousin Butler was too old and feeble to take the appropriate action against Sumner. He could see no alternative but to assume the burden himself (Benson, 2004: 131–132). Brooks did not believe that a challenge to a duel was the appropriate remedy in this kind of situation. This was true for several reasons. Under the code of dueling, noted in former South Carolina Governor John Lyde Wilson's widely consulted 1838 handbook on dueling, gentlemen should only challenge their social equals to an exchange of shots. The reason a duel was the appropriate remedy for an insult between equals was because it allowed each of the parties to demonstrate before their peers that they did not fear death and therefore that they were entitled to retain their membership in the community of gentlemen. In other words, the challenge to a duel was a compliment intended to heal a breach and not primarily an act of hostility (Wilson, 1838). Brooks did not consider Sumner a gentleman who deserved such a compliment. He believed that "the moral tone of mind that would lead a man to become a Black Republican would make him incapable of courage." Moreover, it was widely known that Sumner was a "non-combatant," a man who rejected the values associated with the culture of dueling (Benson, 2004: 135). It would not be considered very courageous to challenge a man to a duel while knowing the challenge would be rejected.

For Brooks, there seemed to be only one appropriate response to Sumner's insults. According to the code of honor, when a socially inferior man insulted a man of honor he should be beaten with a cane or a whip and not offered the compliment of a challenge to a duel. This was the way an enslaver treated an enslaved person and to beat Sumner would be to place him in the same category—the category of a man whose words could be dismissed with contempt. Such a beating punished the enslaved or inferior and demonstrated the superiority of the "master." This would be the way Brooks could publicly affirm his own honor, the honor of his cousin, and of South Carolina. At first, Brooks attempted on two occasions to confront Sumner on the grounds of the Capitol. Having failed to encounter him twice, he finally decided to attack Sumner in the Senate chamber.

What does the Sumner caning tell us about the end of the culture of dueling in America? Most importantly, it demonstrates that in 1856 the culture of dueling was more deeply embedded in the South than in the North. There was no clear and absolute line that separated the two sections on the issue of dueling, but there were important differences, nonetheless. Consider the contrast between the core values of Sumner and Brooks. In 1845, Sumner delivered the keynote speech at Boston's Fourth of July celebration. It was entitled "The True Grandeur of Nations," and he used the occasion to describe his rejection of combat as a path to honor (Benson, 2004: 13–17). His topic focused on the condemnation of warfare between nations, but the same beliefs extended to his ideas about individual combat such as duels. That is why, in 1856, everyone in Congress understood Sumner was a "non-combatant" and not the kind of man who would give or accept a challenge to a duel. In the "True Grandeur of Nations" speech he explained to his audience that

> there can be no peace that is not honorable; there can be no war that is not dishonorable. He is the true benefactor and alone worthy of honor who brings comfort ... where before was wretchedness; who dries the tears of sorrow; who pours oil into the wounds of the unfortunate; who feeds the hungry and clothes the naked; who unlooses the fetters of the slave; who does justice; who enlightens the ignorant; who enlivens and exalts, by his virtuous genius, in art, in literature, in science, the hours of life; who, by words or actions, inspires a love for God and for man ... He is no benefactor, nor deserving of honor, whatever may be his worldly renown, whose life is passed in acts of force; who renounces the great law of Christian brotherhood; whose vocation is blood; who triumphs in battle over his fellow-men.
>
> (Benson, 2004: 14)

In sharp contrast, Preston Brooks came from Edgefield County, South Carolina, a world dominated by a slave-owning elite who placed a high value on a man's willingness to engage in combat as a way of asserting his honor.

Repeatedly during his life, Brooks expressed his core beliefs through his actions. For example, he failed to graduate from South Carolina College because of what the faculty described as "riotous behavior" (Benson, 2004: 26). As he neared his moment of graduation, he had heard a rumor that the Marshall of Columbia, South Carolina, had humiliated his brother by forcibly carrying him to the town guard house. In response to this news, he raced home to collect a pair of pistols with the intent of threatening the Marshall and anyone else who had demonstrated disrespect for his brother. Even after he discovered that his brother was no longer in custody, he continued to brandish the pistols in a threatening manner. Such behavior was considered outrageous enough to get him expelled from college, but it had no negative impact on his standing in his community. In fact, participating or threatening to participate in a violent personal encounter involving honor enhanced the reputation of a man in South Carolina (Benson, 2004: 26).

Similarly, a few years after leaving college, Brooks and several members of his family became involved in a series of confrontations with former college colleague and local political rival Louis T. Wigfall. In the end, Brooks dueled with Wigfall, shooting him through the hip while simultaneously taking a bullet through his own thigh and abdomen. Not surprisingly, for a man who understood combat as a method for asserting honor, it was in the same spirit that Brooks raced to volunteer for South Carolina's Palmetto regiment as soon as he heard that war had broken out with Mexico (Benson 2004: 27). When doctors sent him home after his old dueling wound began to bother him, he lobbied for a quick return and always regretted that while absent he missed much of the combat (Benson, 2004: 27). In sharp contrast to Sumner, Brooks believed that both nations and individuals were required to demonstrate their honor through combat, or as former South Carolina Governor John Lyde Wilson stated it in his code of honor:

> If an oppressed nation has a right to appeal to arms in defence [sic] of its liberty and the happiness of its people, there can be no argument used in support of such appeal, which will not apply with equal force to individuals.
>
> (Wilson, 1838: 3)

While Brooks and Sumner did not share the same attitudes about the connection between honor and violence, it is also important not to exaggerate their differences. Brooks and Sumner should not be thought of as somehow fully embodying the "spirit" or consensus of their sections. Many Southerners understood the tension between Christian values and the culture of dueling—and, like Sumner, sympathized with the Christian view of the world. Most Northerners did not agree with Sumner's rejection of violence for nations or individuals—or we would never have had a Civil War. We must be careful to temper our generalizations here.

Yet it is also clear that Sumner and Brooks did advocate values that embodied something important about the cultures in which they were embedded. Neither man would have been as successful as a leader if they could somehow have traded places—and not just because of their different attitudes towards slavery. Moreover, their confrontation made each man famous, and each won wide support in his region. We have ample evidence—through editorials, mass meetings, correspondence, and petitions—that both men came to be seen as representing values widely shared in their section. As Brooks himself phrased it at one point during the uproar after the caning, "I have lost my individuality in my representative capacity. I am regarded to a great extent as the exponent of the South against which Black Republicanism is war[r]ing in my person" (Benson 2004: 134). That is why pieces of the cane he shattered over Sumner's head came to be seen as valued symbols, or as he phrased it in a letter to his brother, "The fragments of the stick are begged for as *sacred relicts* [*sic*]" (Benson, 2004: 132).

Another significant difference between Brooks and Sumner and their respective supporters was that they experienced the caning in radically divergent ways. It was not just that one man wielded a cane as a weapon and the other man experienced an attack on his head, that one man struck the blows and the other man received them. More importantly, Brooks and his friends understood the caning as a way to affirm his honor. In contrast, Sumner and his friends understood it as a brutal and barbaric criminal assault.

As already noted, for Brooks the choice of a cane rather than a pistol immediately marked the confrontation as a way to show contempt for a social inferior. He wanted it understood that his major motive was to humiliate Sumner—to dishonor him, to treat him with contempt—but not to kill him. This was a crucial point for Brooks. Since a willingness to face death was a central characteristic of a man of honor, if Brooks had killed Sumner, he might have inadvertently given the Senator an opportunity to demonstrate the core quality of an honorable gentleman—a willingness to face death in defense of honor.

This attitude helps us understand the meaning of what has usually been ignored as a puzzling, minor side discussion surrounding the caning. It turns out that some Southern men steeped in the culture of dueling, wondered why Brooks's choice of weapon had been a cane rather than a horsewhip or cowhide (Benson, 2004: 133). At least for some of these men, a whip seemed much less likely to produce significant injury or death, but it would have been quite effective at producing humiliation. This choice and the criticism it generated from some men of honor was so important to Brooks that he addressed the issue in his resignation speech to the House of Representatives. He determined not to use a whip, he explained, because he knew

> that [since] the Senator was my superior in strength, it occurred to me that he might wrest it from my hand, and then—for I never attempt

anything I do not perform—I might have been compelled to do that which I would have regretted the balance of my natural life.

(Benson, 2004: 152)

This point is a bit obscure and needs some explanation for a modern reader. Brooks here implied that in addition to the cane, he carried another weapon or had some other means of killing Sumner in the event he was overpowered. He had originally selected a cane as a weapon because he believed he was more likely to be able to maintain control of it. In other words, Brooks chose a cane and not a whip because it seemed to him less likely to lead to the death of Sumner, a death he "would have regretted" for the rest of his life.

When Andrew Pickens Butler returned to the Senate and delivered his own speech about the assault, he too offered a description that downplayed the murderous intent and alleged brutality of Brooks. Butler insisted that the wounds inflicted on Sumner were the result of the unintended shattering of the cane. First, he denied that Brooks began the attack by hitting Sumner on the head, as some others had claimed, but rather that the first blow was administered to "the face," a traditional site for attacking a man's honor—a site where a man could both symbolically and literally "lose face." Then, Butler continued, "On the second stroke the cane broke. It is the misfortune of Mr. Brooks to have incurred all the epithets which have been used in regard to an assassin-like bludgeon attack, by the mere accident of having a foolish stick, which broke." The cane broke a second time, Butler explained, and it was the breakages that inadvertently added to the brutality of the attack. According to Butler, Brooks's "design was to whip him; but the stick broke, and that has brought upon him these imputations...." Even with the broken cane, Butler believed Sumner received only superficial wounds. As he summed it up, "After all that has been said and done, on a *postbellum* examination, what is it? A fight in the Senate Chamber, resulting in two flesh wounds, which ought not to have detained him [Sumner] from the Senate" (Benson, 2004: 145).

Not surprisingly, Sumner himself had a radically different experience of the attack. Consider his testimony given to the investigating committee of the House of Representatives (Benson, 2004: 136). He described himself seated in the Senate and absorbed in his work when Brooks (who he did not recognize) approached and began to speak. Brooks told Sumner that he had read his speech twice and that it was a libel on South Carolina and his relative Mr. Butler. Then, according to Sumner, "he commenced a succession of blows with a heavy cane on my bare head, by the first of which I was stunned so as to lose sight. I no longer saw my assailant nor any person or object in the room." Not only did he regard the attack as brutal, but it had come without warning, directed at a defenseless man. "I had no arms either about my person or in my desk," he explained. "Nor did I ever wear arms in my life. I have always lived in a civilized community where wearing arms has not been considered necessary" (Benson, 2004: 136–137).

The theme of a brutal assault was also evident in the majority report of the House investigating committee, consisting of Congressmen sympathetic to Sumner (Benson, 2004: 3). The report described Sumner in a "sitting posture" when Brooks approached him. Brooks then hit him with a "large and heavy cane," directly on his "bare head." It noted that Sumner was "[s]tunned and blinded by the first blow ... The blows were repeated by Mr. Brooks with great rapidity and extreme violence, while Mr. Sumner, almost unconscious, made further efforts of self-defense, until he fell to the floor under the attack, bleeding and powerless. The wounds," the report noted, "were severe and calculated to endanger the life of the Senator who remained for several days in critical condition." Finally, the report described the size and weight of the cane and noted that "the weapon used was of a deadly character, and that the blows were indiscriminately dealt, at the hazard of the life of the assailed" (Benson, 2004: 3).

One way to misread this disagreement over the violence of the assault is to think of it as a conversation between men who shared a common set of values, men who all condemned excessive violence. In other words, when Brooks and his supporters characterized the violence as relatively mild in contrast to Sumner and his supporters who focused on the brutality and potentially deadly nature of the attack, they all could have been operating under the same set of shared values—only with different beliefs about the facts. But to accept such an interpretation would be to misunderstand the real nature of the dispute. Overwhelmingly, those who supported Sumner did not believe that a physical attack of any sort on the Senator could be a way of humiliating and dishonoring him. Some saw him as a martyr; others as a brave and unarmed man who withstood the brutal assault of a bully. On the other hand, those who supported Brooks saw him as a man who affirmed his status as an honorable gentleman by resorting to violence in response to an insult. Some might have preferred an assault with a whip rather than a cane. Brooks's brother considered himself among that group. As he summarized his position in a letter, "I might have substituted the cowhide for the Gutta percha, but the difference is too small to complain" (Benson, 2004: 133). In other words, unlike Sumner, Brooks and his supporters looked at the caning through the eyes of men who accepted the values of the culture of dueling.

Another difference between those who were part of the culture of dueling and those who were not concerns their attitudes toward legal remedies as responses to attacks on a man's honor. Many years earlier the position of men embedded in the culture of dueling was best expressed by President Andrew Jackson. After Jackson left office, he asked his successor, Martin Van Buren, to pardon a man who had been accused of trying to shame him by "pulling" his nose (Greenberg, 1996: 19–23). To pull a nose was to humiliate a man by demonstrating contempt for the most prominent projection of himself into the world. It was another way of calling a man a liar. Jackson explained to Van Buren that in cases involving such an attack on a man's honor, his mother had always advised him to "indict no man for assault and battery or sue him for slander" (Greenberg, 1996: 21–22). Jackson's mother understood that in the culture of dueling, a gentleman could not take refuge behind the safety of legal remedies when his honor had been assaulted. Jackson lived in a world where challenges to a man's honor could only be met by pistols, whips, canes, and fists—but not by the law. Resort to the law seemed like the remedy of a coward. This same attitude toward law and honor was equally evident in the Brooks/Sumner confrontation. When Andrew Pickens Butler spoke to the Senate about Brooks's use of a cane to respond to Sumner's insults he wondered aloud, "What was my friend to do? Sue him? Indict him? If that was the mode in which he intended to take redress, he had better never go to South Carolina again" (Benson, 2004: 144). These disagreements were completely parallel to the way supporters of Brooks and of Sumner spoke and wrote about the issue of free speech and the caning. Sumner's supporters considered his speech legally protected by the Constitution and his position as a Senator. Brooks's supporters saw the speech as full of insults, for which violence was the only appropriate response.

What can we learn from this reading of the caning of Charles Sumner that helps us understand the end of the duel in America? Most importantly, it allows us to recognize that for those who considered themselves men of honor, the core values associated with the culture of dueling were completely consistent with and reinforced by the core values associated with the culture of slavery. Consider a few of the connections. Slavery divided the world into a hierarchy of two groups—"masters" on the one hand, and the people they enslaved on the other. Certainly, there were other important statuses in the Old South, but the most important distinction that permeated the culture was the one between free white people and enslaved Black people. Similarly, in the culture of dueling, the most important status distinction was between people with honor and people without honor. But it is important to recognize that the hierarchy of slavery and the hierarchy of honor were two parallel hierarchies that supported each other.

For example, a man of honor could not tolerate being called a liar and could not permit his words or other projections to be treated with contempt. At the same time, white men believed that enslaved people lied all the time and that their words could never be believed. That is why if a hundred enslaved people witnessed the murder of one white man by another, the law recognized no witnesses because enslaved people could not testify in cases involving whites. The words of enslaved people and the words of men considered to have no honor could be treated with a similar level of contempt. Sumner, of course, would still be able to testify in court after he had been caned. But through the eyes of men like Brooks, embedded in the culture of dueling, the caning simultaneously marked Sumner as a man with no honor and as a man who possessed the core qualities of an enslaved person, regardless of how the law treated him.

The connection between honor and slavery can also be seen in attitudes toward confronting death. In the culture of dueling, if a gentleman was insulted and therefore had his honorable status placed under a cloud, one central response was to engage in a duel. As noted already, a duel would allow a man to demonstrate that he possessed the core quality associated with men of honor—that he did not fear death. That is why throughout his life, Brooks repeatedly placed himself in the position of risking his life in defense of his honor. At the same time, one of the central myths that whites believed about enslaved people was that the very fact of their enslavement was evidence that they preferred life to death, even if life meant dishonor. Gentlemen of honor believed that they themselves could never be enslaved because they would rather die than submit to the humiliation of life as an enslaved person (Greenberg, 1996; Patterson, 1982).

Another characteristic of men of honor is that their individual honor was linked to the honor of their family. That is why Brooks saw himself as dishonored both when his brother was arrested and when Sumner insulted his cousin. At the same time, one of the central features of enslavement was that it did not formally recognize that enslaved people had families. Marriage between enslaved people was not recognized by law. Moreover, at any time, parents could legally be sold away from each other and from their children.

Since slavery and the culture of dueling were so intricately connected, it is easy to see why dueling flourished in the slave South and was less entrenched in the free-labor North. This also helps us understand why dueling ended almost simultaneously with the end of slavery. In fact, Northern representatives in Congress noticed the difference as soon as the South seceded. (Freeman, 2018: 270–271). It was the South and slavery that gave energy and meaning to the duel and related violent encounters. Hence, it should come as no surprise that once slavery was abolished it was followed quickly by the demise of the duel.

This central conclusion should not be taken too readily to imply more general conclusions about the sectional conflict and about the connection between dueling and slavery—at least not without considerable additional evidence. Dueling and violent confrontations involving honor flourished in many parts of the world that did not have slavery, including in nineteenth-century Europe. Duels may have been clearly connected to slavery, but they were not uniquely and exclusively connected. This can be seen in many ways. For example, the culture of dueling, despite its compatibility with slavery, had not completely disappeared from the free-labor North by the 1850s. Historian Joanne Freeman has described many fights and challenges involving Northerners in Congress during those years (Freeman, 2018). Northerners may have engaged in these affrays less frequently than Southerners and these encounters may have been more often condemned in the North, but they did exist. In addition, the connection between honor and slavery cannot be used simply to imply that North and South were different societies that ultimately clashed in the Civil War. The North cannot be viewed simply as a "modern," free-labor, capitalist society in contrast to a sleepy, backward "pre-capitalist" slave South (Mayfield and Hagstette, 2017) We have a significant body of scholarship demonstrating that masters sought profits just as relentlessly and ruthlessly as the capitalists who dominated the North. In many ways, they were, in fact, the capitalists of the South.

There can be little doubt that slave and free societies were connected to each other and shared many attributes and values during the years before the Civil War. Christianity prevailed in both sections of the nation. The influence of slavery also permeated both sections. Northern banks loaned money to plantation owners and accepted enslaved people as collateral for their investments. When "a master" defaulted on a loan, many of these banks moved into the business of owning people. Northern companies sold insurance to planters and provided an essential service for enslavers. The industrialization of the North began and flourished in New England textile mills, and these were dependent on cotton grown by enslaved people. Similarly, racism was just as prevalent in the North as in the South. Even the prison, once regarded by many scholars as the quintessential "modern" institution that sought to control people not by whipping their bodies but by more subtle, internal mechanisms of controlling their minds, also equally flourished in the South and the North. Moreover, apart from some issues involving honor, many antebellum Southerners were as obsessed as Northerners with litigation and the rule of law (Baptist, 2014; Beckert and Rockman, 2016; Mayfield and Hagstette, 2017).

But none of these observations undermine the central conclusion of this essay. The Brooks/Sumner confrontation illustrates the link between slavery and the culture of dueling and helps us understand why the two institutions lived and died together.

References

Appiah, K.A. (2010). *The Honor Code: How Moral Revolutions Happen*. W.W. Norton and Company.
Ayers, E.L. (1984) *Vengeance and Justice: Crime and Punishment in the 19th-Century South*. Oxford University Press.
Baptist, E. (2014). *The Half Has Never Been Told: Slavery and the Making of American Capitalism*. Basic Books.
Beckert, S. and Rockman, S. (eds.) (2016). *Slavery's Capitalism: A New History of American Economic Development*. University of Pennsylvania Press.
Benson, T.L. (2004). *The Caning of Charles Sumner*. Thomson Wadsworth.
Bruce, D. (1979). *Violence and Culture in the Antebellum South*. University of Texas Press.
Donald, D.H. (1960). *Charles Sumner and the Coming of the Civil War*. University of Chicago Press.
Freeman, J.B. (2001). *Affairs of Honor: National Politics in the New Republic*. Yale University Press.

Freeman, J.B. (2018). *The Field of Blood: Violence in Congress and the Road to Civil War*. Farrar, Strauss and Giroux.

Greenberg, K.S. (1996). *Honor and Slavery: Lies, Duels, Noses, Masks, Dressing as a Woman, Gifts, Strangers, Humanitarianism, Death, Slave Rebellions, The Proslavery Argument, Baseball, Hunting, and Gambling in the Old South*. Princeton University Press.

Hoffer, W.H. (2010). *The Caning of Charles Sumner: Honor, Idealism, and the Origins of the Civil War*. Johns Hopkins University Press.

Mayfield, J. and Hagstette, T. (eds.) (2017). *The Field of Honor: Essays on Southern Character and American Identity*. University of South Carolina Press.

Patterson, O. (1982). *Slavery and Social Death: A Comparative Study*. Harvard University Press.

Wilson, J.L. (1838). *The Code of Honor, Or, Rules for the Government of Principals and Seconds in Duelling*. Thomas J. Eccles.

Wyatt-Brown, B. (1982). *Southern Honor: Ethics and Behavior in the Old South*. Oxford University Press.

12 Brought Up with Shame

Trans-Generational Perspectives on Disciplinary Correction in Finland during the Twentieth and Twenty-First Centuries

Satu Lidman

When said to a child, "shame" equates inappropriate behavior!
(Man born in 1926[1])

Introduction

Shaming is hurtful in all its forms, although its consequences can be more or less harming depending on its methods, duration, and the resilience of the individual. Whether against children or adults, criminals or the oppressed, corporal punishment always includes an aspect of shame. Chastisement, such as whipping or emotional abuse for "educational purposes," is likely to cause shame; trust, which is so fundamental for healthy close relationships, is replaced with experiences of worthlessness and inherent wrongness. As a means of culturally accepted, even expected, parenting the long history of such disciplinary correction reflects the transformation of familial power relations and the more recent developments in the field of individual rights. The transition of attitudes, behavioral models, and legislation are slow processes consisting of multiple, overlapping layers. On the societal level, chastisement is connected to shared trans-generational traumas. Insensitive upbringing does not, however, inevitably lead to deep traumatization in individual cases.

This chapter investigates shame and shaming in the context of regulating parenting and abolishing disciplinary correction in modernizing Finland. Drawing on interviews with Finns who have been subjected to, or executed, chastisement during different decades of the twentieth century, on the one hand, and societal discussions preceding and concerning a major legislative change in 1983, on the other, shaming is seen as a universal, culturally deep-rooted, and historically constructed phenomenon. As such it profits from interdisciplinary analyses, and thus the approach chosen for this chapter includes elements of oral history and legal history. Shaming and shame experienced due to disciplinary correction are connected to individual memories and emotions, but at the same time also to societal structures, such as transitions of power relations, culture of parenting, and legislation.

DOI: 10.4324/9781003022916-16

A Pan-European Legacy: Chastisement for Order in Family and Society

In the biblical worldview, which was a central factor in shaping everyday life for centuries, to love one's child was closely connected to a demonstration of parental authority: "He that spareth his rod hateth his son: but he that loveth him chasteneth him betimes."[2] Due to this widely quoted, powerful proverb among others, the justification of psychological and physical correction of children was deep-rooted in all European countries and beyond. Being grounded in what was perceived as a God-given and natural hierarchy, such phrases defined ideal Christian parenting and even survived in modernizing, more secular settings. Inevitably, shame and chastisement have, until fairly recently, played major roles in child rearing and simultaneously in attempts to maintain societal peace.

During the long early modern period, raising one's children was not a private matter, although family issues were preferably dealt within the home to avoid public scandals. Upbringing was understood to be an important part of societal order, a duty that parents as honorable citizens needed to fulfill. This aim enabled different kinds of approaches towards one's offspring, including shaming. However, unnecessary cruelty was not permitted, and the limits of appropriate and excessive correction were continually disputed. Advice books on family life encouraged parents to rather pray together with the child, and to patiently explain sinfulness, than reach for the birch rod.[3] Of course, looking through today's lens of children's rights and child psychology, even many of the former milder methods were clearly insensitive if not merely violent. Yet the objective was not to harm the child, but rather to act according to what was thought to encapsulate caring parenthood.

For centuries, didactic literature emphasized the expected roles of different family members as the basis for a good and righteous life. For example, the early sixteenth-century German Franciscan Johannes Pauli chose to teach his readers by telling a story of a criminal who made fun of his father. Being sentenced to death, the man referred to his father, saying: "if you only had punished me in my youth, I would not have ended up with the shame."[4] Neglecting parental duties, such as the moral training of children, was long understood to cause societal problems, even criminality. Failing in these educational tasks could put parents' own reputation at stake: "The rod and reproof give wisdom: but a child left to himself bringeth his mother to shame."[5]

Disciplinary correction was regarded as such a self-evident feature of early modern family life that the lack of discipline could even be perceived of as a form of neglect.[6] Children's behavior could sometimes even lead to the public humiliation of the parents. The ideals of honor, chastity, and the overall Christian moral code were central to both familial education and the state's expectations towards its citizens. Avoiding shame was essential in all areas and phases of life, which is why shaming was supposed to function as a method of teaching manners and punishing for wrong behavior on many levels. Shame was utilized for disciplinary correction within the family, but also as an instrument for making a warning example of someone through a court's decision.[7]

The treatment of unruly children in the past cannot be analyzed outside the wider societal context; public shaming and painful corporal punishments were essential elements of the criminal justice system in all of Europe until the nineteenth century and even later. Witnessing this sort of correction in society—or at least being aware of it as a possibility—could not but reflect in the domestic sphere. Particularly, it supported the image of masculine disciplinary power. If adults could be whipped in a public square as a demonstration of justice, why would the housefather not have the right to chastise his children?[8] The shaming of the wrongdoer was therefore not only seen as just, but also as a well-grounded method to maintain order and promote justice. As such, these shaming processes were connected to the dominant power hierarchy, including the patriarchal gender system.

As an essential foundation of culture and society, patriarchy guaranteed parents, but especially the father, authority within the family unit. All children should remain submissive to their parents and not rise up against them, but, beyond that, girls and boys were raised differently. The virtues for boys consisted of loyalty and respect of (male) authorities as well as honorable manliness and honesty, whereas for girls, chastity, modesty, and nurturing-orientated tasks as wives and mothers formed the basis of idealized existence. Thus, the reasons for chastisement also depended on what was considered shameful behavior in the context of the gendered expectations and honor code, especially when children were about to reach puberty.[9] The cultural structure that allowed control and correction in child rearing had a long-term impact on education, and psychologically it became a shared experience in the Western history of shame.

The post-Enlightenment period saw a new sensitivity to violence in which the rationale and justification of shaming punishments were questioned. Pillories were taken down and public whipping was reduced, or at least hidden from the eyes of the public and executed inside the prison walls. Yet in terms of raising children to become good citizens, shame remained a widely used instrument, although the boundaries of acceptable and inappropriate methods were constantly debated.[10] Abolishing the disciplinary correction of children was, on the one hand, tied to the developing theories of criminal justice and, on the other, to the dignity of the child as a human being.[11] At the turn of the nineteenth and twentieth centuries, attitudes concerning submissive upbringing and the shaming of children in schools and homes were changing. Some were readier to welcome the abolition of disciplinary correction than others; however, in many ways shaming continued to be normalized.

Attitudinal Change: A Slow Transition

> And he [father] liked to chastise us for the smallest reasons. We were not birched but told to go out of the house and shame ourselves.
>
> (Man born in 1924)

In all of Europe, children continued to be brought up with shame long after the era of judicial shaming had ended; yet an ideal father was never a tyrant losing his temper. The trick was rather to demonstrate authority without the need to resort to the birch and, of course, mothers also possessed disciplinary power.[12] Furthermore, in the course of the nineteenth century, attitudes on the husband's right to chastise his wife underwent a transition, but similar kinds of parental power remained the last resort of culturally and legally approved correction. In the beginning of the next century, insensitive educational methods were still commonplace, although they were increasingly criticized.[13]

For modernizing post-war Finland, children represented the future. In the process of rebuilding the nation, children were to be loved and taken good care of—and not chastised too much.[14] In real life, parenting included a wide range of methods, from the authoritative and insensitive to caring and respectful upbringing. Additionally, the meanings that people give to their childhood memories also vary, and they are dependent on context. Older generations might be more understanding towards their parents if they feel that the chastisement was well earned, or that it took place due to harsh living conditions in which adults did not possess the luxury of investing time in their children.[15]

> There were eight of us, and such a crowd cannot be controlled in any other way ... Life was quite miserable, since the war had just broken out when I was born. The whole country was so poor.
>
> (Woman born in 1939)

With time, familial disciplinary methods became somewhat softer, but authoritative perceptions of parent–child relations were not easily replaced. It is therefore not surprising that in a popular parental advice book from the early 1960s, physical correction was considered to be "seldom necessary," yet on some occasions it would be "the only way that a child understands."[16] Despite the then-existing universal principles of human rights, loving parents were still given the cultural right to subjugate their children when they misbehaved—or in order to prevent such behavior—and to expect a different kind of "good behavior" depending on the child's gender.

Finns of different ages who were interviewed on their opinions of physical correction, for a documentary filmed by the national broadcasting company in the mid-1960s, clearly expressed their view that it is the parents' duty to keep order within the family. Children were generally understood to be "in the need of birching" or at least a little slap, and this perception was justified through the interviewees' own childhood experiences. The reporter informed the audience about such trans-generational perspectives in a straightforward way without taking a stand one way or another, but rather neutrally referring to chastisement as something that children learn at home.[17] There were worries about insufficient discipline in society, and conservative commentators connected the tendency of giving up physical correction with the rising rates of boys' juvenile crime.[18] At the time, the majority of the population still saw at least some kind of shaming as an integral part of raising children.

> It's so typical that the child gets flicked and begins to cry and will be put in a corner or somewhere to be ashamed.
> (Woman born in 1940)

> Of course, children must be somewhat chastised normally, but not too much physically. Even a child understands if you guide and talk to him/her the right way from early on.
> (Man born in 1933)

In the societal debates on parenting in the 1960s and 1970s, opinions were divided for and against physical correction. Finland was already a highly secularized society, but even so, authoritative parenting and the right to chastise continued to be legitimized by quoting the Bible. Some were worried about modern educational methods, such as the Summerhill type of democratic or alternative upbringing, as this would make children irresponsible. At the same time, critical voices began to use the term "violence" intending it to replace the idea of "correction," and they saw no excuse for making violence less useful in the case of children.[19] In a documentary from 1966, a daycare institution that explicitly declared physical correction off limits, and anything that could be called "punishment" more generally, was presented as a brave new innovation.[20] Though the conservative ideas of upbringing were not easily brushed aside, a new understanding of a child's psyche was on its way.

> There is always a reason for a child's bad behavior. The child is not feeling all right. All of these [assumptions] that a child does something shameful, it only happens because the child desires to be noticed.
> (Woman born in 1939)

Those who were against authoritative parenting emphasized its negative psychological outcomes, such as anxiety, bitterness, restlessness, and aggression. Ideas on more humane methods started to take root, and professionals recommended that parents encourage and guide their children. The modern

Finnish educational ideology came together in the widespread parenting advice "love and boundaries" (*rakkautta ja rajoja*), meaning creating a safe space for a child to grow without unnecessary control.[21] This new view was preceded by a slow attitudinal change that reflects popular and expert views on parenting in the second half of the twentieth century, but it should also be seen as part of the *longue durée* history of shame and violence.

Parents were now increasingly interested in knowing more about the possible reasons for children's unwanted behavior. They were also educated about the consequences of the chosen educational methods, such as understanding the distinction between internalized morality and the external impact of shaming that only derives from the fear of punishment. Children were to be listened to and adults should be aware of the responsibilities that come with their authority.[22] The expressions of shame faded and finally disappeared from the common way of talking to and about children, and shaming ceased to be the norm, let alone fashionable, as an instrument for upbringing.

> In my opinion, a child should not be ashamed, but one must be sure that he/she understands. Shame is a totally wrong way to go, because it will remain incomprehensible to the child.
>
> (Woman born in 1940)

Documentaries in the 1970s enlightened audiences about the psyche of the battered child by referring to international research from the previous decade. Disturbing images of children's injuries were shown. Now the argument was clear: all adults are responsible to work for the best interest of the child and to not let psychological or physical violence go unnoticed.[23] In 1982, Finnish television repeatedly showed a one-minute educational film to raise awareness of harmful parenting; the clip's central message was that a baby's cry must not be taken as a sign of bad behavior and parents ought to control their aggression.[24] Conservative, pro-correctional voices, or people repeating learned ideas of chastisement as a normal part of family life, were no longer given prominent platforms from which to express themselves.

Attitudinal changes are predominantly generational trends but, of course, there are exceptions. In the early 1980s, the differences between age groups were more visible: younger people adopted a less authoritative understanding of child rearing, which then slowly grew into mainstream opinion. Towards 2020, attitudes have transformed more evenly across age groups.[25] However, campaigning for children's safety at home has remained necessary. Although the issue was not explicitly discussed in the context of shame, the dynamics of shaming continued to impact on a nonverbal, often unconscious level—and sometimes old ways of perceiving shaming can be traced even among younger generations.

Young Children Can Be Told "Shame on You" or Something Similar Because of Their Bad Behavior

> This way the child learns not to repeat the same mistakes again.
> (Man born in 1992)

Today's Finland is a welfare state, often considered as a model country for human rights, and in a global comparison many societal developments have indeed been positive. Nevertheless, changing attitudes concerning disciplinary correction has been a faltering process, which is yet to be concluded. In 2010, in the national action program to reduce corporal punishment, it was still relevant to stress "the human dignity of the child and reciprocal respect between children and parents."[26] The elderly, and even younger adults, remember the time when chastisement was not a crime. In fact, it would hardly be an exaggeration to say that almost everyone knows someone who has been subjected to some kind of "educational" shaming.

Overall, the attitudinal change has been massive, and today a child being maltreated, yelled at, or physically assaulted will generally have the strong sympathies of the public. Actually, the majority of Finns hold disciplinary mental abuse as being even more harmful than physical correction. Almost all participants in a 2017 nationwide survey perceived belittling, raging at, and threatening the child with abandonment as seriously damaging.[27] The perceptions of ideal and inappropriate parenting transformed slowly, but similar trends can be traced in most Western countries.[28] In terms of legislative change, however, Finland became a forerunner.

Legislative Change: Abolishing Harmful Educational Means

In 1979, Sweden was the first country to prohibit the corporal punishment of children, and Finland was the next to follow in 1983. In the global perspective, the pace of such legislative changes was very slow, and it only began to accelerate in the course of the twenty-first century. Still, in 2022, only 14 per cent of the world's children are legally protected from all types of corporal punishment in homes and other contexts.[29] This figure forces us to realize how deep-rooted the chastisement of children is. Though one cannot claim that previous centuries would have seen children as worthless or denied love for them, understandings of childhood have undergone significant transitions fairly recently. The culture of violence and shame prevailed as many adults kept on treating children in families, schools, and institutions worse than their peers, even with cruelty.

In Finland, the criminalization of all kinds of assaults against children followed the long-term development of a human-rights-based understanding of the value of children and their right to safety, an increase in the psychological knowledge of childhood as a specific period of life, changes in the overall standards of education, as well as growth in economic and social wellbeing.[30] During the second half of the twentieth century, theories on child development and psychology were developed and adapted in many countries, but without relevant laws and control mechanisms states could not efficiently supervise parenting.[31] It also took time until legislators showed interest in creating such regulations.

Legally, disciplinary correction in Finnish homes remained a grey area until the early 1980s. Yet the lack of sufficient legislation did not mean a total absence of protection. Criminal law had, since the Swedish regime in the Middle Ages, included various paragraphs on assault, but from the child's perspective there were several weak points. The new Penal Code that was adopted during Russian rule in 1889 continued the tradition of legitimizing "the right to disciplinary correction." In the paragraph 12 of chapter 21, disciplinary correction was clearly excluded from criminal offenses as long as the "injuries" caused by such parental acts were mild.[32] The paragraph remained in force until 1979. Paradoxically, it made visible that disciplinary correction must not be unlimited, although in practice the boundaries and definitions of acceptable and illegal methods were blurred—just like they had been for centuries.

Many conventional educational methods, such as isolating, making individuals stand in the corner, humiliating, slapping, pulling hair, and whipping, were not explicitly criminalized. Legally, they were not perceived in the context of violence, and socially they were normalized.[33] From the 1960s onwards, an increasing number of professionals from psychology and law, as well as those working in the fields of education and social work, noticed these shortcomings; building the post-war welfare state was a political and cultural process that also had to include children's safety.

In the mid-1960s, Finnish criminal law underwent some major amendments. In the related governmental proposal, it was concluded that leaving out the said paragraph 12 would be necessary. The existence of such explicit wording that legitimized the harming of children could "encourage hard-handed educators" to use unacceptable methods, and thus endanger children's health. Yet the idea of the parental right to disciplinary correction in itself was still seen as just, and so it was also concluded that familial discipline "cannot be criminalized as assault."[34] In other words, the violation of a child's integrity was justified within limits. In many ways, this debate seemed only to echo the views of previous centuries, but it was nevertheless the first step in a more thorough legislative turn that took place later.

The exception of the assault paragraph that allowed physical correction was finally removed from the law in 1979.[35] Its content no longer reflected society's understanding of ideal parenting. Yet it was not replaced with a prohibition until 1983. In the documents concerning this amendment it was emphasized that there should remain no space for interpretation; the implementation of the law must be clear as it is meant to prohibit all types of harmful disciplinary methods in all contexts. Parents shall make no exception and courts must be able to sentence them for assault no matter how "educational" their intent had been.³⁶ This was the crucial point in the judicial transformation of disciplinary correction into culpable violence. However, the criminal law did not provide useful provisions in terms of children's psychological maltreatment, under which shaming without physical harm can be placed.

In the legislative process of the early 1980s, some of the provisions of the Act on Guardianship, originally from 1898, were modified and written into the new law called the Act on Child Custody and Right of Access. Until then, the valid legislation had included historically constructed formulations emphasizing the objective that a child must be raised to fear God as well as to exercise morality and chastity. The wording of the law had clearly promoted the spirit that it is up to adults' judgment to decide the ways in which the child's will can be molded. The new law strengthened children's legal position by criminalizing psychological oppression and maltreatment, including the absence of care, constituting neglect.³⁷ On the level of regulations, the Act on Child Custody and Right of Access can be seen as marking the end of the era during which adults had, at least in some cases, the legal right to shame and chastise children in Finland.

With the authority of the law, children's individual needs and wishes were now to be taken into account while ensuring their "wellbeing and balanced development." Society was to "secure a close and affectionate relationship, especially between the child and his or her parents." Every child was seen to have the right to "be brought up with understanding"—and therefore to be "protected from all forms of physical and mental violence, maltreatment and exploitation." Children "must not be subdued, corporally punished, or treated offensively in any other way." The purpose of the law became to ensure children's "growth towards independence, responsibility, and adulthood."³⁸ After these legislative changes, Finland rapidly moved into the forefront in protecting children against corporal punishment and psychological oppression.

Globally, following the Declaration on the Rights of the Child in 1959, the UN Convention on the Rights of the Child in 1989 was an important milestone for the work on violence against children.³⁹ Since then, fundamental human rights have guaranteed the child "inherent dignity" and equal rights with all members of society. This ought to be the "foundation of freedom, justice and peace in the world."⁴⁰ As a member of society and a family, the child—regardless of gender—has stronger legal protection than ever before in history. Societal peace is no longer to be reached through hierarchical correctional means, and, in fact, a child possesses such worth as a person that the violation of these values by a parent, or any other adult for that matter, is seen as especially incriminating.

Despite the UNCRC, which is an international human rights treaty especially designed to protect children, the majority of states still have not amended their national legislations accordingly. Only a few years ago the British government, for example, ruled out the criminalization of parents' physical rebuke of children, including "smacking." In 2009, the United Nations set the goal of prohibiting the physical correction of children all around the world.[41] This is, of course, an extremely important objective. However, according to recent Finnish surveys, the mental abuse of children is more common than physical violence and judicially it is seen as harmful. In practice, mostly due to questions related to evidence, it is much easier to bring physical assaults to court.[42] In order to stop the cycle of trans-generational traumas that are connected to insensitive upbringing, awareness raising initiatives should include a strong emphasis on mental abuse and neglect both in the countries that have criminalized chastisement and in those that are still in the process of doing so. In the end, the attitudes that enable submissive parenting also lower the threshold for physical violence.

In Finland, national surveys to map out perceptions of parenting have been conducted regularly. The first such survey took place just before the legislation change (1981) and the next right after it (1985), while others were to follow during the first decade of the twenty-first century and again in 2014. In each survey, the interviewees were asked to, among other things, take a stand on the following statement: "Physical punishment of children is, at least in exceptional circumstances, an acceptable method of disciplining." In 1981, 47 per cent agreed, but in the latest survey from 2017 only 4 per cent agreed. This seems a promising development, but one should note that although a clear majority (65 per cent) strongly disagreed with the said statement in 2017, almost 30 per cent were ready to accept hair pulling or flicking at a child's head. This means that not all parents perceive such milder means as physical punishment.[43] Judicial developments do not guarantee behavioral change, and despite the trend towards zero tolerance of physical violence there remains work to be done in the field of children's wellbeing.

Behavioral Change: Trans-Generational Traumas

> If you said or did something stupid or naughty, they [adults] told you: "Shame on you! How dare you do something like that!" For example, if you made a mess at the dinner table.
>
> (Woman born in 1943)

Childhood is a phase in human life during which one learns skills of empathy and adopts a model of child–adult relations. Growing up in a safe environment during the first years of life equips us with a kind of resistance to traumatization. However, a child is unlikely to adopt such abilities that the adult does not possess, and a person who has been abused or neglected tends to pass on this trauma to his or her children.[44] In other words, adults are likely to repeat the kind of parenting model they have themselves experienced in their childhood.[45] If parents are not aware of the difference between thinking of the child as "naughty" and making him or her understand why a certain kind of behavior is unwanted, they certainly run the risk of shaming.

Of course, early experiences do not directly predict later life, but they have a great impact on identity and one's ability to engage in human relations. Feelings of unsafety and neglect, as well as having been exposed to or having witnessed violence, increase the risk of becoming a victim or perpetrator of such behavior in adulthood.[46] People who themselves have been subjected to birching, or other humiliating methods, might be angry at their parents when they are younger, but in their adulthood they may be ready to accept authoritative education as beneficial for the child. They are likely to have internalized the idea that this is the way to "teach good manners" and respect towards parents.[47] Without being informed about alternatives, sympathizing with the known model of parenting is a natural way to go.

> I was chastised as a child myself, and I thought that some were chastised too little; they should have had more of it. It was because of some small mischief, throwing stones at telephone poles and such. Almost every young boy had such ideas sometimes.
>
> (Man born in 1926)

Not all abused people resort to violence, but some may lack the tools to manage their emotions and cope in stressful situations, as these are learned skills rather than inherent qualities. Both social and environmental factors alike are important in identity formation, and, in terms of behavior, they are linked with each other as a complex web of possibilities and likelihoods. If a person has been neglected or subjugated to violence as a child, the combined effect of these experiences increases, statistically, the risk of copying similar behavior towards children later in life.[48] Insensitive upbringing results in difficulties in recognizing, naming, and verbalizing one's own emotions, and may strengthen the role of shame and the feeling of worthlessness.

> My mom said to me every day: "You poor thing, you know nothing. I wonder how you're gonna make a living!" Every day. And so, my life has been hard, I've had zero self-confidence.
>
> (Woman born in 1939)

Shame is a powerful emotion, and as such it must be taken seriously. It may damage individuals' sense of themselves and their ability to engage in social relations for a long period of time.[49] Experiences of early neglect and emotionally cold parents are also connected to developing a narcissistic personality.[50] Today, the consequences of the physical and emotional abuse of children are better understood than before, although the social norms maintaining the acceptance of authoritative and insensitive parenting are not easy to change. There is an inevitable causality with such experiences linked to negative mental and physical health outcomes. Hence, not only physical injuries but also psychological harm must be regarded as a serious type of maltreatment.[51]

Most traumatic shame even makes one doubt the right to exist, and for a small child without a yet fully developed identity and deficient skills of verbalizing emotions, shaming may cause such deep trauma. Depending on individual resilience, people are more or less vulnerable to negative experiences, and some may go through stronger emotions of shame than others.[52] Both traumatization and its survival are linked with personal psychological resources, on the one hand, and risk factors, such as early experiences of violence, on the other.[53]

Not everyone who has been exposed to disciplinary correction explicitly perceives it as violence, nor feels bitterness. Yet these kinds of personal emotional interpretations do not mean that such experiences have left no mark.[54] Mental abuse is known to be particularly harmful in close relationships and parental aggression damages a child's self-image and growth in many ways. It also affects his or her perceptions of parenting.[55] In her interview, a woman born in 1943 recalled how she had been regularly beaten for educational purposes in her childhood. She felt this had left "no trauma at all." Yet she was quick to admit that it affected the ways she acted as a mother and grandmother; she copied the method of birching, which she held as "efficient."

> It doesn't kill anybody. It's more like, I think if you would birch kids nowadays it would upset them more than actually hurt them [physically].
> (Woman born in 1943)

During the 1960s and 1970s, she chastised her own children with a birch rod or by pulling their hair when they were "doing stupid things" that were forbidden. In her opinion, the children did not harbor emotions of resentment towards their mother due to those experiences. When taking care of her first grandchildren she used to occasionally "slap them a little bit"—but she never laid a hand on the youngest ones, "not even a finger."[56] Her attitude and behavior had transformed with time and in accordance with societal and cultural changes.

> It just ended like that. All of the sudden I felt I was able to control the situation by other means.
> (Woman born in 1943)

Despite the increasing knowledge on the wellbeing of the child, authoritative parenting was, de facto, still commonplace in the early 1980s, and awareness raising around harmful methods of upbringing remained inefficient.[57] The professionals in the Finnish social and health services, as well as in the field of education, were interested in the mechanisms of trans-generational trauma (*taakkasiirtymä*). The concept was launched within psychology to explain the burden of transition and continuity; when traumatic experiences remain unrecognized, silenced, and ignored, parents tend to pass on related negative emotional structures to their offspring.[58] Experiences of shaming and neglect, whether in the form of mental or physical abuse, certainly need to be included in this vision. Although the mere nature of shame makes the verbalization of it difficult and it must often be read between the lines, silence does not mean absence. As authoritative upbringing and insensitive parenting lack the respect towards the child they feed the continuity of shaming.

Parents who have been subjected to degrading upbringing are more likely to resort to similar solutions with their own children.[59] This trans-generational pattern was also clear in the 2017 national survey in which participants with experiences of corporal punishment were more than twice as likely to accept such methods than those who did not have such memories.[60] Blaming parents for their insufficient skills will not, however, help them to become better educators. Instead, they need guidance on how to intervene without harming the child mentally or physically.[61] Legislative changes are one thing, but it is another question entirely to what extent and how quickly behavior corresponds to such changes. This is an especially important viewpoint when dealing with issues that include trans-generational elements and hence cannot be changed at once.

In Finland, insensitive parenting is widely disapproved of and its negative consequences are well known—even among those who still do not shun the disciplinary correction of children. In fact, in the 2017 survey a little over 40 per cent of parents who admitted that they had resorted to some form of punishment (hair pulling, slapping fingers, whipping, threatening with violence) did *not* approve of such methods. The actual figure may be higher.[62] This may seem like a confusing result, but frankly it shows how behavioral change does not necessarily follow from a transition of attitudes. The experiences of previous generations have an impact either directly through one's own ancestors or indirectly on the level of cultural conventions. It also means that adults may need help in their parenting and that they should not be left to parent alone in society.

To Conclude: Children's Rights Are Adults' Duties

In this chapter, I have investigated shame and shaming in the context of authoritative and insensitive parenting by drawing on the changes and continuities of attitudes, legislation, and behavior in Finland. This history is not exceptional as such but rather a part of a pan-European and universal legacy of bringing up children with shame. Overall, the second half of the twentieth century witnessed a new emphasis on children's rights, which was based on an increasing understanding of childhood, including the consequences of both physical and mental harm. Yet in global practice, children are still not sufficiently protected against the violence that takes place in the name of education. In this respect, Finland stands out by having criminalized such deeds almost 40 years ago.

Nevertheless, the Finnish case illustrates that the cultural transition concerning parenting and violence—during which shame lost its role among the fashionable instruments of child rearing—enabled important judicial developments, although these have not fully changed the learned models of behavior. Attitudes and behavior are not always equivalent to the intensions of legislation and despite Finland's good reputation as a nation promoting equality and human rights, insensitive parenting, including shaming and even physical abuse, is still an issue.[63] Additionally, it is important to note that even when surveys point in the direction of a thorough attitudinal change, at some level the maltreatment of children is likely to remain unreported. During the last decades, many of the developments have been promising, but reaching the aim of zero tolerance is an ongoing process.

In the debates on disciplinary correction and violence from the 1960s onwards, shame and shaming were seldom explicitly mentioned, yet their existence cannot be denied. Without doubt, the emotion of shame has had a deep impact on parenting over generations. Everyone has a right to a safe childhood and the responsibility for this objective is on adults. There is a need for continuous efforts in the fields of awareness raising and parental skills development, since shame-based trans-generational traumas are known to increase the risk of violence. This is both good and bad news: there remains the possibility of abandoning old habits but it will hardly take place rapidly.

Hence, it is essential to understand what trans-generational trauma does *not* refer to. Witnessing or experiencing abuse does not automatically lead to traumatization, victimization, or the use of violence. Investigating trans-generational experiences of shame and violence rather offers us the possibility of becoming aware of the risks and possible consequences of a psychological process that makes a person more vulnerable during life's turning points and crises. Historically, fathers have often been represented as misusing their authority, but of course a child can become the subject of insensitive methods from the mother's side as well. It is therefore important to not fall silent on women's role in the shaming of children. This taboo of motherhood could, in fact, be the next cycle of shame that societies should actively seek to break in order to prevent violence against children.

Recognizing why and in which circumstances one's own parents have used authoritative or insensitive methods of upbringing may help one to understand parents as persons but can also work in favor of violence prevention. Better knowledge on how violence may escalate and how traumatization takes place helps to develop alternative ways of coping in stressful situations. In the process of abolishing corporal punishment in Finland, short-term social isolation combined with the following dialogue with the child has become the recommendation. This "time out" (*jäähy*) indicates that a certain kind of behavior is not acceptable, but the intention is not to awaken emotions of shame in the child. An essential part of this parenting method is to talk to the child when both parties have calmed down. Adults are supposed to not only explain why something is forbidden, but also to listen to the child's viewpoints in order to strengthen their mutual trust, a strategy than can be described as a kind of anti-shaming.

In order to combat trans-generational traumas caused by insensitive parenting in today's society, it is necessary to understand the slow cultural transition in the dynamics of shame and violence. One generation after another disciplinary correction served as legally and culturally approved instruments of upbringing. The focus was in keeping order in the household and, beyond that, in society at large rather than on children's wellbeing, not to mention respecting their integrity. Today, it is the undeniable—and universal—duty of adults to protect children's rights and work for their happiness. Guaranteeing human dignity means that nobody, including children, should be shamed in any circumstances or for any reasons.

Notes

1 The quotes used in this chapter originate from the interviews conducted by the author in 2009–2010 (the results were published in Lidman, 2011). The objective of these interviews was to map out the ways in which individuals perceive shame in general. However, and without asking, they typically connected shame with early childhood experiences in homes and parent–child relations and were willing to discuss it as part of their life experiences. The quotes are translated from Finnish to English by the author.
2 Proverbs 13:24.
3 Lidman (2019). In this article, I have analyzed early modern ideals of upbringing, including discussions on suitable and excessive methods, based on Christian advice books such as Albertinus (1638); Brockenius (1696); de Glen (1641); Rotterdam (1563); Pauli (1522); and Törnewall (1694).
4 Pauli (1522, 18–19).
5 Harington (1998); Proverbs (29:15). See also Rowbotham (2017, 101, 106–107).
6 Toivo (2013, 340). See also Gershoff (2010, 32).
7 Lidman (2008). See also Wettlaufer (2008, 237–243).
8 Lidman (2019, 31–32). On shaming punishments: Nash & Kilday (2010, 26–46); Lidman (2008).
9 Lidman (2019, 26–28); Liliequist (2014). See also Hallman (1963, 7, 116, 131).
10 On modernizing perceptions of violence and punishment: Rowbotham (2017, 103); Nash & Kilday (2010, 10–12); Gershoff (2010, 32–33). See also Wettlaufer (2008, 242–246).
11 Freeman (2010).
12 Lidman (2011, 57–76); Lidman (2019, 34).
13 Lidman (2018); Lidman (2011, 68–70). See also Nash & Kilday (2010, 134–152).
14 Salmi (1945).
15 Lidman (2011).
16 Hallman (1963, 123).
17 Film (1966a). See also Hallman (1963, 116).
18 Film (1966b).
19 Sariola (2014, 2); Film (1966b).
20 Film (1966c).
21 Sariola (2014, 2).
22 Hallman (1963, 112–123); Gordon (1978). See also Gershoff (2010, 37–38).
23 Film (1972); Film (1974).
24 Film (1982).

25 Korpilahti et al. (2020); Hyvärinen (2017, 11); Sariola (2014, 11); Don't Hit the Child (2010).
26 Don't Hit the Child (2010).
27 Hyvärinen (2017, 19).
28 See also Gershoff (2010); Freeman (2010); Vaughan-Eden et al. (2019).
29 Sariola (2014, 11). See also Freeman (2010, 217–219). In December 2022, only 65 states had a full prohibition of corporal punishment of children (for updates, see Global Initiative to End All Corporal Punishment of Children: https://endcorporalpunishment.org/countdown/, accessed 15.12.2022).
30 Sariola (2014, 2, 10–11).
31 On emerging regulations on children's rights, see Freeman (2010, 211–213).
32 Penal Code 1889, 21:12. See also Film (1966b).
33 Film (1966a).
34 HE 68/1966, 7.
35 Ellonen et al. (2008, 57); Don't Hit the Child (2010, 29–30).
36 HE 224/1982, 12. See also Criminal Code, 21:16.
37 Act on Guardianship 1898, 33:2; Act on Child Custody and Right of Access 1983, 1:3. See also Film (1966b).
38 Act on Child Custody and Right of Access 1983, 1:1.
39 Sariola (2014, 3); Freeman (2010, 214–216, 219).
40 UNCRC, preamble.
41 Sariola (2014, 3); Freeman (2010, 250).
42 Fagerlund et al. (2014).
43 Hyvärinen (2017, 10–12). See also Sariola (2014, 5).
44 Schulman (2004, 150, 152 154); Hyvärinen (2017, 22–23).
45 Gordon (1978, 168–169); Lidman (2020, 165). See also Vaughan-Eden et al. (2019, 44).
46 On mechanisms of trans-generational violence: Magdol et al. (1998); Schulman (2004); Costa et al. (2015); Labella & Masten (2017).
47 Lidman (2011); Film (1966a).
48 Schulman (2004, 149–150).
49 Nash & Kilday (2010, 1–6).
50 Schulman (2004, 152–153).
51 Vaughan-Eden et al. (2019); Norman et al. (2012); Levine (1997).
52 Schulman (2004, 149).
53 Levine (1997, 48–50); Lidman (2020).
54 Lidman (2011, 67–71).
55 Korpilahti et al. (2020); Sariola (2014); Schulman (2004, 152).
56 Lidman (2011, 76).
57 Ellonen et al. (2008, 57).
58 Lidman (2020, 166).
59 Ellonen et al. (2016); Peltonen et al. (2014).
60 Hyvärinen (2017, 24).
61 Vaughan-Eden et al. (2019, 44, & 47).
62 Hyvärinen (2017, 22–23).
63 See the national School Health Promotion study (1996–): https://thl.fi/en/web/thlfi-en/research-and-development/research-and-projects/school-health-promotion-study (accessed 16.12.2022).

Non-Printed Sources

Interviews on shame, conducted in 2009–2010, with quotations translated by the author (originally published in Lidman, 2011).

Short documentaries and awareness-raising campaigns, the national Finnish Broadcasting Company, Yleisradio:

Film 1966a. Mielipiteitä ruumiillisesta kurituksesta [Views on physical correction]: https://areena.yle.fi/1-50172155
Film 1966b. Kurinpito kotona ja koulussa [Discipline in homes and schools]: https://areena.yle.fi/1-50172156
Film 1966c. Lastantarha ilman ruumiillisia rangaistuksia [A daycare without physical punishments]: https://areena.yle.fi/1-50172158
Film 1972. Lasten pahoinpitely [Assault of children]: https://areena.yle.fi/1-50242202
Film 1974. Äitinsä pahoinpitelemä lapsi [A child assaulted by the mother]: https://areena.yle.fi/1-50138367
Film 1982. Tietoisku: Ihannevauva [Fact sheet: An ideal baby]: https://areena.yle.fi/1-50111527

Legislation and State Documents

Act on Child Custody and Right of Access 361/1983 (trans. by the Ministry of Justice). http://finlex.fi/en/laki/kaannokset/1983/en19830361?search%5Btype%5D=pika&search%5Bkieli%5D%5B0%5D=en&search%5Bpika%5D=lapsen%20huollosta

Don't Hit the Child! National Action Program to Reduce Corporal Punishment of Children 2010–2015. Helsinki: Ministry of Social Affairs and Health, 2010. http://urn.fi/URN:ISBN:978-952-00-3036-0

HE 224/1982 [Governmental proposition on passing the bill on child custody and changing the law on guardianship]. https://www.eduskunta.fi/FI/vaski/HallituksenEsitys/Documents/he_224+1982.pdf

HE 68/1966 [Governmental proposition on changing chapter 21 of the Penal Code]. https://www.eduskunta.fi/pdf/HE/HE68-1966.pdf

Holhouslaki 34/1898 [Act on Guardianship] (historical). https://www.finlex.fi/fi/laki/alkup/1898/18980034001

Korpilahti, U., Kettunen, H., Nuotio, E., Jokela, S., Nummi, V.M., & Lillsunde, P. (Eds.) (2020). *Väkivallaton lapsuus. Toimenpidesuunnitelma lapsiin kohdistuvan väkivallan ehkäisystä 2020–2025* [A childhood without violence: Action plan for prevention of violence against children]. Helsinki: Ministry of Social Affairs and Health. http://urn.fi/URN:ISBN:978-952-00-4123-6

Rikoslaki 1889 [The Penal Code of Finland] (historical). http://www.mlang.name/arkisto/rikoslaki.html

School Health Promotion survey (1996–). https://thl.fi/en/web/thlfi-en/research-and-development/research-and-projects/school-health-promotion-study

The Criminal Code of Finland 39/1889 (trans. by the Ministry of Justice in 2016). https://www.finlex.fi/fi/laki/kaannokset/1889/en18890039

UNCRC. The UN Convention on the Rights of the Child 1989 (Finland ratified as SopS 59 and 60/1991).

References

Albertinus, A. (1638). *Hortulus muliebris quadripartitus. Thet är: thet qwinlighe könets lustgård* (E. Schroderius, trans.).

Brockenius, Z. (1696). *Huus-taflan, eller en Christelig, kort och enfaldig förklaring om the tre hufwud-ståndren, läre- öfwerhets och huushålds-ståndet, ... uthaf then Helge Skrifft ... stält och sammanfattat uti 10 predikningar af Zacharia Brockenio, pastore in Botkyrckia & Salem.*

Costa, B.M., Kaestle, C.E., Walker, A., Curtis, A., Day, A., Toumbourou, J.W., & Miller, P. (2015). Longitudinal predictors of domestic violence perpetration and victimization: A systematic review. *Aggression and Violent Behaviour*, 24, 261–272.

De Glen, J.B. (1641). *Oeconomia christiana, d. i. vollkommene christliche Hausshaltung* (A. Kolb, trans.). Köln.

Ellonen, N., Kääriäinen, J., Salmi, V., & Sariola, H. (2008). *Lasten ja nuorten väkivaltakokemukset. Tutkimus peruskoulun 6. ja 9. luokan oppilaiden kokemasta väkivallasta* [Experiences of violence among children and youth in the 6th and 9th Grades]. Tampere: Poliisiammattikorkeakoulu.

Ellonen, N., Peltonen, K., Pöso, T., & Janson, S. (2016). A multifaceted risk analysis of fathers' self-reported physical violence toward their children. *Aggressive Behaviour*, 43(4), 317–328. https://doi.org/10.1002/ab.21691.

Fagerlund, M., Peltola, M., Kääriäinen, J., Ellonen, N., & Sariola, H. (2014). *Lasten ja nuorten väkivaltakokemukset 2013—Lapsiuhritutkimuksen tuloksia* [Experiences of violence among children and youth: Results of the child victim survey]. Tampere: Poliisiammattikorkeakoulu. http://urn.fi/URN:ISBN:978-951-815-270-8.

Freeman, M.D.A. (2010). Upholding the dignity and best interests of children: International law and the corporal punishment of children. *Law and Contemporary Problems*, 73(211), 211–251.

Gershoff, E.T. (2010). More harm than good: A summary of scientific research in the intended and unintended effects of corporal punishments on children. *Law and Contemporary Problems*, 73(31), 31–56.

Global Initiative to End All Corporal Punishment of Children. https://endcorporalpunishment.org/countdown/.

Gordon, T. (1978). *Viisaat vanhemmat.* [Orig. Parent effectiveness training 1970, P. Talvio-Jaatinen, trans.]. Helsinki: Laakapaino.

Hallman, N. (1963). Pallerosta kouluikään [From newborn to schoolkid]. *Kodin neuvokki* 6. Helsinki: Yhtyneet kuvalehdet oy.

Harington, J.F. (1998). Bad parents, the state and the early modern civilizing process. *German History* 16(1), 16–28.

Hyvärinen, S. (2017). *Piiskasta jäähypenkkiin—Suomalaisten kasvatusasenteet ja kuritusväkivallan käyttö 2017* [From whipping to time out: Educational attitudes and use of disciplinary violence among Finns in 2017]. Helsinki: Central Union for Child Welfare. English summary available. https://www.lskl.fi/julkaisut/finns-attitudes-to-parenting-and-the-use-of-corporal-punishment/.

*King James Bible*1611. http://raamattu.uskonkirjat.net.

Labella, M.H., & Masten, A.S. (2017). Family influences on the development of aggression and violence. *Current Opinion in Psychology*, 19, 11–16.

Levine, P.A. (1997). *Waking the tiger, healing trauma: The innate capacity to transform overwhelming experiences.* Berkeley: North Atlantic Books.

Lidman, S. (2008). *Zum Spektakel und Abscheu. Schand- und Ehrenstrafen als Mittel öffentlicher Disziplinierung in München um 1600*. Frankfurt a. M.: Peter Lang Verlag.

Lidman, S. (2011). *Häpeä! Nöyryyttämisen ja häpeämisen jäljillä* [Shame! Tracking humiliation and embarrassment]. Jyväskylä: Atena.

Lidman, S. (2018). *Gender, violence and attitudes: Lessons from early modern Europe*. London: Routledge.

Lidman, S. (2019). How to raise good children? Disciplinary correction in early modern advice books. In U. Aatsinki, J. Annola, & M. Kaarninen (Eds.), *Families, Values, and the Transfer of Knowledge in Northern Societies* (pp. 23–39). London: Routledge.

Lidman, S.(2020). *Taivas ja syli. Kertomus parisuhdeväkivallasta vanhoillislestadiolaisessa perheessä* [Heaven and lap: Intimate-partner violence in a Conservative Laestadian family]. Helsinki: Gaudeamus.

Liliequist, J. (2014). 'The child who strikes his own Father or Mother shall be put to Death.' Assault and verbal abuse of parents in Swedish and Finnish counties 1745–1754. In O. Matikainen & S. Lidman (Eds.), *Morality, Crime, and Social Control in Europe 1500–1900* (pp. 19–42). Helsinki: Finnish Literature Society.

Magdol, L., Moffit, T.E, Caspi, A., & Silva, P.A. (1998). Developmental antecedents of partner abuse: A prospective-longitudinal study. *Journal of Abnormal Psychology*, 107(3), 375–389.

Nash, D., & Kilday, A.M. (2010). *Cultures of Shame: Exploring Crime and Morality in Britain, 1600–1900*. Basingstoke: Palgrave Macmillan.

Norman, R.E., Byambaa, M., Rumna D., Butchart, A., Scott, J., Theo, V. (2012). The long-term health consequences of child physical abuse, emotional abuse, and neglect: A systematic review and meta-analysis. *PLoS Med*, 9(11): e1001349. https://doi.org/10.1371/journal.pmed.1001349.

Pauli, J. (1522). Schimpf und Ernst. I Teil der ältesten Ausgabe von 1522. In J. Bolte (Ed.), *Alte Erzähler*. Berlin: Herbert Stubenrauch, 1924.

Peltonen, K., Ellonen, N., Pösö, T., & Lucas, S.D. (2014). Mothers' self-reported violence toward their children: A multifaceted risk analysis. *Child Abuse & Neglect*, 38(12), 1923–1933. http://dx.doi.org/10.1016/j.chiabu.2014.10.016.

Rotterdam, E. von (1563). *De civilitate morum puerilium. Höfische und züchtige Sitten*.

Rowbotham, J. (2017). When to spare the rod? Legal reactions and popular attitudes towards the (in)appropriate chastisement of children, 1850–1910. *SOLON Law, Crime and History*, 7(1), 98–125.

Salmi, T. (1945). *Terveitä, iloisia lapsia. Käsikirja vanhemmille, kasvattajille ja opettajille* [Healthy, happy children: A handbook for parents, educators and teachers]. Helsinki: Kustannustalo.

Sariola, H. (2014). *Herra Koivuniemi pantu viralta—30 vuotta ruumiillisen kurittamisen kieltämisestä* [Thirty years from abolishing disciplinary correction]. Helsinki: Lastensuojelun Keskusliitto.

Schulman, G. (2004). Väkivalta ja sietämättömien tunteiden kierrätys [Violence and the circulation of unbearable emotions]. *Suomen lääkärilehti*, 3, 149–155.

Toivo, R.M. (2013). Violence between parents and children: Courts of law in early modern Finland. *The History of the Family*, 18(3), 331–348.

Törnewall, P.J. (1694). *Dygdz och odygdz spegel i huus-håld och gemehna lefwerne, allom i hwart stånd till nyttig påminnelse, och vnderwisning*.

Vaughan-Eden, V., Holden, G.W., & Schieffer LeBlanc, S. (2019). Commentary: Changing the social norm about corporal punishment. *Child and Adolescent Social Work Journal*, 36, 43–48. https://doi.org/10.1007/s10560-018-0592-y.

Wettlaufer, J. (2008): Evolutionäre und pädagogische Aspekte des sozialen Schamgefühls. Zum sozialen Gebrauch von Emotionen im Mittelalter und in der frühen Neuzeit am Beispiel der Schand- und Ehrenstrafen. In J. Kurig & A.K. Treml, Münster (Eds.), *Neue Pädagogik und alte Gehirne? Erziehung und Bildung in evolutionstheoretischer Sicht* (pp. 237–248). Beiträge zur Evolutionären Pädagogik. Interdisziplinäre Bildungsforschung in evolutionstheoretischer Perspektive, Bd. 2. Berlin: Verlag Dr. W. Hopf.

13 Plato, MeToo, the Honorable, and the Others

Hege Dypedokk Johnsen[1]

Introduction

Throughout history, honor and shame have been intimately connected with one of the most headache- and heartache-causing aspects of human nature: our sexuality. This is a fact we are constantly reminded of, not simply in our own private lives. A few years ago, MeToo kickstarted the debate on sexual harassment.[2] With its intensity and extraordinary number of engaged people, the campaign soon became a worldwide and subsequently historical phenomenon. It was a powerful reminder of how crucial our views, laws, and customs concerning sexual assaults actually are—and how these are in flux. As a Plato scholar who takes a special interest in the history of sexuality, for me the MeToo movement provoked the following questions: How were sexual assaults regarded in ancient Athens? And what (if anything) is offered and argued on the subject of sexual assault in Plato's writings?

These questions require an interdisciplinary approach and analysis, with tools and methodologies derived from philosophy, philology, history, and gender studies. I will approach the questions in the following, tripartite way. First, I comment on the Ancient Greek and modern English vocabulary on sexual assault. Second, I provide an account highlighting the gendered dimensions of honor, and how women in ancient Athens were divided into groups of various status: the "honorable" and the "others."[3] This helps us grasp how sexual assaults were regarded in ancient Athens. As we shall see, the social status of a woman subjected to sexual assault had legal implications around the appropriate punishment. Third, I turn to Plato.[4] Some may wonder whether what he has to offer on the topic of sexual assault amounts to very little—indeed, there is no "Plato's dialogue on rape." Nor is the broader subject of sexual assault thoroughly discussed in any of his many dialogues. There are, however, two interesting paths one may follow in order to untangle his writings on the issue: (1) analyzing the passages in which the subject of sexual assault is discussed; and (2) analyzing how psychological states relating to sexual assault may be understood based on Plato's moral psychology. I intend to follow both paths, using Plato's dialogue the *Laws*. Several Plato scholars have pointed out the importance of

DOI: 10.4324/9781003022916-17

shame in this dialogue.⁵ To the best of my knowledge, however, none have connected the views on shame in the *Laws* to the topic of sexual assault, and the shame that tends to accompany it. In this third part of the chapter, I also flesh out a way in which our understanding of what I call *the shame-paradox* may be improved by looking at honor, shame, and sexual assault through a Platonic lens. In short, what I refer to as the shame-paradox is the paradox that although "everybody" agree that it is the abuser—*not the victim*—who ought to be ashamed, victims of sexual assaults typically feel ashamed. Moreover, a significant number of victims also experience shaming by others.

Finally, while sexual violence indeed can be directed against and perpetrated by both men and women, the reader should note that my focus will be on cases in which the victims are women.⁶ Although the number of studies focusing on other groups in the Athenian society (women, children, prostitutes, and foreigners) has increased since the 1970s, it is not an overstatement to say that research on classical Athens in general, including the research on sexuality specifically, predominantly focuses on freeborn Athenian men.⁷ By focusing on women and emphasizing the gendered dimensions, I hope to contribute to the larger, feminist and historical project of restoring *herstory*. ⁸ I conclude this chapter by drawing the threads together, and by explicating why silence-breaking is courageous alongside honoring the silence-breakers for placing the shame that typically arises due to sexual assault/harassment where it belongs—with the wrongdoer, not the victim.

The Vocabulary of Sexual Assault

As MeToo conspicuously revealed, our vocabulary of the subject of sexual assault may seem confusing. What is the definition and differences between terms and expressions like "sexual assault," "sexual harassment," and "rape"? "Sexual assault" refers to the wider category of actions of sexual violence, whereas "sexual harassment" involves many forms of unwelcome and humiliating actions: from actual or attempted rape or sexual assault, to sexual gestures and comments. Roughly, rape is a kind of sexual assault which usually involves non-consensual, sexual penetration (orally, vaginally, and/or anally).

An obstacle one soon faces while investigating sexual assaults in ancient Greek literature is that there is no single, specific term for "rape" in ancient Greek; nor for "sexual assault." Rather, there are several terms, and typically combinations of terms, signifying sexual assault. Roughly put, charges of sexual assault were in classical Athens prosecuted either as (i) general charges of violence (*bia*, under *dike biaion*), as (ii) illegal, non-marital relations (*moicheia*, under *graphê moicheias*), or (iii) as charges of *hubris* (under *graphê hubreos*).⁹ First, (i) *bia* may be translated with *violence*, and its derivative verbs refer to physical, violent actions. There are no sexual connotations to *bia*, per se. However, if the ancient Greek text says that a girl, woman, or boy is subjected to *bia*, we are more often than not reading about a sexual assault. If the text says that a woman became pregnant after an incident of *biasmos*, she most likely got pregnant as the result of rape (cf., e.g., Omitowoju, 2002: 18).[10]

Secondly, (ii) *moicheia* is used only in cases where a man has been illegally sexually involved with a free woman belonging to another man, in the sense that she is under his protection and surveillance (*kyreia*). Typically, the guardian (*kyrios*) of a woman was her closest male kin until she married at around 14 or 15.[11] *Moicheia* is often translated as "adultery"/"seduction," and the noun *moichos* as "adulterer"/"seducer." These translations may be misleading, however. For one thing, *moicheia* has a wider scope than modern usage of the term "adultery," as it is also used in cases with unmarried women. Secondly, the terms "adultery" and "seduction" sound *voluntary*, while *moicheia* indicates some sort of persuasion/seduction. Sexual assaults *not* involving physical violence (*bia*), but "only" verbal "persuasion," would supposedly be reckoned as *moicheia*. This kind of "seduction" does not meet modern standards of consensual sex.[12]

Today, sexual consent is regarded as the key component distinguishing sexual assaults (including rape) from legal, sexual intercourse. Sexual consent, however, does not seem to have been the main issue in ancient Greek laws on sexual assault. Instead of consent from the woman in question, the central issue was whether the sexual relation was *without her guardian's consent*: if it was, the relation would be regarded as offensive and shameful to the guardian and his household (*oikos*). This is, for example, revealed in a speech by Lysias (*On the Murder of Eratosthenes*, [1], 4.):"Eratosthenes had an intrigue with [*moicheia*] my wife, and not only corrupted her but inflicted disgrace upon my children and an outrage [*hubris*] on myself by entering my house." Here Euphiletos defends himself on trial by claiming that the murder of Eratosthenes was legally justifiable (on what grounds will be made clear when we revisit the juridical circumstances shortly). Noteworthy, according to some original material, including a passage of this speech, sexual seduction in the context of *moicheia* was punished *harder* than sexual assault characterized by violence (*bia*).[13] It is noteworthy that there are different interpretations of this passage and of the importance of sexual consent: some argue classical Athens qualifies as an obvious "rape culture," others reject this description.[14]

The third (iii) term, *hubris*, is a wide-ranging and complex term, used both as legal term and one describing sentiments and actions. In modern English, *hubris* refers to arrogance: "an extreme and unreasonable feeling of pride and confidence in yourself."[15] In the Liddell Scott Jones dictionary of Ancient Greek, however, the explanation reads: "wanton violence, arising from the pride of strength or from passion, insolence." According to Cohen (1991b: 172), in surveying all the usages of the words *hubris* and the related *hubrizein, hubristes,* and *hubrisma*, "one finds that more than fifty per cent of all occurrences refer in a general way to some unspecified kind of wrongful, insulting, insolent, or excessive behaviour." *Hubris* often describes violent assaults bringing disgrace upon the victim, for the pleasure of the abuser. However (and this is the crux), when an act is characterized as an act of *hubris*, the shame reflects back on the abuser. This is because the acts of *hubris* were thought to crave a perverse sense of honor and pleasure, on the abuser's behalf. This point is noted in Aristotle's definition of *hubris* (*Rhetoric*, II, 2, 1378b5):

> for insult [*hubris*] consists in causing injury or annoyance whereby the sufferer is disgraced, not to obtain any other advantage for oneself besides the performance of the act, but for one's own pleasure; for retaliation is not insult, but punishment. The cause of the pleasure felt by those who insult is the idea that, in ill-treating others, they are more fully showing superiority. That is why the young and the wealthy are given to insults; for they think that, in committing them, they are showing their superiority.

The prime example in ancient literature is perhaps Achilles, who kills his beloved's killer, Hector, then slits his heels and passes a girdle through them, before fastening the girdle to his chariot and dragging Hector's dead body around, continuing to mistreat the body for the next 12 days.[16] Of most interest for our purposes here, however, is the strong sexual connotation of *hubris*. This is not preserved in the modern usage of the term and therefore easily overlooked. In classical Greek literature, we find manifold connections between sexual desire and *hubris*. *Hubris* is also specifically connected to sexual violence: the rape of women, in particular, is frequently referred to as hubristic. In fact, we may say that acts of sexual assault are acts of *hubris*, and that rape constitutes a subcategory of *hubris*: "*Hubris* as rape created shame on the part of the victim and a perverse sense of honor or 'raising above' on the part of the perpetrator" (Ludwig, 2002: 171).

The Honorable and the Others

The women living in classical Athens around 400–300 BCE may be divided into two main categories: "the honorable" and "the others." In the following, I elaborate upon both categories, conveying the gendered dimensions of honor in classical Athens, and showing how the social status of a woman subjected to sexual assault had legal implications. "The honorable" refer to female Athenians born free from slavery. In contrast to free men, the women (even those not born into slavery) merely had the honor they were ascribed through their family's status. Whereas we today typically associate "honor" with a personal feeling of pride, the ancient Greek term *timê*, usually translated as "honor," denotes a more objective description of a person's value in society. One may here distinguish between *acquired* honor and *pre-ascribed* honor. Freeborn men could acquire honor through honorable deeds: such as military service, political, intellectual, or artistic activities, etc. This kind of honor founded on *merits* is what Aristotle regards as true honor (cf. *Nicomachean Ethics*, 1124a1). Their individually acquired honor would then be added, so to speak, to the honor/value they were pre-ascribed through their family's status.

In contrast, the ways of acquiring individual honor for women—even "the honorable" ones—were significantly limited. "The honorable" women could, however, *lose* their honor/value. They would then be excluded from the category of "the honorable" and degraded into "the others." Non-marital sex could cause such degradation; whether consensual or not, since sexual consent (as we have seen) played a less significant role in ancient Athens than it does today. One might think that if consent was irrelevant, then the woman involved in a case of illegal (i.e., not approved by her guardian) non-marital sex could not be sanctioned. This is not the case, however. If a married woman was found guilty of illegal sex, she could risk a number of things: getting divorced and evicted from her household, being refused participation in religious festivities (thereby taking away her religious duties, a great disgrace), being denied wearing ornaments (i.e., the tokens revealing her social status and value), and being beaten.[17]

Contrary to what one might think, the honorable Athenian women were referred to as citizens (by *astos* and *politês*; female forms of *astê* and *politis*, often translated as "citizen"). They did not have equal rights, however, nor did they participate in the political life like male citizens, and they lived quite separately from men outside their household (excepting festivals, funerals, and weddings).[18] Classical Athens was a patrilineal society, in which the father's status alone determined citizenship: until 450 BCE. That year, Pericles, the great statesman and general during the Golden Age of Athens, passed a resolution: from now on, a woman's status as a citizen was a condition for her children's status as citizens.[19] Before the resolution, the status had been given to all children of male citizens. The resolution implied that children of a woman without citizenship would not become citizens. In this way, the law ensured that *only "honorable" women give birth to "true Athenians"* (and only "true Athenians" became citizens). The "honorable" women thus became necessary in order to keep the otherwise patrilineal, upper-class society going, and, moreover, it became extremely important to protect, oversee, and preserve their honor. Besides the Athenian women born "honorable," some concubines (*pallakai*) could be included amongst "the honorable." A concubine is typically described as a non-Athenian woman having a long-term relationship with an Athenian man, living relatively permanently in his household, either instead of a wife or as part of a *ménage à trois* (cf., e.g., Blundell, 1995: 124). Some of them were free, but without citizenship, thus their children would not automatically become citizens. Due to the resolution, these children would be sort of *semi-legitimate* Athenians.

"In law an Athenian woman had no independent existence. She was always assumed to be incorporated into the *oikos* which was headed by her *kyrios*" (Blundell, 1995: 114). Nor could women "appear before the court or even give evidence in any direct way" (Omitowoju, 2002: 17), so if a case of sexual crime were brought to trial, it would be by the *kyrios*. The (sexual) honor of "the honorable" was protected by Athenian law, more precisely by the exception of the Draconian law. Draco was the first Athenian lawgiver to make a written constitution public (around 621 BCE). The first of Draco's laws said that a man who had murdered ought to face trial. There was, however, an important exception from the law: If a man found another man "next to," or perhaps rather "on" (*epi* + *dative*), his wife, mother, daughter, sister, or his free concubine, then he could murder him *without being punished for it*.[20] The "man" here refers to a freeborn, Athenian man with citizenship. This is the juridical grounds on which the previously mentioned Euphiletos bases his defense. Draco's laws were so harsh that "Draconian law" is a phrase common in several languages, even today, and is used to convey that a law is unreasonably strict. When moderated in 409 BCE, however, this exception remained. The distinction between the two categories of women is demonstrated in this exception of the law, as it exclusively applies to "the honorable," i.e., a male citizen's wife, mother, daughter, sister, or free concubine. These women had a *kyrios* who, with law in hand, could kill a man if he found him *in flagranti* under his own roof. The exception applied only if the intruder was found inside the house where the woman lived, and it does not distinguish between perpetrator or lover, but gave the offended man permission to kill either. More often, however, a fine was paid. There were also other, more brutal and humiliating, kinds of punishment executed in public (such as *rhaphanidosis*, the act of inserting a radish into the anus).[21]

What, then, about "the others," the women *not* mentioned in the exception of Draco's law, and thus seemingly without legal protection? It is said that the fine for assault on a free man, boy, or honorable woman was *double*, which may be interpreted as though the fine for assault on a slave was half that amount.[22] If a woman was neither an honorable woman nor enslaved, she had no legal protection. "The others" consists of a diverse group of women with lower status, born unfree and/or as foreigners, or freeborn Athenian women who had lost their value in society. Sub-categories include unfree concubines, courtesans (*hetaîrai*), and prostitutes (*pornai*). *Hetaîrai* are sometimes referred to as prostitutes, but it is useful to distinguish between *hetaîrai* and *pornai*. The courtesans were always free, while the prostitutes were always unfree. The courtesans were entertainers and (girl)friends, whose sexual "services" were typically repaid with something other than cash (cf. Glazebrook, 2016: 704). Among the most famous courtesans is Aspasia. The previously mentioned Pericles divorced his honorable, Athenian wife to live alongside the skilled rhetorician Aspasia (which he did, for about 20 years). Ironically, they never married. Soon before her arrival, Pericles passed a new law forbidding Athenian male citizens to marry non-Athenian women. Freeborn in Miletus, Aspasia did not have the status of an "honorable" Athenian woman (she was occasionally even referred to as a *pornê*), and so their son Pericles Junior was legally a bastard not granted citizenship (though he eventually received it).[23]

The prostitutes worked in brothels for money. One of the most well-known examples is Neaira, who was bought and prostituted by madam Nikarete from Corinth. Neaira was charged for illegally presenting her daughter as an Athenian citizen (somewhere between 343–340 BCE). According to the accusers, her daughter was not a citizen, as Neaira was not an honorable, Athenian woman. A fact, the accusers continued to argue, which moreover made her marriage (to a male Athenian citizen) illegal. The details are presented in the speech *Against Neaira*.[24] The speech provides a rare glimpse into the sex industry in classical Athens, to the women living within it, and, particularly, to how their value/honor was determined. A passage in the speech states: "We have courtesans for pleasure, concubines for the daily tending of the body, [and] wives in order to beget legitimate children and have a trustworthy guardian of what is at home" (Demosthenes, *Against Neaira* [59], 122). It is also said that an Athenian man is *obligated* to divorce his wife if she is having non-marital sex, i.e., if she has an affair or is assaulted: if refusing, he could lose his rights as a citizen (Demosthenes, *Against Neaira* [59], 87; see also Lysias, *The Murder of Eratosthenes* [1], 34).

Summing up this section: classical Athens was a deeply patriarchal society where women had no independent legal existence. They were divided in two categories: "the honorable" (freeborn, noble Athenian women) and "the others" (a diverse group of women with lower status). The sexual endeavors of the honorable women were strongly overseen, as their (sexual) honor was so wrapped up in their value, and their honor needed to ensure citizenship of their children (after Pericles' resolution). This may be one of the reasons why sexual crimes against honorable women were so harshly punished in Athens. Sexual offenders were punished in other Greek cities as well (see Cantarella, 2005: 243), but as far as we know, only in Athens could it be legally permissible to take the wrongdoer's life.

Plato's *Laws* and the Paradox of Shame

Having discussed the legal framework concerning sexual assault in ancient Athens, and the underlying social and gender roles, I now turn to Plato and a philosophical discussion of shame and sexual assault. In the *Laws* we find paragraphs explicitly discussing sexual assault, as well as a thorough discussion of human nature, which is helpful in analyzing how psychological states related to sexual violence may be understood based on Plato's moral psychology. Towards the end of this section, I explore a way in which our understanding of what I call the shame-paradox may be improved by looking at the subject of honor, shame, and sexual assault through a Platonic lens.

In comparison to other Greek writers from the same period, the connections between passionate desire (*erôs*) and *hubris* are particularly strong in

Plato.²⁵ Even so, there are few attempts at analyzing how psychological states relating to sexual violence may be understood based on Plato's moral psychology. This is surprising, as scholars working on Plato's moral psychology often emphasize that while much has changed since Plato (customs, laws, religious beliefs, etc.), human psychology and emotions have not—and that Plato's moral psychology is therefore still relevant for understanding our mind, sentiments, and behavior. It is particularly striking when compared to the robust amount of secondary literature on other kinds of crimes and cases of lack of self-control. In what follows, I untangle the view(s) on shame and self-control conveyed in Plato's *Laws*, in the context of sexual assault.

As mentioned, ancient writers including Plato use *hubris* to denote an act which is offensive to a person's honor, often with a strong sexual connotation. In the *Laws*, sexual assaults are explicitly referred to as acts of *hubris*. It is said that sexual violation of free women (apparently, though unsurprisingly, not against female slaves) or boys may be punished by the one who has been treated with *hubris*, or the offended's relatives. This is listed as one specific condition under which it will be right to regard the killer innocent: "If anyone sexually violates a free woman or boy, *he may* be killed with impunity by the victim of the violence, or by the victim's father or brothers or sons" (*Laws*, 874c4). The constellation of words related to *hubris, bia*, and "sexual pleasures" (*ta aphrodisia*) here signifies rape. Moreover, rape is described as both *dishonoring* and *harmful*, as Cohen (1991b: 175) writes:

> Plato's law of rape (*Laws* 874c4) uses the passive tense of *hubrizein* to describe what the victim has suffered at the hands of the assailant, who may be killed with impunity. It is significant, however, that the act constituting the offence itself is described not by *hubrizein*, but rather *biazomai*. This use of *hubrizein*, it would seem, describes the intentional sexual dishonoring of the victim, not the physical violence used to accomplish it.

The passage is followed by: "If a husband discovers his wedded wife being raped and kills the attacker, *the law* will regard him as innocent" (*Laws*, 874c5).²⁶ This is a clear echo of the mentioned exception from Draco's law. The difficulty in getting the citizens to control their sexual urges is clearly expressed earlier in the dialogue (*Laws*, 836b1–4):

> But there are *sexual* urges too—of boys and girls and heterosexual love among adults. What precautions should we take against passions which have had such a powerful effect on public and private life? What's the remedy that will save us from the dangers of sex in each? It's a great problem, Clinias.²⁷

How to control these urges? The character "the Athenian" states that all human actions are motivated by three needs and desires, which through proper education will lead to virtue, whereas poor education may lead to the other extreme (*Laws*, 782e). These three desires are for (i) food, (ii) drink, and (iii) *ta aphrodisia*, i.e., sexual pleasures (*Laws*, 783c). The desires must be controlled by the powerful influences of *fear* (including shame), *law*, and *correct argument* (*Laws*, 783a5–7). Internally, "moderation [*sôphrosunê*] in sexual matters" (*Laws*, 785a1) is presented as an ideal. The ideal seems to apply to both sexes: for example, the sexes are treated equally in the adultery law (*graphê moicheias*) (*Laws*, 784e1–5).[28] The term sôphrosunê is notoriously difficult, but typically translated "self-control," "sound-mindedness," "moderation," or "temperance."[29] Worth noting, especially for our purposes here, is that *sôphrosunê* is typically contrasted with *hubris* in Plato (see, e.g., *Phaedrus*, 237e–238a).

I will now turn to the paradox of shame in the context of sexual assault: in a case of interpersonal violence, one may typically distinguish between an *aggressor* A, who acts violently, and a *victim* B, who is subjected to the violent act. Through the violent act, the aggressor typically (though not necessarily) inflicts shame upon the victim. This is especially true in cases of sexual assault. In cases of rape, the aggressor (i.e. the rapist) may through the violent act (rape) inflict shame upon the victim: either by intentionally seeking to *put the victim to shame*, or without consideration, though nevertheless causing the victim to *feel ashamed*. However, it is the aggressor—and not the victim—who typically is regarded as the one who *should* feel shameful (not only by modern standards, but also according to Plato and the ancient Greeks). Although "everybody" agrees that the aggressor, not the victim, ought to be ashamed, victims of sexual assault typically feel ashamed. Moreover, and again contrary to what "everybody" agrees to, a significant number of victims are also shamed by others. This is what I refer to as the "paradox of shame."

What, exactly, makes this a paradox? To explain, we need to take a closer look at shame *qua* phenomenon. How do we understand shame today, and how was it understood by the ancient Greeks? In Ancient Greece and the modern Western world alike, shame is regarded a social emotion requiring self-consciousness. There seems to be a difference, however, in how we evaluate shame. Today we typically focus on the negative aspects of shame, and how it is an unpleasant and unproductive emotion connected to distress, self-blame, and self-punishment. In ancient Greek philosophy, and especially in Plato, we find a more positive account of shame. In Plato, shame serves an important morally and epistemologically edifying role. Socrates typically attempts to throw youths into a state of uncertainty (*aporia*), using *shaming* as a technique.[30] Socrates' inducing of shame has the final goal of motivating the interlocutor: if not knowing what you thought you knew (and perhaps have claimed to know) is sufficiently shameful, this might motivate you to seek knowledge—knowledge which will increase your ability to make good decisions.[31] In the conclusion of this chapter, I return to this positive account of shame, arguing for its relevance in understanding the importance of silence-breaking in matters of sexual harassment and assault.

The two most relevant ancient Greek terms in the *Laws* which may be translated with "shame" are *aidôs* and *aiskhunê*. *Aidôs* is the Greek Goddess of shame, modesty, respect, and humility, and the term describes the feeling that restrains men from wrongdoing. On the other hand, *aiskhunê* (from *aîskhos*) means *disgrace*. In the *Laws* (646e10–647a2), *aiskhunê* is defined as "fear for our reputation, when we imagine we are going to get a bad name for doing or saying something disgraceful. This is the fear which we, and I fancy everyone else, call 'shame'." This definition suggests that shame is a kind of fear, more precisely fear of *what others might think*, which furthermore suggests that it is essentially a social phenomenon.[32] As we know, shame is a powerful silencing force. This definition pins down why: because we are afraid of what others may think.

However, even though shame is an essentially social emotion, it has a distinctive link to the self. This point is made in the contemporary philosophical study on shame by Deonna et al. (2012): I am ashamed of *myself* because of *p*.[33] Even though one can leave out the "of myself"-clause, it is always correct to use it, they argue. In comparison, one would never say that one is "guilty of oneself."[34] Whereas we feel guilty because of a particular action, the feeling of shame refers to the whole person: the guilty thought "I did something bad"; the shameful thought "I am bad." This is why shame can have serious negative impacts on a person's self-image. It is here useful to distinguish between *genuine shame* and *toxic shame*. Genuine shame is associated with genuine dishonor and the unpleasant fear-like awareness of having committed something others (and oneself, perhaps) would regard as morally wrong. In contrast to genuine shame, toxic shame is a false, pathological shame evolving over a significant period of time, typically manifested in children and adults who have been abused and oppressed, creating a complex trauma.[35] Toxic shame is always misplaced in the sense that it cannot rationally be ascribed to a moral wrongdoing by the person experiencing it.

In defining (genuine) shame as a fear of the opinion other people would have of us if we acted wrongly, Plato's definition may be said to have a normative aspect, although the phrasing itself is not strictly normative. It suggests that shame is a fear connected to wrongdoing. Returning to the paradox of shame in cases of sexual assault, I believe that the paradox is best understood in terms of this normative aspect. Shame in cases of sexual assault is paradoxical in the sense that it happens in a way opposite to what should—on Plato's definition—happen: there is wrongdoing, but the person wronged, rather than the wrongdoer, experiences the shame. Note that not all sexual assaults (and especially not all cases of sexual harassment) involve physical violence, in which case the term "aggressor" may seem too strong. I therefore use the term "wrongdoer" in what follows, covering all cases where the person has acted wrongly (though it might occasionally sound too soft). The intensity of the shame, however, does not follow the degree of violence, or whether the wrongdoing was intentional or not. Even the ignorant, non-violent wrongdoer may cause the victim serious shame.

Since victims of sexual assault have not acted wrongly, how do we explain the shame they typically feel? First, the shame felt by a victim of sexual assault may be a kind of *bodily shame*, rooted in the incapability of preserving the integrity and control of one's own body and its reproductive functions. Secondly, we must acknowledge the social aspects of this shame: for although "everybody" agrees that the wrongdoer and not the victim should feel ashamed, the victim's fear of others' opinions is not irrational. Over and over again, victims are faced with suspicion and comments like "she should have known better." Though women today can appear before the court (unlike in ancient Athens), there are rarely witnesses to sexual misconduct: the victim therefore needs to be *believed*. If the wrongdoer is a prominent man, or someone the victim somehow depends upon, it is harder for the victim to break the silence after an incident of harassment/assault. It would also be significantly harder to express discomfort regarding unwanted sexual attention, and to reject the sexual advances.

Moreover, with the gendered dimensions of honor in classical Athens freshly in mind, is it possible, that, even today, the shame typically felt by victims of sexual assault (and harassment) is connected to fear of *decreased social value*? If so, then are we not collectively as a society failing these victims? Although our modern laws (in contrast to the previously discussed laws of ancient Athens) do not operate *explicitly* with categories distinguishing "honorable women" from "the others" in cases of sexual assault, and through this consolidate some women as "true victims" and others as "insignificant others," the practice arguably still exists. Statistically, very few cases of rape make it to court at all, but for those that do, the way in which the trials unfold depends on the status of the involved. In court as well as outside, people still evaluate the "trueness" of the victim, based on conditions like the relation which the evaluator him/herself has to victim and wrongdoer. If the evaluator thinks the wrongdoer a respectable man and the victim a "nobody," the evaluator may easily trivialize the offense as not being a "real assault" (*that is just the way he is*), with a "true victim" (*I'm sure she flirted with him, why else would he have paid her any attention?*), committed by a "real predator" (*I've never seen that man hurt nobody*).

Concluding Words on Silence-Breaking

In December 2017, a few months after MeToo started to spread virally, *Time* magazine named "The Silence Breakers" speaking out about sexual harassment in workplaces as their "person" of the year. In the editorial, the editor-in-chief emphasized the "individual acts of courage." Why, exactly, is silence-breaking courageous? One of the most common contributors to silence around sexual harassment and assault is shame. In breaking the silence, victims must face this shame. Further, the silence-breaking presents and manifests a shift of the shame inflicted upon the victim by the wrongdoer. Refusing to take on the shame themselves, the silence-breakers instead place it where it belongs, i.e., with the wrongdoer. For such a repositioning to be successful, however, details of what was said and done are required: as feminist and linguist Deborah Cameron writes, "we cannot put that shame where it belongs—with the perpetrators, not their victims—if we cannot describe the details of what was done and what was said."[36] In cases where silence-breakers name their wrongdoer and reveal details of the wrongdoing, they are inflicting shame. Needless to say, *shame hurts*. Persons who are hurt may respond accordingly. This makes the silence-breaking even more courageous.

Silence-breaking implies sharing intimate details. This may feel invasive and shameful. Women's honor has historically (like in classical Athens) been intimately connected to their sexuality, and non-marital sex (including assault) has been the primary reason for decrease in social status and honor/value. Though most of us would like to think that "in the societies of the western modern world, silence-breakers are believed, and their wrongdoers brought to justice," we cannot deny that *naming oneself as a victim* requires risk-taking by individuals. By engaging with this process an extraordinary number of women actively take this risk, ensuring MeToo became an historical phenomenon. Without using the expression "shame-paradox," I find that Professor Boyle (2019: 70) writes accurately about the phenomenon and the repositioning of shame in her book on the movement:

> it is not that Fallon tried to kiss a female journalist which is threatening, but rather that she decided to speak out about the fact, transforming an experience about which she had felt shame and guilt, into one where the shame and guilt lay not with her but with Fallon.
> (Merrick, 2017)

This is the kind of transformation that leads to the accusations that #MeToo has become a "witch hunt" against men. Men are made newly vulnerable when behavior which has historically been rewarded, or joked about, is denaturalized and problematized by refocusing the narrative on how these behaviors were/are experienced by women. To return to Weinstein's non-apology, men no longer know "the rules" (Weinstein, 2017). On this point, there is a certain agreement between feminists and sexual violence apologists. What Weinstein and feminist theorists arguably share is an understanding that his behavior was not inappropriate according to patriarchal logic, but rather an expression of what men are promised, what they are continually told about their position in the sexual order. Of course, where Weinstein and feminist theorists differ is in what responsibility we think individual men should bear for this.

The term *hubris* seems appropriate in describing several cases of "MeToo-*ing*": the wrongdoer overrated his status relative to the woman he wronged. He felt entitled to behave as he did.[37] In many cases, the wrongdoer is never confronted. Moreover, as previously noted, many of these wrongdoers are ignorant of the fact that they have acted wrongly. Now, as Boyle writes, feminists and sexual violence apologists may agree that men no longer know the rules. For many men, this generates shame, and fear of being (a)shamed. In the aftermath of MeToo, I find that several men express frustration and uncertainty (*aporia*?), with variations over, "Am I really supposed to evaluate my every step now, being constantly aware and afraid of any sexual signal I might send out? I won't—I can't." Well, women all over the world are doing this already. All. The. Time.

That shame hurts, however, does not make it necessarily bad. Indeed, in a society, shame can be used for both good and bad purposes. For example, it is used in consolidating hierarchies within the society: people feel ashamed for being poor. They have not done anything wrong, but shame keeps them from protesting against economic injustice, and instead leads to self-blame. Likewise, women subjected to sexual violence typically feel shame, and blame themselves, instead of protesting against the gender hierarchy and the hubristic men acting as though superior to them. On this point, we should bear in mind the formerly introduced distinction between *toxic shame* and *genuine shame*. As argued, toxic shame is *not* connected to moral wrongdoing and is used in oppression. I argue that inducement of genuine shame, on the other hand, as a consequence of genuine, moral wrongdoing, can have a positive disciplinary function within a society. Shame is an emotion which is unpleasant for the individual, but which—eventually, if the shame is genuine (not toxic) and motivates the individual to improve—may have significant positive effects on the society concerned. Though silence-breaking with its shame-repositioning is unpleasant to the wrongdoers individually, it may motivate them to take individual responsibility, hopefully decreasing future wrongdoing. By encouraging shame in sexual wrongdoers, and rejecting the toxic shame of victim-blaming, silence-breaking may also have a preventive effect on potential wrongdoers. As previously shown, whereas we today typically focus on the negative aspects of shame, Plato offers a positive account of shame serving an important morally and epistemologically edifying function. Shame is good, Plato would say, if it improves one's character, is justly distributed and contributes to a harmonious society.[38]

As we saw in Plato's *Laws*, shame is defined as a kind of fear. Moreover, we learned that in a healthy society, self-control (*sôphrosunê*) is presented as the ideal, and to quench the unhealthy desires of the humans living in it, we need the powerful influences of *fear* (understood as shame), *law*, and *correct argument*. Indeed, these influences are important in order to prevent sexual misconduct: a sense of genuine shame when due, well-functioning laws on sexual crime,[39] and correct argument, for justifying the laws and for increasing the awareness of sexual assault and harassment. For this to be achieved, proper education of the individuals (including their desires) is needed, as well as regulations within the domain of what we today typically regard as private. Furthermore, the citizens should defend those who are wronged "as if it were his own brother or father" (*Laws*, 880b1–6), and not punish each other out of the satisfaction of revenge, but due to *benevolence* (*philia*), as they should support each other in improving their moral characters.[40]

For women throughout history, honor and shame have been intimately connected with sex, sexual violence, and *silence*, as shame has a powerful silencing force. The silence-breakers and feminists supporting the MeToo movement are voicing the wrongdoing and repositioning the shame. The *responsibility* of improving societies, lies with (i) the individual wrongdoers (as Boyle argued above) and (ii) the society collectively, and lawgivers specifically. We should note, however, that the majority of wrongdoers are not powerful men. They are our brothers, fathers, sons, friends and colleagues. By breaking the silence and supporting those who do, we do not go "witch-hunting." Yes, we show solidarity with the victims and induce shame in the wrongdoers. But, in fact (as I believe Plato would have put it, and I agree) in doing so, we are also benevolent towards the wrongdoers, providing them with the opportunity to improve.[41] Through silence-breaking, shame-repositioning, and wrongdoers consequently taking responsibility, accompanied by well-functional laws, proper sexual education, and an increase of collective awareness regarding the magnitude of the problem of sexual harassment and assault, we *will* learn from herstory, and the historical phenomenon MeToo, and improve our society. Hopefully.

Notes

1 For a valuable discussion of the ideas in this essay, I thank Helga Forus, Jonas Jervell Indregard, and Hilde Vinje.
2 The MeToo movement started to spread virally in 2017, initiated by Alyssa Milano, following the allegations against Harvey Weinstein. The phrase "Me Too" was first used in the context of sexual assault on social media in 2006, by activist Tarana Burk.
3 Cf., e.g., Cantarella (2005: 238), though she titles these categories "the honest/the seduced" and "the others/the seductresses."
4 I use the Cooper edition (1997) for all references to Plato, unless otherwise noted. For translators of the other ancient Greek texts, please see References.
5 See, e.g., Cairns (1993: 373–378).
6 I.e., not cases in ancient Greek literature where men/boys are victims, or cases where women are sexual offenders (for example Calypso, who keeps Odysseus as prisoner and sexual slave for seven years; see Homer, *The Odyssey*, Book 5).
7 Studies of the *paiderastia* ("love of boys," the erotic educational system) in classical Athens are countless, e.g., Dover (1978). Among the first significant studies on women and sexuality in classical Greece is Pomeroy (1975).
8 The term *herstory* is a description of women's history, written from a woman's and/or feminist perspective. As argued by Kelly-Gadol (1976: 809; cited in Ourabah, 2020: 4): "women's history has a dual goal: to restore women to history, and to restore our history to women." The term "history" (from Ancient Greek *historía*, meaning "knowledge from inquiry") is etymologically unrelated to the possessive pronoun *his*.
9 Cf., e.g., Omitowoju (2002: 69); Scafuro (1997: 211).

10 Though there is no specific word for rape, some stories leave little doubt, like this story in Pausanias, Description of Greece (9.13.5):

> Scedasus, who lived near Leuctra, had two daughters, Molpia and Hippo. These in the bloom of their youth were wickedly outraged (*biazontai*) by two Lacedaemonians, Phrurarchidas and Parthenius. The maidens, unable to bear the shame (*hybreôs*) of their violation, immediately hanged themselves. Scedasus repaired to Lacedaemon, but meeting with no justice returned to Leuctra and committed suicide.

Terms derived from *bia* and *hubris* are here used in the context of sexual assault. Although *biazontai* in the cited translation is translated "wickedly outraged," it could have been translated "raped." Pausanias (110–180 CE) lived long after Plato, but this story is from around Plato's time, and is also referred to in Xenophon, Hellenica, 6.4.7, and Plutarch, Pelopidas, 20.

11 The "honorable" girls were often very young when the ceremony stating the plans for marriage were held. Demosthenes' sister was promised to a man at the age of five; cf. Demosthenes, Against Aphobus, 27.4.

12 I here side with Omitowoju (2002, esp. pp. 73–93). For an alternative view, see Cohen (1991: 100).

13 See, e.g., Lysias, On the Murder of Eratosthenes, [1], 32:

> You hear, sirs, how it directs that, if anyone forcibly debauches [*aiskhunê bia*] a free adult or child, he shall be liable to double damages [i.e., double the amount laid down for violating a slave]; while if he so debauches a woman, in one of the cases where it is permitted to kill him [i.e., in cases where she the wife, mother, daughter, sister or free concubine of a male citizen] he is subject to the same rule. Thus the lawgiver, sirs, considered that those who use force [*bia*] deserve a less penalty than those who use persuasion [*tous peithontas*]; for the latter he condemned to death, whereas for the former he doubled the damages.

Bia, here translated *force*, is contrasted with persuasion by a word connected to *peitho*, meaning "I persuade/seduce," which etymologically is connected to Peitho, goddess of persuasion/seduction.

14 See, e.g., Carey (1995) and Harris (2004; 2006; 2015: 310) for opposite views.

15 Cf. the *Cambridge Dictionary*.

16 This story is to be found in Homer's *Iliad*. For a study of the treatment of Achilles in Plato's *Republic*, see Hobbs (2000). Another example of a hubristic personality in Plato is Alcibiades; see, e.g., Larivée (2012).

17 Cf. Cohen (1991: 99); Llewellyn-Jones (2011: 236). See also Blundell (1995: 163–165).

18 Cf., e.g., Cole (1984: 97); Pomeroy (1975: 79–81).

19 Cf., e.g., Cantarella (2005: 245). That citizenship belonged to persons whose parents on *both* sides are citizens is also referred to in *Constitution of the Athenians*, 42.1., (presumably) by Aristotle.

20 See Cantarella (2005: 240). The part of the law speaking of the exception is not preserved in what remains of the legal text (today in *The Epigraphical Museum* in Athens), but it is quoted in, e.g., Demosthenes, *Against Aristocrates*, 23.53, written around 352 BCE.

21 See Aristophanes, *The Clouds*, 1083; Cantarella (2005: 244); Cohen (2005: 211).

22 Cf. Lysias, On the Murder of Euphiletos, [1], 32.

23 Cf., e.g., Waithe (1987: 75–83); Nails (2002: 58–62).

24 Traditionally reckoned Demosthenes'; today regarded Apollodores', cf., e.g., Hamel (2003).

25 In comparison to other Greek writers from the same period. Cf., e.g., Fisher (1992: 482).

26 The Cooper edition translator T.J. Saunders here uses "being raped" for a term derived from *bia*, while the Loeb edition translator R.G. Bury uses the more literal phrase "being violated."
27 The "dangers" here referred to concern the begetting of the best children (*Laws*, 784d–785a), a topic thoroughly discussed in Plato's *Republic* (Book 5).
28 For further reading, see Blair (2013).
29 When Socrates is asked to explain the concept of ruling oneself, he replies that it is to be *sôphrôn* and master of oneself, one's pleasures and appetites (Plato, *Gorgias*, 491d10–e1).
30 The appropriateness of referring to this technique as "shaming" is reflected in the term *elenchus*, often used in referring to Socrates' questioning, which often is translated as "examine" and "refute," but also (and originally) means to "put to shame," cf., e.g., Furley (1973). A clear example of *elenchein* meaning "to shame/blame" is found in Gorgias' *Encomium of Helen* (paragraph 2).
31 For further reading, see Dypedokk Johnsen (2019).
32 The Athenian introduces definitions of "two virtually opposite kinds of fear" (*Laws*, 646e4), of which this is the second.
33 Cf., e.g., Deonna et al. (2012: 73–74; 82–83).
34 Konstan remarks that there is no clear distinction in ancient Greek between "shame" and "guilt" (Konstan, 2003: 1033).
35 "Toxic shame" was coined by psychologist Sylvan Tomkins in the 1960s.
36 Cf. Boyle (2019: 12).
37 The point that sexual violence committed by men to a large extent is rooted in ideologies of male sexual entitlement is stressed in the *World Report on Violence and Health* (p. 162), by the World Health Organization.
38 Naturally, the "justness" of Plato's ideal of the just state, with its hierarchical system of producers, guardians, and philosophic rulers (cf. the *Republic*), may very well be questioned. However, this is not discussed further here.
39 See, e.g., the new Swedish law (2018) stating that sex without consent is rape, even when there are no threats or force involved.
40 For more on *philia* in the *Laws*, see Sheffield (2020).
41 Although (as Plato scholars know) the question of whether virtue can be taught is a complex one.

References

Blair, E. (2013). *Plato's Dialectic on Woman: Equal, Therefore Inferior*. Routledge.
Blundell, S. (1995). *Women in Ancient Greece*. Harvard University Press.
Boyle, K. (2019). *#MeToo, Weinstein and Feminism*. Palgrave Pivot.
Cairns, D.L. (1993). *Aidōs: The Psychology and Ethics of Honour and Shame in Ancient Greek Literature*. Clarendon Press.
Cantarella, E. (2005). Gender, Sexuality, and Law Gender, Sexuality, and Law. In M. Gagarin & D. Cohen (Eds.), *The Cambridge Companion to Ancient Greek Law* (pp. 236–253). Cambridge University Press.
Carey, C. (1995). Rape and Adultery in Athenian Law. *The Classical Quarterly*, 45(2), 407–417.
Cohen, D. (1991a). *Law, Sexuality and Society: The Enforcement of Morals in Classical Athens*. Cambridge University Press.
Cohen, D. (1991b). Sexuality, Violence, and the Athenian Law of 'Hubris', *Greece & Rome*, 38(2), 171–188.

Cohen, D. (2005). Crime, Punishment, and the Rule of Law in Classical Athens. In M. Gagarin & D. Cohen (Eds.), *The Cambridge Companion to Ancient Greek Law* (pp. 211–235). Cambridge University Press.

Cole, S.G. (1984). Greek Sanctions against Sexual Assault. *Classical Philology*, 79(2), 97–113.

Demosthenes. *Demosthenis. Orationes.* (1907/1921). S.H. Butcher and W. Rennie (Eds). E. Typographeo Clarendoniano.

Deonna, J.A., Rodogno, R., and Teroni, F. (2012). *In Defense of Shame: The Faces of Emotion.* Oxford University Press.

Dover, K.J. (1978). *Greek Homosexuality.* Duckworth.

Dypedokk Johnsen, H. (2019). Socrates' Erotic Educational Methods. *Journal of Philosophy of Education.* 53(2), 309–322.

Fisher, N.R.E. (1992). *Hybris: A Study in the Values of Honor and Shame in Ancient Greece.* Aris and Phillips.

Furley, D.J. (1973). Notes on Parmenides. In E.N. Lee, A.P.D. Mourelatos, & R.M. Rorty (Eds.), *Exegesis and Argument: Studies in Greek philosophy presented to Gregory Vlastos, Phronesis* (Supplementary Volume), 1: 1–15.

Glazebrook, A. (2016). Prostitutes, Women and Gender in Ancient Greece. In S.L. Budin and J.M. Turfa (eds.), *Women in Antiquity: Real Women across the Ancient World* (pp. 703–713). Routledge.

Gorgias. (2005). *Encomium of Helen.* D.M. MacDowell (Ed./Trans.). Bristol Classical Press.

Hamel, D. (2003). *Trying Neaira: The True Story of a Courtesan's Scandalous Life in Ancient Greece.* Yale University Press.

Harris, E. (1990). Did the Athenians Regard Seduction as a Worse Crime than Rape? *Classical Quarterly*, 40(2), 370–377.

Harris, E. (2004). Did Rape Exist in Classical Athens? Further Thoughts on the Laws about Sexual Violence, *Dike*, 4, 41–83.

Harris, E. (2015). Yes and No in Women's Desire. In M. Masterson, N.S. Rabinowitz, &J. Robson(Eds.),*Sex in Antiquity: Exploring Gender and Sexuality in the Ancient World* (pp. 298–314). Routledge.

Hobbs, A. (2000). *Plato and the Hero: Courage, Manliness and the Impersonal Good.* Cambridge University Press.

Homer. (2017). *The Odyssey.* Translation by E. Wilson. W.W. Norton & Co.

Kelly-Gadol, J. (1976). The Social Relation of the Sexes: Methodological Implications of Women's History. *Signs*, 1(4), 809–823.

Konstan, D. (2003). Shame in Ancient Greece, *Social Research*, 70(4), 1031–1060.

Krug, E.G. (et al.) (2002). Ch. 6. Sexual Violence. In *World Report on Violence and Health*, World Health Organization.

Larivée, A. (2012). Eros Tyrannos: Alcibiades as the Model of the Tyrant in Book IX of the Republic. *The International Journal of the Platonic Tradition*, 6(1), 1–26.

Llewellyn-Jones, L. (2011). Domestic Violence in Ancient Greece. In S. Lambert (Ed.), *Sociable Man: Essays on Ancient Greek Social Behaviour in Honour of Nick Fisher* (pp. 231–266). Classical Press of Wales.

Ludwig, P.W. (2002). *Eros and Polis: Desire and Community in Greek Political Theory.* Cambridge University Press.

Lysias. (1930). *Speeches.* Translation by W.R.M. Lamb. Harvard University Press; William Heinemann Ltd.

Merrick, J. (2017). I Won't Keep My Silence: Michael Fallon Lunged at Me after Our Lunch, *Guardian*, November 4.
Nails, D. (2002). *The People of Plato: A Prosopography of Plato and other Socratics*. Hackett Publishing Company.
Omitowoju, R. (2002). *Rape and the Politics of Consent in Classical Athens*. Cambridge University Press.
Ourabah, M. (2020). *The Social Life of a Herstory Textbook: Bridging Institutionalism and Bridging Institutionalism and Actor-Network Theory*. Springer Verlag.
Pausanias. (1918). *Pausanias Description of Greece*. With English translation by W. H.S. Jones & H.A. Ormerod, 4 Volumes. Loeb Classical Library. Harvard University Press; William Heinemann Ltd.
Plato. (1997). *Plato: Complete Works*. J. Cooper (Ed.). Hackett Publishing Company.
Plutarch. (1914, Vol. 1/1917, Vol. 5.) *Plutarch's Lives*. Translation by B. Perrin. Harvard University Press; William Heinemann Ltd.
Pomeroy, S.B. (1975). *Goddesses, Whores, Wives, and Slaves: Women in Classical Antiquity*. Schocken Books.
Scafuro, A.C. (1997). *The Forensic Stage. Settling Disputes in Graeco-Roman New Comedy*. Cambridge University Press.
Sheffield, F.C.C. (2020). Love and the City: Eros and Philia in Plato's Laws. In L. Candiotto & O. Renaut (Eds.), *Emotions in Plato* (pp. 330–371). Brill.
Waithe, M.E. (1987). *A History of Women Philosophers: Vol. 1: Ancient Women Philosophers, 600 B.C. 500 A. D.* Martinus Nijhoff Publishers.
Weinstein, H. (2017). Statement. *New York Times*, October 5.
Xenophon. (1918 and 1921). *Hellenica*. In *Xenophon in Seven Volumes, 1 and 2*. Translated and edited by C. L. Brownson. Loeb Classical Library. Harvard University Press.

14 Shame, Modernity, and Postmodernity in Britain

David Nash

Introduction

Modernity always seemed pleased with itself that it had worked and fought hard to eradicate shame. The nineteenth-century West generally saw this as an assumed part of a wide and deep cultural project, one which was about stabilizing societal reactions to perceived wrongdoing. If we look at a number of developments, we can clearly see this in action. It had been a traditional view that shame had gradually been replaced by guilt within modernity, notably a view similarly seen as outmoded by Jörg Wettlaufer in Chapter 2 of this volume. This view had arguably been a product of modernity's own confidence in its creation of an autonomous self. One that could, on its own, now transcend the primitive draw and subsequent power of communal behavior and sanctions. It was supposedly sufficiently strong and anchored in its own sense of the civilized that it was able to tackle transgressions privately in the form of self- policing—namely as guilt. Individuals could replay events in private and examine their own levels of culpability and thus reproach themselves accordingly. It was also a hallmark of modernism that this process was supposed to fortify individuals for their subsequent forays into social interaction. Although individuals could chastise themselves it was scarcely the case that individuals were actively and regularly afraid of their reproachful self. This has thus entered a situation of negotiation rather than confrontation.

Interestingly this chronological change (and dichotomy) has been seen more recently as substantially outmoded since the suggestion stemmed from a perceived cleavage between public and private. This seemed inevitable since many histories of the coming of modernity do greatly privilege the creation of the private sphere. Such a development is seen as a prerequisite for much of the behavior required to create modern social classes and the arenas they operated within. This perspective was also encouraged by some major theoretical grand narratives (e.g., Norbert Elias and the "civilizing process" and modernization theory) (Elias, 2000 edition). Initially, much commended the nature of these changes.

This chapter seeks to examine the progress of this history by examining evidence from England roughly covering the period 1780 to the present.

DOI: 10.4324/9781003022916-18

Whilst this is obviously related to expertise and knowledge of relevant sources in this area, it might be possible for others to map on the experience of other societies and contexts. One of the most impressive recent attempts to do this has been Ute Frevert's volume *The Politics of Humiliation* (Frevert, 2020). This argues that new perceptions of humankind, bequeathed by the Enlightenment, started to have a serious impact upon the forms of organization that proliferated in the countries of Europe. Frevert notes a growing perception about how growing detachment from the eighteenth century, and still earlier *ancien régime* modes of thought, began to see the individual as a viable entity of cultural and social organization. Frevert describes this as a realization of the power and importance of human dignity. After this, regimes of control and socialization began to factor this element into planning and design which was increasingly reflected in both institutional and building construction. Certainly, there is a noted level of knowledge transfer in this area occurring between European states, sometimes over some considerable geographical and even ideological distances. Julia Barlova, for example, noted the willingness and rapidity of Russian adoption of English ideas of modern, more draconian and authoritarian, approaches to poor relief (Barlova, 2013). Frevert identifies this type of progressivism, and arguably its spread, as indicative of both liberal outlooks and governmental regimes that could be classified as broadly social democratic, or least demonstrating aspirations towards this goal. Obviously this did not prevent such ideas spreading beyond this, such as in Barlova's Russian example. Liberalism and other outlooks embracing change emerged as a war upon a wide front where the pre-conceptions of previous generations were challenged. The customary, which had previously contained its own logic and justification, became marginalized by the reforming zeal of agents of the new modernization. Examples exist in the challenge to customary rite that prevented the poor from gathering marginal resources from fields and woodlands. Their own cultural capital was also challenged by a reforming zeal intent upon removing the immoral (Bushaway, 1982).

A chief area, which saw this form of intervention, involved a quest to restore human dignity through removing instances where shame was a principal agent of socialization and control. Thus, Frevert notes the gradual removal of shame elements of punishment. Symptoms of this are catalogued throughout Europe by Frevert. This occurred within the French Penal Code of 1791 and by 1851 the pillory had been consigned to the past by Prussia, explicitly as a matter of human dignity. By 1843 the Rhine legislature witnessed a situation where all classes voted against the retention of corporal punishments on the grounds that they affronted human dignity and were demeaning (Frevert, 2020: 28, 32 & 33, 36–37). However, Frevert is ultimately skeptical about the overarching explanatory power of the Enlightenment critique of human behavior. Her work has spotted a considerable array of false starts, reversals, and selective re-invention of shame wholly within liberal systems of government and mechanisms associated with discipline. Shame, she argues, was not wholly removed as a phenomenon by concerted government action. It could re-emerge sometimes even as an agent of the humane civilizing ideal it was seeking to promote. This explains why shame was used to socialize children into recognizing collective civilization, something that trumped the wayward power and desires of the individual will (Frevert, 2020: 84–87).

The most important of Frevert's observations is the assertion that the arrival of forms of social democracy were an exercise in devolving honor from what had been the preserve of elites into a commodity. This was now divided amongst classes, which gave individuals the self-worth and dignity, which social democratic forms relied upon for their form and function. Henceforth the quest for the modern democratic citizen was to defend the requisite honor they had achieved and, if possible, add to it at every conceivable opportunity. This devolution of honor created social classes that were an obvious feature of nineteenth-century societies, especially those that industrialized. Frevert suggests that although the state's abandonment of its own sponsored affront to human dignity was Janus-faced in some areas, there is no doubting the obvious withdrawal of this in others. Where the state relinquished control of the mechanism which created and utilized shame this did not lead, as Frevert argued, to the wholesale and total abandonment of shame as simply a primitive form and behavior left behind by modernity.

What Frevert's explorations have revealed is that shame became located in the fundamentals of human interaction. Some institutions, such as schools and junior educational organizations hung on to disciplinary regimes as a method of socializing those who were considered to possess no honor of their own, at least until reaching the age of majority. When this was achieved, other institutions that, in various ways, took up the task of the continued creation of the individual for citizenship commenced similar work on the psyche. Thus, Frevert notes that these institutions and sites where shame remained powerful were areas where ideas of the humane and civilized found themselves suspended for a variety of reasons and periods of time. College fraternity rituals performed the task of the rite of passage into adulthood as well as signaling belonging to another status group. Similarly, initiation in the armed forces, as well as ever present disciplinary codes performed similar functions in these latter organizations. Quite regularly, the armed forces would obviously be a contested site, whereby forms of discipline that persisted within its ranks would display a mismatch with the progress of reform and practice that would occur in the rest of society at large. (Kilday and Nash, 2017: 243–273). Ultimately, Ute Frevert is skeptical of the claims made by liberalism and social democracy. She notes that expressions of humane progress and wishful thinking should not obscure the fact that many of the components of a developing modern society merely ended up relocating the position of shame and humiliation into other spheres. This happened perhaps wittingly around the composition of some regimes and institutions, in the desperation to socialize individuals into humane citizens. But also perhaps unwittingly in that its reforms helped to vacate many areas of life where human nature and agency stepped ("back") in and allowed shame and humiliation to be recast.

What is especially pertinent for our purposes is the centrality of class in this analysis. Thus, one element of this chapter is to critically examine the interplay between liberal social democracy and its influence, alongside the modernist phenomenon of class and its effects. The relationship between these two facets is illuminated through a selective investigation of English social and cultural history over the nineteenth century and beyond. This was, we should remember, the country that was forced into pioneering a recognizably modern class system. This developed rapidly on the back of both industrialization and urbanization within the period in question. England was also a society which was spared the revolutionary upheavals of the nineteenth century which occurred in many other countries—some of which are examined in this volume. This means it is possible to consider the interplay described by Frevert within a society which did not witness cataclysmic political events, some of which that happened elsewhere would otherwise have made investigation of such developments and their continuity of impact at least more problematic.

Modernity in England—Marginalizing the Organic and Inhumane

The early generations of Marxist social historians, in the wake of the social history and "history from below" boom of the 1960s and 1970s, were quite clear that the capitalization of agriculture was also involved in a transformation in attitudes in the countryside to traditional ways of life. In many instances these two transformations went hand in hand. E.P. Thompson was acutely aware of this in his exploration of the eighteenth-century Black Act. This sought to clamp down on forms of rural crime by also implementing an attendant agenda. Thompson noted that property owners were also intervening to prevent tenants and the wider agricultural populace from exercising what had been regarded previously as customary rights (Thompson, 1975). Thus access to the gleaning (gathering) of surplus arable crops after the harvest and the similar gathering of firewood were both increasingly proscribed and prevented by concerted action motivated by changing economic relationships. Thompson deliberately posited this as market forces driving the rural populace into a subordinate economic role (Thompson, 1975). After this offensive upon traditional economic relationships the second phase was an eradication of customary forms of behavior intended to socialize and civilize an otherwise unruly and uncouth population. This offensive was again catalogued by Thompson and Bob Bushaway who saw improving impulses seeking to stamp out everything from coarse and rude folk song to bull baiting and the skimmington ride—the rural populace's impromptu shaming mechanism *par excellence* (Bushaway, 1982: Thompson, 2010).

The eighteenth-century gentry urge to protect property was also analyzed by Thompson and others who saw the creation of the period's "Bloody Code" as the natural outcome of these struggles (Hay et al., 2011 edition). In England the changes to punishment regimes were reactive rather than planned in the latter part of the eighteenth century. These slowly began to use incarceration, which gradually superseded the extreme exemplary corporal and capital punishments within a generation, one that had substantially lost faith in their exemplary element. In England being able to view a miscreant receiving corporal or capital punishment was a more obviously serendipitous affair than the relatively complex structure of indictments and sentences suggested. As we are well aware England's "Bloody Code" handed out capital sentences, but their implementation was an arbitrary occurrence. This was governed often by contexts, individual offense, geographical location and a particular disposition of those who administered and pronounced upon the law's decision surrounding the fate of defendants in individual cases. This arbitrariness meant that high levels of sentences did not equate with actual levels of punishment. Gradually this whole regime was replaced with situations whereby individuals were incarcerated or transported (Beattie, 1986). From encountering an individual's punishment and shame the experience moved to an embedded forgetfulness, one in which miscreants who had been visibly displayed now very obviously disappeared from view.

The eventual removal of many of the capital statutes was seen as a piece of enlightened thinking by several generations and this period also saw the disappearance of the pillory in England (Nash and Kilday, 2010: 68–87). Many arguments which brought about these, and similar reforms, turned upon the idea that the law would cease to attract the respect that was essential to its efficient operation. Such sentiments were offered by commentators as diverse as Voltaire, Beccaria and Benjamin Rush, the last of these emphatically saw shame punishments as indicative of the failure of reason and the proper impact that religion should have on the human psyche (Nash and Kilday, 2010: 97). However, the reformation of the prisoner was also an ideal that permeated the first half of the nineteenth century. In some respects this concept developed from two distinct and ideologically opposed positions. Traditional Tory radicalism found the marketization of society distasteful and railed against the loss of organic connection between social groups that somehow had served to preserve society in a quasi-imagined past. These ideas find their most lucid expression in the ideas of William Cobbett, Thomas Carlyle, and Richard Oastler (Driver, 1946). Repentance and the search for a better self drew distinctly upon ideas of shame and humiliation. Drawing upon religious motifs of penitence criminals and prisoners became objects to save and redeem. What was arguably its opposite number, utilitarianism, had served to create forms of contract throughout society in what contemporary critics described as a "cash nexus"—a phrase often attributed to Carlyle but also to Karl Marx.

Reforming criminals was considered of greater benefit to the whole of society than simply punishing them. The watch word was rationality and this became a justification for experiments in the creation of different punishment philosophies and the individual institutions they would inspire. Enlightenment thought, however, did not dispense with shame where punishment was concerned. David Hume saw inconvenience to the body, and shame filled distress to the mind, as complementary and valuable in the cause of furthering the successful reformation of the offender (Hume, 1797: 489). Jeremy Bentham's much studied and discussed philosophy of panopticism created a prison regime where strict and rigidly enforced isolation and long periods of reflection for individual prisoners was supposed to provoke shame, self-abasement, and remorse. Although the model panopticon was never created the ideas incorporated in this did find their way into the structure and mechanism of some local prisons (Ignatieff, 1989)

It has also been suggested that Poor Law regimes in England similarly went from a situation where customary parish doles of food and resources were essentially organic methods of outdoor relief, to one where modern capitalist considerations predominated. This selfsame utilitarianism started from the premise that the able bodied pauper was a dangerous entity consuming capital. Ideas expressed in a similar manner to Thomas Malthus's concern about subsistence rural economies consuming their own means of support created a system of "less eligibility." This intention was to create massive disincentives to the claiming of relief and to create workhouses where only the destitution of individuals would drive them into an institution that had poor conditions and a deeply resonating stigma. Such a fate was compounded by the passing of the Anatomy Act which allowed the corpses of those who died in the workhouse to be given over for dissection (Richardson, 1988; Sen, 2017). This was a frontal assault upon the Christian doctrine of the resurrection and added an overarching, potentially "eternal," level of shame and stigma to the experience of destitution.

Together these operated hand in hand with burgeoning class narratives and aspirations. Entering the workhouse involved the shame of submitting to a system which believed in the moral failure of the able-bodied pauper. This stigma of entering the workhouse resonates through nineteenth-century history and beyond into the fearsome revulsion buildings such buildings conjured when they became NHS (National Health Service) hospitals after World War II. Yet our picture of their regimes and operation is also fragmentary. Whilst the Poor Law itself claimed to be a universal system the actual implementation of this was devolved, heterogeneous, and piecemeal. Research into the actual operation of the New Poor Law reveals an episodic story. In some instances new regulations were ignored, mitigated, or forgotten with the result that older methods of outdoor relief persisted. In other places a rigid, rational system was quietly toned down and made tolerable for all concerned. There are even instances where the arrival of central authority in shape of inspectors resulted in reproaches for the activities of over harsh local administrators.

Whatever the outcome of incarceration in the workhouse was in individual cases the fact remains that exposure to this system was important in the loss of class status or "honor" described by Frevert. The workhouse provoked fear and loss of credentials as a viable member of the "valuable" working class and the restoration of such honor could be the work of some considerable time. Undoubtedly this was the experience for many. Yet the thrust of recent writing on the work and mechanism of the Poor Law reveals a different story. The system, which as we know was a product of specific lines of thinking, was nonetheless actively molded into practice at every stage by all those involved—from overseer to pauper claimant. The reach and effectiveness of government steers, regulations, and policies emerges as highly questionable. Often a lack of resources and actually the will to enforce policies meant that what was supposed to be a coherent and rational system lapsed into a catalogue of diverse, incoherent, and changing practice. Within this situation elements of the old system remained. Far from rational and prescribed, this "new" system was conceivably as organic and responsive as the old one. Even the supposedly monolithic central authority of the Poor Law Board found itself confronted by insistent letters for paupers pleading their respective cases. What is perhaps remarkable is that such an apparently powerful and faceless authority tasked with implementing this change felt duty bound to answer these individually (Carter & King, 2021).

So far this has served to create a somewhat confusing narrative about the civilizing of society to remove shame elements from human behavior and mechanisms of control. On the one hand, we have a punishment and penal system which unsuccessfully strove for simple improvement and "civilization" driven by deliberate policy. One which rationalized the interactions of individuals and the treatment of outsiders (criminals and the poor), thereby overwriting community driven responses and customs with policies and laws. The role of Marxist historians in this adds a further layer of ambiguity. Thompson and Bushaway (and others) could not help but create a form of respect for lifestyles and organic forms of behavior that in their view had died out, or been driven into submission, as the innocent party bullied by the bad boy of improving capitalism. For individuals subjected to skimmington rides and rough music reassurances from these historians that this was at least organic, communal, and an authentic voice would have been of scant comfort. This romanticism about a lost past is also a strange unexplained contradiction since the industrial society that supposedly replaced it was an engine that should have moved history forward towards a triumphant Marxist outcome. As such this rural Marxist romanticism became an enduring touchstone of the left in England coming to terms culturally with a triumphant capitalism, in the country where it triumphed first (Taylor and Enderby, 2020).

In effect these ideas have continued to assist in promoting the concept that there was a conscious project to subdue by forms of modernizing and civilizing. This in itself seemed logical since Norbert Elias originally considered the civilizing process of removing violence from society to be actively driven by a rising urban merchant class (Elias, 2000 edition). This was also teleological in a manner that Marxists could recognize with a clear transition from primitive to civilized with the achievement of a better society being central to its arguments.

Even if we can identify such a conscious project our evidence suggests that it was not the whole triumph of bourgeois free-market liberalism that Marxists believed and lamented. If such a project really was actively promoted, the will to implement this did not measure up to the levels of control the central idea demanded. The imperative for humane intervention prevented the worst excesses of the panopticon-style prison system, whilst enough experiments with its provisions led to its rapid shelving and the search for a viable system went on. We also know that the Poor Law, with its attendant shame element incorporated into its mechanism, was selectively mitigated by a considerable number of different factors from local intransigence to the inefficiency of central government. In both cases it was also true that insufficient resources were ploughed into both the prison system and the New Poor Law. These failed to create efficient, uniform, and centralized systems that conformed rigidly to any authoritarian blueprint. Finding evidence for this blueprint is difficult but we can be more certain that a compliant population, utterly convinced of the merits of modernizing behavior, did not result from the early nineteenth-century revolution in government. The liberalism identified by Ute Frevert in the English context is not entirely identified with the modernization of the punishment system. The reform of the police and punishment system happened under a government which has come to be known as "Enlightened Tory." Nonetheless the evidence of the New Poor Law's construction does align with Frevert's suggestion that enlightened and utilitarian ideas could, and did, retain the propensity and ability to use shame in the construction of their control mechanisms.

What we need to ponder further is Frevert's suggestion that where government and its mechanisms withdrew from the use of shame, this left the field open for human instincts to somehow restore and rejuvenate shame's presence as a manipulative tool of interaction. The evidence we have here is perhaps mixed. It demonstrates that the persistent will existed to modernize and to seek a society that was less attuned to charitable support for those less fortunate than ourselves. This became associated with the idea that social policy should be driven by rational capitalist concerns. However, we have equally encountered a history of human intervention to retard, curb, and limit the reach of this supposedly rationalist system's logic, sometimes self-consciously advanced as humane reactions to monolithic systems and rules.

Therefore we perhaps need a deeper explanation of the places where human instinct, at least in the English context, felt driven to reach for the mechanisms and behavioral qualities we associate with the concept of shame and shaming. For the nineteenth century we can identify the development of narratives of humanitarianism in behavior and punishment as well as the identification and description of the "primitive" in all aspects of culture. But these narratives also missed crucial developments that were important for later aspects of twentieth- and twenty-first-century cultural depiction in England. The advent of such things as trial by journalism, the culture of celebrity, the creation of cultures of scandal, and "archaeologies of reputation," as well as class identities and the "othering" that resulted from this (Nash and Kilday, 2010)

The devolution of honor described by Frevert appears in Britain primarily in the creation of the class system. Class is an economic and cultural division, but it also created identities through the moral stances the individual classes adopted. Very often attempts to proscribe and censure behavior are expressed through the attempt to shame individuals. In the later nineteenth century this was made possible through the power of the mass consumption of the printed word. This is a truly significant shift in the history of shame. We can note that at the most basic level this meant that more individuals could potentially be involved in the act and experience of shaming. This access to the phenomenon of mass shaming also meant that members of all classes were potentially individuals who could be exposed to shame. Yet there was also the possibility that mass shaming could start to indict whole groups and classes within society. This scaling up of the power of shame meant that within modernity it no longer had its former deep connection with community and locality as a pre-urban society would have understood this. It was now possible for people and groups to shame people who they had never met, but also to engage in this activity as a species of status validation. In other words the maintenance of, or gain in, honor from a successful foray against the chosen target.

We can draw on a number of instances where this occurred. Since the start of the nineteenth century one aspect of the creation of the middle class which had been successful was its skill in defining itself in opposition to other classes. Much has been said about the middle classes' attitudes to the aristocracy and monarchy, seeing these institutions as a deeply unfavorable and distorted mirror image of themselves (Nash and Kilday, 2010: 152–172). Where the middle classes practiced thrift and sobriety this was contrasted with reckless expenditure and consumption, as well as questionable moral behavior at a number of important junctures. We do get a distinct picture of this in some informative and telling episodes. One of these occurred quite early in the century in the guise of the Queen Caroline affair. King George IV's especially poor treatment and court action against his estranged wife Caroline of Brunswick is seen by many historians as a formative episode in the creation of nineteenth-century middle-class consciousness in England (Wahrman, 2010 edition; Nash and Kilday, 2010: 152–172)

Monarchy was also the target of English republicans in the 1860s. After the death of Prince Albert the absence of Queen Victoria from matters of state and civic engagements became something of a national scandal. When the Queen requested money for a number of royal dowries, the situation became inflamed when she was found to have lied to parliament about the condition of the royal finances. These issues were scarcely helped by the sexually promiscuous behavior of Prince Edward the heir to the throne. By no stretch of the imagination were republicans in England likely to incite revolutions, like those that had occurred in many European countries earlier in the century. However, they had some more subtle tools at their disposal that embraced many of the ideas outlined about the power of shame within the printed word, as much as notions of their own identity and potential threats to this (Nash and Kilday, 2010: 152–172)

If republicans in England had actively set out to shame the monarchy then they found that the institution had unwittingly undertaken a great deal of the work for them. Whilst we have already mentioned the scandals that beset the monarchy, what was important in this shame episode of the 1860s was the intent to galvanize the middle classes against the crown. This strategy worked because earlier the first years of Victoria's reign had been characterized by her and Prince Albert actively cultivating connections with the middle classes. This had involved creating a reputation for modest and sober behavior, in stark contrast to the Queen's profligate predecessors. The Victorian monarchy had also taken a major role in reaching out to society by hosting social occasions where the middle classes could portray their own prosperity and further aspirations. With the death of Prince Albert all of these facets of monarchy had disappeared overnight. No longer did the monarch and her family give the middle classes a lead and role model, instead through carefully targeted criticism English republicans were able to tarnish the monarchy more effectively as they exploited middle-class fears. Seeing the monarch to be in league with a dissolute aristocracy undermined middle class ideals of thrift, sobriety and merit. These appeared to be an alternative aristocracy of virtue which aristocracy "blocked" from having a free market in achievement and honor (Nash and Kilday, 2010: 64). Republicans also hinted that the dangers posed by a brutalized working class meant that the prosperous and wealth generating middle class could be caught in a pincer movement that amounted to revolt against their bourgeois way of life.

The leading republican Charles Bradlaugh, in his newspaper the *National Reformer*, wrote an open letter to the Prince of Wales and adopted an authorial voice which referred to the Prince as a fellow freemason. In this Bradlaugh "hoped" in ironic terms that the Prince would obviously not be deeply in debt (which he was) and that he was "obviously" not involved in the surfeit of scandal that surrounded his sexual mores and the fact that he had cuckolded a considerable number of husbands of aristocratic women (which he was also guilty of). The newspaper went further to arouse middle-class fears in its reporting of the Mordaunt Divorce scandal where the Prince had been in the habit of meeting Lady Harriet Mordaunt in secret at her family home whilst her husband Sir Charles Mordaunt was absent. Lady Mordaunt eventually became pregnant with a child other than her husband's and the newspaper sought to convince readers that the Prince of Wales was the child's father. The portrayal of this episode was calculated to profoundly stir middle-class sensibilities since it depicted a morally reckless social "better" entering a family's private space to violate the lady of the house (Nash and Kilday, 2010: 152–172).

Although only one episode, this does successfully show how journalism and arguments written to a modernist readership could mold and target shame against a stakeholder which could be described as a damaging presence in modern society. Swiftly after outrage it was quite possible to ask questions about, merit, worth, and social utility. Now, more than then, the mechanism of modernity watches very closely over the English Royal Family and the choices made by the institution's incumbents now readily reflect deeper conceptions of moral visibility. Indeed the history of the institution over the last 30 years has been an exercise in monitoring and gauging the press and public response to the actions of individuals. Occasionally this has even resulted in a reversal of policy and attitude in the wake of unfavorable public opinion.

Another instance of shame in England's interaction with modernity is provided by some reactions to the crisis of World War I. Whilst initially recruits for the front were relatively easy to come by, some later recruiting initiatives scarcely had the impact that their instigators envisaged. Gradually some commentators became concerned that there was a hard core unwilling to fight for their country. Thus began a "white feather" campaign against these individuals, which marshalled a considerable number of motifs which associated non-service with outright cowardice (Kilday and Nash, 2017: 21–62). White feathers, associated with poor-quality fighting cocks, were presented to men not in uniform usually by women and sought to invoke shame through an assault upon conceptions of masculinity (Kilday and Nash, 2017: 21–62). This last factor had also been central in persuading individuals to volunteer for service in the first place. What perhaps is significant for our purposes here is that the white feather phenomenon was something that evolved within a liberal social democratic society, as a form of shame-inflected compulsion (Kilday and Nash, 2017: 21–62). This conceivably happened because a liberal state found itself in crisis. As such it had recourse to a series of illiberal acts intent upon preserving liberalism. It is no coincidence that some within this society fundamentally recognized the potential contradiction contained within the state's actions.

There is also an important class dimension to this, and to action taken against soldiers at the front who were accused of failing to do their duty in a war, one which had horrifically outpaced military and societal expectations. It is perhaps no coincidence that many of the accounts of those accused of acts of individual cowardice feature the stories of the rank and file and non-commissioned officers. The comparative absence of fully commissioned officers is noteworthy and requires deeper explanation. We might get one answer if we consider the cultural power of ethics associated with leadership and duty. Another possible answer is that disenchantment with the war and what was expected of officers began to be articulated in more covert and genteel terms. Thus, the war poetry of these years very often emanates from the British officer class. Through almost all of these writings disenchantment prevails and attempts to avoid duty become imagined and metaphorical.[1]

There are also some rather more cynical explanations, which consider that the disenchantment of officers and unwillingness to perform their duties was somehow masked and hidden by a society, which failed to face the realities of this. A historian has recently unearthed evidence that the English General Field Marshal Haig asked that more officers be arrested, charged, and shot for cowardice. This was in a belief, infused with desperation, that a significant number were quietly being allowed to absent themselves, or were otherwise disappearing from frontline service. As a recent press report of this outlined:

> "It was a class issue. If you were in the ranks, then you were shot ... If you were supposedly a gentleman, then you were sent home for rest and recuperation in the bosom of your family," MacKinlay said. "Haig clearly wanted to change that."[2]

In more modern times we also encounter a potent example where class narratives about behavior were used to mitigate the suffering of one social class, whilst ensuring acute action was taken against another. The issue of shoplifting became an intense cause célèbre in the 1970s (Kilday and Nash, 2017: 215–241). The arrival of the self-service department store at the end of the nineteenth century has been well catalogued as producing sustained temptation as a social issue. From this period onwards society dealt with a plethora of individuals who stole from retail premises. Some obviously had economic motives but others, from higher social classes, seemingly had more complex reasons for indulging in this form of criminality.

Very quickly, a pathology of shoplifting developed which identified this with aspects of female identity, something that was later to change markedly. Some explanations centered upon the idea of self-image and esteem and attempts to indulge or recover this from a condition where loss of these had occurred. This may also reflect what Ute Frevert has referred to as honor, which here could be seen to have a particular currency within individual shoplifting cases. Later this would be associated with a number of celebrities who both sought the limelight and its trappings as well as indulged in risk-taking behavior. This became well known enough to become a latter-day cultural archetype (Bamfield, 2012: 38).

The shoplifting epidemic of the late 1970s resulted in the issue being debated in parliament in the context of discussion of the 1978 Theft Bill. During the course of the debates around this measure a number of members of parliament noted that the respectable middle-class people were finding themselves ensnared in the crime of shoplifting. This was pathologized as being authored by distress, minor mental maladies, or absent-mindedness. Attention was specifically drawn to how these individuals frequently felt a deep and profound shame at finding themselves at the mercy of the judicial system (Kilday and Nash, 2017: 215–241). These instances were also instrumental in the founding of an NGO (the Portia Trust) which set about the task of decriminalizing the actions of middle-class people who found themselves potentially faced with the law's consequences. This organization linked the consequence of these minor convictions to the equivalent of branding individuals on the forehead with the letter "F" (for felon) (Portia Trust, 1978). Very quickly unofficial decisions by a number of police forces began to mitigate the reality of distraught middle-class individuals finding themselves convicted of shoplifting after a shame-ridden court appearance.

Consequently, the apparatus of modernity, in the shape of department stores, supermarkets, and the predominance of self-service shopping regimes were all indicted. It was also the case that part of the rhetoric of class and its identity was intrinsic to how shame operated within the crime of shoplifting. Complaints from middle-class people were readily heard by members of parliament and representatives of the legal and medical professions. Conclusions from this indicated that some ill-constructed laws and procedures were ensnaring the wrong people (Kilday and Nash, 2017: 215–241). A lot of these dialogues argued that the law was intended to ensnare clearly evil and recalcitrant individuals and that it had no business in catching and vilifying respectable individuals of a higher class (Kilday and Nash, 2017: 215–241). It was noted that these individuals generally had led previously virtuous and blameless lives. Most importantly of all they thus were people who the rest of society would expect to have embraced the concept of shame, and actively indulged it when arrested and accused of wrongdoing in the form of shoplifting (Kilday and Nash, 2017: 233–234)

Thus, the fundamental issue of class emerges once again as a significant driver of how a modern society repackaged and thought about the issue of shame, strategically allocating blame and culpability along class-defined lines. This indicates instances where the issue of shame had been devolved and entirely internalized by a specific social class. The consciousness of this appears to have been actively denied to a lower social grouping as motivation and socialization were deemed to be woefully incomplete, or indeed to have never happened at all. Were he still around Norbert Elias might have recognized this outcome and perhaps even tacitly approved of it!

Conclusion: The Postmodern Condition and Shame

Belief in the postmodern condition posits and inspires the destabilizing of master narratives, including religion, concepts of manners, and sustained confidence in the efficacy of moral codes. Whether this description of modern society, and specifically modern English/British society fits is debatable. What is not contested is the belief in a postmodern society that is widely held by many who are both widely involved in the media and those who actively study its effects upon society. Thus, it is clearly worthy of speculation to consider the potential impact of postmodern analyses that either influence the study of media, or instead become a part of its creation and culture both now and conceivably in the future.

Postmodernism's potential destabilization of the master narratives of civilizing and humanizing societies potentially create responses purely to context, never stretching beyond to wider moral questions. This is the essence of modern shame punishments, notably in America, with location and performativity often central to its visual contextual effectiveness. Something within the modern populist idioms associated with shame does itself potentially explain their popularity by making them immediate and visible, as if appealing to societies now attuned and invested in the idea of visual culture. This means that mechanisms of pre-modern shame are recast and retooled for modernity and postmodernity. Opportunities now exist to globally gossip and display all on social media. Images and behaviors that offend are stored and are potentially "available" forever, whilst individuals' self-policing of content also means such individuals are nervous, yet their portrayal of self is ever more self-consciously crafted or nuanced. There are also now mechanisms for the eradication of poor narratives of individuals. The phenomenon of creating false stories to overwrite shameful episodes in one's past is an increasingly widespread phenomenon (Kilday and Nash, 2017: 282–285)

Examples of such shame responses and tools are reborn and used, on the one hand to expose inappropriate behavior towards individuals (the "cyber stocks" of sex pests who touch women inappropriately on the London Underground), whilst on the other to enable cathartic anonymous confession (Quora). If communications technology has enabled the global village then it is scarcely surprising if we have the global village's "others" who get marginalized, shamed, vilified, and made an example of. This is by no means a one-way street, however. Other meta-narratives have equally been destabilized in attempts to rewrite what some see as a deeply troubling past. We might now think of individuals shot for cowardice during World War I who have now been pardoned, memorialized, and had their reputations restored. We might add to this how narratives of homosexuality as a marginal and disreputable form of behavior have been atomized by cultural and social change. This has even splintered into the two dichotomous narratives of gay pride and nostalgic capturing of distasteful otherness in the form of gay shame (Kilday and Nash, 2017: 243–273)

But many questions remain. Does the postmodern pushing of emphasis upon the context of each incident also function as an impetus behind retributive shame punishment and its comeback? Have the meta-narratives of civilizing and humanizing approaches (what otherwise might be described as rehabilitation) been damaged and undermined? Does this mean shame and punishments again become inextricably linked to context? Does shame now exist episodically and knowledge of these episodes merely consumed as consequences of that context? If this is becoming important, it in part explains the popularity of shame punishments. Such episodes, including the punishing of women wearing placards proclaiming their theft, are shaming processes that are all about local reputation. They relate to incident and location, so that the act of restitution usually involves elements of performativity. This individual isolation of the crime and the flexibility of response to this is again frequently cited as a source of shame punishment's popularity. We might also ask the question: how far does a focus upon context within postmodernity undermine the wider modernist metanarratives of law and justice? Whilst this might create spectacle, how far does it also undermine modernist conception of respect for the law and its quest for rationality?

Thus this chapter ultimately poses the question which needs to be addressed in the context of the modern and postmodern consideration of shame. Whether we are describing a chronology where societal, cultural, and psychological changes are first enabled and then rolled back by events, ideas, tendencies, and the arrest of social and cultural processes. In other words, does shame appear and disappear according to sensibility and fashion? Or instead, does each epoch of necessity find its ways and means of constructing what potentially can be described as the universal emotion of shame, one fulfilling inextricably central needs? Whilst modernism would be, as most forms of liberalism are, disappointed by the violence inherent in the system, postmodernism would be comfortable with either explanation as potentially viable narratives.

Notes

1 For an example of this see Siegfried Sassoon's "Stand To: Good Friday Morning," published in 1918, which concludes with the lines: "O Jesus, send me a wound today, / And I'll believe in Your bread and wine, / And get my bloody old sins washed white!"
2 See https://www.theguardian.com/uk/2001/feb/11/jasonburke.theobserver (accessed 15/6/2021).

References

Bamfield, J.A.N. (2012). *Shopping and Crime*. Basingstoke: Palgrave Macmillan.
Barlova, J. (2013). "Treat them according to the European tradition": The discourse of blaming the poor, the problem of professional beggars and attitudes to poverty in modern Russia. In J. Rowbotham, M. Muravyeva, and D. Nash (eds.), *Shame, Blame and Culpability: Crime and Violence in the Modern State*. London, Routledge (pp. 152–167).
Beattie, J.M. (1986). *Crime and the Courts in England 1660–1800*. Oxford, Clarendon Press.
Bushaway, B. (1982; 2011 edition). *By Rite*. London, Breviary Stuff Publications.

Carter, N. & King, S. (2021). "I think we ought to acknowledge them [paupers] as that encourages them to write": the administrative state, power and the Victorian pauper. *Social History*, 46 (2), 117–144.

Driver, R. (1946). *Tory Radical: The Life of Richard Oastler*. Oxford, Oxford University Press.

Elias, N. (2000 edition). *The Civilising Process: Sociogenetic and Psychogenetic Investigations*. Trans. E. Jephcott. Ed. E. Dunning, J. Goudsblom, and S. Mennell. Oxford, Blackwell.

Frevert, U. (2020). *The Politics of Humiliation: A Modern History*. Oxford, Oxford University Press.

Hay, D., Linebaugh, P., Rule, J., & Thompson, E.P. (2011 edition) *Albion's Fatal Tree: Crime and Society in Eighteenth Century England*.

Hume, Baron D. (1797, 1986 reprint). *Commentaries on the Law of Scotland Respecting Crimes*. Volume II, Chapter XVII: Of sentence and Execution, p. 472 [NLS: ILS: (16–0 RL) Vol.2]. Edinburgh: Law Society of Scotland.

Ignatieff, M. (1989). *A Just Measure of Pain: The Penitentiary in the Industrial Revolution 1750–1850*. London, Peregrine Books.

Kilday, A.-M. & Nash, D. (2017). *Shame and Modernity in Britain: 1890 to the Present*, London, Palgrave Macmillan.

Nash, D. & Kilday, A.-M. (2010). *Cultures of Shame: Exploring Crime and Morality in Britain, 1600–1900*. Basingstoke, Palgrave Macmillan.

Portia Trust (1978). 'Are We all Criminals?' circular submitted to Royal Commission on Criminal Procedure. Evidence of Portia Trust First Submission, BS 19/96.

Richardson, R. (1988). *Death, Dissection and the Destitute*. Harmondsworth, Penguin.

Richardson, R. (2001). *Death, Dissection and the Destitute*. London, Phoenix.

Sen, S. (2017). From Dispossession to Dissection: The Bare Life of the English Pauper in the Age of the Anatomy Act and the New Poor Law, *Victorian Studies*, 59 (2), 235–259.

Taylor, A. & Enderby, J. (2020). From "Flame" to Embers? Whatever Happened to the English Radical Tradition c. 1880–2020? *Cultural and Social History*, 18 (2), 243–264.

Thompson, E.P. (1975). *Whigs and Hunters: The Origin of the Black Act*. London, Allen Lane.

Thompson, E.P. (2010 edition). *Customs in Common*. London, Merlin Press.

Wahrman, D. (2010). *Imagining the Middle Class: The Political Representation of Class in Britain c. 1780–1840*. Cambridge, Cambridge University Press.

Index

Abraham 88
Achilles 226
Aeneid 109
Aikenhead, Thomas 174
Amicitia 98
Anatomy Act (1832) 246
Anonymous of York (Gerard of York? William Bona Anima of Rouen?) 163
Anthropology 2, 35, 37
Aquinas, Thomas 10*Summa Theologiae* 159–160
'Archaeology of reputation' 249
'Ardenne Case' 17
Aristotle 33, 35, 161
 Nicomachean Ethics 227
Aspasia 228–229
Assyrian empire 56
Atchison David R. 191
Athens 223–240
Attila the Hun 51
Audinus 98
Auno 98, 99
Augustine 86–91
 De Civitate Dei 89
Austregisel 97–98, 100

Barlova, Julia 242
Barre, Chevalier de la 52
Beccaria, Cesare 245
Benjamin, Walter
 Deutsche Menschen 11
Bentham, Jeremy
 Panopticism 246, 248
Bible 88, 207
Biblical criticism 175–176
Black Act 244
Blake, William 60
Blasphemy 171–186
 and lifestyles 172

 and NGOs 181–182
 and occupations 172
 and providence 174
 blasphemy laws 4–5, 52
 Charlie Hebdo 179
 Gay News case 179
 in Ireland 183–184
 Jyllands-Posten 179
 'passive' blasphemy 174
 Satanic Verses 179
Bloch, Mark 67, 68
Blood revenge 13, 46–48, 98–102
Bloody Code 245
Bourdieu, Pierre 2, 12
Boyle, Karen 234
Bradlaugh, Charles 250
Braithwaite, John 34
Brooks, Preston S. 187, 188, 193–201
Brown, Peter 87
Brunhild 102, 103
Burchard of Worms
 Decretum 146
Burkhart, Dagmar 3
Bushaway, Bob 244, 247
Butler, Andrew Pickford 193, 197, 199

Cameron, Deborah 234
Carl (son of Thirbrand) 101
Caroline of Brunswick 249
Carlyle, Thomas 245
Chamresind 102
Chanson de Geste 108–109, 111–113, 115–116
Chanson de Roland 108–123
 Roland 109
Charidemus 92
Charlemagne 104
Charles the Bald 56
Charter of the United Nations 181

258 *Index*

Childebert 102
Chinese Empire 56, 62
Chramnesind 97, 99, 100–103
Christianity 173–179
Class 5–6, 244–250, 251–253
Clovis 51, 53
Cobbett, William 245
Constantine (Emperor) 84
Coetzee, J.M.
  Disgrace 3, 16, 20–25
Congregatio fidelium universalium 162
Copernicus, Nicolaus
Council of Basel (1431) 163
Council of Chalcedon (451) 163
Council of Constance (1414–1418) 161–162
Covenant of the League of Nations 180
Criminal Law 33
Criminology 34
Cynics 25

Danes 55–56
Dante 161
Darwin, Charles 65
d'Ailly, Pierre 161
d'Auxerre, Robert 55
de Beaulieu, Geoffrey 161
de Cramaud, Simon 162–163
de Torquemada, Juan 164
de Troyes, Chrétien 110–111
de Win, Paul 142
des Champs Gilles 162
Declaration on the Elimination of
  All Forms of Intolerance and of
  Discrimination Based on Religion or
  Belief 181
Decree *Haec Sancta* 161
Decree *Frequens* 161–162
Decretum Gratiani 149, 159
Demosthenes
  Against Neaira 229
Denmark
  Tønder 146
Descartes René 35
Dilcher, Gerhard 143
Diogenes 25
Deuteronomy 50
Dossey, Lesley 88
Draco
  Draconian Law 228, 230
Dreyfus Affair 64
Duelling 11, 19. 20, 187–202
Dunham, Jennifer 57, 63

Ealdred 101
East Asia 29
Eberulf 98
Ehrismann, Otfried 126
Egyptian empire 56
Elias, Norbert 24–35, 67, 124, 174
  civilising process 115, 177, 181, 241, 247–248
  Theory of Civilisation 124
Embarrassment 32–33, 35
Emming, Jutta 4
England 5–6, 20, 60, 143, 145, 176–179, 241–256
  monarchy 249, 251
  New Poor Law (1834) 246–248
  Poor Law Board 247
  'white feather' campaign 251
Enlightenment 34, 66, 177, 242
Envy 65–66
European Commission 180
European Court of Human Rights 180, 183
European Union 57

Fabliaux 111–113, 115
Febvre, Lucien 67
Feinberg, Joel 179
Fessler, Daniel T. 28
Fifth Lateran Council (1512–1517) 164
Finland 203–222
  Act of Guardianship (1898) 211
  Act on Child Custody and Right of Access (1983) 211
  Amendments to Criminal Law (1960s) 210
  Russian Penal Code (1889) 210
First Vatican Council (1970) 164
Flanders 143
Flaubert, Gustav
  Madame Bovary 17
Foote, George William 176
Fontane, Theodore
  Effi Briest 3, 16–20
  L'Adultera 17
  Schach von Wuthenow 17
Fourth Lateran Concile (1215) 33
France 4, 62, 107–123, 143, 149
  Beaumont-en-Argonne 149
  Gascony 146
  Penal Code of 1791
  Rouen
    Etablissements 148
  Toulouse 145

Frankish society 52–53, 103
Fraternity rituals 243
Freeman, Joanne B. 188, 200
Freidman, Thomas 61–62
French Revolution 66
Frenz, Barbara 142
Freud, Sigmund
   Introductory Lectures on Psychoanalysis 65
Frevert, Ute 5–6, 34, 176–177, 179–180, 243–244, 247, 248, 249, 252
   The Politics of Humiliation 242
Fukiyama, Francis 51

Gaul 4, 104
Gellner, Ernest 52
Gerald of Aurillac 50
Germany 9–16, 20, 30, 67, 145, 146–147, 172–173
   and political opponents 15
   Berlin 149
   Cologne 147
   conception of honor 15
   Dortmund 149
   FDR 12
   'Final Solution' 14–15
   Freiberg 144
   Germanic Law Codes 47
   Güstrow 149
   Hamburg 149
   Invasion of Poland 14
   Korbach 143
   'Kreisau Circle' 15
   Law for the Protection of German Blood and German Honor 14
   Lübeck 143, 145, 148, 149
   Nazi era 11, 14–15
   Occupation of Rhineland 14
   Rhine Legislature 242
   Rostock 143
   Speyer 149
   Strasburg 143
   Westphalia 143
Gilmour, David 82
Godspell 179
Goffman, Irving 180
Goerdeler, Carl Friedrich 16
Graeber, David 54
Grail Romances 115
'Great Schism' 159, 160, 161–167
Greek empire (ancient Greece) 56, 61, 224–228
   Prostitution in 228–229
Greenberg, Kenneth 5

Gregory of Tours 4, 53, 91, 97–106
Gromer, Georg 142
Gubo, Darara 180–181
Guilt 2, 18, 31, 36

Hague, Field Marshal 252
Hatlen, Jan Frode 4
Hector 226
Himmler, Heinrich
   Posen Speeches 14
Hirschmann, Frank 143
Hobbes, Thomas 35
Holy Roman Empire 4, 142–143, 149
Honor 1, 2, 3, 4, 5, 17–18, 30, 37, 46, 51, 54–55, 62–65, 69, 81–82, 85–86, 97–99, 107–139, 164, 187–202, 243
   and dignity 11
   and family 84–85, 90–91
   and gender 47, 58–61, 81–83, 87–88, 109–110, 125–129, 132, 135–136, 223–240
   and homosexuality 61
   and hunting 53
   and male violence 61–62
   and marriage 59
   and military discipline 243
   and paternity 82–83
   and prostitution 13
   and rape 59–60, 68, 224–225, 230–33
   and religion 51–52, 87, 98–101
   and rumour 86
   and sexuality 58–61, 82–83, 85–89, 133, 146, 223–240
   and wife beating 60
   discourses of honor 9–16, 30, 109–110
   dishonor 10, 31, 86–88, 109–111, 114, 232
   honor cultures 3, 46–48, 58–59, 81–82, 93, 104, 107–123, 124, 150, 204
   honor killings 35, 58, 61, 68
   in Arab society 47
   in Arabic language 31
   in Early Modern period 33
   in English language 10, 11
   in French language 10
   in German language 10–13, 30, 131
   in Latin language 31
   in tribal societies 47–48, 52–53, 55–56, 59, 82, 103–104
   loss of honor 47
   preservation of honor 10–11
Houlebeque, Michel 179
Hume, David 246
Hussein, Saddam 63–64, 68–69

260 Index

Igel, Karsten 143
In Bruges (2008) 48
India 176
In iudicio civium 98
Inhorn, Marcia 90
Iran 64
Iraq 63
Ireland 182–184
Isenmann, Eberhard 143
Italy 143
International Covenant on Civil and Political Rights (ICCPR) 181

Jackson, Andrew 198–199
Jesus Christ Superstar 179
Jews
 dhimmi regulations 52
 Judensau 52
 medieval murder of 51–52
Johnsen, Hege Dypedokk 5
Jones, George 49
Jouglet 112–113
Justinian 53, 84–85
 Digest 84

Kaiser Wilhelm I 19
Karras, Ruth Mazo 125
Kautsky, John 52
Kenosis (self-renunciation) 24
Kery, Lotte 142
Khaldun, Ibn 46, 49
Khomeini, Ayatollah 64
King George IV 249
Knightly tradition 13
Ku Klux Klan 188

La Queste del Saint Graal 114
Lactantius 91–92
Landes, Richard 4
Late Antiquity 81–96
Le Chevalier de la Charrette 113
Le Couronnement de Louis 113
Le Goff, Jacques 161
Le Prestre crucefié 111
Le Roy, Pierre 162
Lewis, Helen B 36
Lex familiae Wormatiensis 145
Liberalism 5, 242–244, 248, 251
Libido dominandi 69
Lidman, Satu 5
Lienert, Elisabeth 126, 134
Livy 32
Lotharingia 143

Low Countries 142, 148 171–172
Lying 63
Lysias 229
 On the Murder of Eratosthenes 225, 229

Malthus, Thomas 246
Marsile of Padoue 164
Martial 92
Marx, Karl 245
Marxism 244, 247–248
MeToo 223, 224, 233–235
Megalothymia 58, 69
Mençonge 116
Mendoza Hurtado de 31
Menschenrechte (human rights) 34
Middle Ages 4, 29, 32–35, 48, 55–56, 67, 104, 107–158, 172, 210
Miller, William Ian 33
Modernisation theory 241
Monitum 45
Monty Python's Life of Brian (1979)
Morgan, Robin 61
Mourdant Divorce scandal 25251
Müller, Jan-Dirk 135–136

Nash, David 4–6, 34
National Health Service (UK) 246
National Reformer 250
Nayler, James 174
Neaira 229
Neolithic period 52
Nequam-book 143
New Conciliarism 164
Nibelunglied 4, 125–136
Nike rioters 53
Nussbaum, Martha 34

Oakley, Francis 164
Oastler, Richard 245
Ockham, William of 164
Onēidophobia 57, 58, 61, 63, 64, 68, 69, 102

Palestinians 61
Papacy 4, 159–167
 in Avignon 162
Patria potestas 89
Pauli, Johannes 204
Paulinus of Nola, 87
Pericles 228, 229
Peristiany, John 12
Petrarch 161

Pitt-Rivers, Julian 12
Plato 5, 49, 223–240
　Laws 229–230, 232, 235–236
Poitiers 99, 100
Pope Benedict XIII 160, 161, 163
Pope Celestine V 161
Pope Eugene IV 163
Pope John XXIII 164
Pope John XXIII (anti-pope) 162
Pope Martin V 161
Portia Trust (UK) 253
Potestatis plenitudo 161
Primate behaviour 60
'prime divider' societies 56–58
Prince Albert 249, 250
Prince Edward (later Edward VII) 250–251
Prostitution 13
Prussia 242
Punishments 4, 5, 13, 33, 140–158, 171–175, 203–222, 255
　banishment 150
　capital punishment 245
　corporal punishments 5, 92–93, 150, 203–222, 243, 245
　pillory 145, 147–148, 242, 245
　carcan 147
　cyppus 147
　rough music 247
　skimmington ride 244, 247
　stones of shame 145, 147, 148–149

Queen Caroline affair 249
Queen Victoria 249–250
Quora 254
Qur'an 59, 60

Raoul de Cambrai 115–116
Roman d'Énéas 109
Roman Empire 2–3, 32, 56, 85, 88, 92–93, 97–98, 103
　and family 83–84
　and masculinity 88–89
　and women 84–86
Roman Republic 85
Rosenberg, Alfred
　Der Mythus des 20: Jahrhunderts 14
Ruricius 88
Rush, Benjamin 245
Rushdie, Salman 179
Russia 242

Said, Edward 67
　Orientalism 182

Sancho, Lisa 4
Sawyer, Erin 88–89
Scandinavia 49
Scheler, Max 12
Schoeck, Hans 65
Scott, James 54
Scotland 174
Second Vatican Council (1960) 164
Secularisation 34, 207
Sendgerichte 145
Sère, Bénédicte 4, 142
Shame 1, 2, 3, 4, 5, 27–38, 46, 51, 57–58, 69, 81–83, 93, 97, 107–158, 164, 188–202, 231, 235, 241–256
　and blasphemy 176, 182–185
　and blushing 28, 38, 143
　and charivari 145, 147
　and conceptions of the Jews 48
　and dishonorable trades 13
　and emotions 28, 30–31, 37, 46, 81, 115, 124, 133–136, 140–141, 213–216, 231
　and environmentalism 36
　and humiliation 33–34, 37, 113, 115
　and international diplomacy 182
　and neuroscience 37
　and Onēidophobia 57, 58, 63, 64, 68, 69, 102
　and patriarchy 205
　and penance 33, 141
　and physiology 37, 83
　and psychoanalysis 36, 65
　and psychology 37, 65, 171, 204
　and punishment 4, 13, 33, 140–158, 171–175, 203–222, 255
　　banishment 150
　　pillory 145, 147–148, 242, 245
　　carcan 147
　　cyppus 147
　　rough music 247
　　skimmington ride 244, 247
　　stones of shame 145, 147, 148–149
　and religion 37
　and sex pests 254
　and sexual assault 5, 223–225, 231, 233
　and sexuality 145–147, 223–240
　and shoplifting 252–253
　and sin 33, 141
　and the Bible 32
　and the body 2, 28–29, 35, 132
　biology of 27–30, 37, 83
　Christian conceptions of 3–4, 30, 33, 37, 91–92, 140

262 *Index*

   in Ancient Greece 35–36, 61
   in Arab society 61
   in Arabic language 31
   in Dutch language 148
   in Early Modern period 33–34
   in English language 31–32
   in French language 31
   in German language 31, 32, 147–148
   in Latin language 32
   in Old English language 31, 32
   in Old Frisian language 32
   in Old High German language 32
   in Old Norse language 32
   in Old Saxon language 32
   in Spanish language 31
   in Swedish language 32
   in tribal society 45–51, 57–58, 65–66
   transgressing norms 28, 30
Shakespeare, William 32, 38
   Julius Caesar 11
Sichar 97–103
Simmel, George 12, 35
Slander 85–86, 147, 149
Socrates 231
Spain 173
   Catalonia 145
Spargo, John W 145
Spinoza, Baruch 35
St Ambrose 88, 91
St Jerome 84, 85–86
St Louis (Louis IX of France) 161
St Paul 163
   Letter to the Philippians 24
Stearns, Peter 34
Stewart, Frank Henderson 12
Sumner, Charles 187–201
   "The True Grandeur of Nations" 194
Switzerland
   Basel 162
   Schaffhouse 162

Taakkasiirtymä (trans generational trauma) 214–215, 217
Tangney, June Price 36–37
Tawney, R.H. 174
Taxil Léo 176
Teetaert, Amédée 142
Theft Bill (UK 1978) 252–253
Theodora 53
Theodosian Code 85
Therasia 87
Thompson, E. P. 244–245, 247

Thorsen, Jens-Jorgen
   Sex Life of Christ 179
Thucydides
   Peloponnesian Wars 61
Thurbrand 101
Tolstoy, Leo
   Anna Karenina 17
Tranquilla 102
Treaty of Versailles (1919) 14
Treaty of Westphalia (1648) 180
Triuwe 136
Trusen, Winfrid 142

Uhtred 101
United Nations 212
   Charter 180
   Declaration on the Rights of the Child (1959) 211
   Special Rapporteur on Freedom of Religion and Belief 181
   Special Rapporteur on Religious Intolerance 181
   UN Convention on the Rights of the Child (1989) 211
   UNCRC 211
   Universal Declaration of Human Rights 12
Universal Declaration of Human Rights (UDHR) 181
Universal Declaration of Islamic Human Rights 181
USA 187–202
   Civil War 188–190
   'Crime against Kansas' 190–193
   Missouri 191
   South Carolina 193, 195, 199

Valerius Maximus 32
Van Buren, Martin 198–199
Vengeance 50
Venice Commission (1990) 181
Verbis contumeliosis 141, 150
Verschworene Bürgergemeinde 141
Violence 58–60, 89, 97, 98–104, 198, 205, 208–210, 224–226, 228
Vogt, Ludgera 12
Voltaire 245
Volusianus 87–88, 93
Von Regensburg, Berthold 144
Von Stauffenberg, Claus Schenk Graf 15–16
von Strasburg, Gottfried
   Tristan 125
Von Tresckow, Henning 16

Wales
 Hywel Daa 29
Weapons of Mass Destruction (WMD) 63–64
Weber, Max 12, 67, 174
Weinstein, Harvey 234
Wettlaufer, Jörg 3–4, 171, 241
Whitehouse, Mary 179

Wilson, John Lyde 193, 195
World War I 251–252, 254
Wood, Keith-Porteus 185

Yeandle, David 30

Zabarella, Franciscus 163
Zingerle, Arnold 12

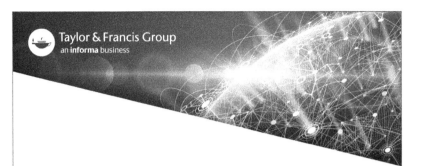

Taylor & Francis eBooks

www.taylorfrancis.com

A single destination for eBooks from Taylor & Francis with increased functionality and an improved user experience to meet the needs of our customers.

90,000+ eBooks of award-winning academic content in Humanities, Social Science, Science, Technology, Engineering, and Medical written by a global network of editors and authors.

TAYLOR & FRANCIS EBOOKS OFFERS:

- A streamlined experience for our library customers
- A single point of discovery for all of our eBook content
- Improved search and discovery of content at both book and chapter level

REQUEST A FREE TRIAL
support@taylorfrancis.com

Milton Keynes UK
Ingram Content Group UK Ltd.
UKHW031502071224
451979UK00020B/228